# THE FATHER, THE SON AND THE HOLY SPIRIT

*SOCIETY*
*OF BIBLICAL*
*LITERATURE*

# DISSERTATION SERIES

William Baird, Editor

**Number 61**
THE FATHER, THE SON AND THE HOLY SPIRIT
The Triadic Phrase in Matthew 28:19b

Jane Schaberg

Jane Schaberg

# THE FATHER, THE SON AND THE HOLY SPIRIT

## The Triadic Phrase in Matthew 28:19b

*SCHOLARS PRESS*

Published by
Scholars Press
101 Salem Street
P.O. Box 2268
Chico, CA 95927

# THE FATHER, THE SON AND THE HOLY SPIRIT
## The Triadic Phrase in Matthew 28:19b

## Jane Schaberg

Ph.D., 1980
Union Theological Seminary
New York

Advisor:
J. Louis Martyn

©1982
The Society of Biblical Literature

Library of Congress Cataloging in Publication Data

Schaberg, Jane
    The Father, the Son and the Holy Spirit.

    (Dissertation series / Society of Biblical Literature ; no.
61) (ISSN 0145–2770)
    Thesis (Ph.D.)—Union Theological Seminary, 1980.
    Bibliography: p.
    1. Bible. N.T. Matthew XXVIII, 16–20—Criticism,
interpretation, etc. I. Title. II. Series: Dissertation series
(Society of Biblical Literature) ; no. 61.
BS2575.2.S28 1981      226'.206          81–14466
ISBN 0–89130–543–2                       AACR2

Printed in the U.S.A.

. . . In that abyss
Of radiance, clear and lofty, seem'd, methought,
Three orbs of triple hue, clipt in one bound:
And, from another, one reflected seem'd,
As rainbow is from rainbow: and the third
Seem'd fire, breathed equally from both.  O speech!
How feeble and how faint art thou, to give
Conception birth.  Yet this to what I saw
Is less than little.  O eternal Light!
Sole in Thyself that dwell'st, and of Thyself
Sole understood, past, present or to come;
Thou smilest on that circling, which in Thee
Seem'd as reflected splendour, while I mused;
For I therein, methought, in its own hue
Beheld our image painted: steadfastly
I therefore pored upon the view.  As one
Who versed in geometric lore, would fain
Measure the circle; and, through pondering long
And deeply, that beginning, which he needs,
Finds not: e'en such was I, intent to scan
The novel wonder, and trace out the form,
How to the circle fitted, and therein
How placed: but the flight was not for my wing;
Had not a flash darted athwart my mind.
And, in the spleen, unfolded what it sought.
     Here vigour fail'd the towering fantasy:
But yet the will roll'd onward, like a wheel
In even motion, by the Love impell'd,
That moves the sun in Heaven and all the stars.

                    Dante, Paradiso, Canto 33
                    [translated by Henry F. Cary
                    (New York: Collier, 1937)
                    425-26]

TABLE OF CONTENTS

PREFACE

This study was undertaken because of a personal fascination
with the idea of the Trinity. My interest is not based on a
thorough knowledge of all the intricacies of dogmatic debate and
development, nor on a preference for one specific articulation
of the dogma over others. It is based rather on the conviction
--as Jung puts it--"that a dogma which has been such a bone of
contention for so many centuries cannot possibly be an empty
fantasy,"[1] and on the conviction that something found useful
and challenging spiritually demands critical investigation.
This dogma has been called by Whitehead one of the greatest
achievements of the human intellect,[2] by Rahner the fundamental
mystery of Christianity.[3] In our century, however, the bone of
contention has been long buried, the idea of the Trinity having
become for many (to change the metaphor) a museum piece with
little or no relevance to the crucial problems of contemporary
life and thought, an example of the absurd lengths to which
theology has been carried, and "a bizarre formula of sacred
arithmetic."[4] Its formulation in classical theology (there is
in God one divine "nature" and three "persons") and the qualifications this formulation requires today have to a great extent
relegated it to the realm of inaccessible mystery, of the boring, of blind and "loyal" faith.[5] It has also been regarded as
"the rubbish the churches have added" to the NT.[6] But we have
been made aware by artists working with "found objects" of the
value of broken scraps of junk, of the discarded. And whether
the "rubbish" has been added or is found in some form in the NT
strata is an open question, one that will be pursued in the
following pages.

In this regard we may note that several recent works have
claimed a new understanding of the Trinity to be crucial to the
deepening of contemporary insights concerning human liberation.[7]
In such recent efforts, however, the biblical texts such as
Matt 28:19b which lie behind the dogma have not yet received
adequate critical treatment. This seems in part a symptom of
what Dahl has called the neglect in the discipline of NT theology of detailed and comprehensive investigation of NT statements

about God.[8] Because it involves a neglect of areas of agreement that are taken for granted without sufficient examination, this silence cannot but give a lopsided picture of the relationship of Christianity to Judaism;[9] it can lead to a loss or weakening of the vital sense of identity between the Trinitarian God and the God of Israel.

Within the broad context of an interest in the biblical bases of the Trinitarian dogma, attention is narrowed here to a study of the triadic phrase in Matt 28:19b ("in the name of the Father, and of the Son and of the Holy Spirit"), in an attempt to understand the "original metaphor"[10]--or an original metaphor --at the biblical source of this doctrine. We are looking, in other words, for "that beginning" Dante needed. This study will take us backwards into the book of Daniel and beyond into Canaanite mythology and the Enochic traditions, and raise the question of Israelite conceptions of human participation in the heavenly council. It will concern an understanding of Matt 28: 16-20 in the spectrum of a wide variety of adaptations of Daniel 7, so that both the uniqueness and antiquity of the particular vision presented by Matthew can speak.

I would like to thank those who helped me in this work by their criticism, encouragement, interest and sense of humor: in particular my family, especially my mother; the communities at 91st Street, New York City; Maryland Avenue, Saint Louis; 17th Street and Longacre, Detroit; my colleagues in the Religious Studies Department at the University of Detroit, Justin Kelly and James J. Buckley; my friend Patty Geoghegan; Barbara Butler, R. Shabsai Wolfe and Kathy Wofford for assistance with the re- search, proofreading and typing. To the members of my disser- tation committee--Professors J. L. Martyn, R. E. Brown, J. A. Sanders (now of the School of Theology at Claremont), G. Landes and G. Wainwright--special thanks for teaching a rigorous dis- cipline and the excitement of creative discovery.

[1]C. G. Jung, "A Psychological Approach to the Trinity,"
*Psychology and Religion: East and West* (New York: Pantheon,
1958) 2.199.

[2]Cited by E. Schweizer, *The Good News According to Matthew*
(Atlanta: John Knox, 1975) 534; he gives no reference and I have
been unable to locate the statement in Whitehead's works.

[3]K. Rahner, "Trinity," *Theological Dictionary* (ed. Cornelius Ernst; New York: Herder and Herder, 1965) 469.

[4]See E. J. Fortman, *The Triune God* (Philadelphia: Westminster, 1972) xiii.

[5]Rahner suggests that the ultimate reason for a general
lack of attention to this doctrine is that in an age of public
and worldwide atheism the question of God is urgently concerned
with God's existence, not with God's inner mystery. Moreover,
since Augustine the "immanent" Trinity has been to the fore in
discussion, obscuring the "economic" Trinity, so that it is
hard to see what actual Christian existence has to do with the
Trinity ("Trinity in Theology," *Sacramentum Mundi* [ed. K. Rahner; 6 vols.; New York: Herder and Herder, 1970] 6.304).

[6]R. M. Grant reports this remark of a college president in
conversation with him (*The Early Christian Doctrine of God*
[Charlottesville: University of Virginia, 1966] 97).

[7]Notably Letty M. Russell, *Human Liberation in a Feminist
Perspective* (Philadelphia: Westminster, 1974) and J. Moltmann,
*The Crucified God* (New York: Harper and Row, 1974; especially
chap. 6); "The 'Crucified God': a Trinitarian Theology of the
Cross," *Int* 26 (1972) 278-99. Russell argues that "by their
nature and work all three Persons of the Trinity transcend the
categories of masculine and feminine, yet the human metaphors
used to speak of all three of them include human characteristics
of all types. Even the immanent Trinity...can be said to transcend, and also to include, all the characteristics familiar to
us by analogy to human love. Because of the experience of God's
self-communication to the world in the work of the economic
Trinity, it is possible to affirm the immanent nature of the
Trinity as a dynamic communication of love between the 'persons'
of the Trinity. In spite of their distinction of function, the
Creator, Liberator and Comforter share in one divine communication of love to humanity which is experienced in different ways"
(p. 102; cf. p. 96). See also other feminist works such as
Margaret Farley's "New Patterns of Relationship: Beginnings of
a Moral Revolution," *TS* 36 (1975) 627-46. Other important books
illustrating a revival of interest in the Trinity include: R.
Panikkar, *The Trinity and the Religious Experience of Man* (New
York: Orbis, 1973); H. Ott, *God* (Atlanta: John Knox, 1971) esp.
40-62; B. Cooke, *Beyond Trinity* (Milwaukee: Marquette University, 1969); N. Pittenger, *The Divine Triunity* (Philadelphia:

United Church, 1977); K. Rahner, *The Trinity* (New York: Herder and Herder, 1970).

[8]Nils A. Dahl, "The Neglected Factor in New Testament Theology," *Reflection* 73 (1975) 5-8. Theology in the strict sense of the word he deems the neglected factor. Dahl remarks that "most treatments of NT Christology pay astonishingly little attention to the relationship between faith in Christ and faith in God, or to the transfer of divine names, attributes and predicates to Jesus, or to the emergence of 'trinitarian' formulations" (p. 5).

[9]Dahl discusses his understanding of causes that contribute to the neglect, including a pronounced christocentricity with roots in the nineteenth century, the common assumption that the most important elements in the NT are those which are "specifically Christian," and the fact that by and large the concept of God found in the OT and interpreted in contemporary Judaism is taken for granted ("The Neglected Factor," 6). W. D. Davies claims that the relative paucity of materials dealing directly with the doctrine of God in the NT is explained by the fact that faith in the messiah became the primary mark of the believer ("From Schweitzer to Scholem: Reflections on Sabbatai Svi," *JBL* 95 [1976] 540 n. 54). To this discussion should be added the suggestion that the incompleteness of our knowledge of first-century Judaism may cause us to be unaware of the extent and nature of certain theological elements which are not only taken for granted but subtly developed.

[10]Cf. J. A. Sanders, "Dissenting Deities and Philippians 2:1-11," *JBL* 88 (1969) 283 n. 17.

CHAPTER I

SURVEY OF CRITICAL OPINION REGARDING THE
MATTHEAN TRIADIC PHRASE

A. Introduction: Matt 28:16-20

The central focus of this dissertation is the question of
the origin and meaning of the triadic phrase in Matt 28:19b:
"in the name of the Father and of the Son and of the Holy
Spirit." The phrase occurs in the final pericope of the Gospel
(Matt 28:16-20).

> 16. Now the eleven disciples went to Galilee, to the
> mountain to which Jesus had directed them. 17. And
> when they saw him they worshipped him; but some doubted.
> 18a. And Jesus came and said to them, 18b. All authority
> in heaven and on earth has been given to me. 19a. Go
> therefore and make disciples of all nations, 19b. bap-
> tizing them in the name of the Father and of the Son
> and of the Holy Spirit, 20a. teaching them to observe
> all that I have commanded you, 20b. and lo, I am with
> you always, to the close of the age. (RSV)

> 16. Οἱ δὲ ἕνδεκα μαθηταὶ ἐπορεύθησαν εἰς τὴν Γαλιλαίαν
> εἰς τὸ ὄρος οὗ ἐτάξατο αὐτοῖς ὁ ᾿Ιησοῦς, 17. καὶ
> ἰδόντες αὐτὸν προσεκύνησαν οἱ δὲ ἐδίστασαν. 18a. καὶ
> προσελθὼν ὁ ᾿Ιησοῦς ἐλάλησεν αὐτοῖς λέγων, 18b. ᾿Εδόθη
> μοι πᾶσα ἐξουσία ἐν οὐρανῷ καὶ ἐπὶ γῆς. 19a. πορευ-
> θέντες οὖν μαθητεύσατε πάντα τὰ ἔθνη, 19b. βαπτίζοντες
> αὐτοὺς εἰς τὸ ὄνομα τοῦ πατρὸς καὶ τοῦ υἱοῦ καὶ τοῦ
> ἀγίου πνεύματος, 20a. διδάσκοντες αὐτοὺς τηρεῖν πάντα
> ὅσα ἐνετειλάμην ὑμῖν. 20b. καὶ ἰδοὺ ἐγὼ μεθ᾿ ὑμῶν
> εἰμι πάσας τὰς ἡμέρας ἕως τῆς συντελείας τοῦ αἰῶνος.

Minus Judas the betrayer, whose remorse and death Matthew
has already narrated (27:3-5), the eleven have journeyed to
Galilee in obedience to the command of the "angel of the Lord"
to Mary Magdalene and the other Mary: "Go quickly and tell his
disciples that he has risen from the dead, and behold, he is going before you to Galilee; there you will see him" (28:7; cf.
Mark 14:28). The mountain of meeting is not named, and no
mountain is mentioned in the command or in the resurrection accounts of the other gospels.[1] Matt 28:16-20 is, however, the
culmination of seven mountain scenes in this Gospel;[2] most
critics regard the mountain in verse 17 as symbolic.

1

The risen Jesus is seen, but not described. There is no
effort made to narrate the numinous effect or change in his appearance, nor to insist on his physical reality. He is worshipped by the eleven, as he is by Mary Magdalene and the other
Mary in 28:9, but here in the final scene the worship is mixed
with doubt. That is, the eleven (or--less likely--some of the
eleven) worship with a hesitant, divided faith.[3] Jesus draws
near and speaks the words of the great commission. A new note
is struck in this Gospel by the statement that he has received
all power "in heaven and on earth" (v. 18b). According to
Matthew, Jesus already had in his ministry the ἐξουσία to teach,
heal, forgive sins, perform exorcisms and cleanse the temple
(see Matt 7:29; 21:23-24, 27; 8:9; 9:6, 8). But here in the
appearance on the mountain his ἐξουσία has unlimited, cosmic
dimensions.

Furthermore, a new commissioning of the disciples is based
on this total empowering of Jesus. In the first place, their
mission is now to "all nations," that is, to all the peoples of
the earth, to Jews and Gentiles.[4] This comes as a surprise, in
view of the restriction of the mission of the disciples (10:5-6)
and of Jesus himself (15:24) to "the lost sheep of the house of
Israel." A wider mission has been hinted at and anticipated
earlier in the Gospel,[5] but it is only in the death-resurrection
of Jesus that limitations are abolished; the kingdom of God is
thought to break into this age in a new, fuller way. In the
second place, the disciples are now for the first time portrayed
as commissioned to teach. Throughout his ministry, Jesus has
been presented as teaching;[6] in the missionary discourse in
chapter 10, the disciples had received the power to cast out
devils, heal, perform other miracles and preach. But the power
to teach has been reserved until this final moment (contrast
Mark 6:30). The commands of the earthly Jesus are to be the
content of the disciples' teaching; that is, they are to trans-
mit his radical reinterpretation of Torah in the light of the
obligation to love, even one's enemies (5:44; 7:12).[7]

The other specification of the general commission to make
disciples is the command to baptize. The only other references
to baptism in the Gospel of Matthew concern the baptism of John

(3:1-17, 21:23-27). In the Synoptics neither Jesus nor his
disciples are presented as having baptized during his ministry.
In contrast, the Fourth Gospel provides the probably accurate
historical information that Jesus and his disciples did for
awhile continue the practice of the Baptist.[8] The triadic
phrase we will be examining is associated with the action of
baptizing: it is to be done "in the name of the Father, and of
the Son and of the Holy Spirit." What seems to be spoken of
here is initiation or incorporation into the eschatological
community.

The pericope ends with the promise of presence "until the
close of the age." There is no speculation on when or how the
end will come. Focus is not on the imminence of the end, which
Matthew elsewhere correlates with the coming of the Son of Man
(cf. 24:3, 13:39-41), but on the task ahead. Jesus does not
depart or ascend or disappear. His presence, so to speak,
merges into history, into the lives of the commissioned. The
impression is strong that this Jesus has already ascended. The
scene, that is, is "a Christophany of the resurrected ascended
one."[9] He has not been "taken" from his disciples, but rather
draws near to them and draws them in a new way. The narrative
remains open.[10]

This final Matthean pericope is, in the words of Meier,
one of those great pericopes in the bible "which constantly en-
gender discussion and research, while apparently never admitting
of definite solutions."[11] It is widely considered to be of
central significance theologically and thematically to the entire Gospel of Matthew and the key to its understanding.[12] Every
important Matthean theme is caught up here in this carefully
constructed and heavily redacted passage.[13] At the same time,
there is a strangeness about the scene that prompts a few
critics like J. A. T. Robinson to argue that "as a climax to
the Gospel, it is so completely out of line with the rest of
Matthew's eschatology that I cannot believe he himself created
it."[14] Meier more carefully notes that the pericope shows
there may be a great deal more "realized eschatology" in Matthew's theology than is usually admitted.[15] The unique features
of the scene also show that it is "simultaneously both more and
less than an Easter story."[16] The question of the *Gattung* of

the pericope and that of the precise amount of tradition and
redaction in it are still debated.[17]

In spite of the careful attention of scholars to this pericope, the tendency has been to abstract the triadic phrase, "in
the name of the Father and of the Son and of the Holy Spirit,"
from discussion of the pericope as a whole. It has not been
generally considered an integral part of the passage nor a clue
to its meaning and Christology, nor has analysis of the pericope
been thought to elucidate the phrase. Critical opinion concerning the triadic phrase is found for the most part in isolated
remarks in commentaries, in early chapters of works which treat
the development of the dogma of the Trinity, and occasionally
in appendices to theologies of the NT which emphasize lines of
thinking which move beyond the NT. There seem to be several
reasons for the lack of focused treatment of the phrase in its
Matthean context. (1) The danger of reading too much into the
phrase from the perspective of later Christian dogmatic controversy and piety may have made it an unattractive subject for
some exegetes.[18] (2) The mention in the phrase of Father, Son
and Holy Spirit seems to some to have a self-evident meaning:
the names of God, the Messiah, and the Spirit of prophecy and
inspiration are simply linked. (3) The triadic phrase is considered by others a late, fourth century interpolation into the
Matthean text, representing the developed Trinitarian thinking
of the church. (4) Most regard the triadic phrase a traditional liturgical formulation of the Matthean church, the baptismal
formula in current use in that community. Matthew's use of it
is seen as merely a concession to practice; the phrase is not
understood as meaningfully rooted in its Gospel context. The
development of the tradition which produced the phrase, and the
meaning it might have had for the community which produced it,
go largely unexplored.[19]

Each of these points will be discussed in this chapter and
the following chapters, as we examine the triadic phrase from
several different angles. We turn first to a summary of research regarding the classification of the phrase, its uniqueness in relation to other NT triadic material, its grammatical
meaning, and then to discussion of theories regarding its

incorporation into the final pericope and regarding its origin
and development.

### B. Matt 28:19b and Its Relation to Other
### NT Triadic Passages

1. Definition of Terms: triad, trinitarian, Trinitarian

    In works which treat the NT roots or sources of later
Trinitarian dogma, we find the following distinctions made.
Material is considered "triadic" if, regardless of titles used,
the three figures of Jesus, God and Spirit appear in a fashion
that indicates their coordination in the mind of the author
and/or the tradition being used.[20]  Included as well in the
discussion here are the instances in which the presence of
God is implied in a divine passive or in which angels appear
in the place of the Spirit.[21]  In the investigation in subsequent chapters of triadic passages in Daniel and in intertestamental works, a triad is considered to be a union of three
closely related figures or forces depicted (temporarily or permanently) in one heavenly place or in one heavenly action.

    There is no agreement among scholars as to the exact number
and content of triadic texts.  As Martin notes, "Acceptance or
rejection of a given passage among the hard core of texts considered by nearly all commentators usually hinges upon the manner in which the term *pneuma* is interpreted in each instance."[22]
In some instances, it can be argued that the term refers not to
the Spirit of God, but to the spirit understood as a component
of Christ's inner life or personal existence or his functioning
in the world, or to an energy or psychological force (human or
divine).  For example, 1 Tim 3:16 speaks of Christ "who was
manifested in the flesh, vindicated in the spirit, seen by angels, preached among the nations, believed on in the world,
taken up in glory."  See also 1 Pet 3:18: "Christ also died for
sins once for all, the righteous for the unrighteous, that he
might bring us to God, being put to death in the flesh but made
alive in the spirit."[23]  Rom 1:3-4 also contains a contrast between flesh and spirit, but it should be included as a triadic
text: "the gospel concerning his Son, who was descended from
David according to the flesh and designated Son of God in power

according to the Spirit of holiness by his resurrection from
the dead." The idea of Jesus having been "vindicated in the
spirit" or "made alive in the spirit" is a contributing factor
to the idea of the Spirit's role in the resurrection of Jesus.
It is also sometimes difficult to determine where a unit begins
and ends, and, therefore, whether mention of the three members
of the triad in contiguous verses really constitutes a triadic
text. John 3:34-35 and Luke 10:21-22, which will be discussed
later, are examples of texts which should be classified as triadic passages, but are never so regarded.

Triadic NT texts are often classified as (1) triadic formulas, in which the three are closely united in a phrase or
sentence that seems grounded in worship or liturgical use but
does not seem integral to the NT writer's argument; (2) triadic
thought patterns, in which the three appear in a brief statement of an author's thought; (3) triadic schema or ground plans,
in which mention of the three appears to structure a fairly extensive argument of the author.[24] Mention should also be made
of narratives which contain the triad: for example, the Synoptic narratives of the baptism of Jesus (cf. John 1:32-34) and
the infancy narratives (cf. Matt 1:18-23 and Luke 1:35). Matt
28:19b is widely considered an example of the first classification, and texts such as John 14:16 ("And I will pray the Father,
and he will give you another Counselor, to be with you forever")
are considered examples of the second. Wainwright finds a
threefold schema in the outline of Romans,[25] an example of the
third classification.

Most of the controversy concerning the triadic texts dis-
solves into the question of their interpretation in the light
of later Trinitarian dogma. Is the Trinity an entirely post-
biblical doctrine, or do some or any of these NT texts antici-
pate or approximate the notion of three divine persons in one
Godhead or divine nature? Since the doctrine was formulated in
philosophical terms that are not used in the NT, the answer to
that question is judged to be found by asking two further questions: (1) Can we detect in a given text any indication that
the Spirit is thought of as a person or a being similar to the
other two members of the triad? (2) Is there any indication

that the unity of the three is stressed or implied?  Theoretically, if the answer to both the above questions is affirmative,
it is claimed by most critics that the text under consideration
should be considered "trinitarian."  That is, the text does an-
ticipate or approximate or lay the foundation for a doctrine of
a coequal trinity of persons.  This does not mean that there is
a formal and explicit doctrine of the Trinity in the NT.  There
may be no evidence of a conscious effort to establish a triadic
conception of God, a tri-unity, but there is indication that
thoughts were moving in that direction.

     These questions are easier to pose than to answer.  The
situation is complicated by these further points: first, the
word "person" cannot be used without a great deal of qualifica-
tion.  As Rahner and others have insisted, the contemporary
meaning of the term (an individual center of consciousness,
concrete spiritual being, center of exercised existence, life,
freedom) is quite different from its meaning in the Trinitarian
controversies and formulations of dogma (a distinct self, capable of relation, ὑπόστασις, mode of subsistence).[26]  The later
concept of "person" is in itself a product of reflection on the
biblical material, which deals with aspects (such as "corporate
personality") that are difficult for us to grasp fully.  It is
illegitimate, therefore, to dismiss a text as trinitarian because one does not find in it three persons in the contemporary
sense of the term.  Paul's conception of Christ, for example,
as Moule points out, transcends the merely individual.[27]  The
Spirit, as many have noted, is never addressed as a "You" in
either the OT or the NT.  Daniélou considers the word "angel"
to be the old-fashioned equivalent of "person."  "Angel" was
thought of as having an essentially concrete force, and conno-
tated an eternal supernatural being manifesting itself, a distinct spiritual substance.[28]  The "personal" aspects taken on
by the intertestamental idea of the Spirit were borrowed from
the idea of angelic spirits.[29]  As the *mal'ak Yahweh* in the OT
was often a manifestation of God, angels in the intertestamental
period could also be thought of, in some cases, as extensions
of the power of God.  They do not really qualify as independent
"persons" in the contemporary sense.  It seems necessary, therefore, when working with biblical or intertestamental materials,

to operate without a strict definition of person, and to be content with clues that point in the direction of some self-
distinctness and relational capacity, however vague.[30]

Second, there is a further complication in the fact that
unity may be stressed without any intended implication of equality. Angels participate in and belong to the heavenly realm
and intertestamental figures such as Melchizedek and the translated, transformed figures Enoch and Elijah and others also belong to this realm, having in a sense crossed the gulf between
divinity and humanity. The term "elohim" is applied to Melchizedek five times in 11Q Melchizedek,[31] and Philo calls Moses
θεός. Unity may be considered by some NT writers quite apart
from the question of equality: see John 10:30 ("I and the Father
are one") with John 14:28 ("the Father is greater than I").

A third complication is introduced into the discussion by
the insistence of some critics that we can detect "trinitarian"
thinking only if we can detect an awareness on the part of NT
writers of the "problem" of the relation of Jesus, God and
Spirit, that is, the problem of reconciling Jewish monotheism
with the divinity of Jesus and the personhood of the Spirit.
Insofar as the doctrine is answer to a problem, according to
Wainwright, the doctrine of the Trinity emerges in the NT, although there is no formal statement of a position. The "trinitarian problem" arose in the Fourth Gospel, and partially in
other NT writings. Only in the Fourth Gospel is there an attempt to answer it, to show Father, Son and Spirit different
from each other yet one, and therefore only in the Fourth Gospel is there trinitarian thinking.[32] The flexibility of Jewish
monotheism in the Greco-Roman period, however, indicates that
we are in danger of formulating the "problem" anachronistically.
Furthermore, attempts to read NT material in terms of answers
to such a problem may result in blocking our perceptions of
more authentic origins of the material.[33]

Because of these complications, the word "trinitarian"
will be used here sparingly, to refer to instances where unity
of the three figures (God, Jesus and Spirit) is implied or
stressed, and where the Spirit can be considered to have vaguely
"personal" characteristics. The notion of equality is not

clearly implied, nor are the texts necessarily seen as an answer
to the "trinitarian problem."[34]  The terms "Trinity" and "Trinitarian" are reserved for the stage of formal doctrine at which
God is clearly perceived as tri-personal, coequal.  The biblical
material does not reflect this stage.[35]  It will be seen, however, that some of the biblical imagery and symbolism we will
examine does present in its own way startling claims which
challenged early thinkers.  Our effort will be to recover those
challenges.

## 2. The Classification of Matt 28:19b and Its Uniqueness in the NT

     Matt 28:19b is classified almost without exception as a
"triadic formula" with roots in the Church's worship and liturgical expression.  It is further classified by many as "Trinitarian" as the term has been defined above in the strict doctrinal sense.  Those critics who consider the phrase a late
interpolation into the text and even some others who consider
it a part of the received text, understand it as a close ap-
proximation to the developing Trinitarian theology of the
Church: Father, Son and Holy Spirit have been united here under
the rubric of one "name," that is, one presence or power or one
essence.  Implied or even explicit, according to this interpretation, are the notions that the unity of God involves a triad
and that this is a triad of equal persons.  Moule, for example,
remarks that Matt 28:19b may belong to a stage at which there
is a genuinely Trinitarian conception of God, arguing that
"when 'the Father' and 'the Son' seem to be taken beyond the
merely parabolic, and used almost as independent technical
terms, we are, perhaps, witnessing a tacit recognition of the
character of the Deity as involving reciprocity and dialogue."[36]
He considers that this text may be a product of a period which
held a truly Trinitarian conception of God, but that it is
doubtful whether any of the other NT phrases are in this category.[37]  Rahner argues that while there is no systematic doctrine of the "immanent" Trinity in the NT, the nearest to such
a proposition is Matt 28:19b.[38]  Fortman takes exception to the
assertion of Wainwright that this formula in Matt 28:19b has no

Trinitarian doctrinal implication.[39]  He asks, "Could the evangelist put the Father, Son and Spirit together in this way
without insinuating or implying that for him the Son and Holy
Spirit are distinct from the Father and on the same level with
the Father, who is obviously God?  Can it really be denied that
the sacred writer here presents the three as at once a triad
and a unity?"[40]

Schweizer, whose work on Matt 28:16-20 is unusual in that
it contains an extended excursus on the triadic phrase, is more
cautious.  He insists that this passage goes beyond all other
NT triadic passages, because it brings all three together in a
single name, and this is crucial to what is being said.  But he
does not believe that this deals with any developed doctrine of
the Trinity; rather, "behind the threefold formula stands the
conviction that in the Son as well as in the Spirit, God himself
becomes present, without any restriction or dimunition...."[41]
He goes on to say that this implies a profound conception of a
nonisolated, active, nonstatic, nonabstract God who is love.
He links this idea with that of an "original act of love" implied "both after Matthew and in his period" by the Christian
community when it spoke of the Son who was already present with
the Father before creation.[42]

G. F. Moore and Hans Kosmala do not classify the Matthean
phrase or discuss it in a manner similar to that of the critics
considered above, but their insights and opinions are of interest here.  The former would, I think, be inclined to classify
the Matthean phrase as simply "triadic."  Moore remarks that it
is anachronistic to read the phrase "in the name of the Father,
Son and Holy Spirit" as a Trinitarian formula, and that it is
unnecessary to suspect in it the influence of Gentile Christianity.  He considers it as a statement by (Jewish) Christians
for Gentile converts.  Speaking of the phrase as it appears in
the *Didache* 7:1-3, Moore says it is a statement of monotheism,
messianism, and prophetic community.  Jewish believers thought
it appropriate for Gentile converts to confess their faith in
the one true God, the Father, and in his Son the Messiah, and
in the Holy Spirit of inspiration in the society of believers
and especially in their prophets.  It was considered sufficient

in the case of Jews or Samaritans (who had no need to profess monotheism) to baptize in the name of the Lord Jesus or Jesus Christ.[43] In a somewhat similar vein, Kosmala thinks that the threefold formula was not needed as long as the gospel was preached only to Israel: Israel knew and believed in God the Father, knew of the Holy Spirit who, emanating from God, had inspired the prophets. What it did not know was the name of the Messiah and, therefore, the name of Jesus was the center of the earliest Christian message. The need for the teaching about "the three divine powers," according to Kosmala, arose as a result of the early Christian mission among the Gentiles (cf. 2 Cor 13:14, 1 Cor 12:2, Eph 2:11-12, 3:2, 4:17). In the "Hellenistic" world it was necessary to make the name of Jesus known *together with* "the Father and Creator who had planned everything, and the Holy Spirit, the active divine power."[44]

The above theories and classifications, with the exception of Moore's, regard the Matthean triadic phrase as stating or implying ontological identity among the members, and so, in the opinion of some critics, passing beyond the bounds of "Hellenistic Jewish Christianity."[45] Its conception in a "Hellenistic" environment is assumed. Kilpatrick gives "the surprising Trinitarian formula" of 28:19b as evidence that Matthew "reflected no weak or noncommittal Christology." This scholar considers the Gospel of Matthew thoroughly Christian, its Judaism subordinate to its Christology, and its Christology the main thing which separated it from Judaism.[46]

Before discussing other factors operating in the above classifications and interpretations of the Matthean triadic phrase, it is well to consider briefly the uniqueness of that phrase in relation to the fifty or so NT passages considered triadic by various critics. The Matthean phrase is unique in four respects. (1) Only Matt 28:19b draws the three members of the triad into a unity of some sort by seeming to attribute one "name" to all three. The titles of the three are in the genitive case, following one *nomen regens*. There is one other NT text that bears some relation to this. Luke 9:28 attributes δόξα to the Father, the Son of Man, and angels: "when he (the Son of Man) comes in his glory and that of the Father and of the holy angels," (ὅταν ἔλθῃ ἐν τῇ δόξῃ αὐτοῦ καὶ τοῦ πατρὸς καὶ τῶν ἁγίων ἀγγέλων).  In contrast, there are many texts in which the three names or titles are separated by different *nomina regentia* and other material.  One example is the formula of blessing in 2 Cor 13:14: "The grace of the Lord Jesus Christ and the love of God and the fellowship of the Holy Spirit be with you all."  See also Jude 20-21: "But you, beloved, build yourselves up on your most holy faith; pray in the Holy Spirit; keep yourselves in the love of God; wait for the mercy of our Lord Jesus Christ unto eternal life."  The significance and meaning of the phrase "into the name" in Matt 28:19b will be discussed in the following section of this paper.

(2) Matt 28:19b is the only text in which the three members of the triad are simply joined together by name, three names in a row, with no mention made of their functions in the Christian life or their roles in the story of Jesus or of other essential elements of the Christian faith.  Again, there is only one other authentic NT text which bears some relation to this, and again the third member of the triad is angels: "In the presence of God and of Christ Jesus and of the elect angels (ἐνώπιον τοῦ θεοῦ καὶ Χριστοῦ Ἰησοῦ καὶ τῶν ἐκλεκτῶν ἀγγέλων) I charge you to keep these rules without favor" (1 Tim 5:21).[47]

(3) Matt 28:19b is the only NT text in which the three are linked in what appears to be a baptismal formula.  Elsewhere in Acts and in the Epistles, baptism is spoken of as in, on, or into the name of (the Lord) Jesus Christ.  Acts 2:38 reads, "Repent, and be baptized every one of you in the name of Jesus Christ for the forgiveness of your sins."  See also Acts 8:16; 10:48; Rom 6:3; 1 Cor 1:13, 15; 6:11.  In the opinion of almost all critics, this indicates the threefold name was added to an originally monadic formula and represents a later liturgical development.[48]  The Matthean triadic formula is unique also in that nowhere else in the four gospels is there another phrase that looks like a baptismal formula.  Not even baptism "in the name of Jesus" is recorded in the gospels, which speak only of the baptism of John, the baptism of repentence, the baptism of the "coming one" who will baptize with the Holy Spirit (Mark 1:8 and John 1:33) and with fire (Matt 3:11, par. Luke 3:16),

and of baptism as a metaphor for the death of Jesus (Mark 10:
38-39 and Luke 12:50)[49] and release of the Holy Spirit.  In
spite of the fact that it seems clear that baptism was practiced
from the earliest days of Christianity, there is also no other
text besides Matt 28:19b which attributes this practice to a
command of Jesus.[50]

There are many passages, however, in which the triad occurs
in a baptismal context.[51]  Acts 2:38 continues, "and you shall
receive the gift of the Holy Spirit.  For the promise is to you
and to your children and to all that are far off, every one of
whom the Lord our God calls to him" (Acts 2:38-39).  In 1 Cor
6:11 there is the same combination of a (possible) mention of
baptism in the name of the Lord Jesus Christ, and a triad: "but
you were washed, you were sanctified, you were justified in (ἐν)
the name of the Lord Jesus Christ and in the Spirit of God."
The triad occurs again in a baptismal context in Titus 3:4-6:
"but when the goodness and loving kindness of God our Saviour
appeared, he saved us, not because of deeds done by us in righteousness, but in virtue of his own mercy, by the washing of
regeneration and renewal in the Holy Spirit, which he poured
out upon us richly through Jesus Christ our Saviour."  A triad
appears in the Synoptic accounts of the baptism of Jesus: Jesus
(beloved Son), Spirit of God (Holy Spirit in Luke), voice (of
the Father) (Matt 3:16-17, Mark 1:10-11, Luke 3:21-22).  In
John 1:33-34 we find the triad of Holy Spirit, God's elect
one,[52] "the One who sent me to baptize with water."[53]  Barth
points out that "the Father, the coming Messiah (or Son) and
the Spirit mentioned in the Baptist's preaching became manifest
in connection with Jesus' baptism."[54]  A triad occurs in Peter's
speech to the Gentile Cornelius at Joppa apparently in an account of Jesus' baptism: Peter tells "how God anointed (ἔχρισεν)
Jesus of Nazareth with the Holy Spirit and with power (δυνάμει);
how he went about doing good and healing all that were oppressed
by the devil, for God was with him" (Acts 10:38).  Ephesians 2:
13-22 is an example of a baptismal motif, connected with the
idea of restoring the lost "image of God" according to which the
first human was created.[55]  In this passage we find the triad
Christ Jesus, Spirit, Father: "through him (Jesus) we both

(those who are near and those who are far off) have access in
one Spirit to the Father" (v. 18). 1 Peter 1:2 is addressed to
the exiles "chosen and destined by God the Father and sanctified by the Spirit for obedience to Jesus Christ and for sprink-
ling with his blood." This address precedes the first part of
the epistle (1:3 to 4:11) in which allusions to baptism are so
numerous that this section, according to Fitzmyer, should be
regarded as a baptismal exhortation incorporated into the
letter.[56]

(4) Finally, the Matthean triad in 28:19b is unique in the
Gospel of Matthew in its particular combination of titles, "the
Father," "the Son" and "the Holy Spirit." Matthew does have
other triadic passages, but with different titles. The baptismal scene contains the triad of Beloved Son, voice (of God) and
Spirit of God. The infancy narrative contains the triad Holy
Spirit, Jesus, God (1:18-23). Matthew unites Jesus and the
Spirit of God in the coming of the kingdom of God through exor-
cism in 12:28 where it is probable that he has changed the more
primitive phrase, "the finger of God," in the parallel in Luke
11:20, to a mention of the Spirit. Matthew alone uses Isa 42
1-4, with its triad of Yahweh (speaking), servant, and Spirit
(12:18-19). Matt 12:32 (parallel in Luke 12:10) reads, "Whoever says a word against the Son of Man will be forgiven; but
whoever speaks against the Holy Spirit will not be forgiven."
If a divine passive is intended here, this can also be included
as a triadic passage.

In addition, Matthew has three triads of Son of Man,
Father, and angels, all in the context of judgment or parousia
(25:31-46, 13:41-43, 16:27--the first two only in Matthew).
Matt 24:36 also contains the triad of Son, Father and angels,
taken from Mark 13:32. Matthew alone contains the triadic passage in 26:53 ("Do you think that I cannot appeal to my Father,
and he will at once send me more than twelve legions of
angels?").[57]

The Matthean scene of the death of Jesus may also be considered triadic, if it can be argued that in changing Mark's
word for the final moment, "he expired," (ἐξέπνευσεν, Mark 15:
37, 39)[58] to "he yielded up the spirit" (ἀφῆκεν τὸ πνεῦμα, Matt

27:50; cf. John 19:30, παρέδωκεν τὸ πνεῦμα), Matthew is thinking
of more than Jesus' life force or breath. This is unlikely,
however. Matthew is probably stressing Jesus' courage and
voluntary acceptance of death. The reference in Matt 27:50 is
to the spirit of life given by God and now given back by Jesus;
no reference to the Holy Spirit is intended here.[59] The scene,
then, can be considered triadic only in embryonic form. In
this it corresponds to such passages as 1 Pet 3:18 and 1 Tim
3:16.[60] The notion of voluntary acceptance of suffering and
death, even at the beginning of his ministry, may be an important motif in the Synoptic accounts of the baptism of Jesus,[61]
which can also be read as anticipations of the resurrection.
Barth notes that the declaration of the heavenly voice and the
descent of the Spirit in the baptismal narratives correspond to
the "justification" of the crucified one by his resurrection
(1 Tim 3:16).[62] The above references to triadic texts in Matthew indicate that he may have been conscious of the significance
of the triad, and preserved and stressed it at crucial moments
in the story. The particular combination of titles found in
28:19b, however, is found nowhere else in his Gospel.[63]

The combination of titles, "the Father," "the Son" and
"the Holy Spirit" is found in one other passage in the NT: in
Luke 10:21-22. This significant text, and the related text
John 3:34-35 which contains the almost identical triad of "the
Father," "the Son" and "the Spirit" will be discussed below in
connection with the tradition behind Matt 28:16-20.

In great part, the fact that the Matthean triadic phrase
is unique in the four respects considered above has influenced
its classification as a "Trinitarian" phrase. Its grammatical
form and the particular titles used became standard both in
baptismal ritual procedure and in Trinitarian theology. But
the criteria we set in the previous section for classification
either as "trinitarian" or "Trinitarian" have not been met. A
closer look at other aspects of the phrase in Matthew's Gospel
is required before the discussion is temporarily closed concerning its classification. A full discussion of the meaning of
Matt 28:19b must be postponed until we have a grasp of (1) the
traditions Matthew may have been using, and (2) the theological

statement made both in the tradition and in the final Matthean
pericope.

3. "Into the Name"

In discussions of the triadic phrase in Matt 28:19b as
Trinitarian, it is often implied or explicitly stated that the
"name" theology of the OT is operative here.  The divine Name
is seen as a holy reality, almost with an existence in its own
right, a symbol of the presence of Yahweh.  This idea is based
on the ancient belief that name is a manifestation of soul, a
part of the personality, the influence and authority of the
person.  In the OT and in intertestamental Judaism, the Name
can be described as the essential revelation of God's being.
Matt 28:19b is read by some as intending the extention of the
one Name or power to all three members of the triad.  The transfer of the name κύριος to the exalted one in the pre-Pauline
hymn Phil 2:6-11 shows that the idea of one Name given to all
three might not be impossible, even at an early period.[64]  It
is not clear, however, that this was the intention of Matthew.
The phrase could also be understood to mean "in the name of the
Father, and (in the name) of the Son and (in the name) of the
Holy Spirit."  Grammatically, either interpretation is possible.[65]

The use of the triadic phrase in later documents is also
ambiguous.  In the *Didache* 7, we have instruction given concerning the rite of baptism, and the triadic phrase used twice is
identical to that in Matt 28:19b.[66]

> 7:1  Now about baptism: this is how to baptize.  Give
>      public instruction on all these points, and then
>      "baptize" in running water, "in the name of the
>      Father and of the Son and of the Holy Spirit."
>
>   2  If you do not haverunning water, baptize in some
>      other.
>
>   3  If you cannot in cold, then in warm.  If you have
>      neither, then pour water on the head three times
>      "in the name of the Father, Son and Holy Spirit."[67]

No further information is given here regarding the understanding
of the "name."  Two chapters later, however, when laying down
regulations about people who are entitled to participate in the
Eucharist, the author describes them as "those who have been

(1:23),[83] there is no indication in Matthew that the "name" of
God has been given to Jesus, much less to the Holy Spirit, as a
focus of their unity.

Another angle of investigation involves the possibility
that εἰς τὸ ὄνομα may simply be a common phrase, without the
overtones of the OT "name" theology.  In Hellenistic inscriptions
and papyri, εἰς τὸ ὄνομα is frequent with a financial meaning:
a sum of money is paid "into the account" of someone.  The phrase
implies a transference of property or a passing into ownership.
Soldiers also took an oath, and pseudonymous documents were
written εἰς τὸ ὄνομα.[84]  The meaning then, in the Matthean context, would be that the baptized person was dedicated to Father,
Son and Spirit, becoming their property.  A transference has
taken place.[85]  Lars Hartman, however, warns against assuming
too easily that technical commercial or military terms were used
to supply the imagery in the NT.  We cannot assume that the same
meaning was carried from one context to another.  He is of the
opinion that the phrase was more neutral and carried different
meanings.[86]

An explanation of the phrase based on the Hebrew-Aramaic
expression לְשׁוּם or לְשֵׁם, a term found in the Mishnah and Talmud[87]
and elsewhere, leads to a similar interpretation, though the
Semitic phrase is more elastic.  Here שֵׁם does not have the
strict meaning, "name," but the phrase means "with regard to,"
"with reference to," "for the sake of," "because of," "in the
interests of," "with the obligation of venerating," "for."  It
is a flexible phrase, and can denote both the basis and purpose
of that which is named.  The meaning in the baptismal context
would have to do with the relationship between the baptized and
the Father, Son and Spirit.[88]  Hartman again cautions, this time
against finding too precise a grammatical aspect and of distinguishing too sharply between a causal and final meaning of the
phrase, which is itself neutral, its meaning depending on its
context.[89]  In ritual matters, the phrase was used "to introduce the type, reason, or purpose of the rite as well as its
intention."  With respect to baptism, the phrase could indicate
a kind of "fundamental reference," characterizing the rite,
qualifying it, distinguishing it from other rites, defining it.[90]

Is it possible, then, that in Matt 28:19b we have a definition
of a type of baptism, that of Father-Son-Spirit, distinguished
from the simple Jesus type of baptism?  The evidence from the
Mishnah and Talmud, however, is much later than the NT.

There is a further interpretation based on a Semitic idiom,
but one which is used in the OT and which could have a technical
meaning in ritual matters.  Barth and others interpret εἰς τὸ
ὄνομα in analogy to the Hebrew formula קרא בשם, "calling on the
name."  According to this theory, at the administration of baptism there was a proclamation or invocation, making clear reference to the rite's cause, purpose and distinctiveness.[91]  Hartman thinks that the arguments in favor of the hypothesis that
the name (of Jesus, or of the triad) was actually uttered at
baptism are not very strong, but that it is possible that such
an action took place.[92]  Most scholars who argue along this line
imagine that the names of the three were invoked by the baptizer,
not by the one being baptized.[93]  Or, in line with what is known
of early baptismal rites in the second to fourth centuries, the
basic element of the ritual may have been the three interroga-
tions concerning belief in each of the members of the triad.
Tertullian (De Corono 3) understood this practice to be grounded
in the command in Matt 28:19b.[94]  The declaration of belief demanded of the candidate and corresponding to the triadic formula
might have been simple assent to each question.  Occasionally,
the candidate may have made an explicit declaration of faith.[95]
The repeated description of baptism as "in the name of the Lord
Jesus" (for example, in Acts 8:16, 19:5 and 1 Cor 6:11) seems
to imply that the formula which is preserved, "Jesus is Lord,"
had a place in that rite.[96]  Acts 22:16 indicates that the baptized person was to speak out: Ananias tells Paul, "Rise and be
baptized, and wash away your sins, calling on his name" (ἐπι-
καλεσάμενος τὸ ὄνομα αὐτοῦ).  No fragments, however, of a triadic confession or statement of faith have been preserved unless,
as some argue, Luke 10:21-22, par. preserves a primitive baptismal hymn, and texts such as Mark 8:38, Rev 3:5 preserve something of the understanding that a baptismal confession on earth
corresponded to a (triadic) heavenly confession.  There is no
evidence, however, that the Holy Spirit was spoken to or invoked as a person.[97]

Acts 8:36-38 (Western text) is an illustration of a dialogue between baptizer and candidate preceding baptism.  A
statement of faith is elicited by Phillip from the eunuch, although here it is not by question, as in the later writings.[98]
In John 9:35-38, Jesus asks the former blind man if he believes
in the Son of Man.  "He answered, 'Who is he sir, that I may
believe in him?' 'You have seen him,' Jesus replied, 'for it is
he who is speaking with you.' 'I do believe, Lord,' he said
and bowed down to worship him."  The response of faith is missing in several significant manuscripts, and contains some non-
Johannine characteristics.  Brown suggests that verses 38-39
may be an addition stemming from the association of John 9 with
the baptismal liturgy and catechesis, but that baptismal symbolism may have been intended in the story by the Evangelist.[99]
There are, then, no clear instances authentic to the NT text of
a dialogue pattern or a question-answer pattern preceding the
ritual of baptism, although there are clues that this practice
may have been quite early.

The preceding gives a slightly different nuance to the
understanding of Matt 28:19b as a "liturgical formula."  The
word "formula" is often used in a very loose manner, and can
mean anything from the reproduction of the actual "official"
words used in a rite, to a concise summary of some element of
faith or practice.  If the above theory is correct, that εἰς τὸ
ὄνομα τοῦ πατρὸς καὶ τοῦ υἱοῦ καὶ τοῦ ἁγίου πνεύματος in Matt
28:19b commands that the name(s) of the three be called or mentioned by the baptizer and/or by the candidate, perhaps in
dialogue form, then Matt 28:19b is not necessarily a formula
that exactly reproduces the words uttered in the rite.  The
person baptizing, that is, is not necessarily instructed to say
"I baptize you in the name of the Father and of the Son and of
the Holy Spirit," nor is the candidate to say "I believe in the
name of the Father and of the Son and of the Holy Spirit."  The
first formula, the words of the baptizer which later became the
stereotyped form, was not even in existence by the fourth century, according to Kelly.[100]  There is a point, then, to the
contention of several scholars that it is a mistake to treat
Matt 28:19b as a liturgical formula (meaning the actual words

used in baptizing) which it later became, and not as a description of what baptism accomplished, or its nature, aim or results.[101]  Massaux's study of the influence of the Gospel of
Matthew in the early church before Irenaeus has shown the popularity of that Gospel among later Christian writers, who ap-
pealed to its account of the words of the Lord as authority for
rubric and ethical rulings.  The Gospel of Matthew "created the
climate of ordinary Christianity."[102]  But what was later taken
as rubric was not necessarily so intended by Matthew.  If Matt
28:19b is giving specific instructions about how to baptize,
calling on the Father, Son and Holy Spirit, it is the only clear
evidence in the NT material of such a practice.  *Didache* 7,
which may depend either on Matthew or on a common tradition or
custom, shows us the triadic formula firmly established in liturgical practice, perhaps as early as the end of the first century.  If Matt 28:19b, on the other hand, is merely mentioning
the characteristics of the rite, and the resulting fellowship
of the baptized with members of the triad, there is ample evidence in the NT that baptism was so understood (see, for example, Acts 2:38-39, 1 Pet 1:2, 1 Cor 6:11, Titus 3:4-6), and this
evidence comes from all NT periods.  In either case, what is
most important to our investigation here is that there is no
indication of emphasis on the one ὄνομα shared by the three.

It is impossible to decide with certainty which of the
above interpretations of the phrase εἰς τὸ ὄνομα in Matt 28:19b
is closest to the Evangelist's thought and to the way his early
readers would have understood the phrase.  Most likely, in my
opinion, the phrase characterizes the rite and may indicate that
the three names are mentioned or invoked by baptizer or baptized.
Least likely is the idea that the author intended to express the
belief that the one Name or power or essence of God was extended
to the three members of the triad.  That the text was later considered to imply this is understandable for three reasons. (1)
The word םשׁ was loaded with theological importance that was not
lost, even under the pressure of changing idioms.  (2) Matthew's
own Christology and his understanding of the Holy Spirit were
open to such an understanding, and the development of Christology and Pneumatology eventually required it in some circles.

(3) Christian baptism was considered from the beginning to involve the action and presence of Jesus, God and Spirit.  In
time, Matt 28:19b was read as a rubric, and became the phrase
used in the rite of baptism.

The phrase εἰς τὸ ὄνομα, then, is ambiguous, even though
by its brevity it pulls the three members of the triad into a
unity that is unique in the NT.  To insist that it means that
one Name is shared by all three is clearly an anachronistic interpretation.  The phrase does not warrant such metaphysical
implications laid upon it; it does not indicate that God is
perceived as a unity of three equal persons, nor is it evidence
of an analysis of interrelations.  It cannot be used as evidence
that Matt 28:19b is a "Trinitarian" statement.[103]

## 4. Matthean "trinitarianism"?

A sketchy and preliminary answer to two questions is required here.  In section 1 above, on the definitions of the
terms triad, trinitarian and Trinitarian, the word "trinitarian"
was used to refer to texts which exhibited two characteristics.
(1) In them, the Spirit can be considered as vaguely personal,
and (2) the unity of the three figures, Jesus, God and Spirit,
is stressed or implied.  In order to decide whether Matt 28:19b
qualifies as a "trinitarian" passage, it must be asked whether
these two factors are present.  At this stage of our investigation, we confine ourselves to a glance at the Christology and
Pneumatology of the Gospel as a whole, moving on the level of
the most apparent meaning of the final redactor.  Later it will
be shown that awareness of the traditional elements in 28:16-20
offers new perspective on this aspect of the triadic phrase.

Concerning the first factor, there are in Matthew eleven
passages classified in Schmoler, *Handkonkordanz*,[104] as referring
to "Dei spiritus, spiritus caelestes": 1:18, 20; 2:11, 16; 4:1;
10:20; 12:18, 28, 31; 22:43 and 28:19.[105]  In only one of these
passages does the Spirit perform a "personal" function, that of
speaking, but here it is called the Spirit of the Father.  In
Matt 10:20 the twelve disciples are promised that when they are
delivered up, what they are to say will be given to them then,
"for it is not you who speak, but the Spirit of your Father

speaking through you" (cf. Mark 13:11, Luke 12:12, Acts 7:10).[106]
In the Matthean passage, the Spirit of the Father is represented
as a being or force which takes possession of the persecuted
ones at the moment of crisis and speaks through their mouths,
either as their defense attorney or, more likely, as the one who
bears witness to Jesus (10:18). This may be no more than the
force of prophetic inspiration.[107] There is no "teaching" done
by the Spirit, as in John and Luke. Perhaps Matthew intends to
present the Spirit as personal in 4:1 ("Then Jesus was led up
[ἀνήχθη] by the Spirit into the wilderness"), but more probably
he is softening Mark's verb (ἐκβάλλει) and identifying the power
that animates Jesus. Matthew does not seem to have paid a great
deal of attention to the Holy Spirit. His thinking does not go
much beyond that of Qumran (cf. 1QH 12:11-13, 13:18-20, 14:12-
13, CD 2:12) and that found in the NT concerning the spirit of
prophecy. At Qumran we find as well the idea of the holy spirit
as guide and protector (1QH 7:6-8, 9:32). Matthew's major contribution, however, was to link the Spirit closerly with the
Father (10:12)[108] and, in his infancy narrative, with Jesus
(1:18, 20). But he did not, as far as we can tell from these
texts, clearly consider the Spirit a "person."

     To the second question, whether Matthew implies the unity
of the three figures, Father, Son and Spirit, an affirmative
answer can be given. There is no passage in Matthew where Jesus
is explicitly called "God," but the name Emmanuel is given to
him (1:23). This is not the name the child finally receives,
but as Kingsbury points out, "this ostensible anomaly...only
serves to call attention to the nature of the term Emmanuel: it
is a name not in an appelative sense, but in the sense that it
sets forth the significance of a person, viz., Jesus Messiah:
he is 'God with us.'"[109] Conceived of (ἐκ) the Holy Spirit
(1:18, 20), Jesus is empowered to make available the saving
presence of God on earth, in a sense bringing the realm of the
holy into time and space.

     Related to Matthew's exposition of "Emmanuel" is his iden-
tification or assimilation of Jesus with the figure of the Wisdom of God, already identified in Jewish tradition with Torah[110]
and with the Spirit.[111] Suggs has suggested that Matthew took

over Wisdom speculation from Q, in which Jesus and John the
Baptist had been presented as the last and greatest "envoys" of
Wisdom; their message was rejected and they were killed. Matthew
in several places altered Q (e.g., 23:34) in order to indicate
a full identification of Jesus with Wisdom; Jesus is no longer
merely the final messenger of Wisdom but is Wisdom incarnate,
and hence the embodiment also of Torah.[112] Whether or not one
accepts the details of Suggs' thesis,[113] he has, in the opinion
of several critics, accurately perceived the heights of Matthean
Christology. The close coordination between Jesus and Wisdom
indicates that for Matthew, Jesus is no merely historical individual, but a being who belongs to the heavenly realm. In 18:20
Matthew presents Jesus as the Shekinah: "For where two or three
are gathered in my name, there am I in the midst of them"; cf.
*m. 'Abot* 2:2: "But if two sit together and words of the Law (are
spoken) between them, the Divine Presence rests between them, as
it is written, 'Then they that feared the Lord spoke one with
another; and the Lord hearkened, and heard, and a book of remembrance was written before him, for them that feared the Lord,
and that thought upon his name'" (Mal 3:16).[114]

According to Matthew, the kingdom of heaven manifested itself in the person, words and deeds of Jesus with such force
that the kingdom can be considered to be a present reality in
Jesus' own day and in his afterlife. The attitude people assume
toward Jesus is their attitude toward the kingdom.[115] That
kingdom of heaven is regarded by Matthew as the kingdom both of
Jesus the Son of Man and of God, the Father.[116] Jesus, as the
one to whom total authority in heaven and on earth has been
given (28:18), will in the end use that authority to judge all
nations (7:21-23, 13:36-43, 25:31-46).

In a series of works, Birger Gerhardsson has shown that the
gospel of Matthew returns again and again to contemplation of
the *Shema'* (Deut 6:4-5) in the light of the life and teaching
of Jesus of Nazareth. Gerhardsson has argued that the temptation narrative (Matt 4:1-11) is constructed on the basis of a
midrash on the *Shema'*: in contrast to the unfaithful son,
Israel, Jesus is shown to be the righteous, faithful Son of God
who loves God with heart, soul (life) and strength.[117] The

parable of the sower in chapter 13 is constructed on the same
basis,[118] as is the Matthean crucifixion scene.[119]  In Matt 22:
37-40, Jesus is presented as arguing that Deut 6:5 is "the
great and first commandment," and Lev 19:19 is "a second...like
it."  Here is a carefully formulated hermeneutic program: "On
these two commandments depend all the law and the prophets" (v.
40).  Gerhardsson calls it "nothing less than the Matthean
Church's principles for interpretation and application of the
inherited holy scriptures"[120] and its understanding of the
principles of Jesus.  Matthew sees Jesus as the person who is
perfectly "one with" God, the person who perfectly proclaims
and lives out God's own oneness.  Jesus is loyal to God *alone*

These few examples should suffice to show that Matthew
clearly thinks of Jesus as drawing his existence from, and
operating out of the power field of God in a unique sense.  The
Spirit which is of God (10:20, 3:16) belongs as well to that
realm.  In the final pericope (28:16-20), the disciples are
afforded a vision of the risen and ascended Jesus--"in heaven"
and because of the promise of presence with them (v. 20) on
earth "always, to the close of the age."

This extraordinary conception we cannot consider "trinitarian" in the sense in which that term has here been defined,
since there is no decisive evidence in Matthew's Gospel that
the Spirit is considered "personal."  Therefore, the phrase "in
the name of the Father and of the Son and of the Holy Spirit"
(28:19) will be simply classified as "triadic" in the following
pages as attempts are made to probe for its meaning both within
and behind the Gospel setting.  Whether the phrase had another
meaning at a pre-Matthean stage is a question we will pursue
below.

## C. The Incorporation of the Triadic Phrase
into Matt 28:16-20

We turn now to an examination of theories concerning the
incorporation of the triadic phrase into the final Matthean
pericope.  Three theories will be treated in this section: (1)
that the triadic phrase is a late (second to fourth century)
interpolation; (2) that the triadic phrase is a traditional

baptismal formula which has been joined to other traditional
elements either by Matthew or before him; (3) that the triadic
phrase, and in fact the pericope as a whole, is a Matthean
composition.

1. The Triadic Phrase as a Post-Matthean Interpolation

a. *Conybeare's Argument from the Eusebian Evidence*

     The church historian Eusebius (c. 262-339), bishop of
Caesarea, quoted Matt 28:19 sixteen times without the triadic
phrase (writing instead, "Go and make disciples of all nations
in my name") and only five times in accordance with the received
text.  Conybeare noted that the shorter reading occurs in Eusebius' works before the Council of Nicea in 325, and the longer
one afterward.  This led to the tentative conclusion that the
shorter reading is original, and the longer created around 130-
140 to conform to liturgical usage, appearing perhaps first in
the African Old Latin texts, creeping then into the Greek texts
at Rome, and finally establishing itself in the East during the
Nicene epoch.[121]  It has been shown, however, that in contexts
in which Eusebius refers to Matt 28:19 using the shorter form,
the longer form was not required in connection with the point
being made.  The use of the longer, in fact, would have marred
the development of his thought.[122]  Moreover, examination of
representative passages from Eusebius illustrates the tendencies
of that writer to free and inexact quotation, and to group together various NT passages relating to the same subject.  The
longer reading occurs in contexts where such topics as the
Trinity, the "mystical regeneration" (of baptism) and the distinction of Son from Spirit as a separate person are being discussed.  These facts, according to Hubbard, "argue for the conclusion that the shorter reading is not based upon textual evidence but represents instead a free use of 28:19 with 'in my
name,' a phrase widely used in the NT."[123]

     The most telling argument against Conybeare's theory of
interpolation is that there is absolutely no NT manuscript evidence to support the shorter reading.  Conybeare thought that
the disappearance of the shorter reading from the manuscripts
could be explained by the fact that the dominant party in the

Church, which supported the consubstantiality of the Son and
Spirit with the Father, was able to correct all extant manuscripts thoroughly.[124] This seems unlikely and is, in any case,
unprovable.  It is significant that there is no other patristic
evidence apart from Eusebius to support the theory of a shorter
original.  Moreover, Eusebius himself was "anti-Trinitarian" in
that he rejected the doctrine of consubstantiality as propounded
by the Council of Nicea;[125] this may have influenced his quoting
of Matt 28:16-20.  The parallel to the Matthean triadic phrase
in *Did* 7:1, which has been discussed above, is not of clear
value in this debate because its date is disputed.[126]

b. *Other Arguments That Support the Shorter Reading*

     There have been several recent attempts, based on evidence
other than the Eusebian, to show that the shorter reading is
original to the Matthean text.  Several of these have been summarized and countered by Hubbard, whose arguments are strong
and need not be repeated or supplemented here.[127]  In addition
to these attempts, Beasley-Murray contends that the opening
declaration of Matt 18:18b demands a Christological (not triadic) statement to follow it.  "All authority in heaven and on
earth has been given *to me*" leads one to expect as a consequence,
"Go, make disciples *to me* among all the nations, baptizing them
in *my* name, teaching them to observe all *I* commanded you."[128]
This original version has been thought to represent the fulfillment of the vision of the exaltation of the Son of Man in Dan 7:
13-14 (Matt 28:18b an allusion to Dan 7:14) conceived along the
lines of the old oriental coronation of a king: verse 18 declares the assumption of universal authority by the Risen Lord:
verses 19-20a are the proclamation of his authority among the
nations; verse 20b announces his power in the guardianship of
the disciples.  "In such a scheme there would be no ground for
bringing in the triune name, for baptism is the appropriation
of the disciple-subject to the Son of Man."[129]  As will be seen
below, the suggestion of a link between verses 18b and 19b is
extremely valuable, but it does not necessitate the positing of
an originally monadic baptismal phrase.  I hope to show that
both verse 18b and verse 19b are drawn from Danielic traditions.

c. *Conclusions*

   The theory that a short version of Matt 28:19 was original
to the text, and that the triadic baptismal phrase is an interpolation has won fairly wide acceptance.  It is one way of explaining the uniqueness of the triadic phrase (in terms of its
formal grammatical structure, its connection with baptism, and
apparently its relation to Matthean theology, interests and use
of titles).[130]  The phrase is unique because it is foreign and
an interpolation.  The Synoptic tradition--and indeed the whole
of the NT--does not seem to have prepared the reader for a
phrase of such strange implications, especially if it is read
in the light of its *Nachleben*.  Vermes expresses a common opinion when he dismisses "the trinitarian formula appended to the
gospel of Matthew 28:19" as "representative of the latest stage
of doctrinal evolution and consequently out of place in a historical investigation of Jesus and his age."[131]

   But it is anachronistic to call the phrase "trinitarian,"
and the phrase does bear some relation to other NT triadic passages.  The theory that it is an interpolation cannot be upheld.
The lack of manuscript evidence, and of patristic evidence besides Eusebius's, for the shorter reading is significant.
Awareness of the tendencies of Eusebius to quote inexactly, to
conflate, and to oppose developing Trinitarian thought, lessen
the importance of his testimony.  Each of the other arguments
for the originality of the shorter reading has been also judged
to be weak.  The exegete, therefore, is justified in proceeding
on the assumption that the triadic baptismal phrase in 28:19b
is authentic to the received text.

2. The Triadic Phrase as a Traditional Baptismal Formula;
   Its Relation to Other Traditional Elements in the Final
   Pericope

   The most common opinion of NT critics is that the triadic
phrase in Matt 28:19b is a traditional baptismal formula,[132]
current in the Matthean community and incorporated by Matthew
in order to concretize the command of the risen Jesus to "make
disciples."[133]  As such, it is regarded by many as having no
further relation to its present context in the final pericope

or to the Gospel as a whole.  The Evangelist is simply supplying
a detail of his community's liturgical life.  He is not invent-
ing that liturgical practice, but grounding it in a command of
the risen Jesus.  Goulder, for example, thinks that this "agrees
with Matthew's ecclesiastical concern and his habit of justify-
ing established church procedure with a word of the Lord."  Matt
28:19b supplies the dominical authority for baptisms (presumably
administered in Eastertime) in Matthew's community.[134]  The triadic phrase is thus understood as a detached insight, the background and meaning of which remain obscure.  The pericope as a
whole does not illuminate the phrase, nor does the Matthean
concept of baptism.  The form and language of the triadic phrase
are claimed to be non-Matthean.[135]  Some regard it as a development and incorporation of Pauline theology;[136] others as a
phrase that may have stood in the lost ending of Mark.[137]  In
any case, the triadic phrase is thought to be a "community construction," probably developing out of a Christological (monadic)
form, or existing side by side with that form in certain communities.  The fact, as noted above, that baptism is spoken of in
Acts and the Epistles as "in" or "into" the name of (the Lord)
Jesus Christ, lends weight for many to the theory of "expansion."[138]

It is often the notion that the triadic phrase is a "baptismal formula" that precludes consideration of Matthean composition or even redaction of it.[139]  However, the phrase may
have originally been intended to describe the nature, aim or
results of baptism, or to indicate that the three names are
mentioned or invoked by baptizer or baptized.[140]  It is odd
that, for the most part, scholars who consider the phrase a
"community construction" do not speculate on either the "community theology" that produced it, or Matthew's theology as a
development of or reaction or response to that community thinking and practice.

There are three distinct theories concerning how and why
the traditional triadic phrase was incorporated into the final
Matthean pericope as that pericope was formed.  (1) It was
added, probably by Matthew, along with two other independent
traditional sayings, to a brief, pre-Matthean tradition of a

post-resurrection missionary charge.  This theory will be considered as it is presented by R. H. Fuller.  (2) The triadic
phrase was added by Matthew from his community's liturgical
practice to a primitive proto-commissioning narrative.  This
theory has been developed in detail by Hubbard.  (3) The triadic
phrase was embedded in a pre-Matthean "liturgical tradition"
which Matthew redacted.  The theory of Strecker (and its expansion by Meier) will be analyzed.

     (1) Fuller thinks that the pre-Matthean missionary charge
read simply, "Preach the gospel," and contained the command to
baptize.  An independent parallel is found in the Markan Appendix 16:15-16.  There was no pre-Matthean narrative of a charge,
but Matthew himself has picked up the suggestion in Mark 16:7
of a Galilean resurrection appearance.[141]  The pre-Matthean
charge has been modeled on already existing charges of the
earthly Jesus (cf. Matt 10:5).  Besides being found in the
Markan Appendix 16:16, the association of baptism with the word
of the Risen One is implied in Luke 24:45 and John 20:23, which
mention forgiveness of sins, a notion often in the NT in close
and primary connection with baptism.  The community early understood the implications of the call to evangelize in the light
of its heritage from John the Baptist.[142]  Matthew has redacted
the missionary charge, suppressing all reference to the evange-
lization of Israel,[143] adding his emphasis on "making disciples"
and on teaching,[144] and--of special interest here--changing an
original monadic baptismal formula ("baptize in my name") to
the triadic.[145]  Fuller does not develop this last suggestion
further with regard to Matthean interests or theology, but as
we will see in section C of this chapter, he thinks the Matthean
triadic phrase results from the development of a Jewish apocalyptic triad.  The Matthean phrase brings out the "triadic implications" inherent in the early community's experience of the
gospel.[146]  Matthew has, therefore, reinterpreted the earliest
tradition about an appearance to the twelve in Galilee, which
came to him via Mark 16:7.  He understood this "not as the
founding of the eschatological community, but as the inaugura-
tion of the mission."[147]

To the mission command, Matthew has joined two other traditional sayings: (a) the saying about the authority of the
exalted one: "All authority in heaven and on earth has been
given to me" ('Εδόθη μοι πᾶσα ἐξουσία ἐν οὐρανῷ καὶ ἐπὶ γῆς,
Matt 28:18b), and (b) the promise of presence: "and behold, I
am with you always, to the close of the age" (καὶ ἰδοὺ ἐγὼ μεθ'
ὑμῶν εἰμι πάσας τὰς ἡμέρας ἕως τῆς συντελείας τοῦ αἰῶνος, 28:
20b). That these sayings are traditional is shown by the fact
that they are paralleled elsewhere in the Jesus tradition. The
first, (a) Matt 28:18b, is paralleled in Matt 11:27: "All things
have been delivered to me by my Father" (πάντα μοι παρεδόθη ὑπὸ
τοῦ πατρός μου; cf. Luke 10:22) and in John 3:35: "The Father...
has given all things into his hand" (ὁ πατὴρ πάντα δέδωκεν ἐν τῇ
χειρὶ αὐτοῦ). The common source of this tradition is Dan 7:11
LXX, which Fuller believes was first applied to Jesus as the
exalted Son of Man by the Hellenistic-Jewish community.[148] The
second traditional saying, (b) Matt 28:20b, is related to the
tradition in 18:20: "For where to or three are gathered in my
name, there am I in the midst of them." It is perhaps related
also to the saying in P. Ox. 1: "Lift up the stone and there
you will find me; cleave the wood and I am there."[149] Fuller
thinks that Matt 28:20b, 18:20 and the agraphon are all derived
from a common original which was circulated as a saying of the
exalted Lord. It originated as an utterance of a Christian
prophet, who modeled it on Jewish beliefs about the Shekinah
(cf. m. 'Abot 3:2). The utterance reflects, says Fuller, a
faith in the presence of the risen Jesus in the Christian assembly, in anticipation of the parousia.[150]

The fact that it was Matthew himself who fused the mission
command with these two independent logia is clear to Fuller because of the large number of Mattheanisms that these verses
contain.[151] Many other scholars agree that three traditional
sayings have been joined by Matthew in this pericope,[152] and
that the pericope is formed of three independent logia, whose
motifs are nowhere else joined.[153] Several criticisms, however,
can be offered concerning this theory. It does not take sufficient account of the similarities between Matt 28:16-20 and the
post-resurrection commission narratives in the other gospels

and Acts, nor is it based on a sufficiently thorough analysis
of Matthean redaction.  Furthermore, the possibility of a relationship among the traditional elements in Matt 28:16-20 is
unexplored.

(2) The second theory, proposed by Hubbard, is that the
triadic phrase was added by Matthew to a narrative of a primitive
missionary charge.  While Hubbard considers 28:16-20 to consist
of the same three elements discussed above (the saying about
authority in v. 18b, the missionary charge in vv. 19-20a, the
promise of presence in v. 20b), only the missionary charge is
said to come from the tradition.  The declaration of authority
and the promise of presence are called "Matthean redactional
elements," although they are also "themes known before Matthew's
time."  The former is reflected in Matt 11:27 (Q) and the latter
in passages which speak of the Lord's or the Spirit's assisting
presence.[154]  The missionary charge is found in the primitive
apostolic commissioning, reconstructed in this way:

| | |
|---|---|
| *confrontation:* | Jesus appeared to the eleven. |
| *reaction:* | When they saw him they were glad, though some disbelieved. |
| *commission:* | Then he said: preach (the gospel) to all nations.  (Baptize) in my name for the forgiveness of sins. |
| *reassurance:* | (and behold) I will send the Holy Spirit upon you.[155] |

This reconstruction is regarded as the tradition common to Matt
28:16-20, Luke 24:36-49, John 20:19-23 and the Markan Appendix
16:14-18.  The primitive narrative is a (written?) statement of
credentials for preaching; it is the narrative of an appearance
of the risen Jesus, the experience of which is an essential
element of what constitutes a person an apostle and transfers
authority to that person.  The proto-commissioning is "one step
removed from the actual account of Jesus' Easter commission on
the lips of an original disciple."[156]  A universalistic emphasis
has been added by someone involved in the Gentile mission.[157]
To this whole, Matthew has added elements from his own distinctive perspective.  He has added, for example, the location in
Galilee (drawn from Mark), the mountain (Matthew's mythological
symbol), the emphasis on the authority of the Risen One (drawn

directly from Dan 7:14 and indirectly from that passage via the
saying in Matt 11:27).[158]  The emphasis on obedience to Jesus'
commands and the promise of Jesus' abiding presence are also
Matthean redaction, the latter catching up the God-with-us
theme in 1:23.

Concerning the triadic phrase, Hubbard notes that the passages he has compared from Matthew, Luke and John all have express mention of God "the Father,"[159] and a reference of some
kind to the Holy Spirit,[160] which with mention of Jesus form a
triad, even if not a triadic phrase.  The original tradition,
however, mentioned only Jesus and the Spirit: the reference to
the Father found its way independently into all three accounts.[161]
What the proto-commissioning provided was material for the composition of Matt 28:19b: it provided mention of forgiveness of
sins and possibly of baptism in Jesus' name, and the promise of
the Spirit's assistance.  This made the incorporation of the
triadic baptismal formula (sanctioned by the liturgical use of
Matthew's community) consistent and understandable.[162]

This theory is not without serious difficulties.  One important inadequacy is that the difference is not spelled out
between finding and redacting an element in the tradition, and
using a "theme" that is known and exerting its influence via
other sayings.  The vagueness of the phrase, "themes known before Matthew's time," in reference to the saying about authority
(28:18b) and the promise of presence (v. 20b), indicates that
the method of determining redaction is less rigorous at this
point than it should be.  Several of the verbal and thematic
"parallels" found in the resurrection appearance accounts are
not convincing.[163]  The approach presented by Hubbard, however,
is valuable especially with regard to our study, in that it
shows that elements of the triadic phrase are echoed in the
other accounts and may be related to earlier tradition.  The
primary thesis of Hubbard, that the proto-commissioning and the
Matthean pericope are strongly influenced by the form of an OT
commission narrative, is an insight which we will explore in a
later chapter.

(3) The third theory to be examined here is that there was
a certain pre-Matthean unity in the sayings (including the

triadic phrase) in verses 18-20. Georg Strecker's position is
that there was already in the liturgical tradition of Matthew's
community a "word of revelation." This unit roughly ran: "All
authority in heaven and on earth has been given to me (28:18b).
Baptize in the name of the Father and of the Son and of the Holy
Spirit (v. 19b). I am with you always" (v. 20b). The reason
for considering these elements already joined is that the sayings and their parallels were not handed down as totally independent logia. They did not float isolated in the tradition,
but demanded some wider context.[164] It is argued that this is
supported by word statistics: the reconstruction contains no
specifically Matthean vocabulary.[165] Furthermore, the faith
underlying all three motifs in the "word of revelation" is faith
in the exalted Lord of the community.[166] The pre-Matthean tradition, then, dealt with the manifestation of the power of the
exalted one in the administration of baptism.[167] Later, according to Strecker, the unit was redacted in typically Matthean
language and with the addition of Matthean elements such as the
theme of universality. The stress is on the commission, not on
the enthronement of the exalted one, which is spoken of in the
past tense.[168] Matthew makes the tripartite liturgical tradition the vehicle of (a) the one great post-resurrection appearance of Jesus to the eleven in Galilee; and (b) the great missionary commission to all nations, who are to be taught the
commands Jesus gave during his earthly life.[169]

One objection that has been raised to this analysis concerns the emphasis in the original tradition on the baptismal
command. The existence is questioned of a "tradition in which
a declaration of universal authority and a promise of the abiding presence of Jesus support simply a command to baptize."[170]
But the command to baptize was certainly considered of great
significance in the early communities. Furthermore, it is not
at all clear that the declaration of authority and promise of
presence "support simply" the command. The tradition isolated
here may be read as stressing the declaration of authority and
its consequences.

Another objection is that Matt 28:18-20 seems to be the
only passage where these motifs are joined in the tradition.[171]

This, however, is not the case: in Acts 1:6-12, a similar tradition can be detected.  As Meier has seen, it deals with an
appearance of the risen Lord on a mountain, and has a tripartite
schema concerning (a) the exaltation of Jesus (Acts 1:9-11:
Jesus "was lifted up, and a cloud took him out of their sight";
"two men" tell the apostles that "this Jesus who was taken up
from you into heaven will come in the same way as you saw him
go into heaven"; cf. Matt 28:18b); (b) the command to start a
mission (Acts 1:8b: "you shall be my witnesses in Jerusalem and
in all Judea and Samaria and to the ends of the earth"; cf.
Matt 28:19a or 20a); (c) the promise of assitance (Acts 1:8:
"But you shall receive power [δύναμιν] when the Holy Spirit has
come upon you"; cf. Matt 28:20b).[172]  The promise of Jesus' *future* presence (Acts 1:11) offers a further parallel to the promise of Jesus' *abiding* presence (Matt 28:20b).

The structural similarity between Matt 28:16-20 and Acts
1:6-12, plus linguistic and stylistic study of the Matthean
pericope, have convinced Meier that Strecker's reconstruction
should be expanded.  Behind the heavily redacted final scene of
Matthew's Gospel lies pre-Matthean tradition which involved:

    (a)   an appearance of the risen Christ in Galilee, on a
            mountain to which he had ordered his disciples to go;

    (b)   a statement concerning exaltation or enthronement;

    (c)   a command to baptize or, alternately, some sort of
            command to begin a mission;

    (d)   perhaps a promise of continuing divine support in
            this mission.

Meier cannot say what the exact wording of this tradition was.[173]
As will be seen in the excursus on Mattheanisms in Matt 28:16-
20, my analysis supports both Strecker's contention that his
reconstruction of the traditional "word of revelation" contains
no specifically Matthean vocabulary, and elements of Meier's
expansion of that reconstruction.  The following points are
also important: the cloud imagery of Acts 1:9 may contain faint
allusion to Dan 7:13 (and perhaps Ezekiel 1), and this may bear
some relation to the supposed allusion to Dan 7:14 in Matt 28:
18b.  The ascension scene in Acts is also triadic: the Father,
the Holy Spirit and Jesus are mentioned.[174]

The pertinent significance of the work by Strecker and
Meier on the final Matthean pericope lies in the fact that they
have posited a pre-Matthean connection between Matt 28:18b (the
saying about authority) and verse 19b (the command to baptize,
which contains the triadic phrase).[175]  Later on in this chapter, it will be seen that it has been suggested that both of
these verses are related to Daniel 7 traditions.  No critic has
taken the further step, however, of exploring how these two
verses might be related to one another on the basis of the connection to Daniel 7.  The thesis will be presented that such an
exploration illuminates the meaning of the Matthean triadic
phrase.

3. The Triadic Phrase and the Entire Final Pericope as a
   Matthean Composition

The final opinion to be examined here concerning the incorporation of the triadic baptismal phrase into Matt 28:16-20 is
that the phrase is neither a post-Matthean interpolation nor
pre-Matthean tradition, but Matthean composition.  J. D. Kingsbury considers the phrase so "thoroughly 'Matthean' in style
and vocabulary that it can readily be ascribed to the evangelist
himself."[176]  He argues on linguistic, stylistic, conceptual
and theological grounds for thorough redaction and Matthean composition of the whole pericope.[177]  The position with regard to
the triadic phrase in verse 19b is as follows: Matt 18:20 shows
that Matthew is acquainted with the "theologically weighty"
phrase, εἰς τὸ ὄνομα.[178]  As for the three names in the triad,
πατήρ with reference to God is one of Matthew's preferred
terms.[179]  Matthew renders υἱός absolutely four times.[180]  The
association of the ἅγιον πνεῦμα with baptism occurs in Matthew
as early as the speech of John the Baptist (Matt 3:11, par.; cf.
Mark 1:8).  In the narrative of Jesus' own baptism, Kingsbury
holds, Matthew had prefigured his concept of Christian baptism,
which is to be in the name of the Father and of the Son and of
the Holy Spirit.  In the baptismal scene, the Father calls Jesus
"my Son" and empowers him with the Spirit (3:16-17) for his
ministry.  In Christian baptism, "one becomes a disciple of
Jesus and a son of God and is empowered by the Spirit for

ministry: the disciple continues the work of the earthly Son of
God."[181]  It is by the narrative of the baptism of Jesus, then,
that the triadic baptismal phrase in 28:19b must be interpreted,
since that phrase is an allusion to the narrative.[182]

The triadic phrase provides the key to the kind of Christology informing the final pericope.  Jesus is given in verse
19b the title "the Son," a variant of the more comprehensive
title "the Son of God."  This means that the text must be elucidated from the standpoint of the category of divine sonship,
not from the categories of Kyrios or Son of Man.  The final
pericope is seen by Kingsbury to have strong affinity with
other parts of the Gospel besides the baptismal narrative in
which the title "Son of God" is prominent.  For example, the
motifs of doubt and worship (28:17) recur in combination in
only one other place in the NT: in the pericope of the walking
on the water (Matt 14:31-33), and this story culminates in the
confession, "Truly you are the Son of God" (v. 33).  The saying
about authority (28:18b) "echoes" Matt 11:27.  The promise of
presence (28:20b) is a "post-Easter reiteration" of the name
Emmanuel (1:23) given to the "Son" conceived of the Holy Spirit.
Furthermore, the mountain mentioned in 28:16 is the setting of
other pericopes in which Jesus is spoken of as the Son: the
transfiguration (17:1-5), the temptation (4:1-10) and the mountain of lonely prayer from which Jesus comes to the disciples
(14:22-23).  The reference in 28:16 to the disciples coming
"into Galilee" where they will begin the ministry of the church
to all nations parallels the departure in 4:12 of Jesus, the
tested Son of God, into Galilee to begin his ministry to
Israel.[183]

Kingsbury's careful analysis of each of the other verses
in the final pericope convinces him that the entire unit has
been composed by Matthew himself,[184] but not on the basis of a
pre-Matthean unit or units of post-resurrection tradition (contrast the positions of Fuller, Hubbard, Strecker, Meier).  Each
of the themes in 28:16-20 must be considered, in Kingsbury's
view, as a channel from Son of God material in the previous
part of the Gospel to the central title "Son" in the triadic
phrase in 28:19b.  With intentional artistry Matthew has

composed the whole as a final expression of his Son of God
Christology.  The meaning of that title, which Kingsbury thinks
is Matthew's major Christological title, is elaborated throughout
the Gospel and here brought to a climax.[185]  The title expresses
the deepest mystery of Jesus' person, can be known only by a
revelation (cf. 16:17) and is the most exalted confession of the
Christian community.  The title is a "private" one, used only
by "transcendent personalities" and believers.[186]  In contrast,
the title Son of Man is "public," the one by which Jesus refers
to himself in interaction with crowds and their leaders, with
the betrayer Judas, the one he uses of himself as he tells his
disciples what his enemies will do to him and what impact his
death will have.[187]  At one point, these two titles will co-
alesce: at the parousia, the appearance before all, believers
and unbelievers, of Jesus as the Son of Man coming for judgment
(25:31-46).  At the point of coalescence, the secret of the
person of Jesus will be disclosed to all, and he will be seen
in the majesty of God by world and church.[188]  The title "the
Son" appears in the triadic phrase in 28:19b because this final
scene is a "private" one, but orientated toward "the close of
the age" (v. 20b).

The triadic phrase, then, in Kingsbury's opinion, has not
been interpolated nor inserted into a unit of redacted, traditional material.  It is not simply a phrase borrowed from the
liturgical practice of the community, placed here on the lips
of the resurrected Jesus to legitimize that practice.  It is not
present in 28:19b because a monadic phrase has been expanded in
the course of Christian thought and life into a triadic.  It is
not present because elements in a traditional account of a post-
resurrection commissioning have suggested it.  It is not a
"community composition" but a composition by Matthew himself,
created by him as an integral part of the pericope as a whole.
It has intelligent and intended links with the rest of the
Gospel, and within the smaller circle of the final pericope.
Far from being undigested tradition or unharmonized material
which Matthew has not mastered, or in which he has evidenced no
interest, the triadic phrase is a meaningful summary of Matthew's
central insight concerning Jesus.[189]

The major importance of Kingsbury's study with regard to
our purposes here is that (a) he has shown that it is possible
to find meaning in the triadic phrase by looking at it squarely
within its Matthean context, and (b) his full-length treatment
of the Gospel has suggested angles of approach for further
exploration--for example, of the relationship Matthew sees between the titles Son of God and Son of Man.  Several objections
to Kingsbury's thesis, however, must be raised.  The first concerns the narrowness of his methodology.  He claims to have
shown that Matt 28:19b, and indeed all of Matt 28:16-20, is
"thoroughly redactional in nature and not traditional."[190]  It
is probable, because of his stated affinity to the views of
Kilpatrick, that Kingsbury uses the word "tradition" to mean
only written tradition.  Kilpatrick objects strongly to the
view that Matt 28:16-20 was derived from an earlier written
document, such as the lost ending of Mark.  But he does note
that this section of Matthew's Gospel probably goes back to
oral tradition and has a complicated history behind it.  He
clearly emphasizes the traditional elements of a supposed Galilean appearance and a formal commission of the disciples, which
he says "reached the evangelist in an inexact and unwritten
form which he has recorded in his own phrasing."  This is old
tradition which is "broken down and vague in outline."[191]  But
Kingsbury gives the impression that he rules out, or at least
considers unimportant for understanding this passage, even any
oral tradition--whether this be confessional and liturgical
tradition from the church, or an appearance or commission tradition, or an interpretive tradition based on an OT text.  In
the case of the triadic phrase, he regards it so much a part of
Matthean theology that there is no need to posit a liturgical
tradition.  Kingsbury does not even raise the question of what
post-resurrection tradition Matthew might share with Luke, John
and the Markan Appendix, nor of how this might have influenced
Matthew's desire to finish off or supplement or even correct
Mark at this crucial point of the ending of the gospel.  Most
important for the investigation of the meaning of the triadic
phrase, Kingsbury has made no mention of the possible presence
of an allusion to Dan 7:14 LXX in Matt 28:18b.  As the statement

of authority in this verse is significant to our treatment of
the triadic phrase, Kingsbury's analysis of it will be detailed
here.

He argues that the clause "All authority in heaven and on
earth has been given to me" (28:18b) is from the hand of Matthew
"*for* it echoes" (emphasis mine) the words of Matt 11:27a (cf.
also 4:9), on the one hand, and such passages as 7:29, 9:8, 21:
23 (which refer to Jesus' authority), on the other hand.[192]
Because 28:18b relates to and catches up themes that appear
earlier in the Gospel, the conclusion Kingsbury draws is that
somehow this rules out the possibility that 28:18b may be considered based on or influenced by tradition. But, in fact, it
may be the case that the Gospel is designed on the basis of a
tradition behind the final pericope. It is not clear what difference Kingsbury sees between Matthew "echoing" a passage
which is paralleled in other gospels, and Matthew using a tradition. Because of the danger of importing into the text the
"general conception" of the Son of Man, Kingsbury does not explore the possibility of an allusion to Dan 7:14 LXX in Matt
28:18b.[193] But Matthew's Gospel is replete with OT citations
and allusions, which others have shown are essential to Matthew's
meaning.[194] This indicates that each possibility of an allusion
in Matthew merits careful scrutiny. It will be argued below
that an understanding of the allusion in 28:18b is basic to an
understanding of the triadic phrase in verse 19b.

Several other comments should be made here concerning
Kingsbury's treatment of the triadic phrase. With regard to
the linguistic treatment, no Johannine evidence has been considered. But εἰς τὸ ὄνομα is used three times in John (1:12,
2:23, 3:18). While πατήρ may be a preferred word for God in
Matthew, it is used 114 times in John. And υἱός is used absolutely in John 14 times. When this evidence is considered in
relation to the Johannine passages which appear to be related
to the saying about authority in 28:18b (cf. John 3:35 and 5:22
for examples), we might wonder if we have to do in the Matthean
pericope with a "thunderbolt fallen from the Johannine sky" or
with bridge material between the Synoptics and Fourth Gospel.[195]
Furthermore, Kingsbury has claimed that the triadic phrase is an

allusion to the baptism of Jesus, and that in that narrative
Matthew has prefigured his concept of Christian baptism.  This
claim is simply stated and not explored, and no argument is
provided against a judgment such as Stendahl's that "there is
little or no indication that Matthew is aware of Jesus' baptism
as a prototype for the baptism proclaimed by the Church.  The
accent (in Matt 3:16-17) is on Jesus' manifestation as the one
endowed with Spirit."[196]  Strecker likewise argues that Matthew
has not attempted to establish baptism as a sacramental occurrence.[197]  It is necessary to probe for information the Evangelist took for granted: for the connections he understood between
Christian baptism and the baptism of Jesus by John.  Finally, it
must be noted that on the whole, Kingsbury's remarks concerning
the triadic phrase in 28:19b would be just as valid if that
verse ran, "...baptizing them in the name of the Son."  He has
understood the phrase as a Christological statement par excellence.  There is no treatment at all of that puzzling element,
the linking of the three so closely.

The contention that Matthew has himself composed the triadic baptismal phrase goes beyond the evidence Kingsbury has
presented.  But his insight is revolutionary: that the phrase
is meaningful within the context of the final pericope and the
Gospel itself, in the thought of Matthew.  We will return to
that insight at a further stage of this work.

4. Conclusion

Neither the first theory (that the triadic phrase in 28:19b
is a post-Matthean interpolation) nor the third (that it is
Matthean composition) is an acceptable explanation of the incorporation of the phrase into the final Matthean pericope.  In
the next sections, I will follow the lead of Strecker and Meier,
and explore further the second theory, that the phrase is an
element of pre-Matthean tradition, not isolated but embedded in
a traditional unit.  My analysis of Mattheanisms in Matt 28:16-
20 (see Excursus) will indicate that there are also further
elements in the pericope which may be traditional.

*Excursus: Mattheanisms in Matt 28:16-20*

The following are instances of Matthew's linguistic or
stylistic usage. *Verse 16:* The mention of "the eleven disciples"
is possibly Matthean. It agrees with Matthew's tendency to
identify the disciples with the twelve, and is a natural outcome
of his detailed presentation in 27:3-10 of the death of Judas.[198]
As "the eleven" are mentioned in the Markan Appendix 16:14, Luke
24:33 (cf. Acts 1:13-14),[199] this term may be traditional.[200]
Matthew picks up the phrase εἰς τὴν Γαλιλαίαν from Mark 16:7
(cf. 14:28) in Matt 28:7; it is used again as a catchword to
link the account of the women running from the tomb (28:10) to
the final scene.[201]

*Verse 17:* The combination of an aorist participle (ἰδόντες)
before the aorist of the main verb (προσεκύνησαν) is characteristic of Matthew when he is linking two actions in an event.
See also προσελθὼν-ἐλάλησεν in verse 18a, and πορευθέντες-
μαθητεύσατε in verse 19a.[202] The particular participle ἰδὼν/
ἰδόντες plus an accusative or dependent clause is often used
redactionally in the Gospel.[203] The verbs προσεκύνησαν and
ἐδίστασαν are Matthean.[204]

*Verse 18:* Matthew uses προσέρχομαι fifty-two times,[205] but
in only one other instance is it used of an action of Jesus: in
the transfiguration account (Matt 17:7), where it is redactional
as it is here.[206] The clause ἐλάλησεν αὐτοῖς λέγων is paralleled
in passages where Matthew has redacted his Markan source (cf.
Matt 13:3, 14:27, 23:1). I judge verse 18b to be non-Matthean.[207]

*Verse 19:* The participle πορευθέντες recalls the use of
ἐπορεύθησαν in verse 16. This literary device is characteristic
of Matthew's style. Also, the pleonastic use of the aorist participle of πορεύομαι as a circumstantial participle attending an
imperative occurs four other times as redaction in Matthew.[208]
Matthew uses the verb μαθητεύω three times; here and at 13:52
(speaking of scribes trained for the kingdom of heaven) and at
27:57 (speaking of Joseph of Arimathea). Elsewhere it appears
in the NT only at Acts 14:21. The word οὖν is found in Matthew
fifty-eight times, and less frequently in Mark (five times) and
Luke (thirty-one times). Matthew uses it with commands twenty-
one times.[209] Stylistically, the coordination of the

circumstantial participles, βαπτίζοντες (v. 19b) and διδάσκοντες
(v. 20a) with the finite verb μαθητεύσατε is the same pattern
Matthew uses in 4:23 and 9:35 where he has redacted, respec-
tively, Mark 1:39 and 6:6b. In these texts, the ministry of
Jesus is summarized; in 28:19-20 Matthew is summarizing the
post-Easter ministry of the church.[210] The verb βαπτίζω is not
Matthean.[211] Several critics argue that the phrase πάντα τὰ
ἔθνη is Matthean,[212] but it is judged here to be pre-Matthean
tradition.[213] Kingsbury's insistence that the triadic phrase
εἰς τὸ ὄνομα τοῦ πατρός καὶ τοῦ υἱοῦ καὶ τοῦ ἁγίου πνεύματος is
Matthean composition is unconvincing, especially in the light
of the Johannine use of the first two titles and of the presence
of the particular combination of the same three titles in Luke
10:21-22 (cf. John 3:34-35).

   *Verse 20:* The typically Matthean words and phrases in this
verse are: τηρεῖν,[214] πάντα ὅσα,[215] ἰδού,[216] and συντελεία τοῦ
αἰῶνος. This last phrase is present in Matt 13:39, 40, 49;
24:3 and 28:20. Elsewhere in the NT, συντελεία τῶν αἰώνων is
found in Heb 9:26.[217] It is also possible that the verb ἐντει-
λάμην in 28:20 is due to Matthean redaction: ἐντέλλομαι occurs
five times in Matthew, twice in Mark, and once in Luke. It
appears also, however, in Acts 1:2.[218] The word διδάσκοντες is
not typically Matthean, but Matthew's stress on Jesus' teaching
throughout the Gospel marks teaching as one of his primary interests. Furthermore, the absence of a parallel to Mark 6:30
(where the apostles return from their first mission during the
ministry and tell Jesus "all they had done and taught") may
indicate that Matthew is responsible for the mention of them
being commanded to teach here in 28:20. It is a task reserved
until the exaltation of Jesus.

### D. The Origin of the Matthean Triadic Phrase

   In this section, two major theories concerning the background and development of NT triadic phrases will be considered.
The first theory is that triadic phrases and passages developed
out of monadic and binitarian, under the pressure of changing
insights into the Christian reality and under pressure of the
attempt to articulate that reality in different situations.

Christian triadic phrases and passages, according to this theory,
are all logically and chronologically later than the one and two
membered materials.  In the case of Matt 28:19b, we would have
an example of a baptismal formula which has developed out of an
earlier Christological one.  This theory will be presented in
the form proposed by Oscar Cullmann.  The trenchant and convincing criticisms offered by J. N. D. Kelly and others indicate
that this may be an oversimplification, and inapplicable to many
binitarian and triadic texts.

The second theory is that some NT triadic texts, of which
Matt 28:19b is one, developed out of an originally Jewish apocalyptic triad.  Under pressure of developing Christian symbolism
and thought, the titles of this triad changed, while the basic
triadic pattern was retained.  With some important modifications
and qualifications of this theory as presented by E. Lohmeyer
and R. H. Fuller, it will be argued that this has much to recommend it as an explanation of the origin of Matt 28:19b, and may
in fact be a clue to the pre-Matthean history of several elements of that Gospel's final pericope.

## 1. The Development of Triadic from Monadic and Binitarian Texts

It is commonly held that some NT phrases and passages which
mention God, Christ and Spirit developed out of monadic phrases
which originally mentioned only Christ, or binitarian phrases
which mentioned Christ and God.  That is, the less complex,
original formulas were expanded into the more complex.  The
simple, single-clause Christological formulas or confessions
are the most frequent in the NT.  These include "Jesus is Lord"
(1 Cor 12:3, Rom 10:9).  The repeated description of baptism as
"in the name of the Lord Jesus"[219] suggests that the formula
"Jesus is Lord"[220] or a similar phrase[221] had a place in the
earliest baptismal rite, and was the earliest summary of the
Christian belief.  This bare, Christological affirmation, it is
argued, constituted the Judeo-Christian nucleus, expressing the
authentic faith of the primitive church in worship, in exorcisms
and even in professions in times of persecution.  This is so
because in the earliest times Christians regarded the confession
of Christ as the essential of their faith.  Faith in God was

self-evident and held in common with Jews.  What was distinctive
was an almost purely Christocentric perspective: proclamation of
Christ as the starting point of every Christian confession.

This Christological affirmation was later enlarged as a
result of theological developments and propagandist requirements.
Cullmann has suggested that the enlargement took place in the
following ways.  (1) Bipartite or binitarian formulas, mentioning Jesus and God, originated in the church's struggle with
paganism.  When those becoming Christians were converted Jews,
only the short Christological statement was needed.  But once
pagans were introduced to Christianity, it was necessary to make
sure their belief was sound on the Judeo-Christian belief in
God the Father.  For this purpose, a confession based on the
*Shema'* was devised.  According to Cullmann, all the contexts in
which bipartite formulas appear are contexts in which paganism
is being consciously opposed.  The most ancient example of this
development is 1 Cor 8:4-6.

> Hence, as to the eating of foods offered to idols, we
> know that "an idol has no real existence" and that
> "there is no God but one."  For although there may be
> so-called gods in heaven or on earth--as indeed there
> are many "gods" and many "lords"--yet for us there is
> one God, the Father, from whom are all things and for
> whom we exist, and one Lord, Jesus Christ, through
> whom are all things and through whom we exist.

Cullmann believes that similar texts, such as 1 Tim 2:5 ("for
there is one God, and there is one mediator between God and men,
the man Christ Jesus"), presuppose an appearance of Christians
before heathen authorities.[222]  (2) Tripartite or triadic texts
developed out of bipartite, because of the association of the
Holy Spirit with baptism.  On the occasion of baptism, or where
baptism was mentioned in a binitarian formula, there was need
to mention the Spirit as the baptismal gift, and so the confession broadened out into a three-membered formula.  Eph 4:4-6,[223]
the ancient liturgical tripartite formulas such as 2 Cor 13:14,[224]
and the "triple invocation of the name in baptism" in Matt 28:19b
are mentioned as examples of this development.[225]  Several other
scholars, while perhaps not agreeing with the details of Cullmann's analysis, also regard Matt 28:19b as an expansion of an
original Christological formula and/or a statement for
Gentiles.[226]

Cullmann considers even the NT binitarian and triadic formulas to be basically Christological confessions. "The first place in the two- and three-membered formulas belongs indeed to God. But this should not mislead us into supposing that the essential element of the Christian confession was faith in God."[227] In these cases, faith in God or faith in the Spirit are really "functions" of faith in Christ. God, that is, is named as the one who raised Jesus, conferred majesty on him, is his father; the Spirit is the Paraclete sent by Christ, or the one who announced him by the prophets.[228] So the motive for the transition from the confession with one article to the formulas with two or three was proclamation of Christ. From this standpoint, however, the development of the Christological formulas into the final triadic form can be seen as a type of Judaizing and a "falsification of the exposition of the essence of Christianity."[229] Cullmann sees the source of the "error" not in the *fact itself* of mentioning God and Spirit, but in the *position* assigned to the mention of God before Christ. This results in a "falsification of perspective" because

> this order threatens to suggest the Jewish representation of Christ, to which the doctrine of the whole New Testament runs contrary, that one must set out from faith in God the Father in order to reach faith in Christ. Against this, the Christian maintains, according to the doctrine of the New Testament, that he reaches God through Christ. The thought of the New Testament is strongly Christocentric: Christ is the divine Mediator and is nearer man; His person is the central object of faith.[230]

That is, "since the believer of the first century believed in the Kyrios Christos, he believed also in God and in the Holy Ghost."[231] Matt 28:19b, then, which, "under the influence of liturgical rhythm and logic, or because the Son himself is the speaker," sets God the Father before the Son, is in less close conformity with the whole of the NT witness than triadic formulas such as 2 Cor 13:14 which mention Jesus Christ before God.[232] In its structure, Matt 28:19b "displaces the center of gravity" and moves away from Christocentrism.

While one may appreciate Cullmann's concern that the members of the triad not be seen in apparent independence from one

another, and his concern that the act of Jesus' exaltation or
resurrection be seen as the central element of NT faith, it
strikes me that his analysis would seem quite bizarre to the
earliest Jewish Christians who, as Cullmann himself admits, held
a self-evident (and I would think primary) faith in God. It is
possible that the triadic phrase in Matt 28:19b, rather than
indicating a move away from Christocentrism, may in its structure indicate a stage of belief that is pre-Christocentric, or
at least a type of belief that existed alongside the Christocentric from the earliest days. Need focus on the act of Jesus'
exaltation or resurrection be in all cases Christocentric?
Might we not posit a faith which expressed this focus in theocentric form?[233]

The whole picture presented above of the evolution of formulas from monadic to binitarian to triadic is weak at several
points. A careful criticism of Cullmann's thesis has been presented by J. N. D. Kelly,[234] and is the basis for some of the
following remarks. While the monadic, Christological formula
may have been the most popular in NT times, this is not evidence
that it was the earliest, nor that the binitarian and triadic
formulas developed out of it. Some binitarian texts (e.g., 1
Cor 8:6) do occur in contexts where paganism is being combatted
or the needs of Gentiles addressed, but the majority of such
texts do not.[235] Identification of God as the one who raised
Jesus from the dead,[236] and the conventional greeting which
links God and Jesus (see Rom 1:7) indicate the coordination of
God and Jesus was instinctive and almost a category of the
thinking of the earliest church. In liturgical settings and
blessings, this coordination was most likely prior to the requirements of the Gentile mission. It may have developed
against a thoroughly Jewish background, under the influence of
Jewish liturgical blessings and solemn descriptions of God, and
solely to meet Jewish Christian needs.[237]

With regard to triadic texts,[238] the proposal to interpret
mention of the Spirit as a replacement of an original mention
of "one baptism" seems far fetched. Eph 4:4 really contains a
seven-fold affirmation and cannot be taken as an illustration
of how the two-fold formula was expanded. "In any case, the

Holy Spirit stood for much more in the eyes of Christians of the first two generations than the gift they had received in baptism."[239]   As noted above,[240] the idea of Jesus being "vindicated in the spirit" (1 Tim 3:16) or "made alive in the spirit" (1 Pet 3:18) is a contributing factor to the idea of the Spirit's role in the resurrection of Jesus (cf. Rom 1:4).  It is possible that triadic texts developed in the context of thinking or celebration of the resurrection as well as in (or in connection with) baptismal contexts.[241]

   In general, the NT shows us monadic, binitarian and triadic texts existing side by side and apparently independently.  All three types of texts may have been deeply rooted in the earliest phases of Christianity, since the church's belief about Jesus only acquired significance in the setting of its belief about God, and since the belief in the Spirit was a part of the consciousness of those who considered themselves living in the Messianic age and in the Spirit's power.[242]   Kelly remarks that, "The truth of the matter would seem to be that the scholars whose theories we are criticizing have been mesmerized by the evolutionary axiom that the less complex must always precede the more complex, and that there must be a line of progressive development."[243]   There was, however, such a line of development in terms of the growing popularity of the more complex, and in terms of later reflection and explicit confession proceeding from the simple to the complex.  The Christological "question" or "problem" does come before the Trinitarian logically and chronologically.[244]   Matt 28:19b, although it uniquely links the Father, Son and Holy Spirit in a way that has led some to argue they are put on one "level" and that personality is being attributed to the Spirit,[245] should not be read as a response to, but is more likely a cause of, the later Trinitarian "question" or "problem."[246]

   With regard to Matt 28:19b, two further points must be made here. (1) Even though there are examples in the NT of a simpler type or form of baptism "in the name of (the Lord) Jesus Christ," the theory that Matt 28:19b evolved out of the simpler cannot be supported by appealing to a general theory that triadic texts developed out of monadic or binitarian.  We

must reckon with the possibility of a triadic type of baptismal
formula (more "developed" in the sense of being a closer ap-
proximation to later thinking) being contemporaneous with the
monadic.[247]   (2) It is possible that a Jewish formula or thought
pattern lies behind Matt 28:19b, as behind several of the other
NT binitarian and triadic texts.[248]  The tendency to coordinate
the three names in one context can be explained, it is true,
from the simple fact that the early Christians were acquainted
with Jewish traditions of God and the Spirit, and under the
impact of the life, death and resurrection of Jesus.[249]  But
the pressure of a triadic Jewish pattern, along with the pressures of reflection on the "new life" of Jesus, would make it
more likely that a Christian liturgical or blessing formula
could take the triadic form quickly and even at a comparatively
pre-reflective stage.  This would not require one to assume, as
Kelly does, that "the conception of the threefold manifestation
of the Godhead was embedded deeply in Christian thinking from
the start, and provided a ready-to-hand mould in which the ideas
of the apostolic writers took shape," and that a "Trinitarian
pattern" was part and parcel of the earliest Christian tradition.[250]  One would assume, rather, that some other meaning and
significance was intended and more obvious to the early framers
of the tradition.  A Jewish pattern may also give a clue to the
reason why the Spirit in the NT retains a relative independence
alongside Christ, whereas the functions of other Jewish hypostases such as Sophia and Logos are transferred to Christ.  The
following section will examine the Lohmeyer-Fuller theory concerning a Jewish apocalyptic triad which, it is argued, had influenced certain NT texts.[251]


2. Development from a Jewish Apocalyptic Triad

        According to R. H. Fuller, the Matthean triad in 28:19b
was "shaped from" an earlier triadic formula found in apocalyptic writings and in apocalyptic contexts in the NT.[252]  In this
he is developing a suggestion of Lohmeyer: "Die älteste Drei-
heitsformel, welche schon jüdische vorgegeben ist...ist Gott,
Menschensohn, Engel."[253]  This triad was found by Lohmeyer in
the Similitudes of *1 Enoch* (chaps. 37-71)[254] in three passages.

The first is a vision of the future Messianic kingdom, seen by
Enoch who has been carried off by a whirlwind to "the end of
the heavens" (39:3).

> Here my eyes saw their dwellings[255] with his righteous
> angels / And their resting-places with the holy. / And
> they petitioned and interceded and prayed for the chil-
> dren of men, / And righteousness flowed before them as
> water, / And mercy like dew upon the earth: / Thus it
> is amongst them for ever and ever. / And in that place
> my eyes saw the Elect One of righteousness and of faith, /
> And I saw his dwelling-place under the wings of the Lord
> of Spirits, / And righteousness shall prevail in his
> days, / And all the righteous and elect shall be with-
> out number before Him for ever and ever. / And all the
> righteous and elect before Him shall be strong as fiery
> lights, / And their mouth shall be full of blessing, /
> And their lips extol the name of the Lord of Spirits, /
> And righteousness before Him shall never fail, (And up-
> rightness shall never fail before Him).
>
>                    *1 Enoch* 39:5-7[256]

The second passage occurs in the context of a scene in
which the dead are resurrected, and the Elect One separates
from them the righteous and holy ones.

> And the Elect One shall in those days sit on My Throne, /
> And his mouth shall pour forth all the secrets of wisdom
> and counsel: / For the Lord of Spirits has given (them)
> to him and has glorified him. / And in those days shall
> the mountains leap like rams, / And the hills also shall
> skip like lambs satisfied with milk, / And the faces of
> (all) the angels in heaven shall be lighted up with joy.
>
>                    *1 Enoch* 51:3-4

The third is a depiction of the judgment of the angels by the
Elect One.

> And the Lord of Spirits placed the Elect One on the
> throne of glory. / And he shall judge all the works
> of the holy above in the heaven, / And in the balance
> shall their deeds be weighed. / And when he shall lift
> up his countenance / To judge their secret ways accord-
> ing to the name of the Lord of Spirits / And their
> path according to the way of the righteous judgment
> of the Lord of Spirits, / Then shall they all with one
> voice speak and bless, / And glorify and extol and
> sanctify the name of the Lord of Spirits. / And He
> will summon all the host of the heavens, and all the
> holy ones above, and the host of God, the Cherubin,
> Seraphin and Ophannin, and all the angels of power,
> and all the angels of principalities, and the Elect
> One,[257] and the other powers on the earth (and) over
> the water.
>
>                    *1 Enoch* 61:8-10

Actually, the triad in these texts is: angels (or: the host of
God), Elect One, the Lord of Spirits.  The title, Elect One, is
regarded by most scholars as one applied (like Righteous One
and Messiah) by the author to the Son of Man.  It is not evidence of a separate source.[258]

By steps which both Lohmeyer and Fuller attempt to trace,
the old triad has gradually been transformed into the Matthean
one.  Lohmeyer found an ancient triad in the NT in the following places.

> Mark 8:38: "For whoever is ashamed of me and of my
> words in this adulterous and sinful generation, of him
> will the Son of Man also be ashamed, when he comes in
> the glory of his Father with the holy angels."

> 2 Thess 1:7-8: "...when the Lord Jesus is revealed
> from heaven with his mighty angels in flaming fire,
> inflicting vengeance upon those who do not know God
> and upon those who do not obey the gospel of our Lord
> Jesus."

> Rev 1:1-2: "The revelation of Jesus Christ, which God
> gave him to show to his servants what must soon take
> place; and he made it known by sending his angel to his
> servant John, who bore witness to the word of God and
> to the testimony of Jesus Christ, even to all that he
> saw."

> Rev 14:10: "...he also (who worships the beast and its
> image, and receives a mark) shall drink the wine of
> God's wrath, poured unmixed into the cup of his anger,
> and he shall be tormented with fire and brimstone in
> the presence of the holy angels and in the presence
> of the Lamb."

> 1 Tim 5:21: "In the presence of God and of Christ Jesus
> and of the elect angels, I charge you to keep these
> rules without favor, doing nothing from partiality."

Lohmeyer found the formula Father, Son, angel in two texts.

> Matt 24:36 (par. Mark 13:32): "But of that day and hour
> no one knows, not even the angels of heaven, nor the
> Son, but the Father only."

> Rev 3:5: "He who conquers shall be clad thus in white
> garments, and I will not blot his name out of the book
> of life; I will confess his name before my Father and
> before his angels."[259]

The inclusion of the Spirit in the formula, Lohmeyer felt,
was prepared for by several factors: (1) by the tendency in the
Similitudes to speak of "the Lord of Spirits";[260] (2) by the
link made by John the Baptist between the coming one (drawn

with the traits of the Son of Man: judge and saviour of the
world)[261] and the Spirit, which was thought of as the power of
imminent eschatological completion; (3) by the conception of
Jesus as Spirit-empowered servant of Yahweh found in Matt 12:18
("Behold, my servant whom I have chosen...I will put my Spirit
on him"). The narration of the baptism of Jesus (with its triad:
beloved Son, Spirit, [voice of] God) was seen by Lohmeyer as
paradigmatic of Christian baptism. Hence the development of a
triadic baptismal formula.[262] Lohmeyer did not attribute the
creation of the triadic formula to Matthew, but to the Galilean
community. He thought it was interpolated by a later scribe
into Matthew's Gospel. Lohmeyer did not speculate in any detail
on the Galilean understanding of the triad.[263]

   According to Fuller's analysis, the triad develops under
the pressure of the "triadic implications" of the early community's experience of the gospel: "in faith the believer is
brought by the Spirit to the eschatological presence of God in
Jesus."[264] The Jewish apocalyptic triad has been Christianized
as it appears in the primitive strata of the NT: (1) God is
called Father, and the work of the Son of Man is linked with
Jesus' work (see Mark 8:38, "the most primitive occurrence" of
the triad in the NT). Fuller thinks, however, that at this
stage there is no explicit identification of Jesus and the Son
of Man.[265] (2) The next stage is the post-Easter church's identification of the Son of Man with the exalted Christ, and the
development of a Father-Son Christology rooted in Jesus' use of
the term 'Abba for God.[266] Examples Fuller gives for this stage
include 1 Thess 3:13, Mark 13:32.[267] (3) Finally, angels are
replaced by the Holy Spirit, facilitated by a general tendency
to substitute spirits for angels in apocalyptic.[268] This gives
us the rudimentary triadic groupings in Paul as, for example,
in 1 Cor 12:4-6, 2 Cor 13:13. The original apocalyptic theology
has been transformed by the Christian historical experience.
Although Fuller indicates that Matthew himself may have edited
a monadic form of the baptismal command in order to produce the
triadic form in 28:19b,[269] he does not discuss in detail this
triad in relation to other elements of the final pericope, nor
does he explore the Matthean understanding of the triad. He

remarks, however, that the Son of Man Christology behind 28:18b
(an allusion to Dan 7:14 LXX) has developed into a Father-Son
Christology in Matt 28:19b.[270]

The Lohmeyer-Fuller theory of an apocalyptic background to
the NT triad found in Matt 28:19b is extremely valuable.  (1)
It undercuts the assumption of some that the triadic text was
the product of, or produced for the benefit of, Gentile Christians.  This assumption is a correlate of the traditional position that the later church's conception of the triune God was
developed exclusively in an atmosphere of Hellenistic philosophy
and owed little or nothing to Judaism.  (2) It directs our attention to the importance of the literature of the intertestamental period.  Few scholars today would speak as Lebreton did
in 1939 of Jewish intertestamental literature as a distortion
and deformation of Jewish theology, and as merely human tradition in contrast to the revelation of God in the OT and NT.[271]
Still, a cursory examination of contemporary works on the Trinity shows that it is common in an analysis of the background of
the dogma to leap from a discussion of OT texts to NT, expressing implicit agreement with Lebreton that "later books of
Palestinian Judaism...are not the sources of our dogma, and
they exercised only a very slight influence on the Theology of
the Trinity."[272]   (3) This theory finds some indirect corrobora-
tion from the thesis presented by Georg Kretschmar.[273]  He argues that the framework of ideas presupposed in the Church's
dogma was ultimately derived from the late apocalyptic traditions of Palestine, which he traces back to the turn of the
first century A.D., and which were developments of the imagery
of the celestial judgment court.[274]  Kretschmar's concern is to
follow the transition from the triadic formula of the late first
century (e.g., 1 Clement 58:2) to the fourth century doctrine
of three subsistent hypostases.  Following Kretschmar, Daniélou
speaks of "the first form of the theology of the Trinity": that
which uses terms borrowed from the vocabulary of Jewish angelology to present the Word and the Holy Spirit.[275]  Neither Kretschmar nor Daniélou includes analyses of NT or pre-NT writings.
But if Lohmeyer and Fuller are on the right track, the influence
of Jewish angelology can be pressed further back.  Jewish

apocalyptic was influential in the formation as well as in the
later interpretation of NT triadic texts.  (4) The Lohmeyer-
Fuller theory focuses attention on pre-NT passages in which
three figures are mentioned, rather than on the development of
isolated concepts and titles.  This is significant because recovery of the narrative or poetic mythological context of the
triad, the dynamic action or situation in which the three figures were customarily mentioned, is important for an understanding of the theological dimensions of the NT triad.[276]

As it stands, however, the Lohmeyer-Fuller theory, that the
Matthean triad developed out of Jewish apocalyptic through a NT
Son of Man Christology, is problematic.  This is because both
scholars use the Similitudes as a base.  Lohmeyer assumes this
work is pre-Christian and Fuller assumes that it at least contains pre-Christian materials.[277]  They believe, without further
analysis, that the triads found in the three passages in the
Similitudes provided the material for the earliest NT triads.
Fuller goes so far as to say that the NT begins to use the triadic formula exactly where the Similitudes leaves off.[278]  The
triadic passages they deal with in the Similitudes contain, as
we have seen, the triad of angels, Elect One, Lord of Spirits.
The most primitive NT triad, in Fuller's opinion, is angels,
Son of Man, (his) Father (Mark 8:38).  But there is no reason
to assume that the phrasing found in the Similitudes' triad is
any closer to Mark 8:38 than that of the more ancient text, the
source of Son of Man speculation, Daniel 7: angels, one like a
son of man, Ancient of Days.  Nothing requires us to place the
Similitudes' triad chronologically between Daniel 7 and Mark
8:38, or explains why the expression Son of Man would be preferred in Mark to the title Elect One, or why the title Lord of
Spirits would be dropped in the NT.[279]  Moreover, several other
passages in the Similitudes can also be considered triadic.[280]
These indicate that the Similitudes must be much more carefully
integrated into a picture of the evolution of the triadic
phrase.

A more basic problem concerns the dating of the Similitudes.
This work is the only one of the five sections of *1 Enoch*
(Ethiopic) which is not represented among the Aramaic fragmentary

MSS of Enoch literature found at Qumran.[281] This fact has led
several scholars to question the conventional pre-Christian
dating of the Similitudes, and in some cases to hold that this
work may draw on Christian ideas of the Son of Man.[282] Although
the Qumran evidence alone is not decisive,[283] the Similitudes
can no longer be confidently regarded as a clear influence on
the NT. The dating problem is at the moment unsolved. To the
point here is that it cannot be assumed that the triads found
by Lohmeyer and Fuller in the Similitudes can be the starting
point in an examination of the NT triadic texts and their development. Caution dictates that it be demonstrated that a
given passage in the Similitudes (or the tradition behind it)
is the presupposition of a specific NT triadic text. As will
be seen, I find no certain example that such is the case with
regard to the material examined, although there are several instances in which it will be claimed that the NT and the Similitudes share common midrashic traditions. The fact that both
the NT and the Similitudes contain triadic passages may result
from their independent uses of these traditions.

      This does not thereby negate the importance of the
Lohmeyer-Fuller theory. Their identification of some early NT
triads as those containing the expression Son of Man (e.g.,
Mark 8:38) and/or originating in an interpretation of Daniel 7
(e.g., Rev 3:5)[284] argues that an understanding of the uses of
that OT text, which itself contains a triad--Ancient of Days,
one like a son of man, and angels--will provide insight into
the origin, development and meaning of the NT triad. It is becoming increasingly clear (if not yet a scholarly consensus)
that the pre-Christian Jewish midrashic tradition that grew up
around Daniel 7 is extremely complex. We cannot speak simply
of a pre-Christian Son of Man tradition, with fixed title and
coherent concept.[285] Rather, there is a variety of uses of
Danielic imagery. It is within the stream of interpretive traditions flowing from Daniel 7 that the particular tradition or
traditions which will elucidate the roots and meaning of the
triad in Matt 28:19b may be discovered.

      Two further points strengthen the possibility that the
right track is to search for the background of Matt 28:19b in

an interpretation of Daniel 7.  (1) As we have seen, several
scholars recognize in Matt 28:18b an allusion to Dan 7:14 LXX.[286]
If this is the case, there may be an organic relationship between
verse 18b and the triad in verse 19b.  Both Lohmeyer and Fuller
accept the presence of an allusion in 28:18b.  Fuller sees a relationship between the allusion here (and in Matt 11:27 and John
3:35) and the titles Father and Son in all three passages.  He
argues that in all three instances the title Son of Man has disappeared, being replaced by the title Son, with emphasis on the
Father-Son relationship.[287]  But in Matt 28:19b, he suggests,
Matthew may be responsible for the redaction of an originally
monadic baptismal phrase into the triadic.  Verses 18b, 19b-20a
and 20b are considered originally independent logia which Matthew has joined.  Strecker, on the other hand, contends that
there is a pre-Matthean "word of revelation" in verses 18b,
19b-20a and 20b.  He does not, however, explore the dynamics of
this hypothetical reconstruction, nor suggest an apocalyptic
background for the triadic phrase, which he simply takes as a
liturgical formula used in the Matthean community.[288]  Blair
does think that the idea of the Son's "place alongside the
Father and the Holy Spirit (in Matt 28:19b) in a kind of loosely
conceived trinity" is a result of his resurrection and exaltation as Son of Man, future King and Judge of all.[289]  But again
there is no consideration of the background of the triad, nor
is there an attempt to spell out why this triadic imagery should
result from the idea of resurrection and exaltation.  (2) In the
slightly wider context of the Johannine passage, and of the
Lukan parallel to Matt 11:27 (Luke 10:21-22), as in Matt 28:19b,
there is also present a Father-Son-Spirit triad.

*John 3:34-35*

For he whom God has sent
utters the words of God, for
it is not by measure that he
gives the Spirit; the Father
loves the Son and has given
all things into his hand.

*Luke 10:21-22*

In that same hour he re-
joiced in the Holy Spirit
and said...All things have
been delivered to me by my
Father; and no one knows
who the Son is except the
Father, or who the Father
is except the Son, and any
one to whom the Son chooses
to reveal him.

In these three instances, then, there is a possible allusion to
Dan 7:14 joined to a triad of Father-Son-Spirit.

The theory that the triad in Matt 28:19b is related to a
Jewish apocalyptic triad bears further investigation. The occurrence of the triad in the context of a proposed allusion to
Dan 7:14 in three NT texts, and the possibility that other NT
triads may be related to interpretations of Daniel 7 indicate
that the triad found in Daniel 7 may be the Jewish apocalyptic
triad whose development can be traced in different NT triadic
texts. A study of the contexts in which the triad appears
should give (1) some indication of the theological and christological statements being made or implied by triadic imagery,
and (2) indication of whether triadic formulas in the cases
considered developed out of Christian monadic formulas under
the influence of triadic patterns in Judaism and the influence
of specific Christian concerns, or whether the Christian triadic formulas simply develop the Jewish triadic formulas.

[1]Acts 1:12 indicates that Jesus spoke his final words to the disciples from Mount Olivet, near Jerusalem, and from there he was "taken up" into heaven.

[2]The term ὄρος occurs sixteen times in Matthew. When metaphorical uses in pronouncements of Jesus are discounted, there are eleven references, which have been grouped as follows: (1) the mountain of temptation (4:8); (2) the mountain of the sermon (5:1, 8:1); (3) the mountain of private prayer (14:23); (4) the mountain of healing and feeding the crowd (15:29); (5) the mountain of the transfiguration (17:1, 9); (6) the Mount of Olives (21:1, 24:3, 26:30); (7) the mountain of the mission charge (28:16). The first, fourth and seventh are unique to Matthew's Gospel (T. F. Best, "Transfiguration and Mission in Matthew," unpublished paper delivered at the AAR/SBL Convention, Chicago, 1975).

[3]The tension between wavering and adoring is part of the Matthean understanding of discipleship (J. P. Meier, "Two Disputed Questions in Matt 28:16-20," *JBL* 96 [1977] 409).

[4]For the dispute whether ἔθνος means "nations" or "Gentiles," see J. P. Meier, "Nations or Gentiles in Matthew 28:19?" *CBQ* 39 (1977) 94-102, against D. R. A. Hare and D. J. Harrington, "Make Disciples of All the Gentiles (Mt 28:19)," *CBQ* 37 (1975) 359-69.

[5]See 2:1-13; 8:5-13; 10:18; 15:21-28; 4:12-17; 8:28-34; 5:46-47; 18:17.

[6]See 4:23; 5:2; 7:29; 9:35; 11:1; 13:54; 21:23; 22:16; 26:55.

[7]The Torah of the Messiah is understood as bringing the Torah of Moses to fulfillment (R. Hamerton-Kelly, "Matthew, Gospel of," *IDBSup*, 582).

[8]See John 3:22, 26 and 4:1, in which we find the claim that Jesus baptized in Judea with great success. R. E. Brown finds no plausible theological reason why anyone would have invented this tradition, even to support the practice of Christian baptism. The modification in John 4:2 ("Jesus himself did not baptize, but only his disciples") and the absence of the tradition from the Synoptics is evidence that the information that Jesus had once imitated the Baptist's practice was probably taken by some as indication of Jesus' subordination or inferiority to John (*The Gospel According to John* [AB 29; Garden City, NY: Doubleday, 1966] 155).

[9]R. H. Fuller, *The Formation of the Resurrection Narratives* (New York: MacMillan, 1971) 83. The early lists of resurrection appearances and accounts of the appearance to Paul imply the same kind of Christophany. They seem to be based on what E.

Schweizer thinks is the way the resurrection was conceived in
the earliest period: as a direct translation from the tomb to
heaven (*The Good News According to Matthew* [Atlanta: John Knox,
1975] 528).

[10]See B. J. Hubbard, *The Matthean Redaction of a Primitive
Apostolic Commissioning: An Exegesis of Matthew 28:16-20* (SBLDS
19; Missoula, MT: Scholars, 1974) 72.

[11]Meier, "Two Disputed Questions," 407.

[12]O. Michel, "Der Abschluss des Matthäusevangeliums," *EvT*
10 (1952) 21. See also W. Trilling, *Das Wahre Israel* (3rd ed.;
Munich: Kösel, 1964) 4, 21; Günther Bornkamm, "The Risen Lord
and the Earthly Jesus," *The Future of Our Religious Past* (ed.
J. M. Robinson; London: SCM, 1971) 205; Georg Strecker, *Der Weg
der Gerechtigkeit* (Göttingen: Vandenhoeck u. Ruprecht, 1962)
213; Ernst Lohmeyer, "Mir ist gegeben alle Gewalt," *In Memoriam
Ernst Lohmeyer* (ed. W. Schmauch; Stuttgart: Evangelisches Verlagswerk, 1951) 42, 46, 49. P. F. Ellis (*Matthew: His Mind and
His Message* [Collegeville: Liturgical, 1974] 20-22) lists the
themes recapitulated by Matthew in 28:16-20.

[13]See below, excursus on Mattheanisms, pp. 43-44.

[14]J. A. T. Robinson, *Jesus and His Coming* (London: SCM,
1957) 151-52. Robinson thinks that Matthew's eschatology is
purely futurist, and that he found this scene in his pre-
mutilated copy of Mark.

[15]J. P. Meier, "Salvation-History in Matthew: In Search of
a Starting Point," *CBQ* 37 (1975) 213.

[16]Bornkamm, "Risen Lord," 203; see C. H. Dodd ("The Appearance of the Risen Christ: An Essay in Form-Criticism of the
Gospels," *Studies in the Gospels* [ed. D. Nineham; Oxford: Black-
well, 1967] 9-35) for an analysis of the two types of resurrection narratives, concise and circumstantial. He shows that
Matt 28:16-20 has both points of contact with and differences
from the concise type.

[17]Meier, "Two Disputed Questions," 407-24.

[18]Long ago, G. F. Moore warned against Christian interpretation of OT, rabbinic and intertestamental literature which
often set out either (a) to find correspondences, adumbrations,
foreshadowings of the figure of the Son or Logos in the NT, to
collect material to prove Jewish theology had made a place for
being or beings of a divine nature who mediated the ends of the
supreme God in the world as the Son and Spirit did in Christian
theology, or (b) to prove that Jewish theology with its "intermediaries" interposed between a distant transcendant God and
the world was unlike the Christian theology with its lack of
need for intermediaries, its "near" God. For Moore, Christian
philosophical presuppositions controlled these efforts at
proof-texting (see "Intermediaries in Jewish Theology: Memra,
Shekinah, Metatron," *HTR* 15 [1922] 41-85). Similar dangers

exist for NT interpreters: of having one's efforts controlled by (a) the presupposition that dogmatic development is a clear, direct and inevitable development of NT beliefs, or (b) the presupposition that Christian dogma has little or nothing to do with the NT.

[19] It is easy to understand why the triadic phrase appears to be something of an intrusion into the pericope. The risen Jesus speaks of the Son in the third person, and there seems to be no obvious preparation for the strange joining of the three titles, no inherent reason why they are listed in this way, in this context.

[20] "God" (θεός) is used most commonly in the NT to refer to the God of the OT, the one Jesus of Nazareth called "Father." There are, however, NT passages which imply that Jesus is divine (for example, Phil 2:6-7, John 10:30, 14:9) and a few that explicitly use θεός to refer to Jesus (for example, John 20:28). The title θεός in some instances, then, was a term of wider application than just to the God of the OT. The term "triadic" is not used here with the meaning it had and has in Eastern rite Christianity.

[21] Lohmeyer and Fuller, whose theories of the origin of the Matthean triadic phrase will be discussed below, propose that the NT concept of Spirit develops in part out of the concept of angels. They point out that triads can be found in the NT in which the substitution of Spirit for angels has not yet taken place. Fuller also argues that the Son of Man in some NT triads was not originally identified with Jesus.

[22] Francis Martin, "Pauline Trinitarian Formulae and Church Unity," *CBQ* 30 (1968) 200.

[23] Cf. Phil 3:3.

[24] A. W. Wainwright distinguishes between "Threefold formula" and "Threefold pattern" (*The Trinity in the New Testament* [London: SPCK, 1962]. E. J. Fortman speaks of triadic formulas, triadic patterns and triadic ground plans or tripartite passages (*The Triune God*).

[25] Wainwright, *The Trinity*, 257, 22.

[26] K. Rahner, "Trinity," *Theological Dictionary*, 472; "Trinity, Divine," *Sacramentum Mundi* (6 vols.; ed. K. Rahner; New York: Herder and Herder, 1970) 6.296-98, 301-02, 307. Cf. Leslie Dewart, *The Future of Belief* (New York: Herder and Herder, 1966) 143-52.

[27] C. F. D. Moule, "The New Testament and the Doctrine of the Trinity: A Short Report on an Old Theme," *ExpTim* 88 (1976) 17.

[28] Jean Daniélou, *The Theology of Jewish Christianity* (ed. J. A. Baker; Chicago: Henry Regnery, 1964) 118, 143, 146.

[29]See Raymond E. Brown, "The Paraclete in the Fourth Gospel," *NTS* 13 (1966) 124.

[30]There is evidence, for example, that the author of the Fourth Gospel considered the figure of the Paraclete personal or at least as having personal characteristics. He used the Greek masculine pronoun ἐκεῖνας with the neuter substantive τὸ πνεῦμα in 14:26; cf. v. 17. R. E. Brown has shown, moreover, how closely the Paraclete is modeled on the figure of Jesus, and yet their roles are distinct ("The Paraclete," 126-28). Others have emphasized the similarities between the Paraclete and Jewish intertestamental angels (cf. G. Quispel, "Qumran, John and Jewish Christianity," *John and Qumran* [ed. J. H. Charlesworth; London: Geoffrey Chapman, 1972] 146-49). J. L. Martyn quite rightly remarks that the Paraclete has no independent personality and no independent function. He looks like the Johannine Son of Man, and makes Jesus' presence on earth effective (*History and Theology in the Fourth Gospel* [New York: Harper & Row, 1968] 135-36). Still, the two figures are distinct from one another.

[31]See below, p. 173.

[32]Wainwright, *The Trinity*, 247, 250, 264, 30. Fortman (*The Triune God*, 22) also speaks of "the threefold problem" touched tangentially in some NT texts (e.g., Gal 3:13-14, where the promise of the Spirit is related to the crucifixion).

[33]See Robert M. Grant (*The Early Christian Doctrine of God*, 85-90) for a presentation of the opinion that it was Gnosticism (not the problem of reconciliation with Jewish monotheism) which stimulated early Christian concern to articulate the interrelationships among the members of the triad. The charge of atheism leveled against Christians also led them to state their doctrine of God. Grant thinks that the NT presents data for the doctrine of the Trinity, but the "problems" related to the data have not yet been raised. S. D. McBride ("The Yoke of the Kingdom," *Int* 27 [1973] 277-79) argues that there were two stages in the Jewish interpretation of the first line of the *Shema'*. In the first, it was read as an oath of allegiance to the suzerainty of Yahweh alone. In the second, dating from the beginning of the Amoraite period (third century A.D.) and in opposition to both Gnostic and Christian theologies, the *Shema'* became a statement of the metaphysical unity of the single divine Being.

[34]Fortman's term, "elemental trinitarianism," is appropriate here (*The Triune God*, xvi).

[35]See Brevard Childs, *Biblical Theology in Crisis* (Philadelphia: Westminster, 1970) 209: the inner unity among the parts of the triad has not yet been worked out at this early stage. K. S. Kirk remarks that the "doctrine of the Trinity" emerges from the NT only in confused form ("The Evolution of the Doctrine of the Trinity," *Essays on the Trinity and the Incarnation* [ed. A. E. J. Rawlinson; London: Longmans, Green, 1928] 160).

[36]Moule, "The New Testament and the Doctrine of the Trinity," 17.  Moule does not make the distinction between "Trinitarian" and "trinitarian," but only between "Trinitarian" and "threefold," and he does not define his terms with much precision.

[37]Ibid., 18.

[38]Rahner, "Trinity, Divine," *Sacramentum Mundi*, 295.

[39]See Wainwright, *The Trinity*, 252, 266.  Wainwright thinks Matt 28:19b is simply proof that the threefold pattern was accepted when this Gospel was written.  Matthew gave prominence to it but, like Luke, showed no sign of being aware of the "trinitarian problem" of the relation of the three members to one another.

[40]Fortman, *The Triune God*, 115.  Fortman also remarks, however, that nowhere in the NT do we find any Trinitarian doctrine of three distinct subjects of divine life and activity in the same Godhead.  When the three are coordinated on the same divine level in a triadic pattern, there seems to be no realization that a common function would mean community of nature.  It should be noticed that this idea of common function without community of nature pertains also to certain aspects of Divine Council imagery in the OT.

[41]E. Schweizer, *Good News*, 533.

[42]Ibid.

[43]G. F. Moore, *Judaism* (2 vols.; New York: Schocken, 1971) 1.188.  The *Didache* passage and the relation of the phrase to the rite of baptism will be discussed below.

[44]H. Kosmala, "The Conclusion of Matthew," *ASTI* 4 (1965) 136.

[45]See R. H. Fuller's treatment of Phil 2:6-11 in *The Foundations of New Testament Christology* (New York: Charles Scribner's Sons, 1965) 230 and 198 n. 14.  The OT category of "presence" is still central.  Fuller notes that in ontic affirmations (which raise ontological problems) in the NT, the point being made is that "in Jesus there occurs an encounter with the eschatological presence of God directly at work" (*Resurrection Narratives*, 144).

[46]G. D. Kilpatrick, *The Origins of the Gospel According to St. Matthew* (Oxford: Clarendon, 1946) 107.

[47]The "Johannine comma" inserted between vv. 7 and 8 of 1 John 5 mentions "the Father, the Word and the Holy Spirit, and these three are one."  The authenticity of this text is not defended today by any responsible exegete or critic, since it is absent from the manuscripts of all ancient versions except the Latin, and from all manuscripts of the Vulgate prior to

800 A.D. and is not cited by any Greek or Latin father before
the fourth century. It is found only in eight late Greek co-
dices where it has been translated from the Latin, and appears
to have been a gloss inserted into the Spanish or African texts
of the Old Latin version of the NT, originally as an allegorical
commentary (see Bruce Vawter, "The Johannine Epistles," *JBC*, 405;
and Bruce Metzger, *A Textual Commentary on the Greek New Testament* [New York: United Bible Societies, 1971] 716-18).

[48] See Schweizer, *Good News*, 530-31. The theory that trinitarian forms evolved from monadic and binitarian will be discussed below.

[49] J. A. T. Robinson, "The One Baptism As a Category of NT
Soteriology," *Twelve New Testament Studies* (London: SCM, 1962)
161. He comments that the teaching in these two texts is the
same as that in John 7:39. Baptism finds its consummation in
Jesus' death but is not confined to it. O. Cullmann argues that
this association of baptism and death (which was known to the
earliest communities; cf. the pre-Pauline tradition in Rom 6:3-
4) can be traced to the fact that Jesus regarded his own baptism
in the light of Isaiah 42 and 53 as the beginning of his vicarious suffering and a consecration to death (*Baptism in the New
Testament* [London: SCM, 1950] 19). The link between baptism and
death is *not* found in Matthew, who omits the baptismal reference
from the Markan pericope about the sons of Zebedee (Matt 20:20-
28) and has no parallel to Luke 12:50. Trilling remarks that
Matthew understood the baptism commanded in 28:19b as a baptism
into life in God, not into the death of Jesus (*The Gospel According to Matthew* [2 vols.; London: Burns and Oates, 1969]
2.269).

[50] The Markan Appendix 16:15-16 may imply a command: "And
he said to them, 'Go into all the world and preach the gospel
to the whole creation. He who believes and is baptized will be
saved; but he who does not believe will be condemned.'"

[51] A great percentage of the NT epistolary literature has
been said to be "baptismal." It is claimed that form criticism
and the study of cultic traditions can uncover a large number
of texts (for example, Ephesians as a whole) containing baptismal formulas, confessions, hymns, sermons or exhortations. See
M. Barth, "Baptism," *IDBSup*, 87. Barth's own position is that
it is safer to rely only on those texts which speak explicitly
of "baptism" and "baptizing" in the sense of a ritual act. A
wider view is taken here, since even the linking of triadic material with a metaphorical allusion to baptism may be of
significance.

[52] The vast majority of Greek MSS read "the Son of God,"
but see R. E. Brown, *Gospel According to John* (1.57) for the
opinion that that reading is probably the result of harmoniza-
tion with the Synoptic accounts of the baptism and of Christological development.

[53] In John 1:6, John the Baptist is called a man "sent by
God."

[54]M. Barth, "Baptism," 88. The Baptist is represented in the Q material as baptizing "in the name of" (so to speak) God (who is able from stones to raise up children to Abraham; Matt 3:9, par. Luke 3:8). Mark 1:4 and Luke 4:3 represent John as preaching "a baptism of repentance for the forgiveness of sins" (by God). In John 1:33, the Baptist speaks of the one who sent him to baptize with water (presumably God). If the historical Baptist applied to himself Isa 40:3, this application may have originally meant he understood himself to be preparing the way for God. He speaks of the coming one (ὁ ἐρχόμενος) in Matt 11: 3, par. Luke 7:19 (cf. Mark 1:7; Matt 3:11; Luke 3:16; John 1: 27, 30), and of the Holy Spirit with whom the coming one will baptize. This latter idea is in Mark (1:8) and Q (Matt 3:11, par. Luke 3:16); cf. also John 1:33.

[55]Wayne A. Meeks, *The Writings of St. Paul* (New York: W. W. Norton, 1972) 126 n. 5.

[56]J. A. Fitzmyer, "The First Epistle of Peter," *JBC*, 363. Fitzmyer summarizes here the theories of Boismard (that four baptismal hymns can be isolated in the letter), and F. L. Cross (that 1:3 to 4:11 represents the celebrant's part of a Roman baptismal liturgy celebrated at Easter).

[57]An angel is mentioned in Luke 22:43 and also in John 12:29 (which is related to the Synoptic Gethsemane accounts).

[58]Luke 23:46 also uses this term, but Luke adds the citation of Ps 31:6, "into your hands I commend my spirit."

[59]See Donald P. Senior, *The Passion Narrative According to Matthew* (Leuven: Leuven University, 1975) 305-07.

[60]J. N. D. Kelly (*Early Christian Creeds* [London: Longman, 1972] 19) capitalizes the word "Spirit" in both of these passages. The transition to a triadic concept is more apparent, however, in Rom 1:3-4, as we have seen.

[61]See above, n. 49.

[62]M. Barth, "Baptism," 88. The triadic emphasis can be seen to emerge from these considerations of the death of Jesus and the expectations of the Baptist.

[63]Matthew's editing of Mark 13:11 may indicate that he found the relationship between the Father and the Spirit more significant than the title "Holy Spirit." He has changed Mark's use of the latter title to read "the Spirit of your Father" (Matt 10:20).

[64]See, however, George Howard, "The Tetragram and the New Testament," *JBL* 96 (1977) 78-79, esp. n. 72. Based on his theory that the Tetragram was not removed from OT and NT texts until the end of the first century A.D., Howard argues that the original NT texts may have contained less "functional identity" between God and Christ than is thought, the title κύριος not being used yet in the LXX to translate יהוה. But even if this

is so, the use of κύριος for יהוה among Greek speaking readers
may have antedated its written appearance. Howard discusses
what was written in Greek for the sacred name, i.e., יהוה; but
what was pronounced in public reading may have been κύριος.

[65]In Hebrew grammar, a distinction can be clear even without the repetition of the *nomen regens*. In later Hebrew, it is
unusual to repeat it. See the repetition of the *nomen regens*
נֶפֶשׁ in 2 Sam 19:6, and the lack of repetition of the *nomen
regens* דַּם in Isa 1:11. See R. E. Brown, "J. Starcky's Theory
of Qumran Messianic Development," *CBQ* 28 (1966) 54. William
LaSor, however, notes that he has not seen a single example of
the use of one *nomen regens* annexed to two or more genitives in
Hebrew, where the genitives could not be viewed as a single
unit ("The Messiahs of Aaron and Israel," *VT* 6 [1956] 427). In
Greek, two genitives dependent on the same noun, which usually
stands between them, do not occur very often (see Blass,
Debrunner, Funk, *A Greek Grammar of the NT* [Chicago: University
of Chicago, 1971] 93). Two genitives denoting different relations may depend on one noun, however (William Goodwin, *A Greek
Grammar* [New York: St. Martin's, 1965] 231). But the triadic
phrase in Matt 28:19b is not similar to the examples given.

[66]The *Didache* has been dated as late as 200 A.D. and as
early as 50 A.D. Cyril C. Richardson dates it in the form we
have in the mid-second century (*Early Christian Fathers* [Phila-
delphia: Westminster, 1953] 1.165) as does Edouard Massaux
(*Influence de l'Evangile de saint Matthieu sur la Littérature
chrétienne avant saint Irénée* [Louvain: Publication Universitaires de Louvaine, 1950] 6). According to J. P. Audet, the
bulk of the work should be dated before 70 and is from Syria
(*La Didachê: Instructions des apôtres* [Paris: Gabalda, 1958]).

[67]Translation by C. C. Richardson, *Early Christian Fathers*,
Vol. 1. The title of the *Didache*, which critical editions today retain as authentic, orientates us toward Matt 28:16-20,
and may indicate that this pericope was known: Διδαχή κυρίου
δία τῶν δώδεκα ἀποστόλων τοῖς ἔθνεσιν.

[68]Kelly, *Early Christian Creeds*, 66.

[69]See Fuller, *Resurrection Narratives*, 87.

[70]Kelly, *Early Christian Creeds*, 66.

[71]In *Did.* 10:3, in the grace after meals, praise is given
to the "Almighty Master" who has created everything for the
sake of his name. It has been held that the "name" here refers
to Christ (see Daniélou, *Theology of Jewish Christianity*, 151
n. 18), but this is not at all obvious.

[72]Translation by E. R. Hardy, in *Early Christian Fathers*,
Vol. 1, ed. Richardson.

[73]Massaux, *Influence*, 503; see Grant, *Early Christian
Doctrine*, 81.

[74]Kelly, *Early Christian Creeds*, 73.

[75]Cf., for example, Cyril's *Catechetical Lectures* (c. 348), cited by Kelly, *Early Christian Creeds*, 33; Ambrose's *De Sacramentis*, 2, 7, cited by Kelly, p. 37.

[76]Cf. Tertullian, *De Corono* 3: "we are three times immersed, making a somewhat fuller reply than the Lord laid down in the Gospel" (referring to Matt 28:19b); *Adv. Prax.* 26: "For we are baptized, not once but thrice, into the three persons severally in answer to their several names" (cited by Kelly, p. 45); Hippolytus, *Apostolic Tradition* (written c. 215, probably reflecting Roman liturgical practice at the end of the second and beginning of the third century; cited by Kelly, p. 46).

[77]See R. E. Brown, *The Gospel According to John*, 2.759: these are the only verses in John "where God is said to have given the (divine) name to Jesus." An important combination of textual witnesses omit the clause concerning unity. In Rev 19: 12-13, the one in heaven sitting on a white horse "has a name inscribed which no one knows but himself...the name by which he is called is The Word of God."

[78]Giles Quispel, "Qumran, John and Jewish Christianity," 150.

[79]Translation by W. Foerster in *Gnosis: A Selection of Gnostic Texts* (2 vols.; ed. R. McL. Wilson; Oxford: Clarendon, 1974) 2.67. Cf. *Gospel of Philip*, logion 12.

[80]Quispel, "Qumran, John and Jewish Christianity," 150. According to the Valentinians, the Name descended on Jesus in the dove during his baptism in the Jordan (Clement of Alexandria, *Excerpta ex Theodoto* 22:6).

[81]See Quispel, "Qumran, John and Jewish Christianity," 152-54, and Richard N. Longenecker, "Some Distinctive Early Christological Motifs," *NTS* 14 (1966/7) 533-36.

[82]See Matt 1:21-25; 18:20; 19:29; 10:22; 7:21-23.

[83]J. D. Kingsbury, "The Composition and Christology of Matt 28:16-20," *JBL* 93 (1975) 582.

[84]Schweizer, *Good News*, 532. The idea is one of appropriation, dedication, submission, belonging; see W. Heitmuller, *In Namen Jesu* (FRLANT 1:2; Göttingen, 1903). The phrase εἰς τὸ ὄνομα is not used in this sense, however, in the LXX (see 2 Macc 8:4, which speaks of blasphemies committed against God's name). McNeile sees an extension of the idea of belonging in the understanding of "baptism into" as an act "whereby a mystical union is produced." Rom 6:3 speaks of baptism into the death of Jesus; 1 Cor 10:2 of baptism into Moses; 1 Cor 12:13 of baptism into one body, baptism into Christ as "putting on" Christ (A. H. McNeile, *The Gospel According to St. Matthew* [London: Macmillan, 1915] 436).

[85]See A. Oepke, "βάπτω," *TDNT* 1 (1964) 537; R. Bultmann, *Theology of the New Testament* (2 vols.; New York: Scribner's, 1951) 1.40, 137; S. E. Johnson, "Matthew," *IB*, vol. 7, on Matt 28:19b.

[86]Lars Hartman, "Into the Name of Jesus," *NTS* 20 (1973/4) 433.

[87]For example, the phrase םֹיֵּמַשׁ םֵשׁ֥ל is used in the Mishnah seven times all in the tractate *'Abot* (2:2, 2:12, 4:11 twice, 5:17 three times), and in the Tosepta and Mekilta (see references in Hans Kosmala, "In My Name," *ASTI* 5 [1967] 93).

[88]G. R. Beasley-Murray, *Baptism in the New Testament* (London: Macmillan, 1962) 90-92; Joachim Jeremias, *Infant Baptism in the First Four Centuries* (London: SCM, 1960) 29; Herman L. Strack, Paul Billerbeck, *Kommentar zum Neuen Testament aus Talmud und Midrasch* (München: C. H. Beck, 1922) 1.591, 1054-55: "Die Taufe begründet eine Verbindung zwischen dem dreieinigen Gott und dem Täufling, die dieser zu bejahen und zu betätigen hat durch sein Bekenntnis zu dem Gott, auf dessen Namen er getauft ist."

[89]Hartman finds the closest counterpart of the Matthean phrase in the Hebrew-Aramaic םֵשׁ֥ל as used in the earliest Palestinian Christian community, which was not "isolated from the Hellenistic world, as if they did not themselves form part of that world" ("Into the Name," 435 n. 7). New nuances emerged when the phrase was used in an even more Hellenistic environment, and as technical cultic or religious language developed. But he finds Billerbeck's interpretation of Matt 28:19b (see note above) justified.

[90]Ibid., 349-50. Hartman thinks that although Christian baptism was largely inspired by the Baptism movement, the phrase "into the name of Jesus" distinguished the Christian rite especially from John's.

[91]M. Barth, "Baptism," 87. He insists that εἰς τὸ ὄνομα in baptismal texts does *not* mean a transfer into the possession of the Lord, an insertion into salvation history, a magical transformation or a mystical unification with the deity. But see below, n. 93.

[92]Hartman, "Into the Name," 439.

[93]J. Zumstein ("Matthieu 28:16-20," *RTP* 22 [1972] 27) states that by invoking the Father, Son and Spirit on the proselyte, the community introduces that person into the reality of salvation. Trilling speaks of the three names called out over the candidate, each name indicating that a certain aspect of the Christian life in relation to them has begun (*Gospel According to St. Matthew*, 2.269-70). The identity of the baptized, in other words, is given a new dimension.

[94]See above, n. 76.

[95] See Kelly, *Early Christian Creeds*, 48.

[96] Ibid., 15.

[97] If the phrase εἰς τὸ ὄνομα is based on either the expression לְשֵׁם or the formula קָרָא בְּשֵׁם, it is possible that the term "name" does not necessarily indicate that the Holy Spirit is considered a person, i.e., a being with a personal name, in Matt 28:19b. Rather, it may be simply mentioned as a force or power of God. But its connection here (apparently on the same level) with the Father and Son moves it toward personality.

[98] Cf. Metzger (*A Textual Commentary*, 359-60) for a discussion of v. 37; the tradition of the eunuch's confession of faith was current as early as the latter part of the second century.

[99] Brown, *The Gospel According to John*, 1.375, 381-82. Only here in the Fourth Gospel is Jesus worshipped (προσκυνέω).

[100] Kelly, *Early Christian Creeds*, 43-44, 48.

[101] W. F. Albright and C. S. Mann, *The Gospel of Matthew* (AB 26; Garden City: Doubleday, 1971) 363; W. C. Allen, *The Gospel According to St. Matthew* (ICC; New York: Scribner's, 1925) 307. Lars Hartman ("Into the Name," 432-40), as we have seen, discusses the phrase εἰς τὸ ὄνομα as above all a definition, a formula used to characterize the rite when it was presented to others, not necessarily the words spoken at the rite. The theory that the prepositional phrase εἰς τὸ ὄνομα or εἰς alone with regard to baptism (cf. Acts 8:16; 19:5; 1 Cor 1:13, 15; Matt 28:19, cf. 18:20 and Rom 6:3; Gal 3:27; 1 Cor 10:2) signals a reference to the results of baptism, while ἐν τῷ ὀνόματι (Acts 10:48) and ἐπὶ τῷ ὀνόματι (Acts 2:38) signal invocation or confession, is held by several scholars (F. F. Bruce, "The End of the First Gospel, *EvQ* 12 [1940] 206; R. Abba, "Name," *IDB*, 3.502; Albright and Mann, *Gospel According to St. Matthew*, 363; A. H. McNeile, *Gospel According to St. Matthew*, 436). It is hardly possible, however, to tell the difference among these usages, and they seem to be interchangeable (cf. Kosmala, "In My Name," 88).

[102] Massaux, *Influence*, 652.

[103] See Grant (*Early Christian Doctrine of God*, 82) for the argument that not until Athenagoras, a generation after Justin, is there an attempt to work out a "Trinitarian" doctrine.

[104] A. Schmoller, *Handkonkordanz zum griechischen Neuen Testament* (Stuttgart: Würtembergische Bibelanstalt, 1963).

[105] Three others are classified as referring to "hominus animus--anima defunctorum": Matt 5:3, 26:41, 27:50.

[106] In John 14:17 it is said that the Paraclete is in the disciples, and in 14:26 that "the Paraclete, the Holy Spirit, whom the Father will send in my name,...will teach you all things and bring to your remembrance all that I have said to you."

[107]Cf. Matt 22:43 ("David, inspired by the Spirit"); Acts 1:16.

[108]See above, n. 63.

[109]Jack Dean Kingsbury, *Matthew: Structure, Christology, Kingdom* (Philadelphia: Fortress, 1975) 96.

[110]Sir 23:27; Wis 9:9; 6:4, 9; *2 Apoc. Bar.* 5:3-7; Bar 3:37-4:1.

[111]Wis 1:6-7; 7:22; 9:17.

[112]M. Jack Suggs, *Wisdom, Christology and Law in Matthew's Gospel* (Cambridge: Harvard University, 1970). See also Krister Stendahl, *The School of St. Matthew* (Philadelphia: Fortress, 1968) 27, 142.

[113]Marshall D. Johnson ("Reflections on a Wisdom Approach to Matthew's Christology," *CBQ* 36 [1974]) has attempted to sharpen some of the issues raised by Suggs. Among Johnson's most valuable points, I think, are his contentions that further examination is necessary concerning the relation between the Son of Man and Wisdom, and his questioning of the centrality of the Jesus-Sophia motif in Matthew.

[114]Danby translation. The saying is given in the name of R. Hananiah ben Teradian (died 135 A.D.). See also 3:6: "R. Halafta ben Dosa of Kefar Hanania (second half of the second century) said, 'If ten men sit together and occupy themselves in the Law, the Divine Presence rests among them, for it is written, "God stands in the congregation of God"'" (Ps 82:1).

[115]Cf. J. Kingsbury, *The Parables of Jesus in Matthew 13* (London: SPCK, 1969) 18.

[116]William O. Walker, Jr., "The Kingdom of the Son of Man and the Kingdom of the Father in Matthew," *CBQ* 30 (1968) 579. See Kingsbury (*Matthew*, 138, 140, 164, 166) for discussion of the tension between present and future modes of the kingdom.

[117]B. Gerhardsson, *The Testing of God's Son (Matt 4:1-11 and Par)* (ConB, NT Ser. 2; Lund, 1966).

[118]B. Gerhardsson, "The Parable of the Sower and Its Interpretation," *NTS* 14 (1967/68) 165-93. See also idem, "The Seven Parables in Matthew XIII," *NTS* 19 (1972/73) 16-37.

[119]B. Gerhardsson, "Jésus Livré et Abandonné d'après la Passion selon Saint Matthieu," *RB* 76 (1969) 206-27; idem, "Du Judéo-Christianisme à Jésus par le Shema'," *RSR* 60 (1972) 23-36.

[120]B. Gerhardsson, "The Hermeneutic Program in Matthew 22: 37-40," in *Jews, Greeks and Christians* (ed. Robert Hamerton-Kelly and Robin Scroggs; Leiden: Brill, 1976) 134.

[121]F. C. Conybeare, "The Eusebian Form of the Text Mt.
28:19," *ZNW* 2 (1901) 275-88.

[122]B. H. Cuneo, *The Lord's Command to Baptize* (Washington,
1923) 95-110; cited by Hubbard, *Matthean Redaction*, 153.

[123]Hubbard, *Matthean Redaction*, 161.  Hubbard argues that
the special prominence given in Eusebius to the shorter reading
and to the related notion of the importance of Jesus' name indicates that it is "possible but not probable" that Eusebius
had textual support for the shorter reading.  Hubbard's own
exegetical and form-critical findings support the opinion that
Matthew, drawing on the liturgical usage of his church, inserted
the triadic baptismal formula as he redacted a primitive proto-
commissioning.  He concludes that the triadic baptismal formula
has a strong probability of being authentic (p. 175).

[124]F. C. Conybeare, "Three Early Doctrinal Modifications
of the Text of the Gospels," *HibJ* 1 (1902) 96-113.

[125]See B. Lonergan, *The Way to Nicea: The Dialectical
Development of Trinitarian Theology* (Philadelphia: Westminster,
1976) 74-75.

[126]Hubbard accepts a date for the *Didache* in the first
half of the second century, and therefore concludes that it is
possible that both it and the longer Matthean reading sprang
from the liturgical practice of the second century (*Matthean
Redaction*, 162).  If, however, the *Didache* originated much
earlier, it could confirm the authenticity of the longer reading.  Conybeare suspected that the triadic phrase is an interpolation into the *Didache* as well as into Matthew ("The Eusebian
Form," 284).

[127]See Hubbard, *Matthean Redaction*, 163-64, 167-75.  He
deals with the treatments of D. Flusser ("The Conclusion of
Matthew in a New Jewish Christian Source," *ASTI* 5 [1967] 110-20),
Lohmeyer ("Mir ist gegeben," 22-49), H. Kosmala ("The Conclu-
sion," 132-47) and P. Gaechter (*Die Literarische Kunst im
Matthäus-Evangelium* [Stuttgart, 1966] 78-79).

[128]Beasley-Murray, *Baptism in the New Testament*, 83-84.
This scholar does not argue, however, that the triadic phrase
is inauthentic.  He suggests that the monadic Christological
statement was modified by Matthew himself or in his day, to
conform to existing liturgical traditions and needs.

[129]Ibid., 84.

[130]Hubbard (*Matthean Redaction*, 130) remarks that there is
no other triadic formula in Matthew's Gospel.  We have seen,
however, that there are several triadic passages in Matthew.
Kingsbury's attempts to set the phrase in 28:19b squarely within the context of Matthean theology will be treated in section
3, below.

[131]G. Vermes, *Jesus the Jew* (New York: Macmillan, 1974)
200. Vermes probably includes in the "age" of Jesus the time
down to and including the writing of the Synoptic Gospels (pp.
212-13). But his wording is inexact, and open to the rebuttal
that no scholar has claimed the triadic phrase is from the time
of Jesus' ministry. Other scholars who argue that the triadic
phrase is an interpolation include H. B. Green ("The Command to
Baptize and Other Matthean Interpolations," *SE* IV [1968] 62)
and R. Bultmann (*Theology of the NT*, 1.134).

[132]Usually the term "formula" is not defined. See above,
pp. 21-23.

[133]See, for example, Michel, "Der Abschluss," 20, 24;
Strecker, *Der Weg*, 211-12; idem, "The Concept of History in
Matthew," *JAAR* 35 (1967) 229; Bornkamm, "The Risen Lord," 205,
222. Others who share this opinion include Goulder, Schweizer,
Zumstein, Hubbard, J. A. T. Robinson, Gaechter, F. Hahn,
Perrin, Jeremias, Beasley-Murray, Bultmann and Trilling.

[134]M. D. Goulder, *Midrash and Lection in Matthew* (London:
SPCK, 1974) 449, 192.

[135]See Strecker, "Concept of History," 229; idem, *Der Weg*,
209; Hubbard, *Matthean Redaction*, 130.

[136]Goulder, *Midrash*, 52 n. 36, 449.

[137]Albright and Mann, *The Gospel of Matthew*, 362; Robinson,
*Jesus and His Coming*, 131, 132; Allen, *Gospel According to St.
Matthew*, 122. There is no proof, however, that any resurrection
appearances were contained in Mark. Most scholars believe today
that Mark ended at 16:8, and that this was the form of Mark that
Matthew had.

[138]See, for example, Schweizer, *Good News*, 530. The theory
of the growth of triadic formulas out of monadic and binitarian
will be examined below.

[139]Strecker, *Der Weg*, 209; Hubbard (*Matthean Redaction*,
130) remarks, "That Matthew would put into the mouth of Jesus a
triadic baptismal formula without the sanction of the liturgical usage of his church is hard to believe."

[140]See above, section B 3, on the meaning of εἰς τὸ ὄνομα.

[141]Fuller, *Resurrection Narratives*, 80-82.

[142]Ibid., 210 n. 28, 84-86. Fuller accepts the notion that
baptism was practiced from the beginning of the Christian mission. At the early stage, both the rite and its interpretation
"ultimately derived from John's baptism, modified according to
the change of eschatological perspective resulting from the
Easter event" (p. 85).

[143]Fuller argues that the perspective of Matt 28:19 is "palpably late." It presupposes the Hellenistic and Pauline extension of the mission to the Gentiles (*Resurrection Narratives*, 84).

[144]As Fuller points out, the other canonical appearance stories include the charge to preach the gospel, rather than a charge to teach.

[145]Ibid., 88. If he believes that Matthew has another reason, aside from the liturgical practice of his community, for changing the monadic form into the triadic, Fuller does not state and explore it.

[146]Ibid., 86, 92.

[147]Ibid., 91.

[148]Fuller, *Foundations*, 184-86.

[149]Idem, *Resurrection Narratives*, 89.

[150]Ibid.

[151]Fuller accepts the list of Mattheanisms in G. Barth, "Matthew's Understanding of the Law," *Tradition and Interpretation in Matthew* (ed. Bornkamm, Barth and Held; Philadelphia: Westminster, 1963) 131 n. 1, with the exception of the word ἰδού. Fuller, *Resurrection Narratives*, 208 n. 14.

[152]See Bornkamm, "Risen Lord," 206; Zumstein, "Matthieu 28:16-20," 16-17; Michel, "Der Abschluss," 19-21; Barth, "Matthew's Understanding," 131-37; B. Malina, "The Literary Structure and Form of Mt 28:16-20," *NTS* 17 (1970/71) 88; Trilling, *Das Wahre Israel*, 21-45; J. Jeremias, *Jesus' Promise to the Nations* (London: SCM, 1958) 39; F. Hahn, *Mission in the New Testament* (London: SCM, 1965) 64.

[153]Michel, "Der Abschluss," 16-19; Zumstein, "Matthieu 28:16-20," 16-17; Bornkamm, "Risen Lord," 206.

[154]See Hubbard, *Matthean Redaction*, 128-29, 130 n. 1.

[155]Ibid., 114-23. The words in parentheses are the ones Hubbard is unsure belong to this primitive stratum.

[156]Ibid., xi.

[157]Ibid., 128. Hubbard thinks the use of the identical expression by Matthew (28:19) and Luke (24:47), πάντα τὰ ἔθνη, makes it probable that this phrase was present in the proto-commission. The Markan Appendix 16:15 ("Go into the whole world and preach the gospel to the whole creation")--which Hubbard thinks may be an independent tradition--reinforces this view. The absence of universalism in John 20:19-23 is explained by the theological understanding in the second half of the Fourth Gospel of "the world" as under Satan's power (p. 115).

[158]Hubbard, *Matthean Redaction*, 78-83.

[159]Matt 28:19b, Luke 24:49, John 20:21.

[160]Matt 28:19b, Luke 24:49 ("the promise of the Father"), John 20:22.

[161]Hubbard, *Matthean Redaction*, 119.

[162]Ibid., 118-19, 133.

[163]See further criticisms of Hubbard's thesis in the review by D. Senior, *JBL* 95 (1976) 488-89. He finds the basic principle on which Hubbard bases his analysis (that common elements among the three evangelists in this section of the gospel must predicate a common source) not without merit. But the evidence, Senior holds, demands a more refined treatment. He thinks that Hubbard may not give sufficient attention to independent redactional motivation for certain details.

[164]Strecker, *Der Weg*, 210.

[165]While this is true, there are also phrases not included in Strecker's reconstruction of the pre-Matthean tradition which are non-Matthean.

[166]Strecker, *Der Weg*, 211.

[167]Ibid., 255.

[168]Ibid., 210 n. 3.

[169]Meier, "Two Disputed Questions," 411, on Strecker's position.

[170]Hubbard, *Matthean Redaction*, 6-7. Bultmann also heavily emphasizes the baptismal command as the core of the unit. He considers the pericope "a sort of cult legend in virtue of the appended instruction to baptize" (*History of the Synoptic Tradition* [New York: Harper and Row, 1968] 286).

[171]Zumstein, "Matthieu 28:16-20," 18. Each motif, he argues, appears separately: that of v. 18b in Matt 11:27 and John 3:35; that of v. 19b in Mark 16:15; and that of v. 20b in Matt 18:20. He does not respond to Strecker's insistence that the motifs are not totally isolated in the tradition.

[172]Meier, "Two Disputed Questions," 412. See his discussion here of the different redactional tendencies of Matthew and Luke. Matthew speaks of a mountain in Galilee, Luke of the Mount of Olives near Jerusalem. For Matthew, the exaltation is the resurrection; for Luke, the exaltation is a separate ascension forty days after the resurrection. Matthew sees the support for the eleven in the perduring presence of Jesus "who does not depart *from* but comes *to* the church"; Luke sees support in the coming of the Holy Spirit whom Jesus sends after he

departs.  Meier lists Matt 28:19a or 20a for (b) the command to
start a mission.  But he remarks, "One might wonder if, in accordance with Strecker's schema (also tripartite), Matt 28:19b
(some type of baptismal formula) might not be substituted as
the traditional element indicating mission or aggregation to
the church."  Meier does not discuss the triadic phrase in 28:
19b, except to say that it is probably not redactional, since
it never appears elsewhere in Matthew and since Matthew would
not likely introduce a new baptismal formula into his church
(p. 410).  Meier accepts the possibility that the triadic
phrase was embedded in a larger piece of tradition behind 28:
16-20 (p. 414).

[173]Ibid., 415-16.  Element (d) for Meier is the most
doubtful.

[174]There is mention also of Jesus having given commandment
(ἐντειλάμενος, Acts 1:2; cf. Matt 28:20a, ἐνετειλάμην), and of
the Father's authority (ἐξουσία, Acts 1:7; cf. Matt 28:18b) by
which the time of the coming of the kingdom is fixed.  The command in Acts 1:8b is also to a universal mission.

[175]Schweizer also believes that the concluding episode
itself was familiar to Matthew from the tradition of his community, although it is almost impossible to determine to what
extent its wording was already fixed.  From vv. 18-20, the
first and last sayings (vv. 18b and 20b) "are the most likely
parts belonging to the narrative in its earliest form" (*Good
News*, 528-29).

[176]J. D. Kingsbury, "Composition and Christology," 577.
See also his less detailed treatment in *Matthew* (77-78).  J.
Lange,who likewise considers Matt 28:18-20 a Matthean creation,
does claim, however, that the triadic baptismal formula is received tradition (*Das Erscheinen des Auferstandenen im Evangelium nach Matthäus* [Würzburg: Echter, 1973] 313).  Gerhardsson
insists the phrase bears all the marks of Matthean theology.
He considers it to be an expansion of an original monadic formula, designed to appeal to Gentiles ("Monotheism och högkristologi i Mattheus evangeliet," *SEÅ* 37/8 [1972/3] 125-44,
summarized in *NTA* 18 [1973/4] 297).

[177]Kingsbury, "Composition and Christology," 573-84.

[178]Kingsbury admits, however, that in Matt 10:41-42 the
phrase is without the same force ("Composition and Christology,"
578 n. 37).  Goulder (*Midrash*, 482) lists it as a Matthean
phrase.  It is found five times in Matthew and is absent from
Mark and Luke.

[179]It occurs forty-four times in Matthew, thirty of these
times without a Synoptic parallel ("Composition and Christology,"
578 n. 38).  It is used of God five times in Mark, sixteen times
in Luke.

[180]Matt 11:27 (par. Luke 10:22), 24:36 (par. Mark 13:32),
21:38 (redactional) and 28:19b.  Kingsbury, "Composition and
Christology," 578 n. 39.

[181]Kingsbury, *Matthew*, 78; cf. 82, 55-56 on the disciples as sons of God.

[182]Ibid., 77.

[183]Kingsbury, "Composition and Christology," 580-82; idem, *Matthew*, 77.

[184]Idem, "Composition and Christology," 579. Only one portion of the text is difficult to ascribe to Matthew, because its verb is found nowhere else in the Gospel: οὖ ἐτάξατο αὐτοῖς ὁ Ἰησοῦς (v. 16). Kingsbury attributes it to the Evangelist nevertheless, since it refers to 28:10c and is an integral part of vv. 16-17 (p. 575). But see below, Excursus on Mattheanisms.

[185]Kingsbury, "Composition and Christology," 582; idem, *Matthew*, 40-83.

[186]It is used by God (3:17, 17:5), Satan (4:3, 6), demons (8:29) and believers (e.g., 14:33; 16:16; 27:54). D. Senior (*Passion Narrative*, 176 n. 5) draws the opposite conclusion from his review of the nine times Matthew uses the title Son of God. He argues that "Matthew connects the title much more intimately than Mark with situations in which the Messianic identity of Jesus is publically proclaimed."

[187]Kingsbury, *Matthew*, 113-22.

[188]Ibid., 120-22.

[189]Kingsbury speaks of the twofold objective Matthew is pursuing when he associates the conclusion of his Gospel with the Christological title "Son": (1) as regards the horizontal dimension of the history of Jesus, the title relates all the major phases in his life, so that the identification of the person of Jesus of Nazareth and the risen, exalted Jesus is stressed; (2) as regards the so-called vertical dimension of the relationship of Jesus to God, the uniqueness of his person and his divine authority are stressed ("Composition and Christology," 583).

[190]Ibid., 580.

[191]Kilpatrick, *Origins*, 48-49, 96, 37.

[192]Kingsbury, "Composition and Christology," 576.

[193]He argues that in Matthew the motif of exaltation is absent from the words that treat of the coming of the Son of Man (ibid., 580). He is in agreement with the caveat of H. E. Tödt (*The Son of Man in the Synoptic Tradition* [London: SCM, 1965] 290-91) against interpreting Matt 28:18 as a statement about the Kyrios or Son of Man. Tödt, however, does believe that there is something of Dan 7:14 present in Matt 28:18. The "concept of the Son of Man" is absent from the Matthean text, but the "concept of enthronement" deriving from Daniel 7 is present. Tödt's distinctions will be discussed further in Chapter III.

[194]See above, pp. 25-26, for example, Gerhardsson's treatment of Matthew's subtle use of the Shema'.

[195]See Fuller, *Foundations*, 114-15; J. Jeremias, *New Testament Theology* (New York: Scribner's, 1971) 56-61 on Matt 11:27 (Q).

[196]K. Stendahl, "Matthew," *PCB*, 773.

[197]Strecker, "Concept of History in Matthew," 229.

[198]See Meier, "Two Disputed Questions," 409.

[199]John 20:24 notes that Thomas, one of the twelve, was not present when Jesus appeared.

[200]Hubbard, *Matthean Redaction*, 113. It is impossible to be certain of this point, as mention of the eleven may be due to independent redaction by Matthew and Luke. 1 Cor 15:5 lists an appearance to "the twelve."

[201]A Galilean appearance is attested also in John 21, so this element may be traditional. Meier thinks that Galilee was mentioned in the pre-Matthean tradition ("Two Disputed Questions," 416), but he does not offer any support for this claim; rather, his arguments support it being Matthean redaction (p. 408). The mention of the mountain is often thought to be Matthean redaction, since this motif appears often in this Gospel (see above, n. 2). But the instruction given to the disciples in 28:7, 10 says nothing about a mountain. Two unusual linguistic usages follow τὸ ὄρος in 28:16: οὖ which seems to mean "whither," and the simple τάσσω which is a hapax legomenon in Matthew (see Meier, "Two Disputed Questions," 409). Meier takes this to indicate that the whole phrase, τὸ ὄρος οὖ ἐτάξατο αὐτοῖς ὁ 'Ιησοῦς, usually translated "the mountain to which Jesus directed them," is pre-Matthean tradition. As we have seen, he notes that Acts 1:6-11 also deals with the appearance of the Risen Jesus on a mountain. An examination of several other NT uses of the verb τάσσω suggests a different translation for the phrase in Matt 28:16. In Matt 8:9 (par. Luke 7:8) the centurion speaks of himself as a man "set under authority" (ὑπὸ ἐξουσίαν τασσόμενος). In one other text, Rom 13:1, τάσσω is used again with ἐξουσία: "Let every person be subject (ὑποτασσέσθω) to the governing authorities (ἐξουσίαις). For there is no authority (ἐξουσία) except from God, and those that exist have been instituted (τεταγμέναι) by God." We find τάσσω used in one passage with the sense "ordained": Acts 13:48, speaking of Gentiles "ordained (τεταγμένοι) to eternal life." There are also two in which the verb has the sense of "appointed" or "commissioned": Acts 15:2 (Paul and Barnabas and others are "appointed [ἔταξαν] to go up to Jerusalem") and 22:10 (Saul's Damascus experience in which it is said he will be "told all that is appointed" [τέτακται] for him to do). These texts, especially the last two, lead me to suspect that the meaning intended at Matt 28:16 may be that of appointment or commission to the new task. If so, we should translate "to the mountain

where Jesus commissioned them (to make disciples)" and not "to
the mountain to which Jesus had directed them (to go)." A major problem with the former translation, however, is that the
aorist ἐτάξατο following the aorist ἐπορεύθησαν naturally lends
itself to a pluperfect sense. One would have expected a future,
a periphrastic future, or μέλλω with the infinitive ("where he
was to or about to commission them") (J. P. Meier in a letter
to the author). The fact that the simple τάσσω is not used
elsewhere in Matthew still supports the argument that the
phrase is pre-Matthean tradition.

[202]G. Barth, "Matthew's Understanding," 131 n. 1.

[203]Meier, "Two Disputed Questions," 409. He notes that it
is strange, since the seeing is stressed in the preceding context, that it is almost ignored here. This tension leads Meier
to suspect that there may be an element of tradition in the
theme of seeing Jesus (p. 411).

[204]Matthew uses προσκυνέω thirteen times; Mark and Luke
use it only twice. It is used, however, twenty-four times in
Revelation. Five times Matthew alters Mark to describe worship
as the gesture of those who approach Jesus (8:2; 9:18; 14:33;
15:25, 20:20; cf. Hubbard, *Matthean Redaction*, 75). The verb
διστάζω is found in the NT only at Matt 28:18 and 14:31 (a
Matthean insertion into the Markan story of Peter walking on
the water). In both texts we find the Matthean theme of the
obedient/worshipping disciple who nevertheless wavers.

[205]In Mark it is used five times, in Luke ten times.

[206]Meier, "Two Disputed Questions," 410.

[207]On the clause ἐδόθη μοι πᾶσα ἐξουσία as Matthean redaction, see Kingsbury ("Composition," 576), A. Vögtle ("Das christologische und ekklesiologische Anliegen von Mt. 28, 18-20," *SE* 2
[1964] 281-83) and Lange (*Erscheinen*). The latter sees 28:18b
as a "new edition" by Matthew of 11:27 (Q); he is carefully refuted by Meier ("Two Disputed Questions," 413-14). Kilpatrick
thinks that the linking of οὐρανός and γῆ in 28:18b is redactional (*Origins*, 48). See also Kingsbury, who notes that various expressions associating "heaven and earth" appear thirteen
times in Matthew, as compared to twice in Mark and five times
in Luke; in only three cases do the Matthean instances have
Synoptic parallel ("Composition and Christology," 576). But
the conjunction with both nouns in the singular occurs only in
pre- and extra-Matthean traditions (Meier, "Two Disputed Questions," 410). The theory that in 28:18b are found allusions to
Dan 7:14 and 4:17 LXX will be presented in Chapter III.

[208]Kingsbury, "Composition and Christology," 576.

[209]Ibid., 576-77. Eighteen of these times Kingsbury
judges are editorial.

[210]See ibid., 577-78.

[211]The combination of making disciples (μαθητὰς ποιεῖ) and baptizing is found in John 4:1 where Jesus' work (cf. 3:22) is compared to that of John the Baptist: 'Ιησοῦς πλείονας μαθητὰς ποιεῖ καὶ βαπτίζει ἢ 'Ιωάννης. This may indicate that the association of these ideas in Matt 28:19 is traditional.

[212]Cf. Kingsbury, "Composition and Christology," 577; Meier, "Two Disputed Questions," 410.

[213]Cf. Luke 24:47. The phrase occurs four times in Matthew: at 24:9, 14; 25:32 and here at 28:19. The use at 24:9 is indeed redactional; but in 24:14 it is taken from Mark 13:10. I consider it in both 25:32 and 29:19 as based on Dan 7:14 LXX. In these texts, it corresponds to the Aramaic, כֹל עַמְמַיָּא אֻמַיָּא וְלִשָּׁנַיָּא.

[214]Six times in Matthew, once in Mark, not at all in Luke. John, however, uses it seventeen times.

[215]Matthew also uses this phrase six times, and in 23:3 with τηρέω. The word πάσας in v. 20b is probably also redactional.

[216]This word is found sixty-two times in Matthew, seven times in Mark and fifty-seven times in Luke. See Meier, "Two Disputed Questions," 410.

[217]It will be argued that each of the Matthean passages is drawing on Danielic tradition. The term συντελεία appears twenty-two times in the LXX of Daniel.

[218]The occurrence in Matt 17:9 is at the end of the transfiguration scene; there are many links between this pericope and the final Matthean pericope. The promise of presence, ἐγὼ μεθ' ὑμῶν εἰμι, is considered redactional by Kingsbury, Lange, Hubbard and others (see Hubbard, *Matthean Redaction*, 96-97). It does take up the interpretation of Emmanuel in 1:23, and is reminiscent of 18:20, so that the theme of presence appears at the beginning, middle and end of the Gospel. But Meier thinks that all three instances of the motif are traditional (see "Two Disputed Questions," 415, 410-11). This is most probably correct.

[219]Acts 8:16; 19:5; 1 Cor 6:11 and elsewhere.

[220]See Col 2:6; Acts 11:17; 16:31; Phil 2:11.

[221]"Jesus is the Messiah" (1 John 2:22), "Jesus is the Son of God" (Acts 8:37, Western text; cf. 1 John 4:15), "Jesus is the Son of Man" (cf. John 9:35-38).

[222]O. Cullmann, *The Earliest Christian Confessions* (London: Lutterworth, 1949) 32, 42. Cf. 1 Tim 6:13; 2 Tim 4:1. Dogmatic disputes, Cullmann holds, also made binitarian formulas necessary: they had to be used against modalists who confused God and Christ, and against Gnostics who denied the Creator God.

[223]"There is one body and one Spirit...one Lord, one faith, one baptism, one God and Father of us all...."

[224]"The grace of the Lord Jesus Christ and the love of God and the fellowship of the Holy Spirit be with you all."

[225]These are not "confessions of faith" but only "declarations." See Cullmann, *Earliest Christian Confessions*, 43, 36; and idem, *Baptism in the New Testament*, 71. R. P. Martin ("Liturgical Materials, NT," *IDBSup*, 556) argues that one-member confessions developed into two-member statements, and then into a triadic structure. He sees the process taking place under pressure of polemic situations *or* through the rise of the baptismal formula (Matt 28:19b).

[226]See, for example, Moule, "The New Testament and the Doctrine of the Trinity," 16. Gerhardsson and others agree that the expanded triadic formula in Matthew is an indication that by Matthew's time the church consisted of Gentiles and Jews ("Monotheism och högkristologi," 297). R. E. Brown more cautiously remarks, "Almost all scholars would agree that this baptismal formula represents a stage of sacramental development beyond that of the first decades when Christians baptized in the name of Jesus" ("Difficulties in Using the New Testament in American Catholic Discussions," *Louvain Studies* 6 [1976] 151). "More developed" does not necessarily mean "an expansion of." Rather, it seems to mean "closer to the eventual Christian doctrine of the co-equality of three divine persons." More and less developed statements or formulas could exist contemporaneously.

[227]Cullmann, *Earliest Christian Confessions*, 39.

[228]Ibid., 40 n. 3. Cullmann considers Rom 1:1-4 as an example of an ancient Christological confession in which God and Spirit are named as "functions of Christ."

[229]Ibid., 50.

[230]Ibid.

[231]Ibid., 52. Faith in Jesus Christ gave faith in God the Father and in the Spirit its Christian foundation (p. 63).

[232]Ibid., 51.

[233]This is not to claim that the readers of NT times thought in expressly theocentric and Christocentric categories, but to claim that they might be able to feel in certain NT passages more than others a move away from Judaism's theocentric focus.

[234]Kelly, *Early Christian Creeds*, 24-28.

[235]See, for example, 1 Tim 6:13, which Kelly and others believe may be connected with baptism rather than with a judicial process.

[236]Cf. Rom 4:24; 8:11; 2 Cor 4:14; Gal 1:1; 1 Thess 1:10;
Col 2:12; Eph 1:20; 1 Pet 1:21; and the divine passive ἠγέρθη
(Mark 16:6; Luke 24:34; Matt 28:6).

[237]Kelly, *Early Christian Creeds*, 26.

[238]Kelly calls them "Trinitarian" (ibid., 23) and speaks
of the rarely explicit "Trinitarianism" and "Trinitarian ground
plan" of the NT. By this he means the "conception of the
threefold manifestation of the Godhead" in which the ideas of
the apostolic writers took shape. It has been argued above
that this terminology and the attribution of such a conception
to Matthew is inaccurate.

[239]Kelly, *Early Christian Creeds*, 26.

[240]See above, p. 6.

[241]See above, pp. 13-14, for mention of the number of
triadic texts which occur in a baptismal context.

[242]See Kelly, *Early Christian Creeds*, 28. M. Wiles ("Some
Reflections on the Origins of the Doctrine of the Trinity,"
*JTS* 8 [1957] 99) agrees with Kelly that the threefold form was
a basic datum of Christian thought from the very beginning.

[243]Kelly, *Early Christian Creeds*, 27. On the other hand,
it cannot be maintained, as it sometimes is, on the basis of
the belief that Matt 28:19b represents the verbatim words of
Jesus, that there was evolution from the triadic to the monadic
forms.

[244]See H. Küng, *On Being a Christian* (Garden City: Doubleday, 1976) 476: "Both historically and objectively the Christological problem became the source of the often misunderstood
Trinitarian problem."

[245]This is because the Spirit seems to be given a personal
"name" or even the *same* name as the Father and Son. But it has
been argued that there are other more likely ways of understanding the phrase, εἰς τὸ ὄνομα (above, pp. 16-23).

[246]Above, p. 23.

[247]As Matt 28:19b is the only example of a triadic baptismal phrase, it is not clear that there are monadic and triadic
baptismal formulas of equal antiquity.

[248]E. Stauffer suggests that a Jewish triple formula based
on the *Shema'* (such as: one God--one name--one Israel; or,
one God--one temple--one Israel) has influenced NT texts (see
references in *New Testament Theology* [London: SCM, 1955] 326 n.
821; cf. 251. He also gives examples of four- and five-membered
formulas). Another suggestion, which we will examine in the
following section, concerns the triad of God, Son of Man, angels
found in the Similitudes and in the NT. The triad based on the
*Shema'* does not involve the Messiah. The Jewish triads we will
discuss may or may not involve a Messianic figure.

[249]An elementary and formal preference for the number
three as such may also have exercised some influence, but I
would not judge that this is of great importance.  See Stauffer
(*NT Theology*, 326 n. 825) for mention of the early church's
tendency to form impersonal, threefold formulas.

[250]Kelly, *Early Christian Creeds*, 23.

[251]As will be seen, the Jewish apocalyptic triad can be
considered either to influence the development of a Christian
monadic formula into a triadic, or to underlie the creation of
primarily triadic Christian formulas and passages.

[252]R. H. Fuller, "On Demythologizing the Trinity," *ATR* 43
(1961) 121-31; idem, *Resurrection Narratives*, 85-86.

[253]Lohmeyer, "Mir ist gegeben," 30-31, repeated in Lohmeyer, *Das Evangelium des Matthäus* (ed. Werner Schmauch;
Göttingen: Vandenhoeck und Ruprecht, 1962) 413.

[254]This is the second of the five sections of *1 Enoch*
(Ethiopic), and contains three revelations or visions: chaps.
37-44, 45-57, 58-69.  An epilogue takes up the main theme of
Enoch's heavenly journey, bringing him to the palace of God
(M. Black, "The Throne-Theophany Prophetic Commission and the
'Son of Man,'" *Jews, Greeks and Christians* [SJLA 21; ed. R.
Hamerton-Kelly and R. Scroggs; Leiden: Brill, 1976] 63).

[255]That is, the dwellings of the holy and righteous ones.

[256]Translation and rearrangement of the text by R. H.
Charles.  See T. W. Manson ("The Son of Man in Daniel, Enoch,
and the Gospels," *BJRL* 32 [1950] 183) for a different translation and arrangement.  According to Charles, the vision infers
"that the Messianic community will one day be composed of both
angels and men, under the rule of the Messiah and the immediate
protection of the Lord of Spirits" (*The Book of Enoch* [Oxford:
Clarendon, 1912] 75).  Unless stated otherwise, Charles' 1912
edition of the *Book of Enoch* is the one used for this study.

[257]This strange listing of the Elect One with the orders
of angels, and as the only singular in the list, may be the
copyists' mistake; but Charles gives no MSS variation here,
and does not comment on this phenomenon.

[258]Usually the figure with the Lord of Spirits is called
the Elect One (39:6-7; 40:5-6; 45; 49:2, 4; 51:3; 52:5-6; 53:6;
55:3-4; 61:5, 8).  He is called Son of Man in chaps. 46, 48,
62, 69.  In 46:3 it is said that the Head of Days has chosen
the Son of Man (cf. 48:6).  Charles proposed the theory of two
sources in the Similitudes, a Son of Man source and an Elect
One source (*Book of Enoch*, 64-65).  He is not followed in this
by most scholars, but see D. Suter's theory of two distinct
traditions ("Apocalyptic Patterns in the Similitudes of Enoch,"
*SBL 1978 Seminar Papers* [ed. P. J. Achtemeier; Missoula:
Scholars, 1978] 1.3-7).  The title, Elect One, may be drawn
from Isa 42:1 (cf. *1 Enoch* 49:4).  It will be recalled that
the triad--God, Holy Spirit, Elect One--occurs in John 1:33-34.

[259]The title Son does not appear in this verse, but "one like a son of man" (1:13) is speaking; in 2:18 he calls himself "the Son of God."

[260]This title is used 104 times in the Similitudes. Cf. Num 16:22 ("God of the spirits of all flesh"); 27:16; Ps 104:4 ("who makes his angels spirits"). It is reminiscent of the OT title, Yahweh Sabaoth, and may be a parallel to the title אל אלים in 1QM (which Yadin translates "God of angels") and to אדון לכול רוח in 1QH 10:8, 2. The closest NT parallel is Heb 2:9 ("Father of Spirits"). 2 Macc 3:24 has the expression ὁ τῶν πνεύματων...δυνάστης. See Charles, *The Book of Enoch*, 69.

[261]Here, Lohmeyer means the traits of the Son of Man in the Similitudes.

[262]Fuller thinks of the structure of the baptismal narratives as patterned on the Christian baptismal experience, but moving toward the triadic formula ("Demythologizing," 126).

[263]Lohmeyer, "Mir ist gegeben," 22-49. Lohmeyer theorized that primitive Christianity had a twofold origin, in Galilee and in Jerusalem. Galilean Christianity considered baptism, originating in the baptism by John, a necessary condition of salvation. In Galilee a pre-Matthean Aramaic form of the missionary command included the baptismal command and the triadic phrase, originating in the triadic event of Jesus' baptism. See Hubbard (*Matthean Redaction*, 172) for criticism of Lohmeyer's position.

[264]Fuller, *Resurrection Narratives*, 87; idem, "Demythologizing," 125-29.

[265]The meaning in the mind of the evangelist is another matter.

[266]Fuller, *Resurrection Narratives*, 210 n. 31. Cf. E. Schweizer, "υἱός," *TDNT* 8 (1972) 372 n. 268: once the term Father is used, Son of Man has to become Son of God. In contrast, Grundmann thinks that the absolute formula is the oldest christology, which reaches back to the proximity of Jesus himself, and then is developed secondarily into Son of Man and Son of God ("Mt 11:27 u. d. joh. 'Der Vater - Der Sohn' Stellen," *NTS* 12 [1965/6] 46; cited by Schweizer, 371 n. 266).

[267]Fuller, "Demythologizing," 127.

[268]The Spirit of Truth (or Light) and the Spirit of Falsehood mentioned in 1QS 3:18-26 are also called angels, and may be identical with the angels Michael and Belial of 1QM 13:9-12, 17:6-8 (see R. E. Brown, "The Paraclete," 122). In Rev 1:1-2 (cf. 22:16), the revelation communicated to John is by an angel, but elsewhere the Spirit is speaking to the churches (cf. 2:7, 11, 29, etc.). John speaks of himself as "in the spirit" when he receives revelations (1:10; 4:2); an angel carries him away "in the spirit" (7:3; 21:10) to receive visions. These

works and others represent a stage in which the two concepts
(angel and spirit) have not yet coalesced, and the substitution
of Spirit for angel is not complete.  There is mention of the
angel of the Holy Spirit in such late works as *Ascension of
Isaiah* 9:36, 39-40; 11:4, 30.  To oversimplify, angels are
thought to accompany and act upon the human being from the outside.  But the spirit can be regarded as a power within a human
being, that being's own power or a special gift from God, an
invasion.

[269]Fuller, *Resurrection Narratives*, 88.

[270]Ibid., 83.

[271]Jules Lebreton, *History of the Dogma of the Trinity*
(2 vols.; London: Burns, Oates and Washbourne, 1939) 1.108.

[272]Ibid.  Consideration of Philonic and rabbinic concepts
(logos, the Powers, memra, torah, wisdom, shekinah) outweighs
consideration of apocalyptic imagery and concepts.

[273]Georg Kretschmar, *Studien zur frühchristlichen Trini-
tätstheologie* (Tübingen: J. C. B. Mohr, 1956).

[274]According to Kretschmar, there were two strains of
Trinitarian reflection before Nicea.  The first, found in
Origen and Methodius and back to the first century, left its
impression on the Eucharist.  In it, Christ and the Holy Spirit
were conceived as two supreme heavenly powers standing before
God's throne.  The second had closer links with baptism; in it,
God, Christ and the Holy Spirit were ranged side by side as
heavenly witnesses (see review by J. N. D. Kelly, *JTS* 9/10
[1958/9] 373).  Kelly finds Kretschmar's thesis revolutionary
and a welcome shift of emphasis.  He remarks that Kretschmar
has cut the ground from under the suggestion that classical
Trinitarianism was in effect disguised polytheism (Werner and
Loofs), and that he "has assuredly established the relevance
to Christian doctrine in the first two or three centuries of
the bizarre underworld of Jewish speculation, particularly
about the angelic powers" (pp. 374-75).  He finds Kretschmar's
case at critical points may depend "on a brilliant conjecture,
an unprovable insight" but argues that this exciting work will
leave its mark on all future studies of the evolution of patristic doctrine (p. 375).

[275]J. Daniélou, *The Theology of Jewish Christianity*, 119,
117.

[276]Kretschmar speaks of the imaginative angelological
framework of the heavenly court scene being used to picture the
risen and elevated Christ in union with God and the Spirit.  He
insists that the starting point of Christian Trinitarian doctrine is not the question of the authority of the historical
Jesus, nor speculation about divine powers, nor a probing for
the ground of the Incarnation.  It is rather Easter.  Trinitarian doctrine became necessary because of the resurrection;
faith in the triune God depends on faith in the resurrection
of Jesus (*Studien*, 219-23).

[277]Fuller, *Foundations*, 38. He argues cautiously that we cannot assume the Similitudes are pre-Christian in origin, but thinks that they are evidence for a tradition in Jewish apocalyptic that is pre-Christian. In his opinion, the logia of Jesus seem to presuppose a "reduced apocalyptic" in which the future coming of the Son of Man as eschatological judge was part of the traditional imagery.

[278]Fuller, "Demythologizing," 127 n. 8.

[279]Both Mark 8:38 and *1 Enoch* 51:3-4; 61:8-10 refer to a heavenly judgment. But in the passages in the Similitudes, the Elect One is judge, whereas in Mark 8:38 the Son of Man seems to be a witness. The judgment in the former texts takes place in heaven, but in Mark 8:38 it is not certain to where the Son of Man "comes."

[280]In chap. 46, Enoch is granted a vision of "one who had a head of days" and of another whose face "had the appearance of a man." The vision is explained by "one of the angels" (v. 2). In chap. 47, the triad is found of Righteous One, angels and Lord of Spirits (here also called Head of Days). A triad of Head of Days, angels and the seer Enoch (= Noah?) who is called "son of man" appears in *1 Enoch* 60:1-10. Again in chap. 71, we find the Head of Days, angels and the translated Enoch, called "the son of man who is born unto righteousness." (This text will be treated in detail in Chapter V below.) Finally, in two places we find Elect One, Lord of Spirits and the spirit (alluding to Isa 11:2). These are *1 Enoch* 49:2-3 and 62:1-2. The first passage reads, "the Elect One stands before the Lord of Spirits, and his glory is for ever and ever, and his might unto all generations. And in him dwells the spirit of wisdom, and the spirit which gives insight, and the spirit of understanding and of might, and the spirit of those who have fallen asleep in righteousness." The second passage is as follows: "'Open your eyes and lift up your horns if you are able to recognize the Elect One.' And the Lord of Spirits seated him on the throne of His glory, and the spirit of righteousness was poured out on him, and the word of his mouth slays all sinners...." (Note the allusion to Isa 11:4 also. In *1 Enoch* 91:1, the seer Enoch himself says, "the spirit is poured out upon me, that I may show you everything that shall befall you forever.")

[281]See M. Black, "The 'Parables' of Enoch (1 En 37-71) and the 'Son of Man,'" *ExpTim* 79 (1976/7) 5.

[282]Among these scholars are Milik, Dodd, Hindley, Schweizer, Moule, Leivestad, Vermes, Black, E. P. Sanders, Hooker, M. Jas and Mearns.

[283]The position of Milik, that the Similitudes are a Christian Greek work composed around 270 A.D. (*The Books of Enoch* [Oxford: Clarendon, 1976]), is summarized and criticized by J. A. Fitzmyer ("Implications of the New Enoch Literature from Qumran," *TS* [1977] 340-44) and M. Knibb ("The Date of the

Parables of Enoch: A Critical Review," *NTS* 25 [1979] 345-59).
See also J. H. Charlesworth, *The Pseudepigrapha and Modern
Research* (Missoula: Scholars, 1976) 98, and D. J. Harrington,
"Research on the Jewish Pseudepigrapha during the 1970s," *CBQ*
42 (1980) 152.  Charlesworth states that the real issue remains
open: "Are these Jewish Parables pre-Christian and a source for
understanding either Jesus' *ipsissima verba* or the theologies
of the Evangelists?  Or, are they post-Christian and a significant development independent of the canonical gospels, or a
Jewish reaction to Christianity?" ("The SNTS Pseudepigrapha
Seminars at Tübingen and Paris on the Books of Enoch," *NTS* 25
[1979] 322-23).

[284]See the treatment of this text in Chapter VI below.

[285]See further, introduction to Chapter VI.

[286]Several others argue against the presence of an allusion here.  This question will be treated in detail in Chapter
III below.

[287]Fuller, *Resurrection Narratives*, 82-83.

[288]He is in agreement that v. 18b is an allusion to Dan
7:14 LXX, and related in its theme of the cosmic dimensions of
Lordship to Matt 11:27, John 3:35 (Strecker, *Der Weg*, 209 n. 2).

[289]Edward P. Blair, *Jesus in the Gospel of Matthew* (New
York: Abingdon, 1960) 60, 67, 140.

# CHAPTER II

## METHODOLOGICAL CONSIDERATIONS

The wide variety of opinions about the origin, nature and
meaning of the Matthean triadic phrase and its integration into
the final pericope raises many basic methodological questions.
It has been seen in the first chapter that there are three major approaches used by NT critics to understanding the phrase
as an authentic element of the passage.  In the first approach,
most regard it as a traditional baptismal formula drawn by
Matthew from the liturgical life of his community and having no
integral connection with the rest of the pericope.  One is
directed, therefore, to look elsewhere than to its immediate
Gospel context for the significance of the phrase.  General
theories concerning the development of triadic passages, such
as that proposed by Cullmann, provide suggestions regarding the
social situations in which triadic material appears as a response to Gentile needs and pressures.  This approach yields
little solid information (other than speculation about baptismal factors) which would help us to interpret the close linking
of the three particular titles in Matt 28:19b, and Matthew's
reasons (other than a desire to authenticate community practice)
for using the phrase in his final pericope.  The second approach
involves consideration of the triadic phrase as an essential
element of a pre-Matthean traditional unit discernible behind
Matt 28:16-20.  The Lohmeyer-Fuller theory of development of
this triadic phrase from a Jewish apocalyptic triad (when this
theory is modified by the insight that the ultimate source may
be the triad found in Daniel 7, not in the Similitudes which
themselves draw on Daniel 7) opens the possibility that the
triad is linked integrally to the proposed allusion to Dan 7:14
LXX in Matt 28:18b.  Some confirmation of this possibility is
found in the fact that in Luke 10:21-22 and John 3:34-35 there
are both triads with the same titles as that in Matt 28:19b and
possible allusions to Dan 7:14.  The third approach, based on
the theory that the Matthean triadic phrase is a creation of
the Evangelist, is an attempt to explore its meaning in relation

87

to the immediate and wider Gospel context, especially to the
narrative of the baptism of Jesus, and as a focal point of the
major Matthean Christological statement of Jesus' sonship.  At
this point in my study, I have argued that the second approach
is most basic and bears further exploration.

The terms, tradition and redaction, have been used with
insufficient precision in the analyses of Matt 28:16-20 which
have been considered, and the methods of determining traditional
and redactional elements in this pericope differ.  Both vertical
and horizontal methods are used.  The vertical is a verse-by-
verse examination of the text, aimed at identifying Matthean
vocabulary and style and at isolating the Evangelist's redactional techniques.  The horizontal is a comparison of the
Matthean with the corresponding material in Mark and Luke to
determine where there is literary contact, which material is
more primitive, and which theories about sources would best
explain the data.[1]  The use of these methods and wider ones on
Matt 28:16-20, and Hubbard's use of the form critical method,
have produced no consensus.[2]  I do not pretend here to have a
successful interlocking of methods that would completely elucidate the triadic phrase both as a traditional element and as
meaningful in its Gospel context.  But the possible Danielic
substratum of elements of the pericope, including the triadic
phrase, merits more careful analysis that it has been given,
and this analysis will contribute to achieving that goal of
elucidation.

The investigation will profit from (A) an examination of
Matt 28:16-20 on the basis of the discussion so far, in an effort to define major exegetical problems, especially those
which may have bearing on the triadic phrase, (B) a consideration of the problems involved in separating tradition and redaction in Matthew where an OT allusion may be involved, and in
understanding NT adaptations of the OT.  Finally (C), in this
chapter the method of comparative midrash will be described,
and it will be proposed that Matt 28:16-20 is a classic example
of a NT text which can be elucidated by the use of this method
in conjunction with other critical methods.

A. Matt 28:16-20: Major Exegetical Problems

The aim here is to highlight elements of this pericope
which may be related to the meaning of the triadic phrase,
either at a traditional or a redactional level, and to raise
the questions that will chart the course of the following chapters. These particular questions are raised in the light of
that dealt with in the next chapter, namely, whether Matt 28:
16-20 draws upon Daniel.

*Verse 16:* The mountain to which the disciples go is
perhaps not a specific geographical location in the mind of
Matthew, as he has not bothered to alter the command to go to
Galilee which he found in Mark 16:7 (cf. 14:28). Most critics
argue that the mountain is for Matthew the typical site of
revelations, and has mythological significance.[3] There are
seven special mountain scenes in this Gospel, seven scenes in
which Jesus is presented on a mountain.[4] In each of these
seven cases, a "revelation" is not necessarily communicated,
except in the extenuated sense that each of the actions and
teachings of Jesus is a revelation of his identity; only four
of these concern communication with the supernatural world.[5]
Is there some important significance to the fact that the mountain in the final pericope is the seventh? Matthew does not
count the mountains, and shows no extraordinary interest in
patterns of seven.[6] Is the mountain in 28:16 a symbol which
should be interpreted with reference to the fact that Jesus
appears here as already ascended?[7] Is it a symbol, that is, of
the heavens? The mountain in 28:16 may be identified as "the
mountain where Jesus commissioned them" (to make disciples).[8]
Why should a mountain be the site of the commission?

*Verse 17:* It is stated that the disciples see Jesus, but
there is no mention of his physical appearance, in contrast to
the resurrection appearance accounts in Luke and John,[9] nor is
there mention of his being "taken up"[10] or disappearing.[11] The
impression given in Matt 28:16-20, as I have said, is that of
an appearance of an ascended one.[12] Does the account draw on
traditions concerning Enoch and Elijah, the only two figures
regarded in the OT as having transcended death by translation?
The bold use of the verb "worship" with Jesus as its object is

a Matthean characteristic.[13]  Matthew uses it to speak of the
way people come during the ministry to make a request of Jesus
(8:2; 9:18; 15:25; 20:20) and also for the response to Jesus by
the Magi (2:2, 8, 11), those in the boat (14:33) and the women
after the resurrection (28:9).  It is certainly a clue to
Matthew's understanding of Jesus and emphasizes his belief that
the resurrection has not altered his identity.  It should also
be taken into consideration in interpreting the triadic phrase:
is Matthew implying by its use that the Son is due equal honor
with the Father, due the honor usually reserved for God?[14]

   *Verse 18:* Jesus' announcement of his reception of "all
power in heaven and on earth" is the announcement of his reception of the power of God (cf. 11:25).  Does the triadic phrase
in verse 19b function in part to interpret this power as shared
in the divine realm?  If verse 18b does indeed contain an allusion to Dan 7:14 LXX, as will be concluded in the following
chapter,[15] what is the extent of the allusion, and how has it
been modified?  Do other Danielic allusions appear in this
pericope?  Does its presence imply that the translation or
resurrection of Jesus has been conceived along the lines of the
coming of the one like a son of man to the Ancient of Days (Dan
7:13)?[16]  Is Daniel being reinterpreted here within a distinctive stream or streams of interpretive tradition?  Do other
uses in Matthew of Dan 7:13-14 elucidate and prepare for the
allusion in verse 18b?  Nowhere else in the gospels is the role
of the Son of Man appropriated by Jesus speaking in the first
person but without the title, Son of Man.[17]  Does the author
intend an identification of the risen Jesus, Son of Man, with
the Son of the triadic phrase, spoken of in the third person?
Is a transformation or elevation of the status of Jesus
understood?

   *Verses 19-20a:* The commission of the eleven is linked
closely with the statement of Jesus' total authority, by the
word "therefore."  On the basis of his universal authority, he
commands a universal mission.[18]  The central verb of the commissioning is "make disciples," and this is to be done by baptizing and teaching.  Is this command spoken by one in the role
of the Danielic "one like a son of man"?  This needs to be

queried, for the figure in Daniel 7 is one who exercises dominion as a ruler, not as a master of disciples, and there is no
mention of a mission.  What the disciples are commanded to teach
in Matt 28:20a is all that the earthly Jesus had commanded.[19]
Many critics[20] see this element as representing Matthew's presentation of Jesus as a "new Moses."  Does this pericope illustrate the idea that Jesus' prototypes were the Danielic figure
*and* Moses, or has the function of the second been absorbed by
the first, or has the first been reconceived as a teacher without reference to Moses?  Further, why should one in the role of
the Son of Man command baptism?

There is no command to circumcize.  Is this omission evidence, as some have claimed, that the pericope or the tradition
behind it is late, presupposing the settling of the debate regarding the legitimacy of a mission to uncircumcised Gentiles?
Meier remarks that "if you allow that the true people of God
can be formed apart from circumcision, you have dealt a death-
blow to Judaism"; he, therefore, does not designate Matthew's
Gospel as Jewish Christian.[21]  Or, on the contrary, does the
omission indicate that this tradition is early, the presupposition of the debate?

Does the commission given in Matt 28:16-20 involve a sharing of the eleven in the power given to Jesus?  The word ἐξουσία
is not used with regard to them here, but they are authorized
to tasks not given them before in this Gospel, especially to
teach.[22]  In Matthew, the power to bind and loose is promised
to Peter (16:19) and to all the disciples (18:18): whatever
they bind on earth will be bound in heaven, and whatever they
loose on earth will be loosed in heaven.  Whether this power is
the power of imposing or removing an obligation by an authoritative doctrinal decision, or the power to impose or lift a ban
of excommunication,[23] it involves, as do the specific commissions given in 28:19-20a, an empowering to leadership tasks
which are regarded as essential in the formation of a church.
Matthew may intend the earlier passages to be evoked in the
final pericope.

Concerning the triadic phrase, it is probably not to be
understood as a baptismal formula--that is, as the exact phrase

used in baptizing--but rather as a phrase which characterizes
the rite, and perhaps indicates that the three be called upon
by baptizer or person being baptized.[24] It is not properly
speaking Trinitarian, nor, in terms of Matthew's thinking, trinitarian.[25] The significance of the close joining of the three
is not yet clear, nor is it clear why these specific three
titles are used in conjunction, nor why they appear also in
Luke 10:21-22 and John 3:34-35. Is this triad related to the
triad found in Daniel 7? Can aspects of the development of the
triad be traced? Does a monadic phrase lie beneath Matt 28:19b?
If so, what title was likely used?

The connection between the triadic phrase and the narrative
of John the Baptist's baptism of Jesus has been noted, although
Kingsbury's explanation of the relationship from a redactional
perspective is inadequate.[26] We have also found that a triad
occurs often in a baptismal context in the NT.[27] What is the
explanation of these facts? Is the triadic phrase a clue to
differences and similarities between the baptism practiced by
John and that practiced by early Christians?

How is the inclusion of the Son, presumably a human being,
between the Father and the Holy Spirit to be taken? Should the
triadic phrase be interpreted with reference to verse 18b,
Jesus' announcement of his reception of all power, reading verse
18b as a statement that Jesus has been exalted to a divine,
transcendent status? Has he undergone an apotheosis, and been
incorporated somehow into the heavenly realm? How is this conceived in terms of Israelite monotheism? Has a process of
mythologizing occurred? A polytheizing?

*Verse 20b:* Jesus' promise of his presence throughout human
history, "to the close of the age," gives no hint of how near
or far away the end is.[28] The stress on presence makes it clear
that the ascended one has not been removed from human contact.
On the contrary, his presence (like his power) is unlimited by
place or time; it has, in short, the quality of the presence of
God (cf. 1:23; 18:20). This extension of Jesus' presence is
another way of stating belief in his transcendent status, and
therefore significant to interpretation of the triadic phrase.

One important and presently unsolved problem is that of
the form of the pericope. As will be seen in the following

chapter, critics differ in their perceptions of whether the
exaltation of Jesus or the commissioning of the disciples is
central.  A solution to this problem can be reserved until the
meaning of verse 18b and of the mountain symbolism is more fully
probed.  The separation of tradition and redaction in this pericope is crucial, because if (as Strecker contends) the triadic
phrase is embedded in a unit of pre-Matthean tradition, that
unit and conjectures about its Sitz im Leben may contain clues
to the phrase's meaning and origin, and by highlighting Matthew's
redaction, clues to his understanding of it.  The point of entry
into the discussion of this question will be at verse 18b, in an
examination of the proposed allusion to Dan 7:14 LXX.

### B. Tradition and Redaction and the Use of the OT

Although he does not treat Matt 28:16-20, Cope offers
methodological suggestions that are important in regard to that
text.  He argues that one of Matthew's distinctive characteristics is that he uses the OT as a "source" by modeling a passage
on a familiar OT text, with the text providing the logical
framework for the Matthean passage.  Cope insists that the
critic must search for structural relations between some of
Matthew's OT citations and allusions and the material which
surrounds them, and for theological statements which are often
more than just proof-text fulfillments.[29]  The possibility exists that in pericopes modeled on OT passages there may be only
minimal allusion present.  Therefore, exact and fairly extensive evidence for the presence of the underlying OT passage is
necessary.  Allusions must be established by: (1) giving the
parallels in the two passages; (2) listing the differences, and
asking if they can be understood as adaptations of the story or
imagery to Jesus; (3) asking if this connection is found elsewhere.  If so, this is not original Matthean redaction, and in
this case the redactional work of Matthew resides in his use of
a tradition and not in his creation of it.[30]

This focus of attention on the use of the OT is of special
importance in dealing with the Gospel of Matthew.  By Goulder's
count, there are 108 allusive references to the OT in Matthew.[31]
Matthew, according to Goulder, was not an editor in the modern

sense (his literary activity confined to selecting, collecting,
smoothing, adjusting reports he received), but "an editor in
the ancient sense, a *darshan*,[32] rewriting and expounding as appeared necessary for edification."[33]  "His editing was what
other people call composing."[34]  He should also not be regarded
as an "individualist"[35] nor an author in the contemporary
sense,[36] if this means isolating him from his matrix in Judaism.
Analysis of this Gospel demands careful consideration of allusions and imagery which have a texture and a history which the
writer may have intended to evoke or may have unconsciously
evoked, and which his early audience may have heard.  This is
not necessarily a matter of written traditions only, but of
ideas alive and circulating in the Evangelist's world.[37]
"Matthew" is viewed not as a community of scripture scholars,[38]
nor as a writer who simply reflects or represents community
views, but as an author in touch with and influenced by Jewish
and Christian exegetical traditions.

Cope's suggestions concern a method which has not yet been
fully used on Matt 28:16-20, and are valuable in many respects.
The problem with the approach he has described, however, is
that it simply leaps from the NT allusion or citation to the OT
text, and back again.  But before the critic can move from the
detection of an allusion or quotation, to the extent and meaning of adaptation of it by the Evangelist, the critic needs a
sense of the *Nachleben* of the OT passage.  Over two-hundred
years of interpretation and use of OT materials which appear in
the NT are easily overlooked by those who assume that an OT
reference is merely a reactivation of that text as it was interpreted in *its* time (or as the contemporary exegete thinks it
was interpreted or should have been interpreted), and who then
assume the adaptation is the NT writer's redaction.  The possibility does exist that the Evangelist's mind overarched the
interpretations of the intervening years and returned to the
"original meaning."  But the probability is stronger that he
was influenced by the OT text's *Nachleben*, its continual adaptation.  The NT writers inherited an interpreted OT.[39]  The
attempt to examine the life of OT traditions and their influence on a NT text can be seen as a coordination of the methods

and insights of tradition- and form-criticism with those of
redaction-criticism.[40]  Properly speaking, however, it is the
method of midrash criticism or comparative midrash that attempts
to offer a comprehensive view of the development of a tradition,
and a focus on its successive adaptations.

## C. Comparative Midrash

The most detailed statement of the method called comparative midrash and of its relation to other critical methods is
found in J. A. Sanders' article, "From Isa. 61 to Luke 4."[41]
Sanders uses the "broader sense" of the term midrash, meaning
the activity or method of midrashic interpretation, and the
product of that activity, and not confining his considerations
to instances of the literary form or genre of midrash.  In this
he agrees with Renée Bloch that the twofold essence of midrashic
procedure is reference to scripture and contemporization.  The
purpose of midrash is primarily understood to be to call on
scripture to interpret contemporary life and history.  Bloch
speaks of midrashic genre, procedures, tendencies, traits and
even thoughts.[42]  This broader use of the term midrash associates it with the whole phenomenon of the use of scripture in
early Judaism, including the NT.  Large amounts of the Bible
are called midrash by those who adopt this broader definition.[43]

In contrast, a narrower use of the term is proposed by
those who, for the purposes of scientific description, define
midrash strictly in terms appropriate to the classification of
a literary genre.  When midrash is used as a name for a literary genre, "the implication in this *literary* usage is that the
word is based, not on the rabbinic usage of *midrāš* to designate
the *activity* of study or the *activity* of biblical interpretation
or a *type of exegesis*, but on that rabbinic usage which desig-
nates a specific corpus of literature within Jewish oral tradition."[44]  The corpus of literature designated by the rabbis as
midrash is set up as the exemplar, and other works which exhibit
the same primary characteristics are included in the category
of midrash.[45]  The most important primary characteristics are
the basic midrashic structure and the basic aim of commenting
on and actualizing the scriptures to make them intelligible and

religiously relevant in present circumstances.  From the point
of view of literary structure, there are several diverse forms
of literature designated as midrash (exegetical, homiletic and
narrative midrashim).  But the basic midrashic structure common
to all forms labeled midrash is that one which begins with a
text of scripture (either explicitly or implicitly cited) and
proceeds to comment on it in some way.  The material contained
in the midrashic unit is placed in the context of a scripture
text.[46]  The author makes an effort to contribute to the understanding of the biblical account, presenting his composition for
the sake of, or benefit of, or in the service of the biblical
text, which is the primary point of interest,[47] and the subject
of the interpretation.  Wright argues that

> in biblical citations two directions of movement are
> possible: either a biblical text contributes to a new
> composition and is for the sake of the new composition,
> or the new composition contributes to an understanding
> of the text cited and is for the sake of the biblical
> citation.  Only the latter is midrash, since only there
> does the composition actualize Scripture[48]

and aim to focus attention on the original text.  The former
case is mere literary dependence, with biblical text used to
contribute ideas, terminology, authority to the new composition.[49]

Both usages of the term midrash (midrash as a method of
exegesis, a creative and actualizing handling of the biblical
text, and midrash as the name of a literary genre) are legitimate borrowings from the rabbinic vocabulary.[50]  The term is
used in the Qumran literature in a non-technical way.  In CD
20:6, for example, it means study, interpretation or investigation of the Law, and in 4QF1 1:14 it is a title for a passage
of interpretive comments on scripture.[51]  In antiquity, as far
as I know, the term was not ever used to mean either (1) *all*
actualizing scriptural interpretation of early Judaism (both
exegetical procedures and products of those procedures), or (2)
*only* what are recognized today as examples of a literary genre.
The question of the proper use of the term today by biblical
critics cannot be settled on the basis of its uses in antiquity,
and is not a task to be tackled in this work.

But it is important to point out that those who use the
word midrash in the wider sense highlight the truly reciprocal

relation between contemporary experience or event and text.[52]
Both new compositions which are in the service of the biblical
text *and* new compositions which the biblical text serves are
regarded as midrash.[53]  There is no doubt that there is an important distinction between a text which is exegetical in intent, and one which uses scripture as one of its building materials in fashioning an essentially new story,[54] or in interpreting a contemporary event or person or even what is believed to
be a new and unique act of God.  But these two types of texts
are both called midrash by scholars who use the term in the
wider sense.  The latter type is rooted in the understanding of
scripture as not merely a revered record of the nation's past,
but as the revelation of God's will for humanity in all generations, the unshakeable ground of action and identity, the mystery and vision of Israel's destiny.[55]  Even the first type of
text does not usually make the clarification of the biblical
text a goal distinct from the actualization of that text in the
present.[56]

     With regard to the NT use of scripture, it can be argued
that the category of midrash (both in the broader and narrower
senses) is broken or extended in the implied emphasis that
scripture is not "the single and complete revelation" of God's
will unless or until it is understood from the perspective of
the life, death and resurrection of Jesus.[57]  Elucidation of
the OT for its own sake is not the primary aim of NT writers,[58]
but the OT to a large extent guided the process of thought,
created many of the theological issues dealt with in the NT,
and made a tremendous impact "in and on the Christ-event" itself.[59]  Further, there is an analogy between the Jewish midrashic technique of explaining the Bible by the Bible and the
Christian activity of explaining the Bible by Jesus; in some
extended sense the life and word of Jesus represented "scripture" to Christians.[60]  A kind of midrashic activity was one of
the channels through which the risen Christ was thought to continue to speak, and the Spirit to lead and enlighten.[61]

     In this work, the term midrash will be used in the wider
sense, to mean the literary products (whatever their literary
genres) of the Jewish and Christian activity of contemporizing

interpretation of OT texts.  These products may be either exegetical in intent or new compositions to which the biblical
texts have contributed intimately.  As Miller remarks, "The
minimum requirement for the usage of this term as a substantive
will be the presence of a literary unit to which the biblical
citations or allusions clearly belong as formative elements at
some stage in the development of that literary unit."[62]  Brand
new creations *not* intimately based on or commenting on scriptural texts, but only vaguely or incidentally echoing them, and
NT use of Jesus traditions or previous gospel traditions[63] are
regarded as in the midrashic style or as extensions of the
midrashic mentality.  Certain apocalyptic passages will be
classified as either midrash or in the midrashic style, depending on whether the biblical text being pondered and adapted is
taken as authoritative and apparently as the springboard of "new
revelation,"[64] or merely vaguely echoed and not a formative,
essential element of the unit.[65]

Sanders defines the focus of comparative midrash as emphasis on the role an ancient authoritative tradition, whether or
not actually quoted or cited as scripture, played in the life
and history of Judaism and Christianity.  Emphasis is on the
function it served, and the needs it met.  Comparative midrash
pays attention to the manner in which such a tradition (drawn
from Torah, Prophets or Writings) is contemporized and adapted,
and to how other materials are woven with it to draw benefit
from it.  Ideally, all available instances of the contemporization of the tradition are compared to one another.  These instances include the translations, Targums, Qumranian, Christian,
proto-rabbinic, apocryphal and pseudepigraphical materials.[66]

Sketching something of the midrashic history of a passage
cited or alluded to in a text, so as to recover the foil against
which the midrash in the text comes alive, comparative midrash
can help the exegete find the ancient question to which the text
once provided answers.[67]  It is of extreme importance as we attempt to recover the extent of a supposed midrash or midrashic
interpretation, that we recover as far as we can the connections
and associations that may have existed in the mind of the evangelist or of the creator(s) of the tradition--literary or

pre-literary--which was used.  Le Déaut notes that since many of
the haggadic exegeses had become common and traditional, and may
have been continually repeated in the synagogue liturgy, authors
"were able to appeal to texts whose overtones are lost to us and
to traditions for which we have to struggle to recover even the
slightest echo."[68]

Where appropriate, the use of comparative midrash should
aid the NT exegete to:

(1) see if the NT text being discussed is, in its use of a central OT text (and sometimes related traditions), idiosyncratic
or related to a common midrashic tradition;[69]

(2) separate tradition from redaction;[70]

(3) evaluate the activity of the Evangelist as that of an in-
dividual-in-community, rather than that of an independent creator expressing strictly personal outlook and insights;[71]

(4) discuss the structures and substructures of passages in
terms of forms more native to them, and NT writing or composition in relation to the distinctive essence and character of
Torah-writing and adaptation;[72]

(5) acquire a sense of the organic nature of the growth and
development of concepts and imagery rather than a view of them
as developing in neat, linear fashion;[73]

(6) better penetrate and elucidate the areas of common life
shared by Christians and Jews both before and after the split
between them, as well as the areas of distinctive life and
insight;

(7) in addition, although this result may be a long way off,
comparative midrash should help in recovering more of the voice
and creative mind of the historical Jesus, his way of using the
OT and traditions available to him, and in our learning something of the principles and processes that controlled the adaptations of his authentic sayings.

The sense of life and growth is what J. M. Robinson is
after when he writes of the mistake of conceptualizing the
religious world through which early Christianity moved as
"strangely immobile," and individual or collective authors as
static.  He calls for reconceptualization in terms of movements,
trajectories or lines of development through the Hellenistic

world, applying even to the course of one specific religious
tradition within the wider streams of movement.  Attention then
should be given to how one doctrine or tradition may cut or
function in different ways, mean something different, and influence differently at different stages.[74]  My understanding of
comparative midrash is also similar in many ways to Rast's understanding of the method of tradition history.[75]  The interest
of the tradition critic, however, is more in the formation of a
tradition, in how it is incorporated, than in the different
meanings and levels of meanings achieved.  And the body of
material dealt with is exclusively intra-biblical.

    Lindars in *New Testament Apologetic* attempts to trace the
history of exegetical study behind the use of the OT in the NT
by means of tracing shifts of application and modifications of
texts.  By comparing various applications of a given text,
Lindars claims it is sometimes possible to arrange them progressively; "in this way stages of interpretation can be discovered corresponding to the developing thought and interest of
the early church."[76]  Lindars' approach differs from Sanders'
in several ways.  (1) The former argues that the NT use of the
OT is primarily apologetic in motive.  This is in contrast to
focus on the dependence of midrash on a community of interest
and on a kind of delight in the texts themselves.  Lindars does,
however, mention material he calls "pre-apologetic, i.e., de-
rivative from the basic resurrection faith."[77]  (2) The corol-
lary of Lindars' emphasis is an overly sharp distinction between
Jewish and Christian uses of a text.  Lindars finds it possible
that a Jewish homiletic tradition may have been retained alongside the Christian theological message, but his view of "the
Church's own version of the midrash pesher"[78] as based on the
resurrection of Jesus, key to all scriptural meaning, is that
it is utterly distinctive.  He argues that the NT use of the OT
is primarily a mode of expression for early Christian thought,
arising from a contemporary understanding of the meaning of
scripture.  The scriptures are "subservient to God's new declaration in his Son Jesus...God's new word, the 'yes,' the
'now,' of the gospel is Jesus, who demotes the scriptures from
master to servant, as much as he changes the basis of religion

from law to grace."[79]  But, as Borgen sees, the metaphor of
"servant" to characterize the role of the OT in the formation
of the NT is not adequate; the OT's role is also more than that
of a mere mode of expression used in an ad hoc way.  It is rather a necessary and integral part of the new revelation, and
has influenced the interpretive key itself.[80]   (3) Lindars reconstructs developments in what seems an oversimplified fashion
(from proclamation of resurrection to proclamation of pre-
existence; from use of Hebrew to use of Greek texts).[81]   (4)
Lindars devotes less thorough and controlled attention to the
materials outside the canon.

The following chapters will show that the use of the
method of comparative midrash offers new perspectives on the
question of the origin and meaning of the Matthean triadic
phrase, and also on other exegetical problems raised here in
Section A.  The procedure is first in Chapter III to establish
firmly the presence of an allusion to Dan 7:14 LXX in Matt
28:18b, and to examine in preliminary fashion the differences
between these two texts and their immediate contexts.  The second step is to turn in Chapter IV to Daniel 7 itself, and determine as nearly as possible the meaning and function of the
original triad found there and to assess the aspects of the
text which will give rise to later interpretations.  Third, in
Chapter V a survey is made of selected intertestamental uses of
Daniel 7, in order to (a) show the wide range of adaptations of
that text, and (b) focus on those elements of some which are
relevant to the solution of several of the exegetical problems
raised concerning Matt 28:16-20.  The fourth step is to examine
in Chapter VI those uses of Dan 7:13-14 in the NT which deal
with the empowering of the Son (of Man), his vindication, and a
mission related to his appearance, and to discuss the development of the Danielic triad on the basis of an analysis of those
allusions which contain a triad.  Finally, in Chapter VII we
return to a direct focus on Matt 28:16-20 to attempt to (a)
isolate the essence of a traditional pre-Matthean midrash, containing the triadic phrase, and (b) analyze Matthean redaction
of the midrash.

The use of the method of comparative midrash is especially
difficult in this case for two reasons.  (1) There are basic

and important differences of contemporary scholarly opinion
concerning the correct intrepretation of Daniel 7, in particular
regarding its mythological substratum and the identity of the
one like a son of man. This discussion is significant in terms
of understanding later interpretive traditions, and also in
terms of grasping the theological issues at stake when Matt 28:
16-20 with its triadic phrase is considered in a canonical context as an aspect of the biblical bases of later Trinitarian
thought. (2) In spite of the immense body of literature on the
NT "Son of Man problem," there is as yet no full-scale work
which traces the history of interpretation of Daniel 7.[82] The
work in Chapters V and VI is based on a necessarily incomplete
survey of this history, undertaken with an eye to determining
whether several motifs found in Matt 28:16-20 have a prehistory
as elements of Danielic interpretation.

NOTES TO CHAPTER II

[1]Those are the images used by W. G. Thompson (*Matthew's Advice to a Divided Community* (AnBib 44; Rome, 1970) to describe his work; his method is summarized by D. J. Harrington ("Matthean Studies Since Joachim Rohde," *HeyJ* 16 [1975] 378).

[2]Hubbard's method is one of discerning an OT commissioning pattern and then trying to apply it to Matthew and other NT authors. See Meier ("Two Disputed Questions," 407-16) for critique.

[3]See Hubbard, *Matthean Redaction*, 73, and references cited there.

[4]See above, p. 59 n. 2.

[5]Cf. 4:8; 14:23; 17:1, 9; 28:16. As Kingsbury notes, these same four are scenes in which Jesus is spoken of as the Son (see above, p. 38).

[6]It is true that Matthew's genealogy (1:1-17) is made up of multiples of seven (3 x 14); this pattern may stem partly from coincidences in the genealogies Matthew knew, and partly from Matthew's own additions (R. E. Brown, *The Birth of the Messiah* [Garden City: Doubleday, 1977] 70). Matthew also has seven petitions in the Our Father (6:5-13), lists seven vices (15:19; contrast Mark 7:21), seven woes against the Pharisees (23:13-29; contrast Luke 11:52, 42-47), and adds to Mark the saying that Peter should forgive seven times seventy (18:22). But these instances do not indicate the number seven was of great significance for Matthew. Ellis suggests that Matthew has structured his whole Gospel according to the number seven, by adding to the five major discourses the two "minor discourses" of 3:8-12 and 28:18-20 (*Matthew*, 12-13). However, many other "minor discourses" can be found in this Gospel (for example, Matt 11:7-19). It is more likely that if there is an intended link between the words of John the Baptist in 3:8-12 and the final words of Jesus in 28:18-20, it is the link between prediction (of the coming one) and fulfillment.

[7]See above, p. 3.

[8]See above, p. 77 n. 201, my translation. But see the objection of Meier, who finds the proposed translation possible but unlikely.

[9]Cf. Luke 24:16, 36-42; John 20:14, 19-20, 27; 21:4, 12.

[10]Markan Appendix 16:19; Luke 24:51; Acts 1:9; cf. John 20:17.

[11]Luke 24:31.

[12]See above, p. 59 n. 9.  The pericopes about the guard at the tomb and the empty tomb, and the scene in which the women touch Jesus' feet all make it clear that Matthew thinks of Jesus as resurrected; his risen body is present on the mountain, not just his spirit. But nothing is made of this in 28:16-20, and the account alone can be read as a visionary appearance.

[13]Above p. 78 n. 204.  In the other gospels, Jesus is worshipped only in John 9:38 (see above, p. 21); Mark 5:6 (homage by the man with an unclean spirit); 15:19 (false homage of soldiers).

[14]On the mixture of worship and doubt in this scene, see above, p. 59 n. 3.

[15]As the question is hotly debated, and important in terms of any adaptation of the OT text, it merits detailed treatment.

[16]J. P. Meier (*The Vision of Matthew* [New York: Paulist, 1979] 212) argues that v. 18b explains the meaning of the death-resurrection for Jesus himself: it is his exaltation to cosmocrator.

[17]Many times, however, Jesus speaks directly as the Son of Man in the third person.

[18]On the difficulty of reconciling Matt 28:19-20 with 10:5-6, see S. Brown ("The Two-fold Representation of the Mission in Matthew's Gospel," *ST* 31 [1977] 21-32), and Meier ("Salvation-History," 203-15). Also, see above,

[19]See above, p. 2.

[20]Stendahl, "Matthew," 798; J. L. McKenzie, "The Gospel According to Matthew," *JBC*, 114.  On Jesus depicted elsewhere in the Gospel as a new Moses, cf. Hubbard (*Matthean Redaction*, 92-94).

[21]Meier, *Vision*, 31, 213.  He understands baptism as the new initiation rite of the church Jesus promised to found.

[22]See above, p. 2.  In the other post-resurrection accounts, the disciples are commissioned to preach repentance and the forgiveness of sins (cf. Luke 24:47; John 20:23), two aspects of the baptism of John the Baptist (cf. Mark 1:4; Luke 3:3).

[23]The former meaning is most frequent in rabbinic literature, but it is not clear which is intended here (*Peter in the New Testament* [ed. R. E. Brown, K. P. Donfried, John Reumann; Minneapolis: Augsburg, 1973] 98-99) nor whether the verbs have the same meaning and extent in both passages (see p. 100 n. 231).

[24]See above, pp. 22-23.

[25]See above, pp. 8-9, for the distinction made in this work between Trinitarian and trinitarian; see further, pp. 23, 26.

[26]See above, pp. 37-38.  Kingsbury, it will be remembered, argues that the triadic phrase is an allusion to the baptismal narrative, which prefigures Matthew's conception of Christian baptism.

[27]See above, pp. 13-14.

[28]The delay of the parousia is not a concern here, a point which some have read as indicative of a late perspective, in contrast to the imminent parousia hope expressed in 10:23; 16:28.

[29]O. L. Cope, *Matthew: A Scribe Trained for the Kingdom* (Th.D. dissertation, Union Theological Seminary, 1971) 11-12; (CBQMS 5; Washington: Catholic Biblical Association, 1976).

[30]Ibid., 174.

[31]Goulder, *Midrash*, 128-29.

[32]That is, an expounder of sacred tradition, a preacher.

[33]Goulder, *Midrash*, 137.

[34]Ibid., 152.  This is not, however, to express agreement with Goulder's overall picture of Matthew's activity nor with his analysis of Matt 28:16-20.  He considers Matthew to be primarily expounding Mark, first with the aid of Pauline doctrine, and secondly with rabbinic doctrine.  He rules out "sectarian" influence in favor of "mainline" (p. 158).

[35]Cf. R. H. Stein, "What is Redaktionsgeschichte?" *JBL* 88 (1969) 45, 47.

[36]See Cope, *Matthew*, 21 n. 1; J. R. Donahue, *Are You the Christ?* (Missoula, MT: SBL, 1973) 33.

[37]Cf. F. H. Borsch, *The Christian and Gnostic Son of Man* (London: SCM, 1970) 2 n. 1: without continuing awareness of the difference between creative use of a current theme and independent creation, "the study of the Gospels could become a narrowing art distorted by insufficient reference to the wider context of historical movements."

[38]The school hypothesis of Stendahl is not convincing because of the sense of a broader unity in theme of the Gospel than corporate authorship would suggest or allow.  See Cope, *Matthew*, 3 n. 6.

[39]See J. A. Sanders, "From Isa. 61 to Luke 4," *Christianity, Judaism and Other Greco-Roman Cults* (3 vols.; ed. J. Neusner; Leiden: Brill, 1975) 1.75-103.  Wayne Meeks comments, for example, that it is not our modern historical understanding of the OT texts that is appropriated by the author of the Fourth Gospel, but "scripture as seen through two powerful controlling perspectives": the exegetical traditions of Judaism down to

John's time, and the specifically Johannine modifications of
those traditions ("Am I a Jew? Johannine Christianity and
Judaism," *Christianity, Judaism and Other Greco-Roman Cults*,
1.175).

[40]Donahue, mentioning the work of Lindars, Hartman and
Perrin, sees their focus on the NT use of the OT traditions as
the use of form-critical insights helpful in determining traditional material (that is, in the cases he is considering,
early Christian exegetical traditions available to Mark). See
*Are You the Christ?*, 38, 15.

[41]See above, n. 39. See also M. P. Miller, "Midrash,"
*IDBSup*, 596-97.

[42]R. Bloch, "Midrash," *DBSup*, 5.1263-81. Midrash has also
been described as "a way of thinking and reasoning which is
often disconcerting to us." It is an attitude regarding the
relationship between scripture and its adaptation, a part of
Jewish life, part of the sphere of the existential which refuses
to be conceptualized (R. Le Déaut, "Apropos a Definition of
Midrash," *Int* 25 [1971] 269; cf. 274-75). According to Le Déaut,
P. Borgen captures this broader sense in his description of
midrash as "fresh, creative paraphrase...systematic paraphrase
of words from OT quotations and fragments from haggadic traditions" (*Bread from Heaven* [Leiden: Brill, 1965] 58-59; cited by
Le Déaut, "Apropos," 281 n. 82).

[43]See A. G. Wright (*The Literary Genre Midrash* [Staten
Island: Alba, 1967] 19-21) for a list of biblical material which
Bloch and others (including Vermes, Doeve and Sandmel) consider
midrash.

[44]Ibid., 45.

[45]Ibid., 46. By "primary characteristics," Wright means
those verified in all manifestations of the genre.

[46]Ibid., 67.

[47]Ibid., 74, 94, 100, 140.

[48]Ibid., 114.

[49]Ibid., 116. R. E. Brown, insisting that "the purpose of
midrash is to make the OT account intelligible," does not apply
the term midrash to the NT Infancy Narratives, which were
"written to make Jesus' origin intelligible against the background of the fulfillment of OT expectations" (*Birth*, 37).
Brown does, however, emphasize that the "style of exegesis ex-
emplified in midrash" or "midrashic technique" has a place in
the composition of the Infancy Narratives (pp. 561-62), and he
finds Borgen's studies of midrashic technique in John 6:25-59
persuasive (*Gospel According to John*, 1.294; cf. 262, 277-78).

[50]Wright, *Midrash*, 143; cf. Miller, "Midrash," 597.

[51]In the latter text, Brown notes, the usage is moving toward the designation in post-Christian Judaism "for works which gather the legal statements, stories, and homilies of the rabbis around the biblical text, especially the text of the Pentateuch" (*Birth*, 558). At Qumran, the term midrash is not confined to the meaning of biblical interpretation. See further, n. 55 below.

[52]M. P. Miller, "Targum, Midrash and the Use of the OT in the NT," *JSJ* 2 (1971) 44; idem, "Midrash," 595. This reciprocal relation is what B. Childs calls "midrash dialectic" ("Midrash and the Old Testament," *Understanding the Sacred Text* [ed. J. Reumann; Valley Forge, PA: Judson, 1972] 59 n. 13).

[53]Contrast Wright's position.

[54]See J. J. Collins, "Methodological Issues in the Study of 1 Enoch: Reflections on the Articles of P. D. Hanson and G. W. E. Nickelsburg," *Seminar Papers, SBL 1978* (Missoula, MT: Scholars, 1978) 1.317.

[55]Miller, "Midrash," 594. The view of scripture as vision and portent of the future is especially evident in eschatological and mystical interpretation (p. 595). In 4QFl 1:14, the application of Ps 1:1 to the Qumran community is called midrash, and 4QS 5:1 reads: "A midrash for (of?) the instructor concerning the men of the law who dedicate themselves...." Here, midrash is used as the title of the section, which is apparently "a codified body of inferences from the Scriptures with some possible dependence on explicit biblical citations" (Wright, *Midrash*, 41, 39). This is, in other words, a new composition which the biblical texts serve.

[56]See Miller, "Midrash," 595.

[57]Borgen remarks that Christian theological and exegetical activity "challenged the basic and actual structure of Judaism, where the scriptures, as the divine Law of the people, served as foundation." This can be seen, for example, in the replacement of "'Paul's binding to the scriptures as law' by 'the binding to Christ.' There is, therefore, some truth in the understanding that Christ here has taken over the place and role of the scriptures as Law" (Response to B. Lindars, "The Place of the Old Testament in the Formation of New Testament Theology," *NTS* 23 [1977] 69-70).

[58]Lindars, "The Place of the OT," 64. Wright, however, does find isolated examples of the literary genre of midrash in such texts as Gal 3:6-29 and Rom 4:1-25 (on Gen 15:6), Heb 3:7-4:11 (on Psalm 95); see *Midrash*, 104, 111.

[59]Borgen, "Response," 68, 72.

[60]Commenting on John 5:46, Borgen notes that the Evangelist and the Johannine community regarded the scriptures as valid sources of the words and works of Jesus, together with the

gospel tradition received from the disciples ("Response," 73 n.
4). Goulder applies the term midrash (defined as "embroidery
somewhat in the rabbinic manner, aimed at doctrinal reconciliation and edification" [*Midrash*, 4; cf. p. 29]) to Matthew's
rewriting of the authoritative tradition of Mark.

[61]Miller, "Targum, Midrash," 63; cf. LeDéaut, "Apropos,"
276 n. 60.

[62]Miller, "Targum, Midrash," 44. LeDéaut considers that
midrashic context remains as long as scriptural stimulus continues ("Apropos," 276 n. 60). Miller regards it as still correct to refer to "midrashic tendencies and procedures" in the
use of scripture, even where such a literary unit as he describes is not present. Compare Wright (*Midrash*, 102-03; cf.
115 n. 72): he argues that allusions to a biblical text must be
strong and the biblical context maintained, if the work is to
be classified as an example of the literary genre of midrash.
He implies also that the allusions should be immediately recognizable (p. 130).

[63]See above, n. 60.

[64]On the relation between midrash (defined broadly) and
apocalyptic, see Bloch ("Midrash," 1276-78) and Miller ("Targum,
Midrash," 46). It is pointed out that both midrash and apocalyptic in general actualize ancient prophecies and seek to un-
ravel the mysteries of scripture. Both are concerned with past
traditions for the sake of present and future needs.

[65]G. Scholem discusses the differences between rabbinic
midrashim (expositions of biblical passages) and literature
which is essentially description of "a genuine religious experience for which no sanction is sought in the Bible." He places
the apocrypha and apocalyptic writings (along with the Hekhaloth
texts) in the second category (*Major Trends in Jewish Mysticism*
[3rd ed.; New York: SChocken, 1973] 46). Wright (*Midrash*, 136-
38) argues that the literary forms of midrash and apocalyptic
may be combined in a given work (e.g., in Daniel 9 and *4 Ezra*
12:10-38), depending on whether or not the discussion is for
the sake of some biblical text.

[66]Patte makes the obvious and important point that we proceed on the hypothesis that the authors of the pseudepigrapha
used scripture according to a logic similar to that of classical
Judaism, interpreting scripture by scripture and tallying different texts by verbal similarities. But this is difficult to
establish because we are for the most part dealing with translations or translations of translations which at best will cover
up the subtle hints that allow us to understand the mechanism
of interpretations, "and at worst dismiss them, especially when
the relationship with Scripture is no longer the concern of the
translator" (*Early Jewish Hermeneutics in Palestine* [Missoula,
MT: Scholars, 1975] 140-41; cf. 172-75, 207).

[67]Sanders, "From Isa. 61," 103.

[68]LeDéaut, "Apropos," 277.

[69]Literary dependency between two texts using the same midrashic tradition, or common dependence on a source, written or oral, is a further question.

[70]See Cope's suggestions, p. 93 above.

[71]See Miller, "Midrash," 506.

[72]Sanders, "From Isa. 61," 76-77. Torah is considered as having distinctive life-giving power. See also idem, "Adaptable for Life: the Nature and Function of Canon," *Magnalia Dei: The Mighty Acts of God* (ed. F. M. Cross, W. E. Lemke, P. D. Miller, Jr.; Garden City: Doubleday, 1976) 531-60.

[73]D. Hay ("NT Interpretation of the OT," *IDBSup*, 446) notes that "even where Christian authors cite the same OT texts, each usually gives it a unique nuance of meaning. Shifts in application occur, although the development of these cannot be charted with much probability."

[74]"The Dismantling and Reassembling of the Categories of New Testament Scholarship," *Trajectories through Early Christianity* (ed. J. M. Robinson and H. Koester; Philadelphia: Fortress, 1971) 11, 13-14, 16.

[75]See W. E. Rast (*Tradition History and the Old Testament* [Philadelphia: Fortress, 1972] 56) on the use of Jacob traditions in Jos 12:2-6, and his discussion of "reactualization" of Exodus themes in Deutero-Isaiah and in the Deuteronomic history, of how meaning changes as one work is incorporated into a larger and later complex, and of von Rad's "historical theology" (pp. 72-80).

[76]B. Lindars, *New Testament Apologetic* (Philadelphia: Westminster, 1961) 18. Without accepting R. Harris' testimonia theory, Lindars emphasizes the common background of exegesis shared by different NT authors (cf. 19, 263, 37 n. 1; also idem, "The Place of the OT," 62-63). Hay is less confident that stages of development can be charted (see above, n. 73).

[77]Lindars, *NT Apologetic*, 73. E. E. Ellis ("Midrash, Targum and New Testament Quotations," *Neotestamentica et Semitica* [ed. E. E. Ellis and Max Wilcox; Edinburgh: T. & T. Clark, 1969]) suggests that at least in some cases in the NT the use of an OT text as a testimonium is dependent on a prior midrashic treatment of that text.

[78]The term "midrash pesher" is sometimes used in NT criticism to indicate an "actualized exegesis" considered different from rabbinic halakic or haggadic midrash (Lindars, *NT Apologetic*, 15). Some critics, however, are uncomfortable with this distinction (see M. Black, "The Christological Use of the Old Testament in the New Testament," *NTS* 18 [1971/2] 1).

[79]Lindars, "The Place of the OT," 66.   Perrin, as will be
seen, makes a sharp distinction between Jewish and Christian
uses of the same texts to describe the exaltation of Enoch and
the exaltation of Jesus, considering these uses to be "independent."   His unstated presupposition for this judgment may be
similar to Lindars' view.

[80]Borgen, "Response," 70, 74-75; see above, p. 97.   He
agrees with Lindars that the OT has been reevaluated, reinterpreted and transformed from the new center of allegiance to
Jesus Christ.

[81]See Goulder's criticisms of Lindars (*Midrash*, 133-34).

[82]See further, below, introduction to Chapter VI.

# CHAPTER III

## IS MATT 28:18b AN ALLUSION TO
## THE SEPTUAGINT OF DAN 7:14?

As we have seen, it is claimed by some critics that Matt 28:18b alludes directly or indirectly (via Matt 11:27) to Dan 7:14 LXX. Many have noticed the similarity as well between a proposed use of the Danielic text in Matt 28:18b, 11:27 par. and John 3:34-35. Other critics deny the presence of an allusion in the Matthean final pericope, primarily on the grounds that (a) the linguistic similarities between the passages are not sufficiently strong, (b) the concepts and/or the form of Daniel 7 differ too markedly from those of Matt 28:16-20, or (c) other supposedly clearer allusions to Dan 7:13-14 in Matthew indicate that the Evangelist understood and used the OT passage in a way that is incompatible with its proposed use in Matt 28: 18b. In this chapter, an examination of the linguistic and conceptual affinities between the two texts, and a preliminary examination of the form of each will be undertaken. What I hope to show is that the similarities between the texts do support the presence of an allusion. It will be suggested that the strong differences are clues to a radical reinterpretation, the meaning of which can be grasped from the perspective of a knowledge of the ambiguities and implications of Daniel 7 itself and of its midrashic history.

### A. Linguistic Similarities Between the Two Texts

It is a delicate task to decide whether a NT unit contains an OT allusion, especially if this allusion may be part of a covert (invisible)[1] or implicit[2] midrash. The chief or at least initial clue is the extent of paraphrastic repetition of words and phrases of the OT text. There is, of course, no rule of thumb about the number of words or phrases required to make an allusion, nor can we tell by word count alone how close the evangelist intended to keep to the OT reference, whether his language was only colored by the OT, or even whether the phraseology is deliberate or unconscious and only coincidental.

Whether a unit containing an allusion is a midrash (as I am using this term)[3] is a question which demands deeper analysis.

The Aramaic and Greek versions of Dan 7:13-14 are given
below with Matt 28:16-20.

MT:

חָזֵה הֲוֵית בְּחֶזְוֵי לֵֽילְיָא   13
וַאֲרוּ עִם-עֲנָנֵי שְׁמַיָּא כְּבַר אֱנָשׁ אָתֵה הֲוָה
וְעַד-עַתִּיק יֽוֹמַיָּא מְטָה וּקְדָמֽוֹהִי הַקְרְבֽוּהִי׃
וְלֵהּ יְהִיב שָׁלְטָן וִיקָר וּמַלְכוּ   14
וְכֹל עַֽמְמַיָּא אֻמַיָּא וְלִשָּׁנַיָּא לֵהּ יִפְלְחוּן
שָׁלְטָנֵהּ שָׁלְטָן עָלַם דִּֽי-לָא יֶעְדֵּה
וּמַלְכוּתֵהּ דִּֽי-לָא תִתְחַבַּֽל׃

LXX:[4]

13.  ἐθεώρουν ἐν ὁράματι τῆς νυκτὸς καὶ ἰδοὺ ἐπὶ
     τῶν νεφελῶν τοῦ οὐρανοῦ ὡς υἱὸς ἀνθρώπου
     ἤρχετο καὶ ὡς παλαιὸς ἡμερῶν παρῆν καὶ οἱ
     παρεστηκότες παρῆσαν αὐτῷ.

14.  καὶ ἐδόθη αὐτῷ ἐξουσία καὶ πάντα τὰ ἔθνη
     τῆς γῆς κατὰ γένη καὶ πᾶσα δόξα αὐτῷ
     λατρεύουσα· καὶ ἡ ἐξουσία αὐτοῦ ἐξουσία
     αἰώνιος ἥτις οὐ μὴ ἀρθῇ καὶ ἡ βασιλεία
     αὐτοῦ ἥτις οὐ μὴ φθαρῇ.

Theodotion:[5]

13.  ἐθεώρουν ἐν ὁράματι τῆς νυκτὸς καὶ ἰδοὺ μετὰ
     τῶν νεφελῶν τοῦ οὐρανοῦ ὡς υἱὸς ἀνθρώπου
     ἐρχόμενος ἦν καὶ ἕως τοῦ παλαιοῦ τῶν ἡμερῶν
     ἔφθασεν καὶ ἐνώπιον αὐτοῦ προσηνέχθη.

14.  καὶ αὐτῷ ἐδόθη ἡ ἀρχὴ καὶ ἡ τιμὴ καὶ ἡ
     βασιλεία καὶ πάντες οἱ λαοί φυλαί γλῶσσαι
     αὐτῷ δουλεύσουσιν· ἡ ἐξουσία αὐτοῦ ἐξουσία
     αἰώνιος ἥτις οὐ παρελεύσεται καὶ ἡ βασιλεία
     αὐτοῦ οὐ διαφθαρήσεται.

Matt 28:16-20:

16. Οἱ δὲ ἕνδεκα μαθηταὶ ἐπορεύθησαν εἰς τὴν
    Γαλιλαίαν εἰς τὸ ὄρος οὗ ἐτάξατο αὐτοῖς ὁ 'Ιησοῦς

17. καὶ ἰδόντες αὐτὸν προσεκύνησαν οἱ δὲ ἐδίστασαν.

18. καὶ προσελθὼν ὁ 'Ιησοῦς ἐλάλησεν αὐτοῖς λέγων
    'Εδόθη μοι πᾶσα ἐξουσία ἐν οὐρανῷ καὶ ἐπὶ γῆς.

19. πορευθέντες οὖν μαθητεύσατε πάντα τὰ ἔθνη
    βαπτίζοντες αὐτοὺς εἰς τὸ ὄνομα τοῦ πατρὸς καὶ
    τοῦ υἱοῦ καὶ τοῦ ἁγίου πνεύματος

20. διδάσκοντες αὐτοὺς τηρεῖν πάντα ὅσα ἐνετειλάμην
    ὑμῖν καὶ ἰδοὺ ἐγὼ μεθ' ὑμῶν εἰμι πάσας τὰς ἡμέρας
    ἕως τῆς συντελείας τοῦ αἰῶνος.

Matt 28:18-19 contains two words and a phrase, or five
words, that are identical to Dan 7:14 LXX: ἐδόθη, ἐξουσία and
πάντα τὰ ἔθνη.[6]  The word order in Matt 28:18b and Dan 7:14 is
identical: the aorist passive (ἐδόθη) is followed by the dative
preposition (μοι in Matt 28:18b and αὐτῷ in Dan 7:14 LXX) and
by the noun subject (ἐξουσία).[7]  Furthermore, there is a triad
in 7:13 LXX: the Ancient of Days, one like a son of man and
those standing by (οἱ παρεστηκότες) who are angels.[8]  There is
also in both the LXX and NT passages a repetition of the word
πᾶς: in Matthew πᾶσα ἐξουσία (v. 18), πάντα τὰ ἔθνη (v. 19),
πάντα ὅσα ἐνετειλάμην and πάσας τὰς ἡμέρας (v. 20); in Daniel
πάντα τὰ ἔθνη and πᾶσα δόξα (v. 14).

In addition, verbal similarities between two other LXX
passages in Daniel and phrases in Matt 28:18 and 20 indicate
that the book of Daniel is being thought of in Matt 28:18-20,
and strengthen the possibility of an allusion to Dan 7:14 LXX
in Matt 28:18b.  Besides arguing for the presence of that allusion, Schlatter compares Matt 28:18 to Dan 4:14 LXX (= 4:17 MT),
from which he thinks the use of πᾶς and the phrases ἐν οὐρανῷ
and ἐπὶ τῆς γῆς stem.  This passage in Daniel contains the
words of the Watchers in King Nebuchadnezzar's dream: he is
sentenced to insanity to the end that "he may know that the
Lord of heaven has authority over all in heaven and upon earth,
and whatever he wills he does in them" (ἕως ἂν γνῷ τὸν κύριον
τοῦ οὐρανοῦ ἐξουσίαν ἔχειν πάντων τῶν ἐν τῷ οὐρανῷ καὶ τῶν ἐπὶ

τῆς γῆς καὶ ὅσα ἂν θέλῃ ποιεῖ ἐν αὐτοῖς).[9]  The double allusion
to Dan 7:14 and 4:14 LXX produces in Matt 28:18 "a fine contrast
between Nebuchadnezzar, divested of his authority, and the Son
of Man, to whom all authority in heaven and on earth is given."[10]
The allusion to Dan 4:14 is also a way of emphasizing that the
power of Jesus is the power of God.

Gundry claims further that in Matt 28:20, Matthew has retained his set formula, συντέλεια τοῦ αἰῶνος (cf. 13:39, 40, 49;
24:3), but prefixed the phrase πάσας τὰς ἡμέρας to gain an allusion to Dan 12:13 LXX.  In this passage the angel says to Daniel, "For there are still days and hours until the fulfillment
of the end (ἀναπλήρωσιν συντελείας), but you will rest and stand
in your glory at the end of the days" (συντέλειαν ἡμερων).
Since these are the final words of the book of Daniel, they are
especially appropriate for the ending of the book of Matthew.
They hint, perhaps, that the eleven also will stand in their
glory at the end.

### B. Conceptual and Formal Affinities

The linguistic similarity between two texts is only the
first indication of the presence of an allusion; a recognizable
thought connection or imaginative resonance must also exist.[11]
In this case we find the following affinities.

(1) Both passages in context speak of a transfer of power
from a divine figure to a human or quasi-human figure, after a
struggle and victory.  In Daniel the one like a son of man receives power after the fourth and most terrible beast from the
sea has been destroyed (7:11) and the dominion of the rest of
the beasts has been taken away (v. 12).  In Matthew, Jesus who
has risen from death speaks of having received all power (from
God).[12]

(2) Both texts are claims that the transfer of authority
has consequences for all nations.  In Daniel all nations join
with all heavenly beings (πᾶσα δόξα, v. 14)[13] in worship or
service (λατρεύουσα) of the one like a son of man.  In Matthew,
all nations are to be made disciples of the risen Jesus.

(3) It is possible that both scenes are meant to be, in
different ways, visions of heavenly realities.  Dan 7:13 LXX

explicitly calls that scene a night vision (ὅραμα), and in content it is a revelation made to the seer (as he lay in his bed,
7:1) of an eschatological "event." While in Matt 28:16-20 the
word ὅραμα is not used, aspects of the text suggest that the
author is thinking of visionary experience, perhaps in an apocalyptic mode. The appearance of Jesus is sudden, no description
is given and no departure mentioned, and the scene takes place
on the unidentified symbolic mountain, considered by some a
typical site of revelation. The eleven are said to have seen
Jesus (ἰδόντες), but this participle is ambiguous, and could
denote physical or ecstatic sight, as well as the reception of
a revelation.[14] What they see is Jesus as translated into eschatological existence.[15]

(4) Both scenes can be read as dealing with the eschatological event that is the beginning of the end of the final
kingdom. It is not clear in Daniel 7 that the time of evil
beasts (whose lives have been prolonged, v. 12) is over before
the transfer of power to the one like a son of man, nor that
all begin serving him (v. 14) immediately. That is, even in
Daniel the final moment of history may not be pictured.[16] In
Matt 28:16-20, Jesus commissions the eleven for their historical task and promises his presence "to the close of the age"
when, it is implied, the kingdom will be consummated "in out-
ward splendor."[17]

(5) There seems to be a relationship (if not strictly
speaking a parallelism) between the reception of "the kingdom
and the dominion of the greatness of the kingdoms under the
whole heaven" by the people of the holy ones of the Most High
(Dan 7:27) and the reception of a commission by the disciples
in the Matthean pericope. In both cases, the groups (people
of the holy ones, the eleven) appear to be affected by the reception of power by the individual (one like a son of man, risen
risen Jesus).[18]

(6) In Daniel 7, the reception of power by the one like a
son of man is immediately preceded by his coming "on the clouds
of heaven" to the Ancient of Days, to whom he is presented,
presumably by angels (7:13).[19] In Matthew it is implied that
the handing over of "all power in heaven and on earth" to Jesus

was preceded by his movement in death and vindication into the
full presence of God.  In their respective contexts, that is,
both Dan 7:14 and Matt 28:18 depend on the idea of a "heavenly
directed parousia."[20]  The Matthean text may intentionally
evoke Dan 7:13, applying it to the resurrection of Jesus,[21]
apocalyptically understood as a translation into eschatological
existence.  If Matt 26:64 uses Dan 7:13 to speak of the resurrection of Jesus (or, as Lindars puts it, of "the exaltation
which the resurrection attests"),[22] and not of an earthly
directed parousia, the reader has been alerted to expect the
allusion to Dan 7:14 in Matt 28:18, and to understand this
scene as the appearance of the exalted Jesus.

　　(7) Finally, the figures of the one like a son of man and
the risen Jesus are depicted in Daniel and Matt 28:16-20 as
human and more than human.  The one like a son of man appears
abruptly, riding upon (ἐπί) the clouds of heaven and comes
fearlessly into the divine presence in Dan 7:13; in the LXX of
7:14 he is worshipped by every heavenly being (δόξα).[23]  The
risen Jesus in the final Matthean pericope is apparently regarded as the earthly teacher of the eleven (see v. 20a); to
him, however, belongs cosmic power and the power to be eternal-
ly present to them (v. 20b).  In addition, as "the Son," his
name is joined in close association with the Father and the
Spirit in the triadic phrase in verse 19b.

　　Three further elements of Matt 28:16-20 link this passage
with Son of Man material elsewhere in the Gospel.  (1) The
phrase συντελείας τοῦ αἰῶνος (v. 20b) appears in the question
in 24:3 ("What will be the sign of your coming and of the close
of the age?") whose answer is climaxed in 24:30 ("...they will
see the Son of Man coming on the clouds of heaven with power
and great glory"), and in 13:39-40 (the scene of final reaping
by angels sent by the Son of Man).  (2) The verb ἐντέλλομαι
(Matt 28:20) is redactional at 17:9 ("As they were coming down
from the mountain, Jesus commanded them, 'Tell no one the vision
until the Son of Man is raised from the dead'").  (3) The phrase
πάντα τὰ ἔθνη (28:19) appears in 25:32 (where all are gathered
before the Son of Man for judgment).  It is apparent that there
is an intention to activate these Son of Man associations here

in the final pericope. This is further evidence in support of
the presence of an allusion to Dan 7:14 in Matt 28:18.

## C. Differences Between the Texts

It must be recognized as well that there are striking differences between Dan 7:14 and Matt 28:18 and their respective
contexts. Some of these differences have been regarded as reasons to deny the presence of an allusion.

(1) In Daniel 7 the account of the reception of power by
the one like a son of man is told in the third person. The one
like a son of man is himself silent (as are all the heavenly
characters in this scene with the exception of the angelic interpreter, v. 16). In Matt 28:18, Jesus speaks as the one who
has received power. If he has taken over the role of the one
like a son of man, the role is no longer a passive one, but has
an active dimension. In Daniel 7, the one like a son of man
appears, coming on the clouds of heaven to the Ancient of Days
to receive power and dominion, only after Daniel has seen the
rising of four beasts from the sea, the enthronement of the
Ancient of Days, the judgment and destruction of the fourth
beast with its evil horn, and the removal of dominion from the
other beasts. The one like a son of man is not said to participate in the judgment, nor do we see him initiating an active reign. In contrast, the risen Jesus in Matt 28:16-20 commissions and sends forth his disciples and promises his presence.

(2) Instead of one troubled seer as witness in Daniel 7, in
Matthew the eleven witness the scene with mixed emotions, mixed
levels of commitment (28:17).

(3) Whereas Daniel establishes or strengthens the matter
in his heart (7:28 LXX) and is told in the final chapter to
"seal the book until the time of the end" (ἕως καιροῦ συντελείας,
12:4 LXX), the disciples are instructed to (in effect) spread
the news of their experience.[24]

(4) All nations in Daniel will serve or worship (λατρεύουσα) the man-like figure, and there is destruction of the
fourth beast. In Matthew, all nations are to be made disciples
of the risen Jesus, and no mention is made of the destruction
of opposing powers.

(5) It is sometimes claimed that the final Matthean pericope represents the turning away from an unsuccessful mission
among the Jews to a concentration on the mission to the Gentiles,
and a rejection of Israel. That is, "all nations" in 28:19 is
read as "all Gentiles," excluding Israel.[25] Along these lines,
the exaltation of Jesus is seen as indicating a loss for Israel,
a message (although not a final one) of judgment on it and a
removal of its prerogative.[26] This reading of the commission
need not depend solely on the translation of ἔθνος in 28:19 as
Gentiles, which has been shown by Meier to be inaccurate.[27] The
much disputed question of the relationship between Matthew's
community and the synagogue is still an open one. But if the
split had become definitive between these groups, and the above
interpretation of Matt 28:16-20 a correct one, the use of Daniel
7 in the Matthean text would present a startling and direct contradiction to the apparent import of the Danielic passage.
Written during the Maccabean revolution against the Gentile
Seleucids, this work encourages resistance by the vision of
Israel triumphing over its enemies and receiving an everlasting
kingdom (7:27). But it must be noted that in the book of Daniel
it is the true Israel, remaining faithful through the crisis,
not the nation as a whole, which triumphs.[28]

(6) The scene in Matt 28:16-20 takes place on a (symbolic)
mountain in Galilee, although elements of the scene indicate it
was understood as a visionary experience. The scene in Daniel 7
occurs apparently in the heavenly throne room, where "thrones
were placed and one that was Ancient of Days took his seat" (7:
9). The one like a son of man may be presumed to be enthroned,
though this is not stated explicitly. He may perhaps have been
imagined occupying one of the thrones mentioned in 7:9, or even
as sharing the throne of the Ancient of Days, since he is given
total dominion in 7:14.[29] But the inferences that the readers
were intended to draw are not clear.[30] No throne is mentioned,
and there appears at first glance to be no enthronment imagery
in Matt 28:16-20. It will be argued below, however, that the
mountain in verse 16 may be a symbol of the throne of God.

(7) In Dan 7:13 the one coming on the clouds is called "one
like a son of man" (MT: כְּבַר אֱנָשׁ; LXX and Theodotion: ὡς υἱὸς
ἀνθρώπου). Jesus is not called the Son of Man in Matt 28:16-20,

but simply "Jesus" in verse 16 and, apparently referring to himself in verse 19b, "the Son." Some scholars insist that no
title is used of Jesus in this pericope,[31] but many[32] are of
the opinion that the Kyrios title is implicit here. In contrast,
Fuller and Kingsbury, as has been seen, find here an emphasis on
Jesus as Son. Lohmeyer and Fuller consider this an instance of
the development of the Son of Man title into Son (of God).[33]
For Tödt, the absence of the title Son of Man indicates that
there is no intention to allude to the "concept" of the Son of
Man. He recognizes, however, the presence of an allusion to
Dan 7:14 in the idea of enthronement.[34] It must be mentioned
here that it is becoming increasingly clear that scholars can
no longer take for granted that there existed in pre-NT times a
clear "concept" of the Son of Man or even the "title" Son of
Man.[35] The absence of the concept and title from Matt 28:16-20,
then, need not be regarded as an indication of the absence of
an allusion to Dan 7:14. But the absence of the designation
does mean, even if there is an allusion, that we cannot be *certain* that in this scene Matthew thinks of Jesus as the Son of
Man. The other two members of the triads in Dan 7:13 LXX and
Matt 28:19b are titled differently. In place of the Ancient of
Days, in the latter text there is the Father, and in place of
the bystanders (angels) there is the Holy Spirit.

(8) Again, with regard to the one like a son of man of Dan
7:13-14, this figure has an important and essential relationship
to the (people of the) holy ones of the Most High, mentioned in
verses 18, 21-22, 25, 27. The main vision of Daniel 7 extends
from verses 1-14; here the one like a son of man is presented
to the Ancient of Days and receives power and dominion. An interpretation is given in verses 17-18, in which the four beasts
from the sea are explicitly identified as four kings, and it is
said that "the holy ones of the Most High shall receive the
kingdom and possess the kingdom for ever, for ever and ever."
When the vision is further elaborated in verses 19-22, there is
mention of the last horn making war with the holy ones and pre-
vailing over them "until the Ancient of Days came, and judgment
was given for the holy ones of the Most High, and the time came
when the holy ones received the kingdom." This part of the

vision is interpreted in verses 23-27, where the reader is told
that the horn "will wear out the holy ones of the Most High...
and they shall be given into his hand for a time, two times and
half a time" (v. 25).  But after the court sits in judgment and
the dominion of the horn is destroyed, total dominion under
heaven will be given "to the people of the holy ones of the Most
High" (v. 27).  The one like a son of man, then, is not mentioned except in verses 13-14.  The relationship of this figure
to the "holy ones" and the interpretation of that term (קְדוֹשִׁין)
are highly disputed points.  Some scholars claim that the one
like a son of man is a symbol of the "people of the holy ones"
(angels or faithful Jews, or eschatological Israel in communion
with the angels), others that he is an individual (human or angelic) representative or leader of this group, and/or a "collective person."[36]

But the risen Jesus who appears in Matt 28:16-20 is not a
symbol, but a human (transcendent) person with an earthly history.  There is also no clear indication in this text that he
is understood as a representative or as a corporate or collective person, or that the title "the Son" in verse 19b is so
understood.  The only aspect of the passage that gives us some
pause concerning this point is that all nations are to be baptized "into the name of the Father and of the Son and of the
Holy Spirit."  Does this mean that the risen Jesus as "Son" has
become an inclusive personality into whom his disciples can be
somehow incorporated by baptism?

(9) The triad occurs in Daniel 7 in the context of judgment, followed by transfer of authority.  In Matt 28:19b, however, the triad is connected with the command to baptize, predicated on the risen one's prior reception of authority.  No reference is made to judgment.  What relationship, if any, is understood to exist between judgment and baptism?

(10) It has been suggested above[37] that Dan 7:13 may be
presupposed by Matt 28:16-20.  The coming on the clouds of
heaven of one like a son of man to the Ancient of Days would
then have been taken as a way of describing the resurrection-
exaltation as a kind of translation or ascent (similar to Acts
1:9 but with no interlude between resurrection and ascension).

In Daniel 7, however, the one like a son of man is not said to rise from earth to the heavenly court. Some have argued that he seems to be already in the heavenly realm, and to come "wafting across the heavens."[38] We must ask if Matt 28:16-20 (which seems to presuppose the exaltation of Jesus from earth to heaven)[39] is indirect evidence of a reading of Dan 7:13 that supplements that text with or understands it in the light of traditions concerning the translations of individuals like Elijah or Enoch.[40]

(11) The theme of the eternity and indestructability of the kingdom in Daniel is absent from Matt 28:16-20, replaced perhaps by the theme of the constant presence of Jesus with the eleven "to the close of the age" (v. 20b). The term "kingdom" does not appear in this final pericope nor does the idea of sub-jects; instead, we find emphasis on disciple-making, which im-plies the aim of creating a kind of worldwide "school." The risen one appears not as a king but as a master, even a master-teacher (v. 20a), a kind of wisdom figure.

(12) In Daniel subjugation to the one like a son of man seems to be effected miraculously, perhaps automatically,[41] in coordination with the transfer of power. In Matthew, hoever, a further stage is clearly envisioned between the giving of power and the effect this is to have on all nations: that of a mission of the eleven.

(13) The focus of attention in the two scenes is different. In Dan 7:13-14 it is on the coming of the one like a son of man to the Ancient of Days, and on the transfer of power and the eternality of the kingdom. In Matthew the reception of power is an already accomplished fact, an event which has taken place before the final scene begins. Focus is seen by most to be on the commission of the eleven, on the universal extent and even shared nature of authority.[42] Two further points merit greater attention.

(14) It has been argued that the form of Dan 7:13-14 and that of Matt 28:16-20 are different. The former is considered by some an enthronement scene with three elements: (a) enthrone-ment, conferral of supreme authority; (b) presentation and proclamation of the one so authorized; (c) acclamation, recogni-tion by all peoples of the bestowal of these qualities.[43] Other

critics, looking at the broader context of Dan 7:9-14 or chapter 7 as a whole, find here an adaptation of an ANE ritual pattern of enthronement following conflict and victory over cosmic
enemies. This pattern is found in OT psalms which speak of the
enthronement of the Davidic king, especially Psalms 2 and 7,
and in texts such as Zechariah 9.[44]   Daniel 7, it is argued, is
based on a Canaanite enthronement scene, the tradition of which
has perhaps been transmitted in the royal cult at Jerusalem,
and after the exile in folk or learned circles.[45]

Only two NT critics, Jeremias and Michel, have suggested
that Matt 28:18-20 is clearly patterned on the ritual of royal
enthronement or "triple action coronation."[46]   According to
this approach, as Meier points out, "the most important point
in the pericope is not the missionary charge in itself, but
rather the idea of the enthronement or exaltation of the Son of
Man,"[47] in spite of the fact that no throne is mentioned.  However, the three acts of the enthronement ritual[48] are not really
present in Matt 28:16-20.  There is no enthronement proper or
conferral of power[49] narrated in the present tense, and no acclamation.  Rather, there are elements basic to the text which
do not fit this pattern: (a) the coming of the eleven to the
mountain;[50] (b) the commission (vv. 19-20a) and (c) the promise
of presence (v. 20b).  Moreover, the commission is at least *as*
central to the text as the idea of (past) exaltation.[51]

Most scholars now argue that the primary interest of the
passage is in the commission, not in enthronement.[52]  The closest OT example of the form of this passage is considered by
some to be 2 Chron 36:23 (the royal decree of Cyrus, a variant
of the messenger form)[53] or accounts of the commissioning of
individuals.[54]

Of special interest is Hubbard's treatment, which it is
important to detail at this point.  He argues that Matt 28:16-20
conforms to the structure of a "Hebrew Bible Commissioning Gattung," such as is found in at least twenty-nine passages in the
OT (including Gen 11:28-30; 12:1-4a; 28:10-22; Exod 3:1-4:16;
Josh 1:1-11; Jer 1:1-10; Isaiah 6; Ezek 1:1-3:15; 1 Chr 22:1-16).
This form has the following seven elements:

   1.  circumstantial introduction
   2.  confrontation between the commissioner and commissioned

3.  reaction to the presence of deity
4.  commission proper
5.  protest at the commission
6.  reassurance from the deity
7.  conclusion.[55]

Hubbard finds this form in Matt 28:16-20, although the fifth
and seventh items are omitted, and the confrontation is in two
stages:

1.  introduction: verse 16
2.  confrontation: verse 17a
3.  reaction: verse 17b
2.  confrontation: verse 18
4.  commission: verses 19-20a
6.  reassurance: verse 20b.[56]

There are two problems with Hubbard's proposed solution to
the question of the form of Matt 28:16-20.  (a) The supposed
commissioning-*Gattung* is too broad and lacks specificity.  It
could be applied to a number of other OT and NT texts, and is
not distinctively different from the more general *Gattung* of
theophany or angelophany.[57]  (b) Since the *Gattung* is so broad,
it is of little help toward understanding the post-resurrectional
epiphany.  Verse 18b does not fit the *Gattung*.  Hubbard makes it
the second half of the confrontation, which is split in two by
the reaction; but this split-confrontation is found nowhere else
in the OT parallels.  It cannot be thought of as a self-asseveration,[58] as it is really the declaration of the past act of enthronement, the resurrection, which is the basis of the present
commands.[59]

Neither the enthronement-hymn pattern, then, nor the commissioning *Gattung* fits Matt 28:16-20 perfectly.  This leads
some critics to conclude that the proper form-critical category
has not yet been proposed for this pericope.  Others conclude
that no *Gattung* (dealing with the typical) can be satisfactory,
because the pericope is *sui generis* and idiosyncratic, defying
the labels of form criticism.[60]  In line with the discussion
here, no clear association has been yet shown to exist between
the form of Daniel 7 and the form of Matt 28:16-20, and this may
argue against the presence of an allusion to Dan 7:14 LXX in
Matt 28:18b.

In the following chapters, however, we will take a closer look form-critically at Daniel 7 and at Matt 28:16-20. It will be proposed that Daniel 7 is not simply an enthronement scene, but a "throne-theophany commission" of an apocalyptic seer. An analysis of the Matthean passage on the basis of an understanding of its symbolism and traditional associations shows that this pericope also is a "(throne)-theophany commission" of the disciples. The Danielic text may have been used in connection with the mission of the disciples because the idea that the sight of the risen Jesus is an essential part of what constitutes a person an apostle is very similar to--and drawn from-- the OT idea that a vision of the heavenly court constituted a person a prophet[61] or seer. In the context of the allusion, the scene in Matthew's final pericope is understood as the sight of the risen Jesus in the heavenly court. Vision and commission belong together. Form-critically, then, it will be argued that Daniel 7 and Matt 28:16-20 are closely related. The case is strengthened for the presence of the Danielic allusion in Matt 28:18b.

(15) Finally, concluding the list of objections to the presence of the allusion, it has been argued that if Dan 7:14 is is read as an eschatological prediction, Matt 28:18 cannot be considered its accomplishment. This is so because in the Gospel of Matthew, some claim, there is found only one interpretation of Dan 7:13-14, and this is a parousia interpretation. The prophecy is regarded as fulfilled only by the parousia, when the Son of Man is to come back to earth on the clouds. This is an object of hope for Matthew, and therefore inadequate to account for 28:16-20, the situation of which is pre-parousia.[62] This view is in contrast to the insistence of Hartman and others that Matthew has various ways of interpreting the Danielic text.[63] Meier remarks that a priori such an either/or approach (either a parousia use or no use of Dan 7:13-14) leaves no room for Matthew's use of Daniel in a new, creative way.[64] It also rules out without examination the possibility of use in Matt 28:18 of a tradition at variance with his other uses of Dan 7:13-14.

Some scholars, on the other hand, see in Matt 28:16-20 a proleptic or pre-parousia scene. The implication of the passage

is seen by Jeremias to be that "with the death and resurrection
of Jesus the eschatological hour has arrived."[65]  The meaning
of the scene is that in the resurrection the prophecy that the
Son of Man would be enthroned as ruler of the world *has* been
fulfilled.  The idea that the resurrection of Jesus was his enthronement echoes the immediate impression made by the Easter
events.  The disciples experienced the resurrection not as a
unique mighty act of God in the course of history (although this
is how it was later interpreted), but as the dawn of the eschaton, the definitive turning point, the beginning of the new age,
the hour of Christ's entry into his reign.  The disciples "were
witnesses of his entry into glory.  In other words, *they experienced the parousia.*"[66]  For Fuller, Matt 28:18 represents not
the immediate impression of the disciples, but the later church's
reflection.  He argues that here we can see the shift of Son of
Man Christology from the parousia to the exaltation.[67]

This question is further complicated by the views of Hahn
and Tödt.  Hahn insists that because Matt 28:18-20 is about exaltation (which he understands as "lordship over heaven and
earth" and closely connected with the Hellenist Jewish Christian
view of Jesus as Kyrios)[68] and because exaltation is rarely connected with the Son of Man (parousia) concept,[69] the primary OT
reference in Matt 28:18 is not Dan 7:14.  Tödt, as has been
seen, believes that something of the idea-cluster or gestalt of
Dan 7:13-14 is present in Matt 28:18: this is the concept of
enthronement.  But in addition, he says, the Matthean text contains the concept of exaltation, defined "not as the act of enthronement by which the Son of Man is given the authority of
co-regent with God, but as the state of exaltation in the
lengthening period before the parousia."[70]  The concept of exaltation did not evolve directly from the "Son of Man concept"
and in fact is not connected with it in the Synoptics.

Tödt considers Luke 22:69 (where it is presupposed that the
Son of Man exists in a state of exaltation, remaining with God
during the post-Easter period) the only exception to this statement, and a specifically Lukan interpretation rather than a
separate tradition.  Here "the concept of exaltation has been
adopted from a sphere of Christological cognition which is not

immediately connected with the Son of Man concept," but with
the title and concept of Kyrios.[71]  Matt 28:18 is interpreted
as an expression of Jesus as Kyrios, only along the lines of
the Lukan (not the Matthean) understanding of that title.  In
this sense, Luke 22:69 and Matt 28:18 are similar, but in Luke
22:69 the "original meaning of the designation Son of Man" has
not been obscured by the concept of exaltation, as it has been
in Matt 28:18.[72]  Tödt also claims that the "title and concept"
of Son of Man always carry for Matthew the ideas of parousia
and coming judge of the world, both of which ideas are missing
in Matt 28:16-20.[73]  For Tödt, then, if there is an allusion to
Dan 7:14 in Matt 28:18,[74] it is extremely weak and all but
overpowered.[75]

     This brief survey of some opinions concerning the question
of whether or not Matt 28:18 can be considered the fulfillment
of Dan 7:13-14 indicates that there is need for greater termi-
nological clarity.  The word "exaltation" is being used in this
discussion in different senses.  Fuller following Hahn defines
exaltation (Erhöhung) as a term denoting enthronization as
Kyrios and Christ at the ascension, followed by active rule
until the parousia.[76]  This is distinguished from assumption
(Entrückung) or translation, which is considered the view of
the earliest community: that Jesus was taken up to heaven like
Elijah and like Moses in later apocalyptic,[77] and was waiting
in a state of inactivity until his manifestation as Christ at
the parousia.[78]  By "inactivity" Fuller means "not conceived as
reigning"; no attempt is made to evaluate the present status,
dignity or function of the risen one.[79]  Again following Hahn,
Fuller further distinguishes between assumption and ascension.
In the former term, resurrection and assumption from the grave
are hardly distinguishable (see Acts 3:20-21).  In the latter,
assumption is separated from resurrection and is an event subsequent to resurrection.[80]  Elijah or Enoch typology is used in
the NT for both assumption (cf. Luke 9:51; 1 Pet 3:23-24; Heb
4:14; 1 Tim 3:16) and ascension (cf. Acts 1:2, 9, 11; Luke 24:
51b; Mark 16:19; Rev 11:12).[81]

     Two objections must be raised concerning these distinctions:
(a) Matt 28:18 cannot be seen to be about the exaltation of

Jesus, so defined, since there is no indication in the final
Matthean pericope or in 28:9-10 that Jesus is conceived of as
having been enthroned at his ascension (not assumption). The
indication, rather, is that he is thought of as having been assumed from the grave; there is no interval between resurrection
and ascension.[82] (b) The apocryphal and intertestamental literature indicates that the figures regarded as assumed or translated into heaven were not thought of as inactive. Elijah was
known as the helper of those in need (Mark 15:35-36), flying
down to earth from Paradise (*1 Enoch* 89:52; 87:3). "No place is
too distant nor is any means left unused for the protection of
innocence, the saving of the righteous, the healing of the sick,
the establishment of peace and the giving of consolation and
admonition."[83] The functions allotted to Elijah in the heavenly
world include that of soul-bearer (Sir 48:11).[84] He was not,
however, conceived of as reigning, as far as we know.

Enoch is presented in *Jubilees* as a scribe, writing down in
Eden the condemnation and judgment of the world (4:23-24;
10:17)[85] and functioning as priest in the mountain sanctuary
(4:25).[86] He is available for consultation by his son Methuselah
(*1 Enoch* 106). Furthermore, there *is* evidence that he was
thought of as reigning. Wis 2:7-8 speaks of the souls of the
righteous, modeled in part on Enoch,[87] as destined to govern
nations and rule over peoples "in the time of their visitation."
These have been exalted to the ranks of the angelic attendants
in the heavenly court, and have ruling functions.[88] In *2 Enoch*
22, the translated Enoch is clothed with the garments of God's
glory, given heavenly books and initiated into heavenly secrets.[89]
Although the traditions in the last work mentioned may be later
than the NT, the insistence in *Ascension of Isaiah* 9:6 that
Enoch's translation is not fully consummated until Christ's coming[90] may testify indirectly to the fact that traditions of
Enoch ruling[91] were prevalent in the first century.[92] Assumption or translation to heaven, then, can be thought to have
involved installation in a position of power, an act of enthronement. This sort of exaltation to authority should not sharply
be distinguished from assumption. The assumed-exalted Jesus
seems to be speaking in Matt 28:18-20.[93]

In this present work, the term exaltation will be used to mean reception of power in heaven. This may involve implicit or explicit enthronization. The terms assumption, translation and ascent will refer to the movement of a figure from earth to heaven, whether or not the death of the figure is said to have occurred and whether the body or only the soul or spirit is thought to be involved. Ascension will refer to the event of bodily assumption considered distinct from and following the resurrection of that body. Matt 28:16-20 concerns the exaltation of Jesus and seems to imply his bodily assumption. He is not described here as ruling in a political or military sense, but as ruling in the sense of commanding to the missionary task. The impression given by verse 20b is of Jesus as a sort of co-worker with the eleven. The phrase "to the close of the age" indicates that the task is limited.

To summarize, in point (15) we have examined arguments that Matt 28:18b cannot be considered an allusion to Dan 7:14 (or cannot be considered a strong allusion) because (a) the Matthean text does not fulfill the vision of Daniel 7, (b) is out of line with the other Matthean interpretations of that OT text, and/or (c) involves the idea of Jesus' exaltation which is not linked elsewhere in the Synoptics or rarely linked anywhere in the NT with "the Son of Man concept." But several Synoptic Son of Man texts do have to do with exaltation as defined here and as this concept appears in Matt 28:16-20. As Tödt admits, there is an exalted Son of Man in Luke 22:69 and Acts 7:56.[94] Matt 13:37-43 presents the Son of Man working in the world (ὁ κόσμος) and exercising the function of "raising up sons of the kingdom." The reference seems to be to his ministry between Easter and the parousia.[95] It may be true that Matthew's primary interest in the term Son of Man has to do with its associations with the parousia,[96] and that the term (not used in 28:16-20) is only marginally significant to him as a vehicle for setting forth the post-Easter activity of Jesus. But this is not a convincing argument against the presence of an allusion in 28:18b, an allusion which may be part of a traditional unit. At this point in our investigation, we can only say that the similarities among Luke 22:69; Acts 7:56; Matt

13:37-43 and 28:18 strongly suggest that they are related in an exegetical tradition that interpreted Dan 7:13-14 as a description of assumption-exaltation, not of the parousia. Closer analysis of other NT uses of Dan 7:13-14 will show that several other NT texts also belong to this general tradition.[97]

### D. Conclusion

The linguistic and conceptual affinities between Dan 7:14 LXX and Matt 28:18b and their respective contexts are strong. Of the fifteen differences between the texts which have been examined, some may be theoretically explained in terms of re-interpretation and adaptation. Others are only apparent differences which do not stand up under close scrutiny. My conclusion is that the allusion is indeed present and significant, but I shall keep in mind that all are not convinced. What has been achieved here is probability concerning the presence of the allusion, but not certainty. Dan 7:14, in my opinion, has probably been considered fulfilled, partly or proleptically,[98] and thought to provide an understanding of the resurrection of Jesus and of his present status in the heavenly realm and with the eleven. This text appears also to have been used to present a vision of the future in terms of task and goal.

Still, the differences between the two texts cannot be minimized. Zumstein argues that Dan 7:14 has been so reinterpreted that it is no longer a valid point of departure for elucidating Matt 28:16-20.[99] My claim here is slightly different: that Daniel 7 is *only* a point of departure. Understanding of reinterpretation and adaptation must be based first of all on a grasp of the ambiguities and theological dimensions of Daniel 7, which will be examined in the following chapter. Second, knowedge of the pre-Christian midrashic history of that text, as far as that can be recovered, is necessary in order to determine which traditional elements, if any, may have influenced the Matthean text. Third, a close examination of NT texts which allude to or cite Dan 7:13-14, showing the wide range of uses to which this passage was put, can help us to place Matt 28:18b in proper perspective, and approach from another angle the question of tradition and redaction in the final pericope.

The primary focus in this work is on the triad, as it develops
(according to the theory presented here) from Daniel 7 to Matt
28:19b.

[1]See M. Gertner, "Midrashim in the New Testament," *JSS* 7 (1962) 268-69. The form of a covert midrash is usually that of a concise paraphrase or an expanded paraphrastic composition.

[2]E. E. Ellis, in dependence on Gertner, classifies midrashim as either implicit (i.e., an interpretive paraphrase of an OT text) or explicit (i.e., the lemma [a cited OT text] plus commentary). See his "Midrash, Targum and NT Quotations," 62. It is not clear whether the covert or implicit midrashim are examples of (a) the tendency of OT quotes to fade in transmission (see p. 69 n. 44, where Ellis cites Luke 20:9; 20:20 [cf. 12:53] with Markan parallels as examples of this phenomenon) or (b) of early allusions evoking a whole passage in a period before the church's interpretation was contested and more exact reference to the OT passage required (cf. Lindars, *NT Apologetic*, 19).

[3]See above, pp. 97-98.

[4]There are two fully extant Greek forms of Daniel, the LXX and the so-called Theodotion. The complete text of the LXX is now found in only two witnesses: Codex 88 (Rahlfs) and the Syrohexaplar; most of the LXX form is also found in the third century A.D. Chester Beatty-Cologne Papyrus 967. The LXX of Daniel originated around 100 B.C. in Egypt. The reason for the extreme scarcity of witnesses to this form is that in the second or third centuries A.D. the Christian church replaced it with the so-called Theodotion in MSS of the LXX.

[5]Theodotion-Daniel is considered by Di Lella to be a fresh translation of the Hebrew and Aramaic of Daniel, produced in a Jewish community of Palestine or Asia Minor by a scholar who was disturbed by the fact that the LXX of Daniel was at times less than accurate in relation to the Hebrew and Aramaic. As phrases from Theodotion-Daniel (as well as from the LXX form and from at least one other Greek translation which is no longer extant) appear in the NT, this translation was probably made in the first century B.C., and simply incorporated as is into the later Theodotion recension of the second century A.D. (A. A. DiLella and L. F. Hartman, *The Book of Daniel* [AB 23; Garden City: Doubleday, 1978] 77-82).

[6]Each of these is a common element in the LXX, ἐδόθη appearing twenty-seven times (including four times in Daniel; compare twelve times in ϑ Daniel), ἐξουσία appearing seventy-two times (twenty-four times in Daniel; compare eleven times in ϑ Daniel), and πάντα τὰ ἔϑνη eighty-four times (five times in Daniel; compare one time in ϑ Daniel). In no other text besides Dan 7:14 LXX do these three elements appear together. The only other text of any interest as an alternate source of a possible allusion in Matt 28:18 is Sir 17:2: "he gave to them (human beings) few days, a limited time, but granted them authority over the things upon it (the earth) (...καὶ ἔδωκεν αὐτοῖς εξουσιαν

τῶν ἐπ' αὐτῆς)." But Dan 7:14 LXX is a far more probable source than this passage.

[7]Contrast Theodotion: καὶ αὐτῷ ἐδόθη ἡ ἀρχή.

[8]Cf. Luke 1:19 which speaks of Gabriel as one "who stands before (παρεστηκὼς ἐνώπιον) God."

[9]A. Schlatter, Der Evangelist Matthäus (2nd ed.; Stuttgart, 1948) 798, cited by R. H. Gundry, The Use of the Old Testament in St. Matthew's Gospel (Leiden: Brill, 1967) 5.

[10]Gundry, The Use of the OT, 5.

[11]See David M. Hay, Glory at the Right Hand (New York: Abingdon, 1973) 17.

[12]B. Malina makes the point that Matthew does not say why Jesus now has the ability to exercise full authority, why this authority was received from God. But the terminology in 28:18 indicates that "this authority derives from victory under God's aegis....It is not Jesus specifically as risen Lord who speaks in the text, but Jesus as victorious wielder of authority. That Jesus can and does now wield authority might perhaps serve to prove he has been raised. Yet, formally speaking, Matthew does not seem to view Jesus as the resurrected one, but as the victorious one, the one wielding fullness of authority deriving from victory" ("Literary Structure," 101). It is more accurate to say that Matt 28:18 indicates the resurrection was here understood as a victory.

[13]The term δόξα is used of the heavenly radiance but also of angelic beings who possess this radiance (see BAG, 203).

[14]Cf. Fuller, Resurrection Narratives, 31 (on ἑώρακα, 1 Cor 9:1).

[15]Schweizer is of the opinion that the tradition spoke of a heavenly appearance, but that Matthew inserted the Matthean idiom "Jesus drew near (προσελθών) and spoke to them." This insertion connotes Jesus' coming to the aid of those who doubt and is taken by Schweizer as (admittedly faint) evidence that for Matthew Jesus is not here speaking from heaven but walking the earth. However, only twice is the verb προσέρχομαι applied to Jesus in Matthew: here and in 17:7 which is Matthean redaction of the transfiguration scene (cf. Hubbard, Matthean Redaction, 77-78). This and other strong parallels between the transfiguration and the final commission indicate that Matthew intended the latter to be reminiscent of the former, not necessarily that he wanted 28:16-20 to be thought of as an earthbound experience. The transfiguration scene is called a vision (ὅραμα) in 17:9.

[16]The vision of Daniel 7 may have been understood as the initiation of a process: the power given would result in the recognition of that power; the service of all peoples is

probably not pictured as happening at the moment of the transfer
of power.  N. W. Porteous (*Daniel* [Philadelphia: Westminster,
1965] 111) is certainly correct, however, that when he says in
the author's mind the celestial event is "virtually accomplished."

[17] Kingsbury, *Matthew*, 140.

[18] See below, however, for discussion of the complicated
problem of the identity of the one like a son of man, and the
relationship of this figure to the holy ones (Dan 7:18, 21-22,
25, 27).

[19] In the MT, the verb הַקְרְבוּהִי is active, but the passive
is the correct translation of the Aramaic idiom, which occurs
elsewhere in Daniel (2:13, 18, 30; 3:4; 4:4, 13, 22, 28; 7:5,
12).  Cf. DiLella, *Daniel*, 102 n. 242.  R. H. Charles notes that
the LXX of Dan 7:13 (οἱ παρεστηκότες παρῆσαν αὐτῷ) presupposes
a different Aramaic text: קָאמַיָּא קרבו קדמוהי ("they that stood
by drew near before him").  The ones standing by in 7:16 and the
tens of thousands in 7:10 seem to be an order of angels in immediate attendance on the Ancient of Days.  Charles remarks that
if we insert קָאמַיָּא before קדמוהי in the MT, "we could interpret
this class of angels as a like order in attendance on 'the one
like unto a son of man.'"  The text would then run: קָאמַיָּא קדמוהי
הקרבוהי, reading the verb as active not passive ("they that stood
before him [the one like a son of man] brought him near [to the
Ancient of Days]").  The force that draws or propels the one like
a son of man into the divine presence, then, is his angelic escort
or attendants (Charles, *A Critical and Exegetical Commentary on
the Book of Daniel* [Oxford: Clarendon, 1929] 187).  Jeffery understands the LXX to mean that attendants by the throne of the
Ancient of Days bring the one like a son of man near; but the MT
without emendation he says means that certain angelic attendants
who came in the clouds with the one like a son of man bring him
near (A. Jeffery, "The Book of Daniel," *IB*, 6.461).  The idea of an
angelic escort of the one like a son of man may be related to a
proposed Canaanite connection (which will be examined below) between angels and clouds.

[20] The phrase is that of Lars Hartman ("Scriptural Exegesis
in the Gospel of Matthew and the Problem of Communication," in
*L'Evangile selon Matthieu* [ed. M. Didier; Gembloux: Duculot,
1972] 143).  See J. Jeremias (*NT Theology*, 310) for the opinion
that the ingressive aorist ἐδόθη in Matt 28:18 echoes the connection between resurrection and entry into reign.  Those aspects of Matt 28:16-20 which lead us to understand it as a vision imply that Jesus has been transferred to heaven.  This
movement may have been imagined in terms of Dan 7:13, as a
translation or ascent (cf. Acts 1:9).

[21] Hartman thinks such an interpretation of Dan 7:13-14 was
in Matthew's mind here and also in Matt 26:64 (par. Mark 14:62)
and is also present in Acts 1:9, in the Similitudes and in
*4 Ezra*.  In contrast to this ancient heavenly-directed interpretation, the more customary parousia interpretation appears in
Matt 24:30.  Matthew, therefore, according to Hartman, has
various ways of interpreting Dan 7:13-14.  "Presumably the

apocalyptic imagery of Daniel 7 was felt to be semantically
open--as is that of many other apocalyptic texts--so that it
had an impressionistic function rather than a descriptive one;
this may favor a variety of interpretations" (Hartman, "Scriptural Exegesis," 146; cf. 144).

[22]B. Lindars, "The Apocalyptic Myth and the Death of
Christ," *BJRL* 57 (1974/5) 368.

[23]See above, p. 132 n. 13.

[24]In P. D. Hanson's terms, there is in Matthew a rein-
statement of the tension, which he finds to some extent absent
in Daniel, between vision and reality (cf. "Old Testament
Apocalyptic Reexamined," *Int* 25 [1971] 459-60, 464; this is a
discussion of the differences between Isaiah and Daniel on this
point. Cf. also Hanson, "Prolegomena to the Study of Jewish
Apocalyptic," *Magnalia Dei*, 407).

[25]See Hare and Harrington, "Make Disciples," 359-69.

[26]See, for example, Bornkamm ("Risen Lord," 217 n. 48)
agreeing with R. Hummel (*Die Auseinandersetzung zwischen Kirche
und Judentum im Matthäus-evangelium* [München: Chr. Kaiser,
1963] 142).

[27]Meier, "Nations or Gentiles," 94-102.

[28]The term "the true Israel" is applied to the figure of
the one like a son of man by E. W. Heaton (*The Book of Daniel*
[London: SCM, 1956] 186). The kingdom is not given to the nation of Israel, but to a remnant; some among the nation are
"men of violence" (Dan 11:14), those who forsake and violate
the holy covenant (11:30, 32; cf. the term παράνομοι in 1 Macc
1:11). The expression used to describe these people in Dan
11:32a (מַרְשִׁיעֵי בְרִיח) is found in 1QM 1:2 to designate the rene-
gade Hellenizers (Hartman and DiLella, *Daniel*, 299). Only
those whose names are found in the book are delivered in 12:1;
only some awaken to everlasting life in 12:2.

[29]It has been argued that the plural "thrones" in 7:9 is a
plural of majesty. But, although there is no mention in chap.
7 of assessors or assistants to the judge, in view of 4:14 (17)
(which reads, "The sentence is by the decree of the watchers,
the decision by the word of the holy ones") it is clear to some
critics that heavenly powers take part with God in the judgment.
(see Hartman and DiLella, *Daniel*, 217). On the other hand,
Mowinckel remarks that the plural shows that in the original
conception the one like a son of man took part in the judgment
of the world and "was thought of as sharing God's throne, a
divine being in human form" (*He That Cometh* [New York: Abingdon, 1954] 352).

[30]Porteous, *Daniel*, 108; J. J. Collins, "The Son of Man
and the Saints of the Most High in the Book of Daniel," *JBL* 93
(1974) 65.

[31]Malina ("Literary Structure," 100 n. 2) argues that
Matthew does not use any title at all in his description of
Jesus after the resurrection, possibly because all titles have
proven insufficient.  Malina does not treat the triadic phrase.
Zumstein ("Matthieu 28:16-20," 18), Schweizer (*Good News*, 532),
Bornkamm ("Risen Lord," 207) and Lohmeyer ("Mir ist gegeben,"
47) all state that no title is used in this passage.

[32]These scholars include Bornkamm, Lohmeyer, Strecker,
Zumstein, Schweizer.

[33]See above, pp. 50-54.

[34]Tödt, *The Son of Man*, 288.

[35]See above, p. 56.  Tödt does doubt that there was any
definite set of concepts concerning the Son of Man which was
generally accepted in Jewish apocalyptic, but thinks it possible that different Son of Man-type figures seemed to draw
together when seen in a fresh light by the earliest Christian
communities.  He admits the Son of Man concept is not a constant throughout the Synoptics (*The Son of Man*, 30).  But
basically by the term Son of Man Tödt seems to mean the concept
of the radically transcendant eschatological saviour, a heavenly redeemer whose coming to earth as judge would be a feature
of the end time (p. 23).  For a summary of the debate concerning whether or not the phrase, the son of man, was in use as a
title in pre-Christian Judaism, see J. Bowker, "The Son of Man,"
*JTS* 28 (1977) 20-32, esp. 28-32.

[36]This problem will be examined in the following chapter.

[37]See number (6), pp. 115-16.

[38]Lindars, for example, argues that the whole action of
the Danielic vision takes place in the heavenly realm.  The one
like a son of man is exalted, i.e., raised to honor, but not
raised from earth to heaven ("Apocalyptic Myth," 375).

[39]Schweizer claims that for any Jew it was impossible to
conceive of an eschatological role of any man living on earth
without presupposing his exaltation to heaven.  Thus, the sequence, earthly life--exaltation--eschatological role (found in
Wisdom 2-5), was the only pattern available for describing
Jesus' fate ("The Son of Man Again," *NTS* 9/10 [1963/4] 261).

[40]Lindars insists that we should look to these sorts of
traditions *rather than* to Dan 7:13 for the background of the
idea of Jesus' exaltation to heaven ("Apocalyptic Myth," 375).
For Mark 14:62 and Acts 7:56, Schweizer seems to argue that Dan
7:13 was read in the light of Elijah-Enoch traditions ("Son of
Man Again," 259-61).

[41]But see above, point (4), p. 115.

[42]See Hubbard, *Matthean Redaction*, 82; Zumstein, "Matthieu
28:16-20," 19, 25; Malina, "Literary Structure," 101, 89.

[43]Jeremias, *Jesus' Promise to the Nations*, 39. Meier
("Two Disputed Questions," 417) speaks of the three acts of the
ANE enthronement ritual: "(a) exaltation to the divine realm;
(b) presentation to the pantheon or proclamation of the name;
(c) enthronement proper, the handing over of power, accompanied
by acclamation."

[44]P. D. Hanson, *The Dawn of Apocalyptic* (Philadelphia:
Fortress, 1975) 310, 315. See pp. 305-07 for outlines of the
ritual pattern of the conflict myth, integrated into the
ideology of the royal cult, in psalms from various periods.

[45]J. J. Collins, *The Apocalyptic Vision of the Book of
Daniel* (Missoula, MT: Scholars, 1977) 101-02.

[46]Jeremias, *Jesus' Promise to the Nations*, 39; Michel,
"Der Abschluss," 22-23. These critics see the Matthean verses
as similar to the enthronement hymns of the NT, such as Phil
2:9-11, 1 Tim 3:16 and Heb 1:5-14. The Matthean pericope is
considered formcritically a Christological reshaping of the
words of Dan 7:14 and as such a statement of the Easter fulfillment of the Son of Man enthronement scene. G. Barth does not
have an extended discussion of the form, but argues that the
"close connection of authority, dominion and recognition of this
endowment by all nations" indicates that the conception of the
enthronement of the Son of Man in Dan 7:14 has been transferred
to Jesus ("Matthew's Understanding," 133). Others more cautiously speak of an echo or trace of the enthronement form ly-
ing behind Matt 28:16-20, often with no strong connection with
Daniel 7. Cf. Bornkamm, "Risen Lord," 207-13; Hahn, *Mission in
the NT*, 66.

[47]Meier, "Two Disputed Questions," 417.

[48]Jeremias schematizes the verses in this way: (a) v. 18:
assumption of all power by the risen Christ; (b) vv. 19-20a:
injunction to proclaim his authority among the nations; (c) v.
20b: word of Power.

[49]Hubbard argues that Jesus does not assume all authority
in the final scene, but already possesses it in his earthly
ministry. While it is true that several texts speak of his
authority then (Matt 7:29; 9:6, 8; 10:1; 21:24), and in 11:27
Jesus is presented as declaring that "all things" have been
delivered to him by his Father, Hubbard overstates his point.
In 28:18b the power is "all power in heaven and on earth," and
the verb ἐδόθη seems to refer to the resurrection. Bornkamm
remarks that the new thing here is the universal extension of
Jesus' power, though the power of the earthly Jesus had been
"full" ("Risen Lord," 208).

[50]Jeremias and Michel deal only with the *Gattung* of vv.
18b-20.

[51]See the objections to the theories of Jeremias and Michel
presented by Hubbard (*Matthean Redaction*, 9), Trilling (*Das
Wahre Israel*, 23) and Meier ("Two Disputed Questions," 417-18).

[52] According to Schweizer, vv. 18-20 are to be understood as the "instructions and promise of one who has ascended his throne," aimed at bringing about the acknowledgement of Jesus as Lord by all nations (*Good News*, 536).

[53] Malina, "Literary Form," 87-103, and independently, H. Frankmölle, *Jahwebund und Kirche* (Münster: Aschendorff, 1974) 46-61. Again, these theories apply only to vv. 18b-20. Malina tends to reject the idea of the presence of an allusion to Dan 7:14 in Matt 28:18b, although he thinks that 28:18-20 can be explained in part as a stand toward some such haggadah as that found in *Pirqe R. El.* 11 (97 n. 1). Frankmölle sees the Matthean adaptation of the form of the decree enriched by an allusion to Daniel 7 which raises the promise of hope to the universal eschatological level. The further details of the views of these two scholars are summarized and criticized by Meier ("Two Disputed Questions," 418-20).

[54] Besides Hubbard's work, see also Charles Giblin ("A Note on Doubt and Reassurance in Mt. 28:16-20," *CBQ* 37 [1975] 74-75) and X. Léon-Dufour (*The Resurrection and the Message of Easter* [New York: Holt, Rinehart and Winston, 1974] 94-97).

[55] Hubbard, *Matthean Redaction*, 25-67; see p. 65 for the list of the OT passages. The third and fifth elements are the least constant.

[56] Ibid., 69-72. As has been seen, Hubbard found a common tradition underlying the commissioning scenes in Matt 28:16-20, Markan Appendix 16:14-20, Luke 24:36-53 and John 20:19-23 (see his schematization, pp. 103-04, and the discussion of the proto-commissioning, pp. 122-28). Hubbard also thinks that under the influence of the Hebrew Bible generally and of the commissioning tradition particularly, Matthew added certain motifs and words: a circumstantial introduction, statement of authority, the verbs "go" and "command," the theme of "nations," the frequent adjective "all," and the reassurance "I am with you" (pp. 134-35). See above, pp. 33-34.

[57] See the review of Hubbard's work by H. K. McArthur, *CBQ* 38 (1976) 108, and Meier, "Two Disputed Questions," 422-23. McArthur mentions that J. Alsup (*The Post-Resurrection Appearance Stories of the Gospel Tradition*) relates the appearance narratives, including Matt 28:16-20, to "anthropomorphic theophany" presentations in the Hebrew Bible.

[58] Hubbard considers that v. 18b identifies Jesus as the unique possessor of the universal authority of God. "Jesus is saying, in effect, 'I am the One to whom God has given all authority in heaven and on earth.'" The words perform a function similar to the divine self-asseveration ("I am the God of...") which Hubbard found as a sub-element of the Confrontation in seven of his examples of the *Gattung* in the Hebrew Bible (*Matthean Redaction*, 70). But as Meier points out, there is no "I am the One..." and no verb in the present tense in Matt 28:18b.

59Meier, "Two Disputed Questions," 423. Meier remarks that the proto-commissioning may have included also an introduction and a conclusion. If this is the case, Matthew adds no new element to the structure; he merely adds motifs, and moreover disturbs the supposed structure by the addition of v. 18b.

60This is the current position of Meier. He argues that, using some existing tradition, Matthew has heavily redacted this pericope to express his own ideas concerning christology, ecclesiology and eschatology. It is the interplay or dialectic between tradition and heavy redaction that makes this pericope unique ("Two Disputed Questions," 424).

61See Brown, *Gospel According to John*, 2.973.

62See especially Vögtle, "Das christologische und ekklesiologische Anliegen," 267-68; also Zumstein, "Matthieu 28, 16-20," 19. Schweizer is of a similar opinion, only more hesitant: he says that since the coming on the clouds is future in Matt 25: 30 and 26:64, the connection in 28:18 with Dan 7:14 is not certain (*Good News*, 531). Vögtle also denies the presence of an allusion to Dan 7:14 in Matt 28:18 on linguistic grounds, finding little similarity between the texts. But his argument is based on Theodotion and not the LXX which, as we have seen, is closer to Matt 28:18. Meier ("Salvation-History in Matthew," 211 n. 18) notes Vögtle's opinion, and points out that an examination of Matthew's OT citations shows that he was familiar with both Greek versions of Daniel.

63See above, pp. 133-34 n. 21.

64Meier, "Salvation-History," 211 n. 17.

65Jeremias, *Jesus' Promise*, 39. See also Lindars, *NT Apologetic*, 252, 257, 48. He considers Dan 7:13-14 a text of vindication, and as such capable of being considered literally fulfilled in early Christianity and seen as indicating an inaugurated eschatology.

66Jeremias, *NT Theology*, 310.

67Fuller, *Resurrection Narratives*, 209 n. 22. He thinks that this same shift has occurred in Matt 26:64. In Matt 28:18, the enthronement of Jesus as Son of Man is celebrated, presented as a word of the Exalted One. Cf. D. Palmer, "The Resurrection of Jesus and the Mission of the Church," *Reconciliation and Hope* (ed. R. Banks; Grand Rapids: Eerdmans, 1974) 222; W. D. Davies, *The Setting of the Sermon on the Mount* (Cambridge: Cambridge University, 1964) 198; Barth, "Matthew's Understanding," 134 n. 2.

68Hahn, *Mission in the NT*, 66 and 64 n. 3.

69He discounts Luke 22:69 as "clearly editorial," and Acts 7:56 as having no relation to Matt 28:18-20. Moreover, he insists that Matt 11:27 shows that the ἐξουσία idea had "a speci-

fically Christian previous history" and no direct connection
with Dan 7:14 (Hahn, *Mission in the NT*, 66 n. 3). It seems that
assertions have taken the place of supportive arguments here.

[70]Tödt, *Son of Man*, 285 n. 2.  Matt 28:16-20 "refers primarily to that installation which is already effective as exaltation" (290).

[71]Ibid., 291.  Tödt does not think Matt 26:64 is related
to this Lukan interpretation, but rather is orientated on the
parousia and judgment (p. 84).  Nor is Acts 7:56 related to
Luke 22:69 in an underlying pre-Lukan tradition, although it
also speaks of the exalted one as the Son of Man.  And according to Tödt, Matt 13:41 expresses the unique idea of the Son of
Man as Lord of the church on earth, but not as ruler or exalted
one (pp. 72-73).

[72]Ibid., 290-91.

[73]Ibid.  See also Kingsbury, *Matthew*, 112.  Tödt finds
Matt 28:18 unusual in that it proclaims dominion which already
exists at present.  In contrast, he says, dominion is regarded
in Mark 14:62 and Matt 26:64 as an integral part of the parousia to come; in these texts, therefore, the Son of Man concept
is activated.

[74]Tödt, *Son of Man*, 288.  He regards the allusion as "not
improbable."

[75]On the other hand, Hubbard finds that Dan 7:14 has exercised both an indirect (via Matt 11:27) and direct influence on
Matt 28:18.  He remarks, however, that "attempts to draw any
further conclusions appear unwarranted" (*Matthean Redaction*,
82-83).  Both parousia and exaltation (against Tödt) are future
realities.  "Consequently, Jesus cannot be expected to say something like 'I am the Son of man,' nor can he come on the clouds
of heaven (cf. 24:30; 26:64).  Yet, for the present, his possession of universal authority (28:18) enables him to exercise
the functions of the Son of Man as completely as possible" (p.
81).

[76]Tödt, it will be recalled, defines the "concept of exaltation" as the state of exaltation in the lengthening period
before the parousia (*Son of Man*, 285 n. 2).

[77]And, it should be added, like Enoch.

[78]See Fuller, *Foundations*, 198 n. 9.

[79]Ibid., 184.

[80]Fuller, *Resurrection Narratives*, 123.

[81]Fuller notes that the fact that OT assumptions are of
living persons does not seem to have bothered the early Christians (ibid., 213 n. 41).

[82]Contrast Matt 28:9-10 to John 20:17.

[83]Jeremias, "'Ηλ(ε)ίας," *TDNT* 2 (1973) 930-31.  Cf. J. L.
Martyn, "We Have Found Elijah," *Jews, Greeks and Christians*
[ed. R. Hamerton-Kelly and R. Scroggs; Leiden: Brill, 1976]
188-89).

[84]Jeremias, "'Ηλ(ε)ίας," 931 n. 15.  For a discussion of
the Hebrew and Greek of this verse, see below.  P. Marie-Joseph
Stiassny ("Le Prophète Elie dans le Judaisme," *Elie le Prophète*
[2 vols.; Brussels: Desclée de Brouwer, 1956] 2.214) mentions
the legend that Elijah meets souls on the road to paradise and
conducts them to the place reserved for them (*Pirqe R. El.* 15).
Cf. Ginzberg, *Legends of the Jews*, 4.324, and Str-B, 4.766-67.

[85]Cf. *2 Enoch* 22:1-3; *Tg. Ps.-J.* on Gen 5:24.

[86]H. Odeberg, "'Ενώχ," *TDNT* 2 (1973) 557.

[87]This passage will be considered below in Chapter V.

[88]See G. W. E. Nickelsburg, *Resurrection, Immortality and
Eternal Life in Intertestamental Judaism* (Cambridge: Harvard
University, 1972) 60-61.

[89]*2 (Slavonic) Enoch*, sometimes called "The Book of the
Secrets of Enoch," is considered by many scholars to have been
written in the first century A.D., before 70, by a Hellenized
Jew perhaps in Egypt.  Among those who hold this opinion are:
Scholem, Greenfield, Pines, R. H. Charles and Forbes, Hengel,
Borsch.  Those who argue for a Christian origin include
Daniélou, Russell, Vaillant and Milik.  For a summary of views
concerning this work, see H. H. Rowley, *The Relevance of Apoca-
lyptic* (London: Lutterworth, 1963) 111 n. 6, and Albert-Marie
Denis, *Introduction aux Pseudépigraphes Grecs d'Ancien Testament*
(Leiden: Brill, 1970) 29.  Odeberg thinks that Enoch's exalta-
tion in *2 Enoch* is "his institution as the second highest arch-
angel, as a heavenly figure alongside the throne of God"
("'Ενώχ," 558).

[90]Enoch and "those with him" are clad in their higher
garments, but have not yet received the crowns and thrones of
glory reserved until Christ's descent in the last days.

[91]The late work *Sepher haYashar* (eleventh century Spain?)
tells of Enoch taken up to heaven to rule over angels, as he
had ruled over humanity on earth (cf. M. Himmelfarb, "A Report
on Enoch in Rabbinic Literature," *Seminar Papers SBL 1978*, 1.
263-64).  See further, Ginzberg, *Legends of the Jews*, 1.127-30,
for other material in which Enoch is installed as king of the
angels, prince and chief of all heavenly hosts.

[92]Looking only at the OT traditions concerning assumptions,
one might conclude that the assumed figures were inactive,
withdrawn (cf. Hahn, *Titles*, 130).

[93]In this sense, Jeremias is also speaking about exaltation (see above p. 125). Fuller argues that Dan 7:13 can carry
the primitive meaning of assumption, and does so in Mark 14:62;
he considers this text to reflect the view of "non-active waiting in heaven" (*Foundations*, 145-47). As far as I can tell,
Fuller has not fit this assumption view into his schema of the
shifting applications of Daniel 7; does he imply that the use
of Daniel in this sense is prior to its parousia use?

[94]See above, pp. 125-26. This is not to say it is the exact
same concept of exaltation as found in Daniel.

[95]See Kingsbury, *Matthew*, 121. He speaks of the Son of
Man as "ruling" in this text, and considers it related to 28:18
as the titles Son of Man and Son of God are related (p. 120).

[96]Ibid., 114. He lists six Son of Man references which he
thinks deal with the parousia and which Matthew may have added
to his sources: 10:23; 13:41; 16:28; 19:28; 24:30; 25:31.

[97]See below, Chapter VI.

[98]C. H. Giblin remarks on the "fulfillment perspective" in
Matthew's burial-resurrection account, in spite of the fact that
that there are in this section of the Gospel no fulfillment
citations which are characteristic of other portions of Matthew.
He thinks that scriptural allusions have been thoroughly assumed into Jesus' words in this final portion of the Gospel
because Matthew may want us "to understand the fulfillment of
Scripture precisely as mediated by the Son of Man" ("Structural
and Thematic Correlations in the Matthean Burial-Resurrection
Narrative," *NTS* 21 [1974/5] 413-14).

[99]Zumstein, "Matthieu 28:16-20," 19.

CHAPTER IV

DANIEL 7

This chapter is an examination of several aspects of the
OT text which, as the analysis in Chapter III has shown, may
have some connection with Matt 28:16-20.  The focus will be on
some of the obscurities and insights of Daniel 7 that have
generated questions and given rise to different interpretive
traditions in the search for meaning and "deeper meaning" as
the text was contemporized over successive generations.  The
more careful the study at this stage, the more likely the critic is to catch later responses to the text.  Discussion here is
confined to (A) introductory matters; (B) suggested interpretations of the identity of the one like a son of man; (C) further
light cast on this problem by a glance at the traditions upon
which the author is drawing; (D) the form of Daniel 7 (-12) and
(E) the Danielic triad.


A. Introduction

Accepted here is the theory that Dan 2:5 to 6:28 was
originally a collection of Aramaic court tales, perhaps collec-
ted in the diaspora.[1]  They were edited in the time of Antiochus
Epiphanes IV (175-164), when there was still hope for deliverance (chapters 3 and 6), although martyrdom was a possibility
(3:18).[2]  The editor-apocalypticist added chapter 7, using ancient mythical material, and later added the Hebrew chapters
8-12 and the introduction 1:1-2:4.  Chapters 7-12 are modeled
partly on chapters 1-6, but the apocalyptic section shows a
hostility toward the last world kingdom and an emphasis on the
timing of the end which are not present in the court tales.
This could be attributable to a change in situation, rather
than a change in authorship.[3]  The visions of Daniel 7-12 were
composed between the beginning of the persecution in 169 B.C.
and Antiochus' death late in 164; chapters 8-12 were written
after the profanation of the temple in 167.
Chapter 7 is tightly joined both to the chapters that precede and those that follow.  Written in Aramaic like the court

tales, but an apocalyptic vision like those in chapters 8, 9,
10-12, it serves to unite both sections, and is the central
chapter of the book.[4] Of special interest here is the fact
that chapter 7 seems to be a "midrash" on chapter 2 as many
scholars have noted.[5] Both are profound reflections on a theology of history. The schema of four kingdoms is used in both,
and the pattern of dream (vision)-interpretation. In both, the
final kingdom of God replaces all human kingdoms. In chapter 2
a stone "cut out by no human hand" (v. 34)[6] smashes the image
of four metals to pieces which become "like the chaff of the
summer threshing floors; and the wind carried them away, so
that not a trace of them could be found. But the stone that
struck the image became a great mountain and filled the whole
earth" (v. 35). In the interpretation in 2:44-45, the stone is
regarded as the kingdom which God will set up: "it will break
in pieces all these kingdoms and bring them to an end, and it
shall stand forever." No mention is made here of the people to
whom this kingdom belongs; according to Childs, precisely here
the need was felt for midrashic elaboration.[7] In Dan 7:14,
after the destruction of the fourth beast and the removal of
dominion from the other three, an indestructible kingdom is
given to the one like a son of man, who will be served by all
nations. In the interpretation of this vision, the kingdom is
given to (the people of) the holy ones of the Most High (vv.
18, 22, 27). There is an important if strange parallel between
the growth of the mysterious stone into a mountain that occupies all earth space so that all will have to live on it or
around it, and the reception of the kingdom by one figure,
and/or by a whole people.[8] As the mountain is universal in
space, so the kingdom in chapter 7 embraces "all nations."[9]

It has been suggested further that the word stone (אֶבֶן) in
chapter 2 "conceals" the word for son (בֵּן), making the former a
cryptogram for Israel and corresponding to the (one like a) son
(of man) in chapter 7.[10] This assumes that אבנא would be
"deciphered" as חבן, the Son.[11] As Black remarks, the בֶּן-אֶבֶן
wordplay is one of the oldest and best known in the OT.[12] Here
in Daniel, it need not depend on the unpopular theory of a Hebrew substratum for chapter 7;[13] if the author/editor and early

readers were bilingual,[14] the wordplay may have been intended
and caught.  I am certain, however, of no other biblical example
of an author writing in one language supposing his readers will
catch a wordplay in another.  In any case, there are several
indications in later texts that suggest Daniel 2 and 7 were
linked by this means.  It is possible the wordplay was developed
after the texts were written, by those who saw a conceptual connection between the stone that strikes and replaces the image
and then becomes a mountain filling the earth, and the one like
a son of man who replaces the beasts as the possessor of power,
which is worldwide.[15]  It is important to note that the focus of
interest in chapters 2 and 7 is quite different.  While in chapter 7 it is on the eschatological vision of God's final kingdom,
in chapter 2 it is on the wisdom of Daniel and the superior
power of his God to destroy all idols and to reveal all
mysteries.[16]

Chapter 7 is related to the stories of the first part of
the book primarily by the motif of God's power as the basis of
all earthly power: to him "belong wisdom and might.  He changes
times and seasons; he removes kings and sets up kings" (2:20-
21).  "The Most High rules the kingdom of men, and he gives it
to whom he will" (4:17, 25, 32; 5:21).  His intervention inaugurates the final kingdom, which is in essence his: "his kingdom is an everlasting kingdom and his dominion is from generation to generation" (4:3; cf. 4:34 with 7:14, 27).  "His kingdom
will never be destroyed and his dominion shall be to the end"
(6:26).  Sanity is the knowledge that "heaven rules" (4:25-26;
4:34-37).  This motif is maintained in chapters 8-12 only in a
muted, implied fashion.[17]  Instead, attention is occupied by
the details of increasing evil, the battles of angels, the
sufferings of the oppressed (especially the *maskîlîm* who possess
this wisdom) and their survival, and by the calculation of the
length of the time of persecution.

Chapters 7, 8, 10-12 contain four parallel accounts of one
complex of events concerning Antiochus Epiphanes IV.  As such,
these complement each other and should be used to clarify each
other.[18]  These accounts share a common pattern which can be
outlined as follows:

(1) review of history prior to the time of Antiochus
    Epiphanes;
(2) the career of Antiochus, presented as a revolt
    against God and a threat;
(3) intervention of a supernatural power;
(4) the eschatological state of salvation.[19]

Dan 9:24-27 is a similar formulation, but it contains no mythological elements. The statement of what the eschatological
restoration involves in 9:24 is parallel to Dan 7:13-14, 22, 27
and 12:1-3, in that these three passages describe the aftermath
of judgment.[20] The theme of *hybris* and its contrast serves to
relate chapter 7 to chapters 8-12. The one like a son of man
who in chapter 7 is brought into the divine presence is contrasted with the little horn who "magnifies himself" (8:11, 25)
and "exalts himself above every god" (11:36). Antiochus is the
"contemptible person to whom royal power has not been given,"
but who obtains the kingdom "by flatteries" (11:21).[21]

In 12:1-3 we find the promise:

At that time[22] shall arise (יַעֲמֹד) Michael, the great
prince who has charge of your people. And there shall
be a time of trouble, such as never has been since
there was a nation till that time, but at that time
your people shall be delivered (יִמָּלֵט), every one whose
name shall be found written in the book.[23] And many
(רַבִּים) of those who sleep in the dust of the earth
shall awake, some to everlasting life and some to
shame and everlasting contempt.[24] And those who are
wise (הַמַּשְׂכִּלִים) shall shine like the brightness of the
firmament; and those who turn many to righteousness
(מַצְדִּיקֵי הָרַבִּים), like the stars for ever and ever.

The terms מַשְׂכִּלִים and מַצְדִּיקֵי הָרַבִּים are references to the suffering servant song of Deutero-Isaiah, and witness to a pluralization of the figure of the servant in the wise teachers of the
Danielic community.[25] A special group among the people is being
referred to here,[26] those who will be elevated to join the
heavenly host, the angels, and are described in terms elsewhere
used to describe angels.[27] In support of the position that Dan
12:3 is not a simple comparison of the *maskîlîm* to the stars
(angels), but a promise that they will be exalted to the heavenly world and join the angels, similar promises can be cited in
*1 Enoch* 104:2, 6 (the righteous "will shine as the lights of
heaven, and the portals of heaven will be opened" to them; they
"will become companions to the host of heaven") and *Testament of*

*Moses* 10:9 (God "will cause you [Israel] to approach the heaven of the stars / in the place of their habitation, / and you will look from on high / and see your enemies in Gehenna").[28] The *maskîlîm* are saved by being "lifted out of this order into the cosmic sphere of the vision," raised above harsh historical realities.[29]

The exaltation of the *maskîlîm*, like that of the one like a son of man, is not a self-elevation. Basic to the thought of the book is the unstated aphorism that those who raise themselves eventually fall, but those who are raised by God rule permanently in the end. The *hybris* of the human claim to divine status,[30] regarded by the Jews as blasphemy, is set in sharp antithesis here in Daniel to God's vindication of the righteous. This vindication is a transcendence of death, conceived of as a vertical, spatial transition from one sphere of life to another, higher sphere where there is a lasting form of life.[31] Both the death of the righteous and the possibility of human participation in angelic life are central to the thought and imagery of this book. The thrust is toward the moment when there will be one dimension of reality, one stage, one world, when the distinction between heaven and earth will be obliterated.[32] The analysis above has shown that it is likely that the author expected earthly reality to be "raised."[33] But the book of Daniel lacks any clear and detailed description of the kingdom and the means of its coming.[34]

Daniel is a "political manifesto"[35] a statement of active but nonviolent resistance to the Hellenizing policies of Antiochus, written to support the persecuted faithful by providing them with hope in God's intervention (2:34, 44-45; 7:22; 8:25) and the vision of a new order of reality.[36] The writer "sides with those who endure persecution rather than those who take up arms against it."[37] The oppressed are counseled to wait for the end of the "indignation" (11:36), standing firm and taking action (11:32). There is no withdrawal from the political arena, but instead a bold condemnation of the political power of the day, an action that may lead to martyrdom (11:33-35). There is no call to fight; warfare, rather, is left to Michael (10:13, 21; 12:1)[38] and to God. The action of the *maskîlîm* involves

suffering and teaching.  What they make the many understand
(11:33) is that the issue is the question of rightful kingship,[39]
and that the courage to confront and to critique and even to die
can be drawn from the vision of a transformed world order, a new
and legitimate kingdom.[40]  The vision, that is, of transcendence
and of transformation is presented in order to set Israel free
to be righteous, free from the fear of death.[41]

### B. The Identity of the One Like a Son of Man

In the central chapter 7, one like a son of man[42] moves in
or into the heavens as the antithesis of the beasts from the
sea.[43]  His silence and strange passivity balance the bold activity and noise of the little horn.  Brought near the Ancient
of Days[44] with or on the clouds of heaven,[45] he is not specifically said to rise from the earth.  He may be pictured "wafted
in the upper atmosphere with a nimbus of cloud,"[46] moving across
the heavens toward the court suddenly and mysteriously, or he
may be pictured as ascending.[47]  The text is open to either interpretation, and given the vertical imagery discussed above,[48]
it is easy to understand why an upward motion has been read into
the passage by both Jewish and Christian interpreters.[49]  The
one like a son of man does not do battle with the fourth beast,
which is killed without charge, indictment or sentence,[50] nor
does he judge,[51] nor does he leave the heavenly court (contrast
Zech 3:7), nor is he enthroned.[52]  His relationship with the
Ancient of Days is not explicated.[53]  Although other elements of
Daniel's vision (the four great beasts, the fourth beast in particular, the ten horns, the other horn and its "speaking great
things" and its warfare) are interpreted for the seer by an angel, the one like a son of man is not mentioned again in chapter
7 or in the rest of the book of Daniel after his appearance in
7:13-14.[54]  Recent treatment of this figure by Di Lella[55] and
Collins[56] shows that the problem of the identity of the one like
a son of man has not been solved, but that the lines of scholarly disagreement are sharply drawn.  This debate has important
implications not only for the interpretation of Daniel, but also
for the understanding of subsequent reinterpretations of the
Danielic triad.  It is my contention that, while Collins has the

better of the argument in some respects, neither alternative
proposed is satisfactory, precisely because ambiguity is of the
essence of the figure, and the author is straining to express
new theological insights.  Greater attention to the traditions
used and evoked by the author will help in the following section to sketch a compromise position.

The debate concerns whether the one like a son of man
should be regarded as a human or an angelic figure.  Di Lella's
view is that he is a corporate, human symbol for "the holy ones
of the Most High" (vv. 18, 21-22, 25, 27)[57] who are themselves
the persecuted but faithful Israelites suffering under Antiochus
Epiphanes IV.[58]  Collins' view is that he represents primarily
the heavenly host ("the holy ones") and/or its leader, perhaps
Michael, who receives the kingdom on behalf of his angelic army
*and also* on behalf of the righteous of Israel ("the people of
the holy ones of the Most High," v. 27), insofar as they are
associated with the heavenly host in the eschatological era.
Appearance as human is not inconsistent with the angelic aspect,
as elsewhere in the OT and in the pseudepigrapha angelic or
even divine beings are spoken of in this way.[59]

Concern here is with the meaning of the figures in the
chapter as it stands, since the question cannot be solved by
source analysis.[60]  Neither can a solution be found on purely
philological grounds,[61] but only by a careful study of the context in Daniel.  One must not interpret Daniel from his succes-
sors or even from his predecessors.

The major points of Di Lella's argument are the following.
Just as the four beasts (Dan 7:3-7) are not "real" animals, but
symbols of  the pagan kingdoms, so too the one like a son of man
is "not a real individual, celestial or terrestrial, but is only
a symbol of the 'holy ones of the Most High.'"[62]  These must be
primarily the people of Israel, and not angels or Michael together with the heavenly host, because the chapter must have
relevance for its addresses, the disenfranchised Jews; it would
be small comfort to them to be promised that angels will receive dominion.[63]  In addition, the symbols must be unireferential, bearing a one-to-one relationship with the reality being
symbolized.  For reasons of rhetorical consistency, the one like

a son of man cannot symbolize Michael and the angels as well as
the loyal Jews; he must represent "the historically recognizable
Jews who suffered and died rather than apostatize."[64]  The author does use human imagery to depict angels in chapters 8, 9,
10-12, but here the figures are easily recognizable as angels,
in contrast to the one like a son of man and the holy ones of
chapter 7.[65]  On the other hand, statements are made about the
holy ones in verses 21-22 and 25 that indicate that they are
*not* angels: the little horn (Antiochus Epiphanes IV) is said to
wage war against them, and prevail over them, and even have
control over them for three and one-half years.[66]

There are indications also that the one like a son of man
is *not* an angel.  Di Lella draws on the OT use of the term
בֶּן-אָדָם, which he thinks has consciously influenced the author
in his choice of the expression כְּבַר אֱנָשׁ, to argue that the one
like a son of man is one who has been humiliated but visited by
God and raised to glory.  He is granted the eternal kingdom
"despite his lowly estate and past sins."  A sharp contrast is
being drawn between the angelic and human.[67]  Although the one
like a son of man comes with the clouds of heaven, which are
the usual accompaniments of a theophany, Di Lella notes that he
does not come from God or descend as if he had been an angel in
the divine presence.  Rather, he is *brought* before the heavenly
throne; in this way Israel will come into the divine presence
to receive eternal dominion.[68]

According to Di Lella, there is only one indication in the
book of Daniel that the author believes that some of the faithful will share in the splendor of angels.  This is Dan 12:3.
The ones mentioned in 12:2 who will wake to everlasting life,
says Di Lella, are the "holy ones" of chapter 7, the faithful in
in general.  Nothing is said of their elevation to angelic ranks.
But 12:3 singles out a special group among them for special hon-
or, the *maskîlîm* who are the leaders of the anti-Hellenistic
resistance.  This group does not appear in chapter 7.[69]  One
obvious objection to this interpretation is that in 12:10 we
have the prediction, "Many (רַבִּים) will purify themselves and
make themselves white and be refined;[70] but the wicked shall do
wickedly; and none of the wicked shall understand; but those who

are wise (הַמַּשְׂכִּלִים) will understand." Di Lella himself admits
that the latter term seems to refer here not only to the leaders
of the people, but also to the faithful רַבִּים.[71]  If this is so,
there is no reason to insist the exaltation spoken of in 12:3
has no bearing on the destiny of "the people of the holy ones
of the Most High" (7:27) and hence on the identity of the exalted one like a son of man.

     Collins faults Di Lella for following "the all too familiar
tendency of Anglo-Saxon scholarship to ignore the mythic and
symbolic dimensions of apocalyptic language."[72]  The importance
of angelic beings throughout the book of Daniel (e.g., the
battle between Michael and Gabriel and the angelic "princes" of
Greece and Persia in chapter 10) and in other apocalyptic literature shows that the drama played out "on high" is meaningful
and relevant for a human audience.  The interpenetration of the
two dimensions of "reality" cannot be ignored.  The author sees
the angelic hosts in direct confrontation with human enemies,
and the career of Antiochus as a threat to heaven as well as to
the Jews.  As in Judg 5:19-20, the stars fight against Sisera,
and in 1QM 12:7-8 the angelic host mingles with the army of
Israel, in Dan 11:36, Israel's enemy Antiochus comes into conflict with the heavenly host and with God himself, and is even
successful for a time.[73]  Again in 8:10-12, the onslaught of
the little horn passes over from the purely human domain: he
rises up against the host of heaven, casting some of the host
of the stars to the ground, and then proceeds even against the
"Prince of the host."  Here the pattern of the revolt of the
day star, familiar from Isaiah 14, is used to describe Antiochus'
activity.[74]  All of this, says Collins, cannot be reduced to a
purely imaginative description of human arrogance.  The passages
are imaginative, but like all the symbolism of Daniel they are
"grounded in a particular metaphysics and cannot be dismissed as
'mere' metaphor."[75]  The book is concerned with the cosmic dimensions of good and evil, with the vulnerability of the heavens
and the transcendence of human righteousness.  The two-story
universe which is explicit in chapters 10-12 is presupposed in
chapters 7 and 9, and has to be brought to bear on the interpretation of the figures of the "holy ones" and "one like a son of
man" in chapter 7.

Following Ricoeur and others, Collins argues that it is of the essence of a symbol that it have more than one level of reference. "It is extremely doubtful whether a symbol can ever be simply unireferential, at least in literature or in religious language."[76] The beasts from the sea do not symbolize only the four pagan empires or their kings, but give expression to primordial powers of chaos and evil. The descriptions of the Ancient of Days and the one like a son of man indicate that there is an intention to evoke mythological resonances and to "mean" more than is said directly.[77]

Collins reads 7:21-22, 25 as compatible with an understanding of the "holy ones" as angels, in the light of his exegesis of chapter 8 and of the heavenly battle explicitly described in 10:12-11:1 and 12:1. The only serious objection to a purely angelic interpretation of the "holy ones" is the expression in 7:27, "the people of the holy ones of the Most High." This should be understood in connection with 10:21: just as Michael is the prince of Israel, so Israel is the people of the angels.[78] The fact that the people receive the kingdom in 7:27, as the one like a son of man receives it in 7:14 and the holy ones in 7:22, is explained in either of two ways: (1) the heavenly host has already mingled with Israel, so that the people is no longer totally distinct from its patrons, or (2) in 7:27 the people receive the kingdom and the dominion and the greatness of the kingdoms "*under* the whole heaven"; this verse may emphasize the realization of the kingdom on earth. Either interpretation may be correct since the just join the angels after the final judgment (12:3) and share in their kingdom.[79] Dan 7:27, in other words, is seen as a symbolic formulation, equivalent to what Collins calls the assimilation of the *maskîlîm* to the stars in 12:3. The association of the *maskîlîm* with the angels in the eschatological community warrants the eventual use of the term "holy ones" for human beings. In Daniel, according to Collins, this association is future, at the moment of the eschatological victory; the *maskîlîm* and their followers are therefore now called "the people *of* the holy ones."[80]

While it is possible that 12:3 refers to only an élite among the people, it is more likely that the *maskîlîm* who will

be like the stars[81] are all who share in the eschatological
knowledge, who have stood firm and taken action. The interest
of the author is focused on this exaltation. The eschatological kingdom received by the one like a son of man in 7:14 is
the angelic kingdom in which the *maskîlîm* share.[82] The one
like a son of man is the angelic leader of the hosts of heaven
and of those who will become like the angels. This interpretation, then, is strongly based on the structural parallelism
detected within the second portion of the book.[83]

The further identification of the one like a son of man as
Michael is made in order to highlight the correspondence with
the four beasts who are identified as kings in 7:17. If the
one like a son of man is a leader and not merely a symbol for
the collective unit of the holy ones, the natural assumption is
that he is Michael the "prince" who is prominent in chapters
10-12.[84] The triumph of order over chaos coincides with the
elevation of the one like a son of man over the beasts and with
the triumph of Michael and his people over the princes of
Greece and Persia and their peoples.[85] The parallels between
the one like a son of man and Melchizedek in 11Q Melchizedek
(who has also been identified by some as Michael, and who,
Collins claims, is "a heavenly angelic saviour figure") are
striking.[86] Collins thinks if the interpretation of the one
like a son of man as Michael is accepted, then the later development of the "Son of Man" in the Similitudes is more readily
intelligible: in this work he is no longer identified with
Michael but is "at least a heavenly being of an angelic type"
(see *1 Enoch* 46:1). Other remnants of the tradition that understood the Son of Man as the head of the angelic host are
found in NT passages which refer to this figure coming "with
the angels"[87] or to "one like a son of man" as one of a series
of destroying angels.[88]

I agree with Collins on many significant points. The idea
of the interpenetration of the heavenly and earthly dimensions
is basic to the message of this book. The parallelism between
7:13-14 and 12:1-3 is extremely important, and I think the exaltation of the *maskîlîm* and comparison to the brightness of
stars cast light on the identity of the (people of the) holy

ones and of the one like a son of man.[89] The theophanic characteristics of the latter, and the hope expressed in Daniel for
a "kingdom" beyond the reaches of earthly politics and for the
transcendence of death, indicate that the one like a son of man
is not simply a collective human symbol for the righteous of
Israel in their triumph over Antiochus.

There are several reasons, however, why the identification
of the one like a son of man with Michael does not capture the
author's thought. The primary reason is that the one like a
son of man is not a warrior. He appears after the destruction
of the fourth beast, even though--as will be seen--this sequence
may involve a suppression or readjustment of an aspect of the
mythological substratum of this text.[90] Original warrior traits
of this figure seem to have been transferred instead to Michael.
The passivity of the one like a son of man is of central importance to the author, conveying his message that the reward
awaits those who resist nonviolently. Furthermore, the fact
that the figures of the Son of Man and Michael are distinct in
some later reinterpretations can be read as a remnant of recognition that the author of Daniel did not identify them, rather
than as a later bifurcation of one figure. In other reinterpretations, as Collins has seen, the figures merge. This may
be due to a recognition of the parallelisms that do exist between the figures in Daniel. Collins has argued that the one
like a son of man represents or symbolizes the maskîlîm and
their followers in their participation in the angelic life. But
it does not necessarily follow that the one like a son of man
was understood by the author as an angel. A heavenly figure,
that is, a figure exalted in the heavens, is not necessarily
considered an angel. There is a "peculiar and contradictory
duality" about the one like a son of man.[91] This is due in
great part to the fact that the author draws on several traditions in his composition of this scene to express a new belief.
These traditions retain something of their vitality as they are
blended, and are responsible for the ambiguity of the portrait
of the one like a son of man.

In the following section, some of these traditions will be
examined, especially the Canaanite mythological material and

the material drawn from Ezekiel and the Enoch literature. The
impression persists that in Daniel 7 there is found "a distinct
range of mythology which has not been fully integrated into its
present context."[92] It is my contention that aspects of the
process of integration will take centuries, as we are here in
touch with a wellspring of later Trinitarian doctrine.

### C. The Background of Daniel 7

An examination of the background of imagery and thought is
pertinent here only insofar as something of that background may
still be operative in the text, influencing its meaning and its
later reinterpretation. In Daniel 7, the component traditions
are like elements of a living organism.

### 1. Canaanite Mythological Pattern and Motifs

The vision of Daniel 7 may be ultimately but indirectly
derived from the Canaanite myth of the enthronement of Baal by
'El in an assembly of gods, after the defeat of Yamm, sea. The
enthronement is the passing of authority from one god to
another, younger god.[93] In the Ugaritic texts, the will of 'El
is made known in the judgments and decisions of his council on
the sacred mountain. This will is then announced by messengers
or more directly made known to humanity in dreams and visions.[94]
In the last tablet of the Keret Epic, there is a scene of 'El
presiding over his assembly in which he speaks to the gods:
"Sit, my children, on your seats, on your princely thrones."[95]
'El is characteristically pictured as sitting in judgment, with
Baal Haddu at his right hand and seated on his cherub throne
with his right hand raised in blessing.[96] 'El's beard is white[97]
(cf. Dan 7:9), and he is called "god of eternity" or "ancient
god" ('El 'ôlām) and "king, father of years" (malku 'abū
šanima),[98] which calls to mind the Yahweh epithet, "Ancient of
Days."[99] Cross sees 'El as primarily the divine father:

> The one image of 'El that seems to tie all of his myths
> together is that of the patriarch. Unlike the great
> gods who represent the powers behind the phenomena of
> nature, 'El is in the first instance a social god. He
> is the primordial father of gods and men, sometimes
> stern, often compassionate, always wise in judgment.

> While he has taken on royal prerogatives and epithets,
> he stands closer to the patriarchal judge over the
> council of gods.  He is at once father and ruler of
> the family of gods....[100]

Accordingly, one would expect the one coming on the clouds
in Daniel 7 to be called "son of 'El," instead of "one like a
son of man."  This figure does correspond to the storm-god,
Baal, the only member of the Ugaritic divine council who is not
cowed.[101]  He has power but is subordinate to 'El.  The clouds
are commanded by Baal,[102] and he is given the epithet *rkb 'rpt*
("he who rides on clouds") twelve times in the Baal cycle.[103]
It has also been suggested that the term *'nn* in Ugaritic, where
it appears in the phrase [*'il.*] *hd. d'nn* [.], means either
"storm cloud" or "nimbus," related to the Hebrew עָנָן.[104]  Elsewhere, *'nn(m)* applies to messenger boys, frequently called *'nn
'ilm*, "divine messenger boys," and it appears with this meaning
referring to Baal's retinue.  Cross remarks that one might
argue that the divine clouds were messengers of Baal in the
first place, and then *'nn* came to mean "messenger, errand boy":
the clouds that accompany the one like a son of man in Daniel 7
may be related to the idea of Baal's messengers.  This discussion of the Ugaritic material is highly speculative,[105] but it
might in part account for the imagery of the one like a son of
man being "presented" to the Ancient of Days, as well as the
later association of the former with an angelic retinue.  In
any case, it is argued by Collins and others that the depiction
of the Ancient of Days and of the one coming on the clouds is
not derived from the OT, but from mythological traditions represented in the Ugaritic texts.  There is no proof, however, that
derivation from the latter is direct.

There is no extant Canaanite description of the enthronement of Baal by 'El which would provide a direct parallel to
Dan 7:9-14, though there is a text which shows that kingship was
conferred by 'El.[106]  As there is a rivalry between 'El and Baal
in the Ras Shamra texts, it is not clear whether after the victory over Yamm (see below), 'El institutes Baal as world ruler
or is driven out by him.  There may have been an abdication and
the nomination of the younger god as successor, or perhaps an
enthronement to the right of (?) or on the throne of the older

god.[107] In Daniel 7, however, it is clear that there is no
"wresting of power from an old god by a young one,"[108] but the
giving of power by the Ancient of Days to the one like a son of
man, who replaces the beasts, not the Ancient of Days.

In the Ugaritic texts Baal, who stands at 'El's right hand,
is challenged for the kingship by Yamm, sea.[109] 'El abandons
Baal into Yamm's power, but Baal assaults and overcomes Yamm.
In one variant of this myth, Baal is depicted smiting Lotan,
the ancient dragon (the Canaanite ancestor of the biblical
Leviathan), and in another Anat slays Yamm and/or the serpent/
dragon.[110] The conflict with the sea and its monsters, embodi-
ments of the primordial force of chaos, has a central place in
the Canaanite myth, and may be the ultimate source of the image
used by the apocalypticist in Daniel 7 when he describes the
four beasts rising from the churning sea. Although the forces
of the sea and its monsters appear as an isolated motif elsewhere in the Hebrew bible, here they are a part of the mythic
pattern. The sequence of events in the Canaanite myth is as
follows:

(a) the revolt of Yamm, sea, who demands the surrender
    of Baal and kingship over the gods;
(b) the defeat of Yamm by Baal;
(c) the manifestation of Baal's kingship.

In Daniel 7, point (a) is found in the rising of the beasts from
the sea; point (c) appears in the conferral of kingship on the
Baal-like figure. But whereas in the Ugaritic myth Yamm is
overcome by Baal in battle (b), in Daniel 7 there is no battle;
the beasts are destroyed by the judgment of the heavenly council.
The pattern has been broken.[111] Daniel 7 seems to suppress a
tradition in which the one like a son of man slays the fourth
beast, or perhaps we should more cautiously say, the author
chooses not to use (originally Canaanite) battle imagery in
association with the one like a son of man. In addition, the
Canaanite mythological material has been fused with the popular
schema of the four kingdoms, drawn from Daniel 2.[112]

The specific combination of elements found in Daniel 7 and
in Canaanite mythology (God represented as old and white-
haired,[113] and sitting in judgment in an assembly; a being
coming to the heavenly court on or with clouds;[114] the conferring

of a kingdom by the former on the latter; conflict with monsters
from the sea) indicates that Canaanite mythology has influenced
Daniel 7.  The idea of Baal's death and resurrection or resusci-
tation finds an important parallel in Daniel (against Ferch) if
the relationship proposed above between the figure of the one
like a son of man and the (fallen) *maskîlîm* and their followers
(Dan 12:2-3) is seen as significant and the apocalypse regarded
as concerning the "transcendence of death" (but not, of course,
with any cyclical or seasonal meaning).  The mythic pattern and
the elements drawn from it are factors which help to determine
the meaning of the vision and aspects of its later interpretation.  In particular, the element of the clouds, which suggest
a theophany,[115] leads some contemporary critics to argue that
the impression is given in Daniel 7 of two distinct divine beings,[116] or that the author is describing the superhuman majesty of the one like a son of man, his supernatural origin,
divine likeness,[117] or that at least a celestial being in human
form is presented.[118]  Further, as Collins remarks, "Nowhere in
the OT is Yahweh juxtaposed with another heavenly being in the
way the 'one like a son of man' and the 'Ancient of Days' are
juxtaposed here."[119]

It is true that in the OT there is overwhelming evidence
that clouds signal the presence of God: Yahweh descends in the
cloud at Sinai (Exod 34:5), guides in the pillar of cloud (Exod
13:21), is presented in a cloud over the tent of meeting (Exod
40:34), in the temple (1 Kgs 8:10), and upon the mercy seat
(Lev 16:2), is wrapped in clouds (Ps 97:2); his "day" is a day
of clouds (Joel 2:2; cf. Zeph 1:15), and so forth.  It is true
also that nowhere else in the OT (with the possible exception
of Psalm 110) is an exaltation depicted which so lends itself
to being understood as an enthronement (beside God?) in heaven.[120]
The possibility will be explored below, however, that cloud
imagery associated with the translation of Enoch and perhaps of
the prophet Ezekiel, and Elijah's translation in a whirlwind are
evoked in the portrait of the one like a son of man.[121]  In my
opinion, the mythological material has been partly filtered
through such traditions, but this filtering has not totally
diminished the impact of the original mythological substratum.

The mythological components of the vision open Daniel 7:13-14
to the strange di-theistic interpretation.[122]

In view of the enormous time lapse between the Ras Shamra
texts (which belong to the period shortly before Israel's occu-
pation of Palestine, the fourteenth century B.C.) and the book
of Daniel, and in view of the fact that we do not know how the
Canaanite mythology functioned in the interim,[123] I am speaking
here of the indirect influence of mythological traditions, not
of "borrowing."[124] One possible channel of influence in this
case is interest in the figure of Daniel. Ezekiel speaks of a
righteous wise figure of antiquity called Daniel (Ezek 14:14;
28:3), who is probably related to the righteous judge Dnil mentioned in the Aqat legend from Ugarit,[125] and Danel is said to
be Enoch's father-in-law and uncle in *Jub* 4:20. But the evidence is too scanty to provide a clear view of the relationship
of these references, or of the tradition history of the figure
and of works associated with him.[126] In general, there is no
reason to doubt that ancient traditions closely related to
Ugaritic myths were available in the second century B.C. A
strong interest in old materials existed throughout the Hellenistic world, and the use of myths in Jewish apocalyptic should
be seen in this context.[127] Nevertheless, this is no proof that
the author of Daniel knew the Canaanite material directly.

Another possible channel of influence of Canaanite traditions was the pre-exilic Jerusalem cult, and the later adaptation of its ritual patterns and ideology. The OT passages which
most closely resemble Daniel 7 are the royal psalms. These
psalms have been regarded by some as indicative that in the
Jerusalem court the Canaanite myth and ritual pattern was combined with the archaic League tradition of ritual conquest in a
royal festival celebrating the enthronement of the Davidic king
as Yahweh's "son" and perhaps also of Yahweh.[128] A type of
theology is preserved in the psalms that could be called the
national orthodoxy,[129] the high theology of the Jerusalem court,
in which the kingship was rooted in creation mythology and
fixed in eternity.[130] In prophetic literature of exilic and
post-exilic times, hymns were used that were provided by the
defunct royal cult, based on the ritual combat of the divine

king and his cosmic enemies.  Zechariah 9, Hanson argues, is a
paradigm of this prophetic adaptation of the ritual pattern.[131]
Its scenario is the same as that of the vision in Daniel 7: (1)
threat to the divine council; (2) the conflict; (3) the victory;
(4) salvation of the faithful.[132]  The scene in Daniel, then,
may recapitulate the royal liturgy of the Jerusalem cult; this
can be demonstrated according to Hanson by comparison of the
scenario in Daniel 7 with that of "at least a dozen royal
psalms."[133]  Daniel 7 has been called the eschatologizing of
Psalm 2,[134] or of Psalm 110,[135] but literary dependency is not
evident.

The one like a son of man receives the same powers given
to King Nebuchadnezzar in 2:37 and 5:18.  But, given the author's
political stance,[136] there does not seem to be any intention to
depict the enthronement of a human leader like Judas Maccabeus.
Nor is it clear that the text is consciously messianic.[137]  The
author may be aware of the old cultic associations of the pattern he is using, and may intend to evoke these associations.
But he seems to be essentially presenting his belief that the
final and dramatic transition is about to take place, from a
world dominated by a series of brutal tyrannies to a world
ruled by God and by one(s) who would (in contrast to Antiochus
Epiphanes IV) be God's "real" and ultimate manifestation.  The
message concerns the past (the righteous dead) as well as the
future.  Royal mythology and ritual have been revitalized by new
components and the pressure of new needs.  The use of the pattern does not tell us whether (1) the author is thinking of a
royal man ascending to assume rule on a throne imagined to be in
heaven,[138] or (2) that pattern, once used to speak of the earthly king, has now been cut loose and applied to a heavenly being,
the mythological elements returning to their original meanings,[139]
or (3) there is simply the intention to depict a human being
(representative of God's people as the beasts are of their opponents) being given a kingdom.  Later interpreters will see in
Daniel 7:13-14 both a human Davidic messiah and a superhuman
celestial messiah.  The royal psalms may be one channel in which
the influence of Canaanite and other ANE mythology reached the
author of Daniel.  But since the Davidic king is never depicted

in them as riding on the clouds, nor as a celestial being,[140]
it is clear that traditions also reached the author through
other channels.[141]

The Canaanite mythological pattern and motifs used (consciously or unconsciously) by the author of Daniel elucidate to
some extent the apocalyptic triad of Ancient of Days, one like
a son of man and angels (clouds). Examination of this substratum does not solve the problem of the identity of the one
like a son of man. But it does indicate that the author--in
employing this mythological material in a new way to describe
the transfer of power--gave his work a mysterious dimension
that could not be comprehended simply by reference to the theologies of the past, or to the political drama of his time. In
the following section, an analysis of the influence of Ezekiel 1
on Daniel 7 raises again the question of a representation in the
latter text of two "divine" beings.

## 2. Ezekiel 1

It has been argued by several scholars that there is a
clear literary and theological influence of Ezekiel 1 on Daniel
7. The following points summarize the most important similarities between the two texts.

(1) In both visions a flaming throne appears, set on
wheels (Ezek 1:4, 15-16, 21, 26 [cf. 10:2]; Dan 7:9-10). The
wheels in Dan 7:9 no longer seem to have any function, since
the throne is not in motion.[142] Ezekiel does not call the
fiery-wheeled throne a chariot, but it can be imagined to resemble one because of the wheels and the movement; the word
chariot (מרכבה) came to be applied not only to the throne of
this vision but to the vision as a whole.[143]

(2) Clouds figure in both scenes: the throne is accompanied
by a "great cloud" (עָנָן גָּדוֹל) in Ezek 1:4, and the one like a
son of man comes with the clouds of heaven (עִם-עֲנָנֵי שְׁמַיָּא) in Dan
7:13, where it is possible the clouds are conceived as a
chariot.[144]

(3) The representation of the throne as emerging from wind-
driven storm clouds in Ezek 1:4 is reminiscent of the four winds
of heaven stirring the sea, as well as of the clouds transporting the one like a son of man in Dan 7:2, 13.[145]

(4) Four beasts appear in each scene (Ezek 1:5-12; Dan 7: 3-8). The third beast in Dan 7:6, like the *ḥayyoth* of Ezekiel, has four wings and four heads. The appearance and functions of these beings is different in the two texts: in Daniel they represent the earthly kingdoms and forces of chaos, but in Ezekiel they bear the throne.[146]

(5) Both scenes have magnificent displays of fire: Ezekiel's involves the bright cloud flashing fire, gleaming bronze (1:4), burning coals moving like torches, and lightning flashes (vv. 13-14) and a fiery figure on the throne (v. 27). In Daniel, the throne and its wheels are of fire (7:9) and a stream of fire (v. 10) issues forth from the throne; the fourth beast is burnt with fire (v. 11).[147]

(6) Both visions are said to occur in a time of political anguish for Israel, and in their different ways both are expressive of belief in the divine government of the world and of history.[148] The exile is the tragedy behind Ezekiel's first vision. In chapter 10 the sight of the *Kābôd* departing from the temple, and in chapters 43-44 the sight of it returning are a way of showing that Yahweh and Yahweh's relationship with Israel survived the destruction of the sanctuary. The heavenly throne is beyond the reach of Babylonian might.[149] The vision of the Ancient of Days enthroned and of the one like a son of man communicates a similar hope to the readers of Daniel 7: hope in the survival of Israel as a religious entity, and in the imminent end of the time of persecution and profanation. The four *ḥayyoth* with their fourfold faces and wings represent in Ezekiel the four corners of the earth and the world-embracing sovereignty of the one whose throne they are carrying.[150] The throne itself, moved by the power of the Spirit which streams through the *ḥayyoth* (Ezek 1:20-21), is not bound to any one location. In Daniel, the one on the heavenly throne is the source of the power of historical kingdoms; he confers on the one like a son of man the final power over all nations.

(7) Both visionaries are themselves addressed as "son of man": Ezekiel ninety-three times, and Daniel once in Dan 8:17, the only instance outside Ezekiel in which a seer is so addressed. The term may be one of honor, although this is not the most common view, and Bowman (following Kimchi [1160-1235 A.D.]) suggests

that it signifies likeness to the one seen in the vision.[151]
The one who sees the man above is himself called son of man.[152]
This is, however, only one of several ways in which Daniel is
addressed, and there is no indication that the phrase has special significance, linking him with the figure of the vision.[153]

(8) Finally, and most importantly, in both passages a being
is sitting on or above the throne. In Ezek 1:26 it is "a likeness as it were of a human form" (דְּמוּת כְּמַרְאֵה אָדָם; LXX: ὁμοίωμα
ὡς εἶδος ἀνθρώπου); in Dan 7:9 it is "one that was ancient of
days," presumably also in human form, since his clothing and
hair are described. A connection has also been seen between the
being on the throne in Ezekiel and the one like a son of man in
Dan 7:13.[154] The clouds on or with which the latter figure
comes may have been conceived as a moving chariot, or he may have
have been thought of as coming to be enthroned. The transfer
of power to him and the elements of an enthronement form in
this text contribute to this impression. Further, Ezek 1:26
seems to be the counterpart to Gen 1:26, where 'Adam is said to
be made in the image and likeness (דְּמוּת) of 'Elohim.[155] The
exaltation of the one like a son of man is regarded by some
critics as restoring the dominion of 'Adam.[156]

Feuillet sees both the one like a son of man and the "likeness as it were of a human form" as visible manifestations of
the invisible God, in the figure of a human being.[157] Both, he
says, are celestial beings appearing in human form; both, that
is, belong to the category of the divine and are a sort of incarnation of the divine glory.[158] Both are related to the profanation and purification of the temple, and the return of the
glory to it.[159] The difference is that in Daniel 7 we have an
eschatological representation of Ezekiel's vision. And Feuillet
says that, whereas in Ezekiel the *Kābôd* in human form is presumably God,[160] in Daniel the one like a son of man is a separate "transcendental" being.[161] This leads Black to the conclusion that the author of Daniel 7 knows of two divinities, the
Ancient of Days and the one like a son of man. This text, he
argues, "represents a highly significant development of Ezekiel 1
into a theology which seems virtually ditheistic."[162] The second "god" is not a transcendental (i.e., other-worldly) Messiah,[163]

but rather "the celestial Israel," the remnant of the *maskîlîm*
(Dan 12:3). The author, says Black, is contemplating the
apotheosis of Israel in the endtime; the vision should not be
interpreted apart from the interpretation given to the seer in
7:18, 22, 27.[164]

The analyses of Feuillet and Black are not satisfactory
explanations of the mythological substratum of Daniel 7, as
they do not account for the particular imagery of Dan 7:9-14.
Nor do these scholars convincingly elucidate the relationship
that one may see between Daniel 7 and Ezekiel 1. It is clear,
however, that some strong relationship does exist. It is possible that the author understood Ezekiel 1 as somehow giving
him license to portray a "celestial human being," who in Black's
term may even represent the "apotheosis" of the *maskîlîm* and
their followers. But in order to ascertain if and how this may
be the case, we must investigate two further questions: (1) what
was the nature of Israelite understanding of the divine council
and of human participation in that council? (2) Is it possible
that there was an indirect influence of Ezekiel 1 on Daniel 7,
via Enoch traditions? The answers to both of these questions
are ultimately pertinent to our investigation of the Matthean
triadic phrase: the first because it may enable us to understand
how the Son can be joined with the Father and the Holy Spirit in
a phrase which seems to some to imply the divinity of all three;
the second because the background of Enoch speculation is a component part of the Danielic theme of transcendence of death,
that theme which will appear in the Matthean resurrection
narrative.

3. The Divine Council and Human Participation in the Council

The concept of a heavenly council--of "an assembly of divine beings sitting together with Yahweh, discussing and making
decisions concerning affairs of heaven and earth"[165]--has a
long history of use by OT writers. Cross and others believe
that some of the imagery and poetic language concerning the
council of Yahweh originated in the assembly of the gods common
to the mythological *Weltbild* of Mesopotamia and Canaan.[166] The
concept, however, may not have been simply borrowed by Israel.

Its antiquity in the ANE, and the pervasiveness of the ideas
that (a) it was inconceivable for any person, human or divine,
to exist fully in isolation, without a "household,"[167] and (b)
that divine society and government were organized along the
lines of human society, may indicate that it was an almost inevitable concept, rising independently in many places. But the
terminology used in the OT for the council makes it probable
that Israel was influenced by Canaan in the way in which it expressed this concept.[168] That terminology, as a survey of some
of the texts shows,[169] had very little precision. Israel's
understanding of the council is difficult to grasp. It seems
that we can say neither that the conception of the council of
Yahweh was a mere poetic image or literary survival,[170] nor
that it was a vital aspect of early Israelite belief that grew
fainter with progressive demythologization and movement toward
monotheism. It was an element of the living pattern of Israelite
faith, perhaps even a central element, and most scholars argue
that the danger of this originally polytheistic idea-complex was
minimized by Israelite adaptations.[171] These adaptations included stress on the incomparability of Yahweh (see Ps 89:7).[172]
The other beings, as far as our texts indicate, were not worshipped as gods but conceived as of lesser rank and power.[173]
They did not impinge on or impair the exclusive covenant claim
of Yahweh on Israel, but actually by their services supported
that claim. In general, there is in the OT a striking lack of
mythological detail and elaboration, such as descriptions of
banquets or battles of the gods of the council, or of special
functions assigned to individualized subordinate divine beings,
or of the father-son relationship.[174] There is no mention of
interrelationship among the members of the council, no loves or
hates. The only relationship is between it as a body and Yahweh
as its head; "the council exists to praise Yahweh, to fear him,
and to submit to his rule and judgment and to do his will."[175]
The members are for the most part "colorless, secondary supernatural creatures"[176] who are not named, have no distinct characteristics or histories and never really come to life. The
vagueness of their descriptions suggests that they are delib-
erately minimized and generalized.[177]

The description of the council in Daniel 7, however, does
not conform to many of these characteristics.  The supreme figure of the Ancient of Days does not function here to drain off
attention or significance from the other members.  He appears
with his entourage (7:10) but does not seem to be the only or
supreme judge.[178]  To the council comes one like a son of man.
He comes with the clouds of heaven dramatically, as though this
is an identifying characteristic.  Although he is not described
in further detail, he is far from being colorless.  He is related in the interpretation in later verses, by identification
or representation, to the holy ones who may be members of the
council.[179]  To him is given power that belongs to the Ancient
of Days, the power to rule all peoples, nations and languages
forever (7:14).  As he is not said to depart, it is *possible*
that he is considered to be (or to have become) a member of the
council.[180]  This more elaborate characterization and "person-
alization" may be due in part to the influence of originally
Canaanite materials.  Do we have here simply a bold use of old
mythology in the description of the one like a son of man as a
"colorful" angelic member of the council[181] (as Collins and
others have suggested), or is the concept of the heavenly council revolutionized in more startling fashion, by the possible
integration of a human (or once human) being into its midst?

Human participation in the heavenly council is referred to
in several OT and intertestamental texts.  These distinctions
should be kept in mind in the following discussion: (a) some
texts refer to a human being who is taken up into heaven to
witness or to participate in the assembly and then to return to
earth; (b) others refer to a human being transferred to the
heavenly realm, becoming in some sense a member of the assembly;
(c) others refer to a human being taken into heaven and transformed into or made like a celestial, immortal being.  Prophets
claim to have seen the enthroned Yahweh with his entourage
(Isaiah 6; Ezekiel 1; 10), they claim to have heard him in
council deciding destinies (1 Kgs 22:19-23), and they claim
they are commissioned to relay what they have heard (Isaiah
40).[182]  Further, there are prophets who understand themselves
as having participated in the decisions and announcements of

the council, as "standing" (עמד) in that council,[183] becoming
in effect a מלאך or מבשר.[184] In the post-exilic text Zech 3:
1-10, the participation of the prophet is even more direct. His
function there is not only that of a witness or spectator, with
the duty of communicating what he has witnessed, but he joins
in, and his intrusion "brings the whole action to its point of
climax."[185] Furthermore, the high priest Joshua, standing in
the council and purified, is promised rule over God's house and
charge of his courts and "the right of access among those who
are standing here" (3:7) if he obeys. "Right of access"
(מַהְלְכִים) indicates that the high priest is to have free entry
and passage among those who serve in the heavenly court--that
is, along with the angels. He is given a right and status perhaps even beyond that enjoyed by the prophets: access to Yahweh's presence in the council. This is a priestly adaptation
of a prophetic pattern.[186] A Qumran document of slightly later
date than Daniel, *The Testament of 'Amram*, strongly underlines
the assimilation of priests to angels: according to Milik in
the discourse of 'Amram to Aaron we read clearly, "And you will
be called an angel of God" (ומלאך אל תתקרה).[187]

Do any of the pre-Danielic texts concerning human participation in the divine council imply human transformation? The
prophets as divinely commissioned interpreters speak at times
as though there is virtual identification of the human with the
divine. But there is never, according to most critics, loss of
consciousness of the profound difference between God and humanity, no obscuring of the gulf between the human and the divine.
In OT prophecy in general, humanity is flesh and mortal, God is
spirit, and the "sons of God" are conceived as sharing something
of the spiritual nature of God. As participants in the council,
however, prophets seem to have been conscious of an "adoptive
kinship," a sharing of "corporate personality" (in H. W. Robinson's phrase) with the members of the council and with Yahweh.[188]
But nowhere in the OT is a prophet identified as one of the sons
of God or holy ones, or accorded real membership in the divine
council. The prophet remains mortal and is not divinized.[189]
The presence of the prophet in the divine council is temporary:
"he finds himself in the divine assembly, but he does not belong

there....His access to the divine realm is not unqualified
privilege but is bound to the task of relating that experience
to the normal realm of men."[190]  This may also be believed to
be the case with the high priest Joshua, and again no explicit
transformation or divinization is described.[191]

In Daniel 12:2-3 the *maskîlîm* are promised eternal life,
transformation (in that they will be made to "shine like the
brightness of the firmament" and "like the stars,") and, perhaps, exaltation to the heavenly world.[192]  Does the figure of
the one like a son of man bear any specific relationship to that
promise?  Is he meant to represent, that is, not an angelic
figure but a human figure who has been given special access and
status in the heavenly world?  In the biblical accounts of the
translations of Elijah and Enoch, and in the extra-biblical
traditions associated with them, there are indications of the
belief that a human being can join the company of the *'elohim*.
This, says Yehezkel Kaufmann, is "the limit of biblical apotheosis."[193]  It is my contention that these accounts and traditions
concerning Elijah and Enoch may have influenced Daniel's portrait of the one like a son of man, and served as channel and
framework for the incorporation of originally Canaanite mythological materials.  It will be seen later that these traditions
and materials acquire new life in early CHristian speculation.

By the time of the writing of the book of Daniel, Enoch
and Elijah were thought of by some as having acquired permanent
access to the heavenly realm.  By by-passing or passing through
death, they gained an immortality that placed them in the world
of the council and gave them functions in that world.[194]
Elijah's translation "in a whirlwind to the heavens" (בַּסְעָרָה
הַשָּׁמָיִם, 2 Kgs 2:1, 11)[195] provides the grounds for speculation
concerning him as a heavenly figure available to help the human
race and chosen for an eschatological role.  The description of
the assumption[196] merits our attention, since it may be related
to Baal motifs, as is the coming of the one like a son of man
on the clouds.  It has been suggested that the wonder tales
about Elijah and Elisha were important weapons used by the nar-
rator of the cycles to expose the incompetence of Baal, under-
mining popular beliefs concerning him, and to show the superiority of Yahweh and his adherents.  This is clear in 1 Kings 18,

a chapter which is directly concerned with Yahweh *versus* Baal,
and it may be operative at some level in the formation of 2
Kings 2.  (All the Elijah-Elisha narratives, however, should
not be read uncritically as originating under the same polemical impulse.)  Elijah's assumption illustrates the belief that
only Yahweh rules the clouds, and only his prophet can ascend.
In contrast, though Baal is called "he that mounts the clouds,"
he dies and his body lies on the ground: "We came upon Baal
prostrate on the earth" (*mǵny lb'l npl larṣ*).[197]  In place of
cloud imagery, there is the imagery of the whirlwind and "a
chariot of fire and horses of fire" in 2 Kings 2.[198]  Bronner
points out the connections of Baal with fire and lightning as
well as with storm, wind and rain,[199] and concludes that it is
Yahweh's control of these elements, not Baal's, that is the
underlying theme of the translation story.  While this analysis
may not capture all of the mythological resonances of the OT
text,[200] it indicates similarity between the ascending Elijah
and the one like a son of man in their Baal associations, and
perhaps offers a clue to how originally Baal imagery is being
used by the author of Daniel 7.  The chariot and horses of fire
that take Elijah represent the heavenly army,[201] angelic warriors.  As Elijah is borne into the heavens by the chariot and
horses of the angelic host, so the one like a son of man is
borne on (or comes with) the clouds of heaven (which may represent his angelic host or messengers),[202] and is brought into
the divine presence by angels.

    Was Elijah's translation believed to involve a transforma-
tion and membership in the heavenly world?  Several pre-Danielic
texts indicate that this is so.  Martyn puts it cautiously:
"Since he was dramatically taken up into heaven, he was considered to be alive, in heaven with the (other?) angels, and
available, either by being equidistant, so to speak, from every
generation, or by being on the verge of coming at the end-time
...."[203]  This idea is first suggested in Mal 4:5, where Elijah
is identified as the מַלְאַךְ הַבְּרִית, the precursor of Yahweh mentioned in 3:1.  Here his role at the end is to mitigate the
wrath of Yahweh by turning the hearts of fathers toward their
children and of children toward their fathers (4:6).  Sir 48:10

expands this tradition, speaking of Elijah standing "ready,"
evidently reserved in heaven, and of his task to restore the
tribes of Jacob (cf. Isa 49:5-6).[204]   The difficult verse Sir
48:11 may imply the belief that Elijah appears to the pious before they die, or his appearance at the end.[205]   The Greek is
clearly an expansion,[206] its third line expressing belief that
Elijah's translation was not unique, but a fate that could be
shared by others.[207]   The Animal Apocalypse, written around
the time of the book of Daniel, presents Elijah, after the
division of the Kingdom, as the one prophet (sheep) who was
saved and not murdered by the other erring sheep: "and they
sought to slay it, but the Lord of the sheep saved it from the
sheep and brought it up to me (Enoch), and caused it to dwell
there (1 Enoch 90:52; in a tower raised above the earth, cf.
87:4).[208]   If Elijah is the ram of 1 Enoch 90:31,[209] who appears with "those three (angels) who were clothed in white" and
seizes Enoch by the hand, he is thought to be present at the
time of the last judgment (v. 31), the resurrection of the
righteous dead (v. 33)[210] and the gathering of all the dispersed
into the "new house" of God (vv. 34-36).  While we have no pre-
Danielic text which refers explicitly to the transformation of
Elijah into an angel, it is clear that he was thought of by
some as alive in the heavenly world.[211]

    Moreover, it seems that Elijah had become a focus of at-
tention during the years of Seleucid persecution, his translation a sign of deliverance.  It is easy to understand that the
prophet who fought idolatry and syncretism could become a symbol
for the freedom fighter or resister of Maccabean times: "Elijah,
because of his great zeal for the law, was taken up into heaven"
(1 Macc 2:58).  This figure (with its Baal associations) may
have served as a model (though not the only model) for the
Danielic one like a son of man.

    Features of the figure of Enoch have also contributed to
Daniel 7.  The material concerning him in Genesis and Sirach is
only the tip of an iceberg.  The cryptic statement in Gen 5:24
reads simply: "Enoch walked with God, and he was not, for God took
him" (נַיִּתְהַלֵּךְ חֲנוֹךְ אֶת-הָאֱלֹהִים וְאֵינֶנּוּ כִּי-לָקַח אֹתוֹ אֱלֹהִים).   Enoch is
the seventh after Adam, and his unusually short lifespan (365

years; Gen 5:23) is obviously related to the solar year. While
"he was not" could possibly mean "he died,"[212] it seems that
the *whole* of verse 24, and not just this phrase, is a substitute for "and he died" (וַיָּמֹת), which is the last word spoken
about the other descendants of Adam in this genealogy. "He was
not" means he was not *with* the inhabitants of the earth. "Walking with God" in 5:22 as in 6:9 (concerning Noah), means a
closeness to God in righteousness (cf. *Jub.* 10:17), a living
communion which the P writer believed possible only for these
two members of the antedeluvian community.[213] Perhaps there is
a hint here as well of mystical knowledge and familiarity with
divine secrets.[214] In verse 24, however, the phrase seems to
mean his removal from the world, and is in parallelism with the
phrase, "God took him."[215] The verb לָקַח with God as the subject
and a human being as the object is used in 2 Kgs 2:10 for the
translation of Elijah (cf. Ps 49:16; 73:24). Some commentators,
both ancient and modern, have understood Gen 5:24 to mean that
Enoch did die; he was simply a good man who died young, or died
suddenly, but did not descend into Sheol.[216] If this is correct, the intention of the Torah, as Cassuto puts it,[217] was to
convey that Enoch's death was not like the death of other people,
since God redeemed him from the power of Sheol. Other commentators have read this verse as a statement that Enoch did *not*
die, but was instead translated or entered living into immortality.[218] *Fragmentary Targum* and *Targum Neofiti I* on Gen 5:24
express ignorance of Enoch's end.[219]

Whatever the precise nature of the Priestly writer's conception of the end of Enoch, the piling up of three phrases in
verse 24 indicates clearly that the writer saw a difference between the figure of Enoch and those of the other demythologized
ancestors. They "were only ordinary mortals, not gods, or demi-
gods, or even men transformed into divinities, and they had no
mythological associations whatsoever. They were born, they be-
got sons and daughters, and in the end they died; that is all."[220]
But by surrounding the bleak "he was not" (אֵינֶנּוּ) with the two
other phrases (and thus completely changing its ordinary meaning)[221] the author is saying, with restraint and forcefulness,
that Enoch's end was movement into the presence of God.

Grelot, working from an investigation of Mesopotamian traditions and from materials concerning Enoch in the apocrypha and
pseudepigrapha, finds the statements in Genesis 5 loaded with
mythological significance.[222]  Enoch, he thinks, is presented as
the prototype of perfection by his age and his rank after Adam.[223]
According to Grelot, the Priestly writer meant to evoke the tradition that Enoch was transferred to the garden of God, and entered into an eternal life shared with the angels.  By him and by
his escape from death, the original design of God for humanity
was realized, and Enoch was set in contrast to the tragic end of
others in the pre-flood world.  Grelot reads the "taking" of
Enoch as a message of hope for those who walk with God, just as
the Deluge is a threat addressed to sinners.  The Priestly author's insight in Genesis, therefore, is profoundly different
from that of the Mesopotamian stories, where death as the ines-
capable human fact is emphasized.[224]  Grelot also sees the P
account of Enoch as influenced by Ezekiel's vision of a restored
paradise for a purified people, and by the reminiscence of Elijah
and his translation.  Enoch is, in this view, the prototype of
Israelite prophets.[225]  The author of Sirach has Elijah in mind
as he writes that Enoch "also" was taken (49:14b: וגם הוא נלקח
פנים).[226]

Whether we agree with Grelot that the apocrypha and
pseudepigrapha basically give us fuller accounts of some ancient
traditions contained *in nuce* in the verses in Genesis 5, or
whether we take the more cautious view that it is difficult to
know the character and content of the traditions available to
the Priestly writer,[227] it is clear that related mythological
elements existed in the oral tradition, surfacing in later
pseudepigrapha, medieval legends and mystical literature.  (Of
course, not everything that appears in later material belongs
to this category.)  The P narrative indicates the existence of
a fuller narrative or narratives concerning the figure of Enoch,
and the stark mysteriousness of the Torah's mention of him probably also occasioned the creation of new ideas and stories.  The
repetition of וַיִּתְהַלֵּךְ (Gen 5:22, 24) is especially significant.
Two types of Enoch journeys to the heavens are recounted in
*Jubilees* and the Enoch literature: visionary experiences during
his lifetime, and final ascent.  The repetition of the verb in

Genesis may summarize these two types, and probably also
suggested further elaboration.

Genesis 5 and Sirach tell us nothing explicitly about
Enoch's supramundane existence. Nothing, that is, except that
he was thought of as somehow with God, an intimate of God in
and beyond his earthly life span. These brief notations in
themselves--even if we were unaware of the vast realm of Enoch
literature not included in our canon--suggest that by breaking
or stretching the idea of normal human existence and destiny,
Enoch traditions may have helped create in Maccabean times the
possibility of conceiving of a figure at once human and superhuman, the figure of a human being present as quasi-angelic or
immortal in the heavenly realm. They suggest, in other words,
that the Enoch tradition *may have* influenced the portrait of
the one like a son of man in Daniel 7.

A glance at some of the extra-canonical Enoch materials
strengthens this suggestion. In traditions which cannot with
certainty be dated before the composition of Daniel (but are
pre-NT) we find reference to the heavenly dwelling place of
Enoch,[228] his association with the angels,[229] his functions in
the heavenly realm.[230] There is a "steady line of development"
in Enoch speculation,[231] and influence exerted by extraneous
traditions and by polemical situations. But these traditions
can be seen as tapping a potential of the most ancient Israelite
Enoch material: the potential for conceptualizing a human figure
as angelic-human or at once quasi-divine and human. It can be
argued that 11Q Melchizedek presents a human (or once human)
being as a heavenly being. Melchizedek is four times called
*'elohim* in this document, is spoken of as judge in the divine
council, a heavenly deliverer, protector of the faithful and
chief of the heavenly host.[232]

The author of Daniel struggled with the problem of the
fate of the righteous dead, the Maccabean martyrs. His aim was
to inspire the living resisters with an image of their eventual
and eternal triumph. It can be speculated that Enoch who
"walked with God," the one for whom death was not the last word,
would be a figure to whom the mind and imagination of the author
would naturally turn. Traditions about Enoch, "a sign of knowledge to all generations" (Sir 44:16, Hebrew), may have been kept

alive and developed in the circles of *maskîlîm* to which the
author belonged.  In the following section it will be argued
that *1 Enoch* 14 is one such tradition, and that it has been
drawn upon in the creation of Daniel 7.

## 4.  *1 Enoch*  14

It has long been suggested that there is a close literary
relationship between Daniel 7 and *1 Enoch* 14, both texts which
were originally in Aramaic.  Three theories have been offered
as an explanation of the common details of description, phraseology and general picture: (a) *1 Enoch* 14 was the inspiration
of Daniel 7;[233] (b) *1 Enoch* 14 is an imitation of Daniel 7;[234]
(c) the two texts are independent of one another[235] but may depend on a common source.[236]  In my judgment, the first theory
has the most to recommend it.

*1 Enoch* 14 is the full account of a dream-vision, described
in 12:1 as Enoch's being "hidden" (Ethiopic) or "taken" into
obscurity (Greek).  It is told as a mystical ascent to the heavens during Enoch's lifetime; he falls asleep and dreams it by
the waters of Dan, in the land of Dan to the southwest of
Hermon (13:7).[237]  The reason for the ascent is bizarre: the
evil Watchers, condemned by the Most High (10:4-16) and informed
of the sentence upon them (12:4-13:3), ask Enoch to draw up a
petition for them for forgiveness, and to read it in the presence of the Lord of heaven (13:4).  Enoch, then, ascends for
those who cannot ascend.  He receives a commission (cf. 15:1-2):
the "vision of the wrath of chastisement" (4QEn[c] I vi 5) he sees
is to be told to the Watchers, and a reprimand is to be delivered
to them.  Their petition is refused, and it is decreed that they
will never ascend to heaven, but will be bound for all eternity
and will see the destruction of their offspring, the Giants
(14:4-7; 15:3-16:4).

The ascent itself is described as follows in 4QEn[c] I vi 8
to vii 2 (= *1 Enoch* 14:8-20), according to Milik's reconstruction:[238]

> 8.  [And to me in the vision it thus appeared.  Behold,
> clouds in the vision were calling me, and cloud-mists]
> to me were shouting, and lightning-flashes and thunders
> [were hastening me up and...me, and winds in the vision
> made me to fly, and took me] upwards and brought me up
> and made me enter into [heaven.  9. And I entered it

until I drew near to the walls of a building built with
hail stones] and tongues of fire were surrounding them
all around, [and they began to fill me with fear and
to...me.  10. And I entered among those tongues of fire,
until] I drew near to a great house [built with hailstones; and the walls of this house were like stone
slabs, and all of them were (made) of snow, and the]
floor [was built] of snow.  [11. And the ceiling was
like lightning-flashes and like thunder; and among
them fiery cherubim, and their heaven was of water.
12. And a burning fire surrounded] all their walls
[all around them, and the gates were of burning fire.
13. And I entered into that house which was hot like
fire, and cold as] snow; and [there was] no [pleasure
of life in it; and behold, fear covered me and trembling seized me.  14. And I was shaken and] trembling
and I fell [on my face; and it was shown to me in my
vision.  15. And behold I saw another door which opened
before me, and another house which] was greater than
this, and all of it [was built with tongues of fire.
16. And all of it far surpassed (the other) in splendour
and glory and majesty that] I am unable to describe to
you [its splendour and majesty.  17. And its floor was
of fire and its ceiling was of burning fire.  18. And
it was shown to me and I saw in it a lofty throne, and
its appearance] [was like crystal-glass, and its wheels
were like the disc of the shining sun, and its sides]
were cherubim.  19. [And from beneath the throne came
forth] streams (שבלין) of [fire, and I could not look.
20. Great Majesty sat upon this throne, and His raiment
was brighter than the sun and whiter] than much snow....

This passage continues in the Ethiopic and Greek (14:21-15:2):

None of the angels could enter and could behold His
face by reason of the magnificence and glory, and no
flesh could behold Him.  22. The flaming fire was round
about Him, and a great fire stood before Him, and none
around could draw near to Him: ten thousand times ten
thousand (stood) before Him, yet he needed no counsellor.  23. And the most holy ones[239] who were near to
Him did not leave by night nor depart from Him.  24.
24. And until then I had been prostrate on my face,
trembling: and the Lord called me with His own mouth
and said to me: 'Come hither, Enoch, and hear my word.'
25. And one of the holy ones came to me[240] and he made
me rise up and approach the door: and I bowed my face
downwards.  15:1. And He answered and said to me,[241]
and I heard His voice: 'Fear not, Enoch, you righteous
man and scribe of righteousness; approach hither and
hear my voice.  2. And go, say to the Watchers of heav-
en, who have sent you to intercede for them: 'You should
intercede for men, and not men for you.[242]

The similarities between this passage and Daniel 7 are
striking.  Both are descriptions of a human (or humanlike) being borne aloft by clouds into the divine presence.  God is

depicted sitting on a throne which has wheels (Dan 7:9; *1 Enoch*
14:18) and from which issues stream(s) of fire (Dan 7:10;
*1 Enoch* 14:19).[243]  In both texts the dynamic whirling movement
of the throne described in Ezekiel 1 is stilled, and the throne
is set in place in heaven.  Ten thousand times ten thousand
stand before God (Dan 7:10; *1 Enoch* 14:22).[244]  The clothing of
the one on the throne is spoken of as whiter than (or as white
as) snow (Dan 7:9; *1 Enoch* 14:20).  In addition, Dan 7:13 reads:
"I saw in the night *visions*, and *behold*, there came with the
*clouds* of heaven one like a son of man."  *1 Enoch* 14:8 reads:
"*Behold*, in the *vision clouds* invited me."[245]  The unique role
of Enoch is emphasized: he draws near where none of the angels
and no flesh could enter (14:21-22).[246]  Milik calls him "a
hero who is at the same time human and divine."[247]  As Charles
emphasizes, however, Enoch *as a man* writes the petition for the
fallen Watchers (13:6), receives here a dream-vision and not a
final translation, speaks with a tongue of flesh (14:2), and is
terrified like a mortal at the presence of God (14:24).[248]
Both Daniel 7 and *1 Enoch* 14 concern an end to the dominion of
evil, and judgment passed on evil forces (Dan 7:10, 22, 26;
*1 Enoch* 14:4).[249]  Finally, both texts seem to be drawing on
the same complex of OT passages: Deut 33:2 and Ps 68:17 (the
ten thousands); Ezekiel 1 (the throne, fire display, wheels);
Isaiah 6 (God seated on the throne); 1 Kings 22 and Isaiah 6
(the court, judgment theme).

     The theory that Daniel 7 was in part inspired by *1 Enoch* 14
depends on a pre-Maccabean or early Maccabean date for the
Enochian passage.  Chapters 12-16 of *1 Enoch* are from the Book
of Watchers (chapters 1-36).  Milik has presented a convincing
argument for dating the composition of this book around 250 B.C.
An earlier written source has been incorporated into it.[250]  In
addition, the major arguments for regarding *1 Enoch* 14 as earlier than Daniel 7 are the following.  (1) Chapters 1-36 of
*1 Enoch* contain no reference to the persecution of Antiochus
Epiphanes IV and no sharply focused eschatological interest
predominating.  Instead, we find condemnation of the fallen
Watchers, ruminations on Wisdom themes (cf. 2:1-9), and descriptions of what Glasson calls "leisurely journeys to various parts
of the universe, the animals found there, precious stones,

etc."[251]  Daniel 7 illustrates, according to Stone, a "shift of
emphasis" from the broad speculative interests of the older
work to the magnified eschatological interest which came about
under the impact of the Maccabean revolt.  (2) It is easier to
understand the author of Daniel borrowing from the author of
*1 Enoch* 14, than vice versa.  The former is using the description of Enoch's adventures into unknown regions and his ascent
into the heavens in order to describe in some detail the events
of the immediate future.[252]  The ascending figure becomes an
apocalyptic symbol for the coming vindication and triumph of the
holy ones of the Most High.[253]  Why this should be so has been
suggested above: Enoch, as one who transcended death, even in
his lifetime "walking with God," can be understood as symbolic
of the life of the nation which--transformed--will survive the
persecution of Antiochus Epiphanes IV and even the martyrdom
that has been inflicted.[254]  This is not to say that the one
like a son of man in Daniel 7 is completely identified with or
exhausted by the figure of Enoch.  That figure is only one contributing factor, and not the ultimate origin, of the one like
a son of man.  The author of Daniel 7 has used *1 Enoch* 14, and
Enoch is an original[255] of the one like a son of man who comes
to God in Daniel 7.  Rowley speaks of the "improbable sequence"
of the individual figure in *1 Enoch* 14 becoming the collective
figure in Daniel 7, and then an individual figure again in the
Similitudes.[256]  But the distinction between individual and
corporate is fluid, and is not clearly made in the vision or in
the interpretation of Daniel 7.  It does not seem at all improbable that traits of individual figures used in the composition of Daniel 7 could be recognized and re-emphasized in later
interpretations.[257]

There are several important elements in Daniel 7 other
than those already mentioned that cannot be explained as having
been derived from *1 Enoch* 14.  These include: (a) the notion of
God as old, as "Ancient of Days"; (b) the imagery of the four
beasts and the primal sea; (c) the idea of a transfer of royal
power, the humanlike figure's reception from God of the rule of
an eternal kingdom; (d) the emphasis on the clouds.[258]  As has
been seen in the discussion of the Canaanite hypothesis, it is
precisely these elements which have been explained as related

to the Canaanite mythological drama of the transfer of power
from 'El to Baal who comes on the clouds after the forces of
chaos have been destroyed.[259]  The suggestion has been made
that this mythological material may have been available to the
author of Daniel indirectly, via Israelite royal ideology and
traditions concerning the assumption of Elijah.  Now I make the
further suggestion that Daniel 7 combines the originally
Canaanite mythology with Enoch material.[260]  The similarity of
the fates of Elijah and Enoch may have been the link between
the two traditions.[261]

     What has the author of Daniel 7 done with the text of
*1 Enoch* 14 before him?  Here is a possible theory.  He has seen
the motif of Enoch's ascent and contrasting fall of the Watchers
as a paradigm of the events of his own time: as the evil Watchers fall and will not ascend again, so Antiochus who grotesquely
rose up against the holy ones and the Most High (7:21, 25; 8:
10-11) will be destroyed.  As Enoch approached to receive a commission, so the one like a son of man approaches to receive the
kingdom.  If the power of the Watchers, Giants and spirits of
the Giants was taken seriously by the contemporaries of the author of *1 Enoch* 14, a message of relief was delivered by this
passage: their power is limited and controlled.  The author of
Daniel 7 delivers a similar message: the power of the fourth
beast is already defeated on the plane of ultimate reality and
its days are numbered in history.  The figure of Enoch, righteous and alive beyond death, is used to focus hope and faith
in Israelite survival and triumph, believed to have worldwide
significance.  Enoch has become, in the figure of the one like
a son of man, a heavenly representative of the *maskîlîm*.  Details of *1 Enoch* 14 have been stripped away: the trappings of
heaven, the walls of crystal or hailstones, the fearful tongues
of fire, the three houses inside one another like Chinese boxes
--all these elements which serve to state and protect the transcendence of God and to increase the reader's interest and awe--
are omitted by the author of Daniel 7.  Aspects of the Canaanite
mythology are applied to the one like a son of man and to God
enthroned, and the threat of the fourth beast is highlighted.

Scholem speaks of *1 Enoch* 14 as containing the earliest example of the literary description of the phenomenon of the Throne on its chariot as pictured in Ezekiel 1, mysteries of the world of the Throne and of Divine Glory. *1 Enoch* 14 "was the source of a long visionary tradition of describing the world of the Throne and the visionary ascent to it, which we find portrayed in the books of the Merkabah mystics."[262] Daniel 7, drawing on the Enochic passage, can be seen also as a work within this tradition. It is not a text such as those which indulge in splendid catalogues of the appointments of the heavenly world, the dangers of the ascent, the inhabitants and their functions, or the wide range of mysteries revealed there. But it focuses on the revelation of the one mystery now of crucial importance to the author and his audience: the imminence and supremacy of the final kingdom of God and the role to be played there by the one like a son of man and the (people of the) holy ones. Presence before the Throne is promised to authentic Israel (7:18, 22, 27; cf. 12:2-3), awakening it to its identity. The author is calling his readers to believe in the fellowship of the *maskîlîm* and their followers (living and dead) with the angels of the Throne world and of earthly battle. In this instance, the mystical expression is not esoteric.

Ezekiel 1, 2 Kings 2 (Elijah) and *1 Enoch* 14 contain the following elements: (a) a heavenly throne or chariot; (b) a human or humanlike figure ascending or seated upon the throne; (c) clouds or whirlwind transporting the human figure, or mention of strong wind; (d) a visionary aspect of the account;[263] (e) the occurrence of the vision by a river. There is a magnetic field here, of linguistic[264] and thematic affinities. The elements which the texts have in common show that material is present (1) for drawing inferences from analogy (*gezeroth shavoth*, the second of Hillel's *middoth* or rules of exegesis);[265] (2) for constructing a "family" of texts (*Binyan 'ab mikkathub 'eḥad* and *Binyan 'ab mishshene Kethubim*, Hillel's third and fourth *middoth* by which deductions are made based on the fact that certain texts go together because of their similar contents); and (3) for making an exposition of these texts in terms of one another (*Keyoṣe bo bemaḳom aḥer*, Hillel's sixth *middah*).

One aspect of later exegesis of Daniel 7, as will be seen in
the following chapters, is the interpretation of that text by
reference to the very texts on which it draws, especially
Ezekiel 1.[266]   The influence of Ezekiel 1 on Daniel 7 is probably both direct and indirect (via *1 Enoch* 14).

In the next chapter we will examine the relationship between Daniel 7 and *1 Enoch* 71, and raise the question of whether
both of these texts depend on a common tradition (now lost) of
Enoch's final ascent.

### D. The Form and Function of Daniel 7

I have suggested that the structure of Daniel 7 resembles
the mythic pattern found in the Canaanite story of (a) the revolt of Yamm, sea, (b) the defeat of Yamm by Baal, (c) 'El's
enthronement of Baal and manifestation of his kingship.   In
Daniel 7, (a) the revolt of the sea appears in the rising from
the sea of beasts who exercise oppressive dominion, (b) the
defeat of the beasts is by judgment of the divine council, and
(c) the one like a son of man (representing the [people of the]
holy ones of the Most High) receives dominion and glory and
kingdom.[267]   The conflict/enthronement pattern reached the author of Daniel in part through the medium of the royal liturgy
and royal psalms.[268]   But to call Daniel 7 an enthronement
scene is not to classify it precisely.   It is a dream about or
a vision[269] of what Black calls a "throne theophany."   The Ancient of Days is depicted enthroned surrounded by his court
(7:9-10) and the conferral of dominion on the one like a son of
man takes place (vv. 13-14).   The interpretation of the vision
is given to the seer by an angel.   Black argues that this vision
and interpretation is a message given to Daniel to deliver, his
commission.   These two elements, the throne theophany and the
commission, indicate that Daniel 7 should be classified with the
"throne-theophany prophetic commission" scenes found in 1 Kings
22:19-23, Isaiah 6, Ezek 1:1-3:15 and "throne vision prophecies"
in the Enoch tradition (*1 Enoch* 14; 60; 90:20-23, 31-33, 37-38;
70-71).[270]   Daniel 7 exhibits "a very remarkable development" of
the tradition that precedes it.[271]   "The vision itself has become the subject of the prophet's message."[272]

A glance at the texts listed shows that the throne theophany and commission are found explicitly in 1 Kgs 22:19-23,
Isaiah 6, Ezek 1:1-3:15, *1 Enoch* 14-16 and perhaps *1 Enoch* 71.

| Throne Theophany: | Commission: |
|---|---|
| *1 Kgs 22:19:* "I saw Yahweh sitting on his throne, and all the host of heaven standing beside him on his right hand and on his left." | *v. 22:* "a spirit" is commissioned to be a lying spirit in the mouth of the prophets. Micaiah can also be considered commissioned to report the vision (cf. v. 14), but there is no dialogue between Yahweh and the prophet. |
| *Isa 6:1-4:* "...I saw Yahweh sitting upon a throne, high and lifted up, and his train filled the temple. Above him stood the seraphim...." | *vv. 9-10:* Isaiah is commissioned, "Go, and say to this people...." |
| *Ezek 1:26:* "And above the firmament over their heads there was the likeness of a throne, in appearance like sapphire; and seated above the likeness of a throne was the likeness as it were of a human form." | *2:3:* "And he said to me, 'Son of man, I send you to the people of Israel....'" |
| *1 Enoch 14:18-20:* "And I looked and saw therein a lofty throne; its appearance was as crystal....And the Great Glory sat thereon, and His raiment shone more brightly than the sun and was whiter than any snow." | *15:2:* "And go, say to the Watchers of heaven, who have sent you to intercede for them...." |
| *1 Enoch 71:2:* "And I saw two streams of fire [from the throne], and the light of that fire shone like hyacinth. And I fell on my face before the Lord of Spirits." | *vv. 14-17:* Enoch is commissioned (?)[273] as leader of the righteous: "You are the son of man who is born unto righteousness...all shall walk in your ways...." |

In Daniel 7 there is the throne theophany (vv. 9-10) but no
explicit commission.[274]

Black's theory is not developed in detail and with care,
but should not for this reason be disregarded. More apparent
at first is the contrast between the apocalyptic seer Daniel,
who is repeatedly told not to communicate his visions,[275] and
the prophets sent forth with a message. But the sealing of the
vision of the apocalyptic seer is part of the literary fiction

of pseudonymity. The seer from the ancient past is presented
(so to speak) as a "prophet" not for his own generation, but
for a generation to come, the last generation, that of the author's own time. The visions are "for the time of the end"
(9:17), "for days yet to come" (10:14). Daniel is said to
write down the dream and tell the sum of the matter (7:1), but
to keep the matter in his mind (7:28). In the context of the
second part of the book of Daniel, chapter 7 functions as the
inaugural vision of Daniel, which constitutes him a "prophet"
for the last generation.[276] The visions in chapters 8-12 are
not throne theophanies, but further interpretations of that
central vision in terms more and more clearly pertaining to
Maccabean times. Daniel cannot be told to "go" and speak, because the generation to which he is to speak is supposedly yet
unborn. The lack of "explicit urgency" in Daniel[277] in part of
this literary fiction. Daniel's commission appears in 12:4,
where he is told to "shut up the words, and seal the book, until the time of the end." One can modify Black's theory somewhat, then, and speak of Daniel 7 (-12) as having the form and
function of a throne theophany *apocalyptic* commission, understanding the commission to be for the future in terms of the
fiction of the book.

Two other elements of this form appear fairly constant
also, although Black has not mentioned them. These are:

### The Reaction of the Visionary:

*Isa 6:5:* "And I said, 'Woe is me! For I am lost....'" Cf. v. 8:
the prophet volunteers for service.

*Ezek 1:28:* "And when I saw [the appearance of the likeness of
the glory of Yahweh] I fell on my face....'"

*1 Enoch 14:24:* Enoch is prostrate, trembling; when he is
raised up, he bows down (v. 25).

*1 Enoch 71:2, 11:* The seer falls on his face; he cries out
blessings.

*Dan 7:15:* Daniel's spirit within him is anxious and the visions
of his head alarm him. He asks for and receives interpretation
(vv. 16-27). His final reaction is given in v. 28: "my thoughts
greatly alarmed me, and my color changed; but I kept the matter
in my mind."[278]

### The Word of Reassurance:

*1 Kgs 22:22:* The spirit is promised, "you shall succeed."

*Isa 6:6-7:* The prophet's mouth is touched with a burning coal, and he is told that his guilt is taken away, his sin forgiven.

*Ezek 2:6:* Ezekiel is told, "be not afraid" of the people of Israel to whom he is sent (cf. 2:8-9).

*1 Enoch 15:1:* "Fear not, Enoch, you righteous man and scribe of righteousness."

*1 Enoch 71:14:* Enoch is promised, "the righteousness of the Head of Days forsakes you not."

*Dan 12:13:* "You shall rest, and stand in your allotted place at the end of the days."

It will be suggested in the fifth chapter that Matt 28:16-20 is also a (throne) theophany commission, with the elements of (a) (throne) theophany (if the mountain is regarded as a symbol for the throne of God), (b) reaction, (c) commission, and (d) word of reassurance.[279]

## E. The Danielic Triad

In Daniel 7 we find a triad: Ancient of Days, one like a son of man and angels. This triad appears in one heavenly "place" where the thrones are set, and is engaged in the action of a transfer of power. The angels mentioned are the "thousand thousands...and ten thousand times ten thousand" who stand before God as throne attendants (7:10), and "bystanders" (7:13 LXX; cf. v. 16) who introduce the coming figure to the heavenly court and present him to the Ancient of Days. Three aspects of the Danielic triad will be considered here: (1) its prefigurement in early Canaanite material and in Ezekiel 1 and *1 Enoch* 14; (2) the theological context in which the triad occurs in Daniel; (3) the importance of the third member of the triad.

(1) In the Canaanite material, the triad appears of 'El, Baal and the clouds on which Baal rides, if these were understood at any stage as his divine messengers or retinue. This triad is polytheistic and hierarchical. It has been argued here that Canaanite material was available to the author of Daniel 7, via Israelite royal traditions and via traditions concerning the assumption of Elijah. In the latter, there is monotheizing in the application of Baal motifs to the prophet who is taken in a whirlwind and chariots and horses of fire.[280] The humanlike divine figure on the moving throne in Ezekiel 1 is

accompanied by *ḥayyoth* who have the form of *'adam* (Ezek 1:5)
and whose spirit is in the wheels (1:20, 21; cf. 10:17); these
beings are identified in 10:15 as cherubim.[281]    God appears
here with a retinue of angels, and the prophet himself may have
been thought of as ascending with the chariot-throne.[282]

In relation to *1 Enoch* 14, Ezekiel 1 and Elijah traditions
have been made use of to examine the triad consisting of Enoch
the assumed seer, the Great Glory and angels. Angels here include the cherubim-sides of the throne (4QEn^c 1 vi 18; cf. line
11), the "ten thousand times ten thousand" who stand before the
throne (*1 Enoch* 14:22), the "most holy ones" who never depart
from God (v. 23) and the anonymous "one of the holy ones" who
makes Enoch rise up and approach the open door of the throne
room.    The forces which draw Enoch upward are clouds, cloud
mists, lightning-flashes and thunders, winds (4QEn^c 1 vi 8).
The triad here, then, cuts across the levels of being to include God, (super) humanity[283] and angels.    Daniel 7, however,
exhibits what looks like a process of partial re-mythologiza-
tion.    The use of Canaanite and Ezekielian imagery to describe
both the Ancient of Days and the one like a son of man gives
some the impression that "two divinities" are portrayed here,
but this impression is held in check by (a) the association of
the one like a son of man with the translated human beings,
Elijah and Enoch, and (b) the fact that the one like a son of
man represents the suffering (and transformed) *maskîlîm* and
their followers.    The one like a son of man is not depicted as
a human seer, transported temporarily or permanently assigned a
minor role in the heavenly council.    Rather, he is described in
transcendental terms, coming to receive all earthly power, the
power of God.

(2) The triad in Daniel 7 appears not only to give the
readers a view of the inner workings of the heavenly world, a
glimpse of the realm beyond present experience, or comfort in
time of trouble.    The one like a son of man, I have argued,
represents in the author's thinking *not only* a being who has
become transcendent and invulnerable, one who perhaps comes to
belong in some way to this heavenly world. He represents *as
well* the people of Israel in its fellowship with the angels, in

its transcendent life, i.e., the limited apotheosis of Israel.
He is a point of contact between human and divine, a being in
whom two worlds coincide.  The human world he corporately represents and carries before the throne is not that of the whole
nation Israel, but that of those the author deems the authentic
Israel, those who hold firm in persecution even to death.
Within the triad, then, the true Israel sees itself; it learns
its identity from this symbol.  The one like a son of man is
brought to the Ancient of Days to receive the final kingdom.
This reception of power is the moment of triumph of the persecuted Israel over its oppressor, also the moment of the establishment of the eternal and universal kingdom of God.  In the
Maccabean context of the book of Daniel as a whole, this moment
is that of the triumph of the righteous even over death, enab-
ling resistance in the face of death.  The triad functions,
therefore, to demand something of the readers.  It calls for
faith in this expression of the identity of the righteous, the
identity of the true Israel--dead as well as living--and for
action (11:32).  Hellenistic persecution is spoken of in the
fictional context of the Babylonian exile, the archetypical
apex of suffering.  The lesson that had been learned in the
exile, "that the people's dereliction was a theophany at the
same time,"[284] is here applied.  The theophany in this case is
monotheistic but inclusive.

        (3) We do well to ask at this point what might be the
significance of the third member of the Danielic triad, the
angels.  Why is there emphasis in this scene on angels around
the throne, and why is the one like a son of man *brought* into
the divine presence and *presented*?  Why, in other words, is there
a triad instead of a dyad?  It is a commonplace to consider, as
Hengel does, that "fundamentally the whole of angelology was an
indication that the figure of God had receded into the distance
and that angels were needed as intermediaries between him,
creation and man."[285]  The growing sense of the transcendence
of God became increasingly pronounced from the beginning of the
post-exilic period, and the belief in angels formed "a vital
bridge between God and his universe which otherwise would have
been difficult to construct."[286]  The mood that fostered thought

concerning intermediaries was one of abandonment-by-God, the
reverse side of realization of transcendence. Angelology served
to "rationalize the picture of God,"[287] that is, to ensure the
running of nature according to the divine will, to help to explain the origin and continuance of evil in line with a theodicy
which would develop into a modified ethical dualism. The third
member of the triad, then, can be considered as a symbol of the
distance between the first two.

At the same time, intermediaries have also been seen as
ways of talking about immanence, ways of "spiritualizing and
even humanizing...the belief in God's presence."[288] They are
ways of imagining the presence of God's concern and power in
human or quasi-human forms. The image of God in council attended
by thousands, or on the moving throne with the *hayyoth*, an image
necessary in part to accommodate the deities de-deified in the
monotheizing process, prevents the impression of the static remoteness and the isolation of the divine. The angelic form of
life is considered a state intermediate between God and humanity:
angels share the nature of God but not God's being,[289] and represent as well something of the original potential and final
destiny of the human race.[290] The distinction, then, between
human being and angel, and between angel and God, is fluid in a
way that the distinction between human being and God is not.
The presence of angelic figures in ascent stories such as
*1 Enoch* 14, in their function of bringing the seer into the
divine presence, may say as much about changing ideas of human
potential and aspiration as about the remote isolation of God.
The use of these figures may indicate a desire both to avoid the
visualization of God taking the seer up,[291] and to avoid attribution of the power of ascent solely to the human being. The
"otherness" of God is safeguarded, and it is made clear that
the righteous do not redeem themselves or storm heaven. The
angelic guides give ballast to the bizarre and bold notion of
human presence before the divine throne, human capacity to undertake the journey to the "place" where God is. Imagined as
persons concrete and exterior to the human being, angels prevent
a mysticism of absorption into the divine above or the divine
within, but they facilitate by their mediation a mysticism in

which the divine and human come into communion: the human being
elevated to the heavenly court or in the eschatological community is conceived in some cases as having "merged" with the
angels of the court, but without total loss of human identity.

It is the thesis presented here that Daniel 7 is the
source of that imagery and theology which ultimately lead to
the Matthean triadic phrase, "the Father, the Son and the Holy
Spirit." In the next two chapters, an attempt will be made to
trace instances of interpretation of Daniel 7 which have bearing on the question of the development and meaning of the triad.
The interest here is not simply in changes of terminology and
"titles" of the three members, but in the theological context
and import of the triad as well.

## F. Summary

Analysis of Daniel 7 has shown something of the ambiguities
and tensions in the text itself, especially those concerning
the identity and nature of the figure of the one like a son of
man and the relation of that figure to (the people of) the holy
ones of the Most High. The chapter is closely bound to chapters
2 and 12, the former concerning the stone that becomes a mountain which fills the whole earth, and the latter concerning the
destiny of the *maskîlîm* and their followers. The text has been
understood (with Collins) as primarily a statement of belief in
the transcendence of death on the part of authentic Israel,
called passively to resist idolatry and apostasy even when resistance means martyrdom.

Discussion of the background of Daniel 7 enables us to see
this text as an organic whole, its major component parts drawn
probably indirectly from Canaanite mythological material, and
drawn from traditions concerning the translations of Elijah and
Enoch (especially *1 Enoch* 14), and from Ezekiel 1. Daniel 7 is
an example of the revitalization of mythology in apocalyptic and
of bold (even if unconscious) appreciation of mythological
imagery on the part of Israelite writers. In this case, the
imagery connected with a transfer of power from one divinity to
another has been appropriated. Long accustomed to regarding the

originally polytheistic concept of the heavenly council on
their own terms (wherein the origins may have been forgotten),
Israelite thinkers retained the dynamic understanding of God
which it allowed, and (again perhaps unconsciously) demoted all
gods but one to the rank of angels or ministers. A further
dimension of the appropriation of mythological material appears
in the OT idea of human participation in the council. The
translation of Elijah and the abbreviated traditions in Genesis
of the "taking" of Enoch survived in the OT as exceptions to
the fate of ordinary human beings, and these traditions were
also productive of material in which these figures were seen as
members of the heavenly world. The conception of human beings
in fellowship with the angels, or perhaps even of human beings
"angelicized," later finds more explicit expression in the
Qumran writings, especially the Hôdāyôt and 11Q Melchizedek (in
which Melchizedek is called 'elohim). Daniel 7 has been examined here in the context of a thought world which included the
Hellenistic concept of "immortal" and a certain fluidity in the
distinction between human beings and angels. The one like a son
of man, it has been argued, is for the author a symbol of the
apotheosis of Israel. He represents true Israel in its fellowship with the angels. As such, he is a figure whose humanity is
intentionally ambiguous. He is not said to be an angel, although
his relationship with the "holy ones" opens him to this interpretation. He is likewise not said to be a god, although the
theophanic associations carried by the imagery of coming on or
with the clouds suggest divinity. His identity is unstated.[292]

Ezekiel 1, the classical text *par excellence* which sparked
mystical speculation and practices, provided generations of
visionaries with the image of God enthroned on the *ḥayyoth*, of
the transcendent presence in exile. Deeply influenced by
Ezekiel 1 and by *1 Enoch* 14, the earliest literary example of
adaptation of Ezekiel's vision, Daniel 7 (12) is (like these
texts) a throne-theophany commission[293] and a text which belongs
to the earliest stage of Merkabah mysticism. The author of
Daniel fashions a statement of faith and hope which is a response
to the religio-political crisis of his time, a statement of the
survival power of God and of authentic Israel. The triad that

appears in Daniel 7 (Ancient of Days, one like a son of man and
angels) is a symbol by means of which Israel learns its identity and destiny.

How was Daniel 7 interpreted and used in the nearly two-
hundred and fifty years between its composition and the composition of Matt 28:16-20? In the following chapters it will be
seen that important aspects of the midrashic history of Daniel 7
involved the use and reuse of idea- and image-clusters that ac-
crue to traditions behind the text. On the part of some later
interpreters there was also an awareness of the connection between chapter 7 and chapters 2 and 12, as they interpreted
Daniel by Daniel. The linking of Daniel 7 with other texts,
especially Isaiah 11, led to a new messianic understanding of
the former passage, the one like a son of man sometimes considered a warrior-messiah. In certain other instances, prominence was given to an understanding of the one like a son of
man as *Maskîl*, or as ruler, or as martyr, or as judge. The
figure was regarded by some as a corporate being, by others as
an individual.

The ultimate aim of this work is to show that approaching
Matt 28:16-20 from the angle of comparative midrash will offer
solutions to the major exegetical problems raised by previous
examination of this passage.[294] The analysis of Daniel 7 in
this chapter raises the possibility that the mountain in Matt
28:16 may bear some relation to the mountain spoken of in Daniel
2 (as Daniel 7 is understood as a "midrash" on Daniel 2) and so
be part of a Danielic midrash. I have already suggested also
that the form of Daniel 7, that of a throne-theophany commission,
is similar to the form of Matt 28:16-20;[295] this theory depends
in part on the interpretation which I will propose of the symbolism of the Matthean mountain. In addition, the relationship
between the one like a son of man of Daniel 7 and the *maskîlîm*
of Daniel 11-12 may in some way lie behind the presentation in
the final Matthean pericope of the risen Jesus who commands the
disciples to teach what he has taught.[296] Furthermore, the ap-
propriateness of the use of Dan 7:14 in the mouth of the "resurrected and ascended one"[297] is more apparent in the light of the
discussion here of ascent imagery in Daniel. Finally, the

ambiguity concerning the "nature" of the Danielic one like a
son of man is important to keep in mind in the probe for insight into the understanding of the unity among the members of
the triad in Matt 28:19b.  Focus later in this work will also
be on the relation of the Matthean triad to struggles within
the Matthean community to respond to questions of identity and
destiny.  Examination in Chapters V and VI of selected intertestamental Jewish and NT interpretations of Daniel 7 is guided
by interest in the Matthean pericope.

[1]See John J. Collins, "The Court Tales in Daniel and the Development of Apocalyptic," *JBL* 94 (1975) 218-34. They may have been written during the third century, according to M. Noth ("The Understanding of History in Old Testament Apocalyptic," *The Laws in the Pentateuch and Other Studies* [Philadelphia: Fortress, 1967] 207).

[2]For a survey of Antiochus' policies and acts of increasing persecution, see Hartman and DiLella, *Daniel*, 39-42; V. Tcherikover, *Hellenistic Civilization and the Jews* (Philadelphia: Jewish Publication Society of America, 1961) 152-234.

[3]Porteous (*Daniel*, 115) discusses the theory that supplementing "broadsheets" were issued one after another as conditions worsened.

[4]The Aramaic of chapter 7 has often been explained as an attempt to bridge the two sections. Collins (*Apocalyptic Vision*, 15-19) surveys solutions to the problem raised by the two languages. He concludes that there is not enough evidence that the Hebrew portions are a translation from the Aramaic (against H. L. Ginsberg, *Studies in Daniel* [New York: The Jewish Theological Seminary of America, 1948] 41-61; R. H. Charles, *Daniel*, xlvi-xlviii; Hartman and DiLella, *Daniel*, 232; A. Lacocque, *The Book of Daniel* [Atlanta: John Knox, 1979] 13). Rather, the book was composed as a bilingual work (by a final author/redactor who may have been more comfortable in Aramaic) for a bilingual public.

[5]See B. Childs, "The Canonical Shape of the Book of Daniel," unpublished paper delivered at the SBL Meeting, October 1975; E. Bickerman, *Four Strange Books of the Bible* (New York: Schocken, 1967) 102; Hartman and DiLella, *Daniel*, 208. The term "midrash" is used here more loosely than I used it in Chapter II.

[6]Cf. v. 45: "a stone cut from a mountain by no human hand."

[7]Childs, "The Canonical Shape," 5; cf. Porteous, *Daniel*, 50. In Isa 2:2-4 (= Micah 4:1-4) we find the image of the great mountain of the house of Yahweh to which all nations will flow. Isa 51:1 (cf. Ps 118:22) presents the image of a rock or stone as a symbol of the people of Israel. Lacocque argues on the basis of Gen 28:10-22 and 49:24 that the stone in Daniel 2 belongs to the messianic realm (*Daniel*, 52).

[8]Cf. A. Jeffery, "Daniel," 387; see also Ziony Zevit, "The Structure and Individual Elements of Daniel 7," *ZAW* 80 (1968) 385.

[9]A. R. Rhodes ("The Kingdoms of Men and the Kingdom of God: a Study of Daniel 7:1-14," *Int* 15 [1961] 425) remarks that if Jeffery's interpretation of chapter 7 by chapter 2 is correct, 7:14 is to be associated with the conversion of Gentiles in the last days.

[10]Philip Carrington, *Commentary on Mark* (Cambridge, 1960); cited with no page number by Black, "The Christological Use," 12.

[11]It may have also been read as a plural, sons (Black, "The Christological Use," 12 n. 2) or by the Aramaic form of "the son." In Chapter V it will be suggested that *1 Enoch* 52:1-6 implies the wordplay.

[12]Cf. Exod 28:29; Josh 4:6-8, 20-21; 1 Kgs 18:31; Lam 4: 1-2; Zech 9:16; also 1QH 6:26 etc. (M. Black, "The Christological Use," 12 n. 2).

[13]This theory is held by J. A. Montgomery (*The Book of Daniel* [ICC; Edinburgh: T. & T. Clark, 1964] 282); see also the theory of Bevan and Goettsberger of the accidental loss of a Hebrew original and the filling out of the book from an Aramaic translation (O. Eissfeldt, *The Old Testament* [New York: Harper & Row, 1965] 516).

[14]See above, p. 191 n. 4.

[15]But the one like a son of man is not, in contrast to the stone, a destructive force. Perhaps related to the wordplay, a mountain appears often (as in Matt 28:16-20) in the context of an allusion to Dan 7:13-14.

[16]Collins, *Apocalyptic Vision*, 13, 43-44.

[17]For example, the prayer in 9:4-19 (which is probably a later addition) is a confession that calamity is caused by God as punishment (9:14), expressing belief in divine control over the dynamics of history.

[18]Collins, *Apocalyptic Vision*, 132. The four accounts are (1) the vision in 7:1-14 and its interpretation in 7:17-18; (2) the elaboration of this vision in 7:19-22 and its interpretation in 7:23-27; (3) the vision in 8:1-12 and its interpretation in 8:20-25; (4) the narrative account in 10:20-12:3.

[19]Ibid., 133. The fourth element is missing in the third parallel.

[20]Ibid., 162-63.

[21]His pride is presented as far worse than that of Kings Nebuchadnezzar and Belshazzar who, ignorant of the source of their power, "lift themselves up" (5:20, 23).

[22]If 12:1-3 is understood as continuing the prediction of 11:40-45, the timeframe intended by the author is the period after Antiochus' death (Hartman and DiLella, *Daniel*, 305).

[23]In the close parallel to this passage in "The Words of the Heavenly Lights" (4Q Dib. Ham.), probably based on a common tradition, the phrase "the book of life" occurs (Nickelsburg, *Resurrection*, 15-16).

[24]A universal resurrection is probably not envisioned (Nickelsburg, *Resurrection*, 19, 23; Hartman and DiLella, *Daniel*, 307-9).

[25]The nearby occurrence of these terms parallels Isa 52:13 (הִנֵּה יַשְׂכִּיל עַבְדִּי) and 53:11 (יַצְדִּיק צַדִּיק עַבְדִּי לָרַבִּים). There are no other MT texts besides these in Isaiah and Daniel in which the Hiphil of שׂכל and צדק occur in close proximity. Other elements of the description of the servant find their counterparts in the experience of the *maskîlîm* of Dan 12:3; 11:33-35: (a) the servant suffers (53:5, 7); (b) he is condemned as a lawbreaker (53:8, 12); (c) he is put to death (53:8, 9?, 12; cf. Dan 11: 33-35 where the death of some of the *maskîlîm* is mentioned ["And those among the people who are wise shall make many understand, though they shall fall by sword and flame, by captivity and plunder, for some days...and some of those who are wise shall fall, to refine and cleanse them, and to make them white..."]); (d) in God's eyes, he is innocent. In addition, as the servant is exalted (Isa 52:13: he "will be exalted and lifted up and will be very high"), so will be the *maskîlîm* (Dan 12:3). Cf. Nickelsburg, *Resurrection*, 24-26; H. L. Ginsberg, "The Oldest Interpretation of the Suffering Servant," *VT* 3 (1953) 400-404; Collins, *Apocalyptic Vision*, 170. There is also the possibility that the author of Daniel hints at the idea of vicarious suffering and death on the part of the *maskîlîm* who fall (cf. 11:35 with 12:10).

[26]Charles (*Daniel*, 330) and Jeffery ("Daniel," 543) argue that two different classes of heroes are spoken of: הַמַּשְׂכִּלִים and מַצְדִּיקֵי הָרַבִּים. It is more likely that one class is being described under two titles (Hartman and DiLella, *Daniel*, 101; Montgomery, *Daniel*, 471; Delcor, *Le Livre de Daniel* [Paris: Gabalda, 1971] 255-56; Nickelsberg, *Resurrection*, 24.

[27]As Collins remarks (*Apocalyptic Vision*, 136-38), the stars had long been identified with angels in Israelite tradition (Judg 5:20; Job 28:7; cf. Dan 8:10). The stars are members of the divine council in the Ugaritic texts.

[28]Cf. the later works, Wis 3:7-8; *1 Enoch* 39:5; Mark 12:25. In the Qumran scrolls, the members of the community are believed to mingle with the angels even before death (Nickelsburg, *Resurrection*, 144-69). Collins sees Dan 12:3 as possibly an adaptation of the Hellenistic idea of astral immortality, understood as "the admittance of the just to Yahweh's angelic host" (*Apocalyptic Vision*, 137-38). He speaks of the *maskîlîm* being "assimilated" to the angels; in my opinion, this terminology is acceptable only if it means they are "made like to" or "caused to resemble" the angels, not if it means obliteration of the distinction between the angelic and the human. Contrast Lacocque (*Daniel*, 245 n. 45) who speaks of the "angelization" of the elect.

[29]P. D. Hanson, "OT Apocalyptic Reexamined," 476. Hanson calls this "a flight into the realm of myth" (478 n. 19). See also his "Jewish Apocalyptic against its Near Eastern Environment," *RB* 78 (1971) 52. Hanson's emphasis is on the pessimistic view of reality found in apocalyptic, and on the flight of the

apocalypticist from the historical, political task.  But see
below, n. 31 and pp. 147-48.

$^{30}$Antiochus assumed the title (*theos*) *epiphanēs*, "(God)
manifest," in 169, and in 166 added another title, *nicephorus*,
"victorious, or victory bearer," an equally divine epithet
(Hartman and DiLella, *Daniel*, 40).

$^{31}$J. J. Collins, "Apocalyptic Eschatology as the Transcendence of Death," *CBQ* 36 (1974) 30, 34, 37.  Collins stresses
that eschatological formulations are essentially projections of
hopes experienced in depth in the present (p. 41).

$^{32}$B. Lindars, "Apocalyptic Myth," 372.

$^{33}$Contrast G. von Rad (*Old Testament Theology* [2 vols.;
New York: Harper and Row, 1965] 2.302), who argues that in the
book of Daniel "the saving blessing of the coming aeon" is
imagined as coming down from heaven to earth.  In this he
agrees with Charles that the author of Daniel looked for the
setting up of a messianic kingdom on earth (*Daniel*, cxii).

$^{34}$Collins, *Apocalyptic Vision*, 163, 68.

$^{35}$Ibid., 191.

$^{36}$Cf. J. J. Collins, "The Jewish Response to Hellenism,"
*Int* 30 (1976) 313; idem, "The Mythology of Holy War in Daniel
and the Qumran War Scroll," *VT* 25 (1975) 603; von Rad, *OT The-
ology*, 2.315; F. F. Bruce, "The Book of Daniel and the Qumran
Community," *Neotestamentica et Semitica* (ed. E. E. Ellis and
M. Wilcox; Edinburgh: T. & T. Clark, 1969) 229.

$^{37}$von Rad, *OT Theology*, 315.  He cannot, therefore, simply
be considered one of the Hasidim, since the Hasidim joined the
Maccabean revolutionaries during most of the war, although with
different objectives (Collins, *Apocalyptic Vision*, 214; against
Hengel, *Judaism and Hellenism*, 1.175-80; Hartman and DiLella, *Daniel*, 43-45).  Collins discusses the wide range of attitudes within
the Jewish resistance movement (*Apocalyptic Vision*, 194-210).

$^{38}$In 12:1, it is said that Michael will arise (יַעֲמֹד) at
the time of trouble.  This verb could refer to either judicial
or military action.  See Nickelsburg, *Resurrection*, 11-14; he
contends that Michael's role here is not a purely military one
but also judicial; "The war he wages has the character of
judgment."

$^{39}$Collins, *Apocalyptic Vision*, 195, 208.

$^{40}$Collins argues that the wisdom of the *maskîlîm* is based
on the eschatological interpretation of visions and of scriptures; this wisdom enables them and those they teach to choose
the right side in the current conflict, and gives them courage
to undergo suffering and death because of assurance of a glorious afterlife for the righteous (*Apocalyptic Vision*, 208).

[41]The *maskîlîm* are preparing themselves and their people
for transformation which cannot be brought about by militant
action.  The goal they envision goes beyond the restoration of
the national kingdom (Collins, *Apocalyptic Vision*, 208-9).  It
involves the righteous dead.

[42]Di Lella rightly prefers the translation "one in human
likeness" or "one like a human being" or "what looked like a
human being," because these "allow the possibility of women
being included in the symbol" (*Daniel*, 87).  Hartman comments
that the Aramaic בַר אֲנָשׁ means a member of the human race, as
distinct from the Aramaic גְּבַר, a male human being (ibid., 218).
The importance of the courage and suffering of women and children during the Maccabean revolution is documented in later
works (see 2 Macc 6:10; 7:1-41) and it is not impossible the
author of Daniel was aware of this dimension of the resistance,
although he does not mention it.  However, the conventional
translation, "one like a son of man," is retained in this dissertation because of the proposed wordplay בְּרִ-אֱלָהִין related to
chapters 2 and 7 (see above), and because of interest in tracing
the development of titles of the triad.

[43]See Rhodes, "The Kingdom of Men," 413; Zevit, "Structure,"
387 n. 13.

[44]There are expressions in the OT similar to "Ancient of
Days," but not applied to God.  The biblical concept of God's
eternal existence (see Ps 9:8, etc.) and "the popular notion of
God as an old man" (Hartman and DiLella, *Daniel*, 218) may have
provided the author with permission to use the phrase but not
the inspiration for it.

[45]The MT reads עִם עֲנָנֵי שְׁמַיָּא (7:13).  Some have claimed
that the preposition עִם is a corruption or correction of an
original עַל or בְּ which lies behind the LXX (ἐπί) and Peshitta,
and which would suggest a theophany (Charles, *Daniel*, 186;
Montgomery, *Daniel*, 313).  But the author of Daniel uses עִם
interchangeably with בְּ (see Dan 2:43, 5:30); עִם can be translated, therefore, by either ἐπί or μετά (R. B. Y. Scott, "Behold, He Cometh with Clouds," *NTS* 5/6 [1958/60] 129).  Since
clouds accompany an apparition or intervention of God sixty-six
times in the OT, the clouds in Dan 7:13 (whether understood as
the "companions" of the one like a son of man, as celestial
scenery or as means of transportation [chariot]), are regarded
by many critics as indicative of a theophany (A. Feuillet, "Le
Fils de l'homme de Daniel et la tradition biblique," *RB* 60
[1953] 187, 192-93; cf. Colpe, "ὁ υἱὸς τοῦ ἀνθρώπου," *TDNT* 8
[1974] 420; J. Muilenberg, "The Son of Man in Daniel and the
Ethiopic Apocalypse of Enoch," *JBL* 79 [1960] 201).

[46]Montgomery, *Daniel*, 303.

[47]Several critics relate the clouds to those of scenes of
Moses' ascent or translation.  Vermes (*Jesus the Jew*, 186-87)
mentions *b. Yoma* 4a; *Pesiq. R.* 20:4; see also Josephus' account
of Moses' final departure (*Ant.* 4:326).  Di Lella mentions the

cloud into which Moses passed at Sinai (Exod 24:18); see his
"The One in Human Likeness and the Holy Ones of the Most High
in Daniel 7," *CBQ* 39 (1977) 19.  T. W. Manson ("The Son of Man
in Daniel," 174), Lacocque (*Daniel*, 137), and J.A.T. Robinson
(*Jesus and His Coming*, 45) read Dan 7:13 as an ascent.  See
further, below, on the ascent of Enoch and Elijah.

[48] See above, pp. 146-47.

[49] The contrast with the beasts from the sea, however, is
heightened by *not* having the one like a son of man rise from
the sea in 7:13.  A downward motion has also been read into the
text (see above, n. 33).

[50] Delcor, *Le Livre de Daniel*, 153.

[51] In 7:22 it is said that judgment "was given for (or: to)
the holy ones of the Most High."

[52] See above, p. 134 n. 29.

[53] Do they co-rule or is the Ancient of Days replaced?

[54] The wind, the sea, the characteristics of each of the
beasts, the clouds, the fire from the throne, the appearance of
the Ancient of Days, and other aspects of the vision are without
an interpretation.  This suggests to some critics that an ancient myth or mythological fragment is being historicized and
possibly expanded or transformed by the author.  See Muilenberg,
"The Son of Man," 199 n. 3; Porteous, *Daniel*, 96, 110, 120.
Mythological tradition has been blended by the author with the
four-kingdom schema; the beasts that rise from the sea belong
to the same complex of mythic material as the scene of empowering (Collins, *Apocalyptic Vision*, 127-29).  The Canaanite mythological traditions will be treated below.

[55] Hartman and DiLella, *Daniel*; cf. DiLella, "The One in
Human Likeness."

[56] Collins, *Apocalyptic Vision*; cf. idem, "The Son of Man
and Saints of the Most High."

[57] In 7:27 there is reference to the "people of the holy
ones of the Most High" receiving the kingdom.  While it is
grammatically possible to construe the Aramaic expression as a
possessive construct chain (as does Collins, *Apocalyptic Vision*,
142-43), Di Lella argues that it is more properly understood as
an epexegetical or appositional construct chain ("the people,
i.e., the holy ones of the Most High") or as a hendiadys ("the
holy people of the Most High"; cf. 8:24).  As the "holy ones"
are said to receive the kingdom in vv. 18, 22, these individuals
are the same as "the people of the holy ones" (Hartman and
DiLella, *Daniel*, 95-96).  Contrast Lacocque, *Daniel*, 127.

[58] Among those who hold a similar view are Manson ("The Son of
Man," 174), D.S. Russell (*Method and Message*, 326), M. Hooker (*The*

*Son of Man*, 13), Mowinckel (*He That Cometh*, 349-50), Montgomery
(*Daniel*, 317-24), Delcor (*Le Livre de Daniel*, 39, 153-67); see
other references given by Di Lella (*Daniel*, 97 n. 234). F. M.
Cross understands the one like a son of man as "the young Ba'l
reintegrated and democratized by the apocalyptist as the Jewish
nation" (*Canaanite Myth and Hebrew Epic* [Cambridge: Harvard
University, 1973] 17). Perrin is of the opinion that the
choice of a humanlike figure was probably a pure accident, as
any other cryptically designated figure would have served the
author's purpose equally well, representing the Maccabean
martyrs ("The Son of Man in Ancient Judaism and Primitive
Christianity: A Suggestion," *BR* 11 [1966] 20-21).

[59] Similar views are held by J. Coppens ("Le Fils d'Homme
Daniélique et les Relectures de Dan., vii, 13, dans les Apo-
cryphes et les Ecrits du Nouveau Testament," *ETL* 37 [1961] 215-
28), L. Dequeker ("The 'Saints of the Most High' in Qumran and
Daniel," *OTS* 18 [1973] 108-87), Zevit ("Structure," 395), J.
Barr ("Daniel," *PBC* [ed. M. Black and H. H. Rowley; London:
Nelson, 1962] 598), R. Leivestad ("Exit the Apocalyptic Son of
Man," *NTS* 18 [1972] 247), B. Lindars ("Reenter the Apocalyptic
Son of Man," *NTS* 22 [1975] 55), M. Noth ("The Holy Ones of the
Most High," *Laws in the Pentateuch* [trans. D. R. Ap-Thomas;
Philadelphia: Fortress, 1966] 215-28), J. A. Emerton ("The
Origin of the Son of Man Imagery," *JTS* 9 [1958] 229). Tödt
(*Son of Man*, 31) speaks of the figure as more than an angel.
Porteous (*Daniel*, 110) calls him somehow both human and divine.
Zevit identifies the one like a son of man with Gabriel, not
Michael. Collins lists those who like himself identify him
with Michael (*Apocalyptic Vision*, 149 n. 7). Some of the
scholars who consider the one like a son of man as an angel,
however, assume that the "holy ones" are primarily the eschatological Israel (ibid., 124). Charles thinks that the writer
was inferring that the faithful remnant of Israel would be
transformed into heavenly or supernatural beings; the phrase,
"the holy ones of the Most High" was chosen to express "the
divine or supernatural character of God's chosen people as
contrasted with other peoples on earth" (*Daniel*, 187, 191).

[60] It is unnecessary to discuss in detail the various attempts to distinguish strata in the chapter. Arguments against
the unity of the chapter are based on the impression that the
fourth beast and/or the one like a son of man and holy ones of
the Most High (v. 18) have been progressively reinterpreted.
See Ginsberg, *Studies in Daniel*, 16-18; Hartman and DiLella,
*Daniel*, 13-14; L. Dequeker, "Les Saints du Très-Haut en Daniel
VII," *ETL* 36 (1960); Noth, "The Holy Ones of the Most High,"
194-214; Colpe, "ὁ υἱὸς τοῦ ἀνθρώπου," 420-23. But Collins
argues that the chapter is a unit; there is no need to posit
radically different stages of interpretation or interpolations
(*Apocalyptic Vision*, 126-32). DiLella is of the opinion that
the meaning of the expression "the holy ones" remains the same
throughout the apocalypse, even if one or more glosses have
been added (*Daniel*, 85).

[61]The phrase בַּר אֱנָשׁ is used in the OT only here in Dan
7:13. Di Lella briefly reviews the use of its Hebrew equivalent, בֶּן אָדָם, which appears 108 times in the OT, 93 in the book
of Ezekiel, where the prophet himself is being addressed (cf.
Dan 8:17 where the seer Daniel is spoken to), and elsewhere as
a lofty designation for "man" in poetic and solemn contexts
(*Daniel*, 85-86). In Dan 10:16, the seer is touched by כדמות יד
בן אדם (DiLella's preferred reading on the basis of Theodotion,
6QDan and the LXX; the MT has the plural, כדמות בני אדם; cf.
p. 256). The reference is presumably to the angel who first
appears in 10:5. The occurrences of the Aramaic equivalents in
the Sefire Stele III and Genesis Apocryphon from Qumran are examples of a generic use ("a human being, someone"). The use of
related forms and of the plural in Aramaic parts of Daniel show
us generic and collective and pronominal meanings (p. 86). It
is clear that the term is not a title, and not the name of a
well-known figure (Collins, *Apocalyptic Vision*, 124) but simply
the normal expression for a human being. The preposition "like,"
rather than indicating a mysterious dissimilarity to the human
(this is Tödt's position; *Son of Man*, 23), may simply show that
the terms used are considered inadequate (Feuillet, "Le Fils de
l'Homme," 186); the preposition is stylistically common in the
description of a dream (Vermes, *Jesus the Jew*, 170). In most
cases, קדושים in the MT and ἅγιοι in the deutero-canonical books
of the OT are angels; in the pseudepigrapha and Qumran literature the evidence is inconclusive (cf. Collins, *Apocalyptic
Vision*, 125; Hartman and DiLella, *Daniel*, 90-91).

[62]Hartman and DiLella, *Daniel*, 87. He is not a mysterious
figure of the past or present, nor one who will appear in the
eschatological future (p. 97).

[63]Ibid., 91.

[64]Ibid. He sees the other figures in this text as unireferential: the Ancient of Days is the God of Israel; the
"little horn" is Antiochus Epiphanes IV; the four beasts are
four kingdoms. Di Lella recognizes, however, that the Animal
Apocalypse (*1 Enoch* 83-90)--which he argues should be regarded
as a source for determining the meaning of the symbolism of
Daniel 7--employs a multireferential symbolism (p. 93). He
finds support for his thesis that Daniel 7 uses only unireferential symbolism in his reading of the stone in chapter 2 as a
unireferential symbol of the loyal Jews. He argues that there
is no indication here that the eternal kingdom spoken of has
anything to do with angels or their leader (p. 100).

[65]Ibid., 94. Cf. 8:15-16; 9:21; 10:5-6; 12:6-7.

[66]Ibid., 91, 95.

[67]Cf. Ps 8:5-7; 80:18-20; Job 25:4-6 (and perhaps 15:14-16).
Di Lella thinks this interpretation is bolstered by the senti-
ments of the interpolated prayer in chapter 9 (*Daniel*, 99).
Colpe, on the other hand, while admitting that the psalms show
that the phrase בֶּן־אָדָם could be used in the pre-apocalyptic

tradition collectively, to personify Israel, does not consider
that these texts are the root of the son of man concept in
apocalyptic ("ὁ υἱὸς τοῦ ἀνθρώπου," 407). Moreover, the interpolated prayer expresses a completely different Deuteronomistic
view of the crisis and highlights the newness of the visionary
view (Collins, *Apocalyptic Vision*, 185-87). It cannot be used
to explicate chapter 7.

[68]Hartman and DiLella, *Daniel*, 101-2. If there is intention to evoke Psalm 8 (which, like Genesis 1, refers to the status
of woman and man in God's design), the vision of the subjection of
beasts to the one like a son of man--that is, of the subjection
of the kingdoms of the world to the true Israel--may represent
"nothing less than a new creation, the final redemption of God's
people and the accomplishment of his aboriginal purpose" (Heaton,
*Daniel*, 186; cited by Di Lella, *Daniel*, 98).

[69]Ibid., 100-101. Di Lella concedes that the stars symbolize the angelic host.

[70]Cf. 11:35.

[71]Hartman and DiLella, *Daniel*, 313. Moreover, it is difficult
to see what real difference the author would see in the "everlasting life" of the resurrected and the exalted life of the *maskîlîm*.

[72]Collins, *Apocalyptic Vision*, xviii.

[73]Ibid., 133, 136. Di Lella interprets Dan 11:36 to mean
simply that Antiochus has assumed divine honors (*Daniel*, 301).

[74]Cf. 8:24 where it is said that the power of Antiochus
destroys "mighty men and the people of the holy ones." The
fact that the author never names Antiochus contributes to the
mysterious, cosmic dimension of his work.

[75]Collins, *Apocalyptic Vision*, 140.

[76]Ibid., xix.

[77]See below for discussion of Canaanite and Ezekielian
traditions in Daniel 7.

[78]Collins, *Apocalyptic Vision*, 143, following Coppens, "Le
Fils d'Homme," 63. See above, n. 57, for DiLella's reading of
this verse.

[79]Collins, *Apocalyptic Vision*, 143, 166.

[80]Coppens, like Collins, argues that 7:27 refers to the
people *belonging to* or *enjoying the protection of* the holy ones,
not to a people *composed of* the holy ones ("Le Fils d'Homme,"
13-14; contrast Barr ["Daniel," 592-602] and the interpretation
of Charles [above, n. 59]). Cf. Collins (*Apocalyptic Vision*,
141) on 8:24-25: this passage can be read as a reference to
Israel only if we assume that Israel has already merged with
the heavenly host. This may be the correct interpretation,

because although in 12:3 the faithful do not join the angels
until after the resurrection, the angels may be thought to
merge with Israel at the time of battle.

[81] The transformation is not restricted to the resurrected
martyrs or to the *maskîlîm* who "fall" (11:35); Collins sees in
12:3 a broader, more inclusive promise than that in 12:2.

[82] Collins, *Apocalyptic Vision*, 173-74. Lacocque (*Daniel*,
239) goes further: the resurrection is the transfiguration of
the faithful Israelite into the one like a son of man.

[83] See above, pp. 145-46.

[84] Collins, *Apocalyptic Vision*, 144. Lacocque's view is
that the figure of the one like a son of man is inclusive, and
the angel Michael is one of its aspects (*Daniel*, 242, 133).
The holy ones (a single community of angels and human beings)
participate in him. Lacocque emphasizes, however, the human
dimension of his person and of the holy ones (p. 131). He is
the prototype and *telos* of righteous humanity; in him Israel
sees its own transcendence as a being alongside God (pp. 127-28,
132).

[85] Cf. Collins, "The Mythology of Holy War," 602. The
"standing" of Michael in the heavenly court (with mention of
the book in 12:1) may be considered to correspond to the "coming" of the one like a son of man to the court in 7:13-14 (the
books opened in 7:10, however, seem to be the books of the deeds
of all, not the register of the names of the righteous).

[86] Both are exalted, and the opponents of both are judged.
Other variants of belief in this type of figure are Michael in
the Qumran War Scroll and the angel of God's vengeance in *Testament of Moses* 10. See Collins, *Apocalyptic Vision*, 145.

[87] Cf. Matt 16:27; 25:31; 13:41; 24:21; Mark 8:38; 13:27;
Luke 9:26; and also 1 Thess 4:16; 2 Thess 1:7.

[88] Rev 14:14. Cf. Rev 12:10 where the kingdom is awarded to
Christ after Michael has defeated the dragon. See Collins,
*Apocalyptic Vision*, 144-46.

[89] The *maskîlîm*, in my judgment, can be understood as a
pluralization of the figure of the one like a son of man (though
this does not exhaust the meaning of that figure) as well as of
the suffering servant of Second Isaiah. It should be emphasized that their humanity is not lost by the promise of their
transformation to an exalted state resembling that of the angels.

[90] Fire (from the throne?) accomplishes the destruction in
7:11.

[91] This is Lohmeyer's insight, discussing the NT Son of Man
(*Das Evangelium des Markus* [1951] 6; cited by Tödt, *Son of Man*,
19). Lohmeyer speaks of the eschatological Son of Man as fore-
most a completely transcendent figure who belongs to the coming

world, to God's side, but at the same time as a human figure,
a Jew.

[92]Lindars, "Apocalyptic Myth," 373.

[93]Among those who accept this Canaanite hypothesis are
Colpe ("ὁ υἱὸς τοῦ ἀνθρώπου," 415-19), Delcor (*Le Livre de
Daniel*, 149), Emerton ("The Origin of the Son of Man Imagery"),
Cross (*Canaanite Myth*), E. Schweizer ("The Son of Man Again,"
256), Lacocque (*Daniel*, 129), Collins (*Apocalyptic Vision*, 98-
106). Zevit ("Structure," 390) and Porteous (*Daniel*, 98) are
cautious, stressing the speculative nature of this theory and
the improvability of conscious borrowing by the author. Vermes
(*Jesus the Jew*, 169-70), Di Lella ("The One in Human Likeness,"
3-5; *Daniel*, 87) and Hooker (*Son of Man*, 13) consider an earlier mythological or semi-mythological background irrelevant to a
probe for the meaning of Daniel 7. A. Ferch ("Daniel 7 and
Ugarit: A Reconsideration," *JBL* 99 [1980] 75-86) challenges the
Canaanite hypothesis on the grounds that "incidental correspondences" between Daniel 7 and the Ugaritic texts are outweighed
by significant differences, especially of description, function
and context. I judge his challenge to be unsuccessful, but
valuable because aspects of his treatment point up (a) the com-
plexity, partial preservation and various opinions concerning
the translation, ordering and meaning of the Canaanite texts;
(b) the tentative nature of the theory of Canaanite influence;
(c) the extent of adaptation and transformation of mythological
motifs by the author of Daniel.

[94]Cross, *Canaanite Myth*, 177.

[95]*Corpus des tablettes en cunéiformes alphabétiques* (=
*CTCA*) (ed. A. Herdner; Paris: Imprimerie Nationale, 1963)
17.5.20-28; quoted by Cross, *Canaanite Myth*, 188.

[96]Ibid., 185. Ferch ("Daniel 7," 82-83) finds no real
parallel to the judgment scene in Daniel 7.

[97]"Thou art great, O 'El, verily thou art wise / Thy hoary
beard indeed instructs Thee" (*CTCA* 4.5.66); Cross, *Canaanite
Myth*, 16.

[98]*CTCA* 6.1.36; 17.6.49. See Cross, *Canaanite Myth*, 16-19.
Contrast C. H. Gordon, "El, Father of Šnm," *JNES* 35 (1976)
261-62; cited by Ferch, "Daniel 7," 82.

[99]Collins, *Apocalyptic Vision*, 100; Cross, *Canaanite Myth*,
16. Against Colpe ("ὁ υἱὸς τοῦ ἀνθρώπου," 416-17) who does not
find the parallels with the Ancient of Days convincing.

[100]Cross, *Canaanite Myth*, 50. 'El and Baal in some texts
are spoken of in father-son terminology. 'El in a number of
his epithets is portrayed as father and creator: 'abū banī 'ili,
father of the gods (*CTCA* 32.1.25, 33), and is even called Baal's
father and progenitor (*CTCA* 3.5.43; 4.1.5; 4.4.47). But Cross
points out that we are dealing here with a fixed oral formula
which could be used of any of the sons of 'El, that is, of any

god.  'El was also called Father of man ('abū 'adami; CTCA
14.1.36; 14.3.150, etc.); see Canaanite Myth, 15.

[101]Ibid., 40.  At times Baal plays the role of intercessor
or advocate in addressing 'El (ibid., 179-80; CTCA 15.2.11-28).
Cross remarks that one is reminded of the role of the mal'ak
Yahweh, the advocate in the heavenly court, identical with the
heavenly vindicator or witness in Job.

[102]CTCA 5.5.6-11; 10.2.32-33; cf. J. C. de Moor, "Clouds,"
IDBSup, 169.

[103]Colpe, "ὁ υἱὸς τοῦ ἀνθρώπου," 417.  In a listing of
Baal's entourage, the term 'rpt is used in CTCA 5.5.6-11 (Cross,
Canaanite Myth, 147).  Cross speaks of "the (deified) storm
clouds (or cloud chariot) accompanying him or on which he rides"
(ibid., 17).  Contrast E. Ullendorff, "Ugaritic Studies Within
Their Semantic and Eastern Mediterranean Setting," BJRL 46
(1963-64) 243-44.

[104]CTCA 10.2.33.  Cross, Canaanite Myth, 147.

[105]Ibid., 165-66 n. 86.  De Moor ("Clouds," 169) rejects
the purported etymological relationship between Ugar./Heb. 'nn
(cloud) and Ugar. 'nn (servant--of Baal and other gods).

[106]When Baal is supposed dead, 'El offers to make one of
the sons of Asherah king; the sons, however, prove inadequate
and are rejected (CTCA 6.1.53-67; Collins, Apocalyptic Vision,
101).  Nickelsburg points out that in Daniel 8 and 11 the inso-
lence of Antiochus is described in language akin to that of the
"Lucifer" myth of Isaiah 14.  He suggests that "perhaps Jews at
the time of Daniel recognized in Isaiah 14 the myth of the
fallen god Athtar, identified this god with a (the) chief demon,
and reapplied the myth here to a king who surely appeared to
them to be the embodiment of the anti-God" (Resurrection, 15;
cf. Collins, "Court Tales," 226 n. 47).  This Athtar (Venus-
star) in the Ras Shamra texts is proposed as a substitute for
Baal, when Baal is in eclipse during the dry summer season.  He
is, however, too small to fill the throne, and is forced to
come down to earth and reign "god of it all."  In Isa 14:3-20,
Helel ben Shahar (the morning star or bright one, son of the
dawn) says in his heart, "I will ascend to the heavens; above
the stars of 'El I will set my throne on high...I will ascend
above the heights of the clouds, I will make myself like 'Elyon"
(vv. 13-14).  He is instead brought down to Sheol.  See J. Gray,
"Day Star," IDB, 1.785.  G. Cooke ("The Sons of [the] God[s],"
ZAW 76 [1964] 34) sees the influence of this Canaanite myth both
in Isaiah 14 and Ps 82:7.  The recognition of the presence of
something of this myth in Daniel 7 reinforces the impression
that the one like a son of man is an ascending figure, his ascent set in contrast to the ascent and fall of the evil one.

[107]Cf. Colpe, "ὁ υἱὸς τοῦ ἀνθρώπου," 416, 418-19.  On the
struggles within the Canaanite assembly of the gods, see also
H. Ringgren (The Religions of the Ancient Near East [London:
SPCK, 1973] 144-53) and R. N. Whybray (The Heavenly Counsellor
in Isaiah [Cambridge: Cambridge University, 1971] 37-38).  The
latter speaks of the possibility of a sort of dual kingship of

'El and Baal.  Ferch ("Daniel 7," 83-85) thinks it is not certain that the conferral of kingship on Baal must be inferred.

[108]Colpe's phrase.

[109]*CTCA* 2.

[110]*CTCA* 5.1.1-5; 3.3.35-39.  See Collins, *Apocalyptic Vision*, 98.  Cf. Ferch, "Daniel 7," 79-81.

[111]See above, p. 154.  Ferch rightly notes that Daniel 7
omits a battle between the one like a son of man and the beasts
("Daniel 7," 80), but does not attempt to explain this (or any
other dissimilarity) in terms of Danielic adaptation.

[112]Collins, *Apocalyptic Vision*, 104, 127-28.  The four
beasts are here manifestations of the chaotic power of the sea.
It is widely agreed that the four-kingdom theme, which derived
from a Persian schematization of history, functioned in oriental resistance of Hellenization.

[113]Delcor (*Le Livre de Daniel*, 149) finds the expression
עַתִּיק יוֹמִין astonishing.  Charles calls it an "irreverence" of
which no apocalypticist would be guilty, and emends the text by
inserting a comparative in 7:9: "one like an Ancient of Days"
(*Daniel*, ix, 181).  The LXX reads ὡς παλαιὸς ἡμερῶν in 7:13,
but Montgomery regards this as an ancient error for ἕως (*Daniel*,
304).  There is no comparative in 7:9 LXX.  See above, p. 195 n. 44.

[114]The image of Yahweh riding on clouds (Isa 19:1; cf. Deut
33:26) or making the clouds his chariot (Ps 104:3) is derived
from the storm imagery of the Baal theophanies, Yahweh having
assimilated some of Baal's characteristics.

[115]See above, p. 195 n. 45.

[116]See Emerton, "The Origin of the Son of Man Imagery,"
231-32.  The one like a son of man is clearly "inferior" to the
Ancient of Days, since kingship is given to him by the latter;
but Baal is also "inferior" to 'El in the Ugaritic texts.

[117]See Colpe, "ὁ υἱὸς τοῦ ἀνθρώπου," 420.

[118]Feuillet, "Le Fils de l'Homme," 192-93.

[119]Collins, *Apocalyptic Vision*, 100.

[120]See above, p. 118.

[121]See above, pp. 195-96 n. 47, for suggestions relating
the clouds of Dan 7:13 to Moses' ascent in rabbinic literature
and in Josephus.  These traditions are later than the ones explored here.  I see no evidence that Exod 24:18 has influenced
Dan 7:13 (against Di Lella).

[122]See Colpe, "ὁ υἱὸς τοῦ ἀνθρώπου," 419 n. 152.  Lindars
argues that "the origins of the vision in a mythological enthronement ceremony of a celestial figure may be nearer to the
surface than is usually realized" ("Reenter," 55).

[123]Colpe, "ὁ υἱὸς τοῦ ἀνθρώπου," 418-19.

[124]Cf. J. J. Collins, review of U. B. Müller, *Messias und Menschensohn in jüdischen Apokalypsen und in der Offenbarung des Johannes* (Gütersloh: Mohn, 1972) in *JBL* 93 (1974) 622.

[125]*CTCA* 17-20.

[126]Collins, *Apocalyptic Vision*, 2-3. See M. E. Stone, "The Book of Enoch and Judaism in the Third Century B.C.E.," *CBQ* 40 (1978) 485-86. A Daniel is also an angelic figure in *1 Enoch* 6:7 (seventh in a list of fallen angels); cf. 69:7.

[127]Collins, *Apocalyptic Vision*, 102-4. He thinks it is probable that the mastery of archaic traditions displayed in Daniel was the product of learning, not of simple folk-traditions.

[128]Some critics argue that according to an ANE cultic pattern that may have been pervasive if not rigidly stereotyped or uniform, the celebration of the enthronement of a king was embedded mythically and ritually in the celebration of the enthronement of a god. A yearly ceremony of the king's authority *may have* been part of a ritual drama depicting the god's primordial victory over chaos and the creation of order. The king enthroned on earth symbolized the god enthroned in heaven, and ruled by divine power. The degree to which Israel modified, adapted and rejected elements of ANE royal ideologies is strongly debated (see G. Fohrer, *History of Israelite Religion* [New York: Abingdon, 1972] 142-50).

[129]Hanson, "Jewish Apocalyptic," 44; cf. idem, *Dawn of Apocalyptic*, 300-307.

[130]Cross, *Canaanite Myth*, 262. Cross finds a Canaanite formula of divine sonship of the king in metrical form in Ps 98: 27-28; 2:7; and also in 2 Sam 7:14a and Isa 9:5. Ps 110:3 (now corrupt) in its original form probably also designated the Davidic king as son of God. Some argue that these texts evidence belief in the divine character of the monarchy. (For example, in Ps 45:7, the king seems to be addressed as 'Elohim: "Your throne, O 'Elohim, endures forever and ever.") Critics are quick to point out, however, that the Israelite conception was of the adoptive sonship of the king, or of fundamental legal legitimation, and was not identical or even compatible with the conception of the king as a natural, physical son of God (Cross, *Canaanite Myth*, 247). That is, at his accession the Israelite king was believed declared a son of God by the deliberate decision of God. By the act of God, he could be considered to have entered the sphere of the divine. Insofar as he was promised God's fidelity, he entered into a permanence above the vicissitudes of history. He was honored by God, not set on a par with God. Israel maintained a recognition of the mundane, secular nature of the monarchy and of all kings as mortal. We cannot be sure, however, how precisely or imprecisely the general Israelite populace interpreted the formula of adoption and the myth and ritual pattern that appears in the texts; nor do we know what was envisioned if and when the drama in these texts was acted out.

[131]Hanson, *Dawn of Apocalyptic*, 310, 315.

[132]Hanson, "Old Testament Apocalyptic Reexamined," 475.

[133]Ibid. See his *Dawn of Apocalyptic* (305-7) for outlines of the ritual pattern of the conflict myth, integrated into the ideology of the royal cult, in psalms from various periods.

[134]Bentzen, *King and Messiah*, 74, 20. Delcor (*Le Livre de Daniel*, 166) is highly critical of Bentzen's thesis. Admitting a certain general resemblance between the psalm and Daniel 7, Delcor argues that nothing proves the latter was inspired by the former.

[135]D. M. Hay, *Glory at the Right Hand*, 26.

[136]See above, pp. 147-48.

[137]Colpe remarks that the figure of the one like a son of man suggests messianic ideas without himself being a messiah ("ὁ υἱὸς τοῦ ἀνθρώπου," 421). The one like a son of man cannot simply be identified as another earthly king or even as the future earthly anointed one like David, but in time a messianic association was acquired (Vermes, *Jesus the Jew*, 170).

[138]F. H. Borsch, *The Christian and Gnostic Son of Man*, 116-17; cf. idem, *The Son of Man in Myth and History* (Philadelphia: Westminster, 1967) 142.

[139]See Hay, *Glory at the Right Hand*, 26; Emerton, "The Origin of Son of Man Imagery," 231.

[140]Collins, *Apocalyptic Vision*, 101.

[141]M. Hooker has noticed the chaos-enthronement pattern in Daniel 7, and she further emphasizes the elements of a creation myth behind the text and the connection between the one like a son of man and Adam. She argues that the pattern of the vision in Daniel 7 has been shaped by the primitive myth of creation, involving the following motifs: the emergence of the beasts from the sea, their defeat by Yahweh, and the bestowal of dominion on a human figure. The one like a son of man is Israel, the only truly human nation, the only real descendants of Adam, king of Israel. The enthronement in Daniel 7 means that the dominion of Adam is restored (Hooker, *Son of Man*, 17, 24, 29). The myth is seen as somewhat at odds with its interpretation, in which the holy ones of the Most High are present from the beginning, not created after the victory; cf. Lacocque, *Daniel*, 124, 128.

[142]G. A. Cooke, *The Book of Ezekiel* (ICC; Edinburgh: T. & T. Clark, 1951) 16. This is the case as well in *1 Enoch* 14:18, which Cooke thinks imitates Daniel 7; see below, however, for discussion of the relationship between these texts. In *1 Enoch* 61:10 and 71:7, the wheels are personified and become an order of angels, as in *Ḥagigah*, *2 Enoch* and *Testament of Abraham* 17.

[143]In Jewish tradition, מרכבה becomes an accepted term
referring to visions of the throne, the heavenly palace or
palaces (היכלות), divine hierarchies, and the Glory, dependent
in some way on Ezekiel's vision.  See Scholem, *Major Trends in
Jewish Mysticism* (46) for discussion of the variety of terminology used in the course of the centuries for descriptions of
the contemplation of God's Glory and the throne.  He posits an
essential continuity concerning the Merkabah in the three
stages of this tradition: (1) its early beginnings in the
period of the second temple, in the "anonymous conventicles"
of the old apocalyptics, groups which produced a large portion
of the pseudepigrapha and apocalypses of the first centuries
B.C. and A.D.; (2) its second stage that of the Merkabah speculations of the Mishnaic teachers known to us by name, groups
of pupils of R. Yohanan ben Zakkai; (3) the third stage that
of the Merkabah mysticism of talmudic and post-talmudic times
(pp. 40, 42-43, 47).

[144]Cf. Ps 18:10-11 where God is pictured as riding on thick
darkness (עֲרָפֶל), a cherub, and wings of wind, and above, p. 156,
where the imagery connected with Baal is mentioned.

[145]Scott, "Behold, He Cometh," 129.

[146]W. Meeks hints at an identification between the beasts
with human faces in Ezekiel 1 and 10, and the one like a son of
man in Daniel 7 ("The Man from Heaven in Johannine Sectarianism," *JBL* 91 [1972] 59 n. 54).  He does not develop the suggestion, and the obvious difference is that the one like a son of
man comes to, not with, the heavenly throne of God.

[147]In addition, the verb זהר is used in the OT only at Dan
12:3 to mean "to shine" (rather than "to warn, admonish, in-
struct"; cf. BDB, 263-64), and it and the noun זֹהַר ("shining")
in this text seem to be drawn from the description in Ezek 8:2
of "the form that had the appearance of a man" (LXX: ἀνδρός;
MT אֵשׁ), a being described in the same way as the figure on the
moving throne in 1:27.

[148]See J. Bowman, "The Background of the Term, 'Son of
Man,'" *ExpTim* 58/9 (1947/48) 285.

[149]W. Zimmerli, *Ezekiel* (ed. F. M. Cross and K. Baltzer;
trans. R. E. Clements; Philadelphia: Fortress, 1979) 1.54; S.
Spiegel, "Ezekiel or Pseudo-Ezekiel?" *HTR* 24 (1931) 264-65;
S. H. Levey, "The Targum to Ezekiel," *HUCA* 46 (1975) 142.

[150]W. Eichrodt, *Ezekiel* (London: SCM, 1970) 58.

[151]Kimchi rejects the view that Ezekiel is called "son of
man" so that he might not grow proud and consider himself an
angel because he had seen the vision.  "But my opinion is that
because he had seen the face of a man in the Heavenly Chariot,
God made known to him that he, Ezekiel, is good and acceptable
in His sight, since he is son of man, not son of ox, not son of

eagle." He has more in common with the "man" on the throne than with the *ḥayyoth* (cited by Bowman, "Background," 284).

[152]Delcor (*Le Livre de Daniel*, 167) thinks that the term "son of man" has different meanings in Daniel 7 and in Ezekiel 1. He holds that the figure in the former text is simply a symbol of the Jewish people, including its Messiah or king, who is human in contrast to the beasts, and who has no relation to the prophet Ezekiel or the figure on the moving throne. Delcor does, however, find a link between the angels of Dan 8:15 and 10:16 and Ezek 1:26-27. See also Porteous (*Daniel*, 152) on the description of the angel in Daniel 10 as an echo of the language of Ezek 1:26-27.

[153]Does the prophet Ezekiel himself, בֶּן־אָדָם, bear any relationship to the one like a son of man of Daniel 7? It might be cautiously implied in Ezek 3:12 that the prophet, lifted by the Spirit, ascends with the heavenly throne. If the word בָּרוּךְ is corrected to בְּרוּם in this verse, it reads: "Then the Spirit lifted me up, and as the *Kābôd* of Yahweh arose from its place, I heard behind me the sound of a great earthquake" (the sound of the wings of the *ḥayyoth*). See Cooke, *Ezekiel*, 41. Levey ("The Targum to Ezekiel," 145) remarks that the instances where the prophet is lifted by the Spirit (3:12-15; 8:3; 11:1, 24; 43:5) "have overtones of the mystic ascent of the Merkabah devotee." But this is not sufficient indication that this imagery is responsible for the portrait of the one like a son of man.

[154]O. Procksch, "Die Berufungsvision Hesechiels," *BZAW* 34 (1920) 141; W. Eichrodt, *Theology of the Old Testament* (2 vols.; Philadelphia: Westminster, 1967) 2.32-34; Emerton, "The Origin of Son of Man Imagery," 231; von Rad, *OT Theology*, 2.312 n. 27.

[155]Borsch, *Son of Man*, 138.

[156]See above, p. 205 n. 141. Those who share Hooker's opinion include R. G. Hamerton-Kelly (*Pre-existence, Wisdom and the Son of Man* [SNTSMS 21; Cambridge: Cambridge University, 1973] 41) and I. Engnell ("The Son of Man," *A Rigid Scrutiny* [ed. J. T. Willis; Nashville: Vanderbilt University, 1969] 238).

[157]Feuillet, "Le Fils de l'Homme," 170-292, 321-46. However, God is not "invisible" in Daniel 7.

[158]According to Feuillet, the word "glory" in Ezekiel refers only to the mysterious human silhouette sitting on the throne; this is distinct from the throne itself and from the *ḥayyoth* ("Le Fils de l'Homme," 182). In 8:1-2 he notes that the glory is manifest without the chariot.

[159]Feuillet, "Le Fils de l'Homme," 188-89, 192, 195. The P tradition, Feuillet thinks, which understood the *Kābôd* as a concrete form of the apparition of divinity, is in line with the thought of Ezekiel, and prepares for the vision in Daniel 7. This line of thinking is partially prolonged in the rabbinic conception of the Shekinah. See Zimmerli, *Ezekiel*, 1.123: *Kabôd* is a technical term in P and Ezekiel for the appearance of Yahweh in light.

[160]Ezek 1:1 calls the whole experience "visions of God"
(מַרְאוֹת אֱלֹהִים).  Verse 28 seems to imply that this means visions
in which God was seen; that is, the genitive is objective (but
cf. 8:3, 40:2).  Among those who agree that 1:26-27 is a theophany are Cooke (*Ezekiel*, 21), Colpe ("ὁ υἱὸς τοῦ ἀνθρώπου,"
419 n. 151), Emerton ("The Origin of Son of Man Imagery," 231),
Fohrer (*Israelite Religion*, 78, 169) and Delcor (*Le Livre de
Daniel*, 167).

[161]See Feuillet, "Le Fils de l'Homme," 321-42.

[162]M. Black, "Throne-Theophany," 61.  Neither Feuillet nor
Black discusses the hypothesis of influence of Canaanite mythology.

[163]Black argues that if this were the case with an original vision which the author of Daniel is using only symbolically,
then (if I understand him correctly) the ditheistic position
implied in the original vision may have arisen from a "desire
to remove the anthropomorphic language of Ezek 1:26 from a description of deity" (ibid., 62).  But this makes little sense
in the light of the equally anthropomorphic description of the
Ancient of Days.

[164]Ibid.  Black views this as a development of such think-
ing as is found in Ps 80:17, which speaks of the place of the
nation (or the nation represented by the king) at God's right
hand; cf. the more explicit imagery in *Assumption of Moses* 10.
According to Black, the next logical step is a messianic inter-
pretation such as that found in the Similitudes ("Throne-
Theophany," 63).  See also his treatment of Daniel 7 in "Die
Apotheose Israels: eine neue Interpretation des danielischen
'Menschensohn,'" *Jesus und der Menschensohn* (ed. R. Pesch and
R. Schnackenburg; Freiburg: Herder, 1975) 92-99.

[165]D. Neiman, "Council, Heavenly," *IDBSup*, 187.

[166]F. M. Cross, "The Council of Yahweh in Second Isaiah,"
*JNES* 12 (1953) 274 n. 1; R. E. Brown, *The Semitic Background of
the Term "Mystery" in the New Testament* (Philadelphia: Fortress,
1968) 3; H. Ringgren, *Israelite Religion* (Philadelphia: Fortress, 1966) 95; Whybray, *The Heavenly Counsellor*, 34-39.

[167]Whybray (*Heavenly Counsellor*, 83) notes that, according
to the Israelite concept of "personality," the idea of God as
an isolated monad outside of the context of a society would
have been totally incomprehensible.  G. A. F. Knight (*A Biblical
Approach to the Doctrine of the Trinity*) and A. R. Johnson (*The
One and the Many in the Israelite Conception of God*) stress the
importance of the concepts connected with divine council as
background to later Trinitarian thinking.

[168]Whybray, *Heavenly Counsellor*, 30-41; Cross, "The Council of Yahweh," 27 n. 1.

[169]E.g., Job 1-2; Psalms 28; 82; and 89; Deut 32:8; 1 Kgs
22:10-23; Isaiah 6; Zechariah 3; Jer 23:18.  Passages such as

Gen 1:26-27 and 3:22 which suggest a pluralistic conception of the deity are probably related to the idea of the council. Cooke treats several of these passages in "The Son(s) of (the) God(s)."

[170]Neiman ("Council, Heavenly," 188) makes the interesting suggestion that at most the concept of the council is a "literary fiction to dramatize Yahweh's thought, using the analogy of a human king surrounded by his courtiers."

[171]Cooke, "The Son(s) of (the) God(s)," 26, 45.

[172]In certain OT passages there is the clear idea of a council debating and deciding (Isaiah 6; Job 1-2; 1 Kgs 22:19-23); this moves beyond the concept of an entourage.

[173]This is not to deny that from the time of the migration into Canaan there was a syncretistic tendency characterized by the borrowing of Canaanite gods who were worshipped alongside Yahweh and had their own cult centers. But as Ringgren points out, this religious syncretism came about without premeditation and was never theoretically systematized; see also Whybray, *Heavenly Counsellor*, 41.

[174]See Cooke, "The Son(s) of (the) God(s)," 28-29, 46. Poetical references to mythical fragments can be found, however, in Isa 24:21; 14:12-20; Psalm 82; Deut 32:8-9, and elsewhere.

[175]Whybray, *Heavenly Counsellor*, 47.

[176]Cross, "The Council of Yahweh," 274 n. 1. See also Brown, *Semitic Background*, 4: the members are angels who "at most suggest and carry out commands of Yahweh, who alone renders the final decree."

[177]Whybray (*Heavenly Counsellor*, 46) thinks that this indicates an absence of a fixed tradition, which in turn may indicate that the concept of the council, though persistent, did not occupy a central position in Israel's belief system. He thinks the idea of corporate personality explains the persistence of the idea of the council.

[178]As has been seen, the plural "thrones" in 7:9 indicates to some that assessor angels participate in the judgment (cf. 7:26). Dan 4:17 gives the impression that Watchers or holy ones do more than just proclaim the decision: the sentence and decree concerning Nebuchadnezzar is said to be by their decree or word; the author may intend to depict a similar process in chapter 7.

[179]Cf. Prov 9:10; 30:3; Ps 89:5, 7; Job 5:1; 15:15 and especially Dan 4:17 where "holy ones" are members of the assembly.

[180]In chapter 10, a supernatural "man clothed in linen" is described in a way that recalls the human appearance in Ezekiel 1; this person may be Gabriel, named in 8:16. The angel Michael

is named in 10:21 and 12:1, and has an important function, perhaps judicial, in the latter text. Again, these are not completely colorless or vague characters.

[181]Cross, Hanson and others stress that elements in Daniel
and other apocalyptic works which have a Canaanite parallel most
likely belonged to an underground mythological stratum in Israelite religion, kept alive in the royal ritual and ideology.
This stratum breaks ground in the late OT and intertestamental
period, under pressure of the inadequacies of the Deuteronomistic theology and of the tensions of religious persecution--as
well as under pressure of foreign influences.

[182]Oracles of the type of Isaiah 40 are described by Cross
as divine directives to angelic heralds or as divine proclama-
tions delivered by a herald (see "Council of Yahweh," 275).
Though the visual element is missing, and the prophet just
transmits what he overhears, the conception of the heavenly
council is presupposed.

[183]Cf. Jer 23:18; Job 15:8. The verb עמד can be a technical term for participation (Cross, "The Council of Yahweh,"
274-75 n. 3). It occurs in the OT primarily in judicial contexts: the disputants in a law suit stand (Deut 19:17; Josh
20:6; Ezek 44:24; Isa 50:8); the accusing angel stands (Zechariah 4; cf. *Jub.* 48:9) as does the defending angel (*Jub.* 18:9;
Dan 12:1).

[184]Cross, "The Council of Yahweh," 275; cf. idem, *Canaanite
Myth*, 186-88.

[185]N. L. A. Tidwell, "Wā'ōmar (Zech 3:5) and the Genre of
Zechariah's Fourth Vision," *JBL* 94 (1975) 352. Only in this
text and in Isaiah 6 is there participation in the sense of
giving advice.

[186]Cooke, "The Son(s) of (the) God(s)," 40.

[187]4Q 'Amram[a] (J. T. Milik, "4Q Visions de 'Amram et une
Citation d'Origène," *RB* 79 [1972] 94). Milik thinks 4Q 'Amram
may have been written around 150 B.C. or earlier. *Testament of
Levi* 2-5, 8 situates the ordination of Levi in heaven (cf. 8:11)
and suggests strongly that the earthly priesthood of the Levites
is a replica of the heavenly priesthood of angels: it is said
that Levi will stand near the Lord and be his minister (λειτουρ-
γός), as in 3:5 angels of the presence are the ones who minister
(οἱ λειτουργοῦντες).

[188]H. Wheeler Robinson, *Inspiration and Revelation in the
Old Testament* (Oxford: Clarendon, 1946) 162, 167, 169-79.

[189]See Cooke, "The Son(s) of (the) God(s)," 47.

[190]P. D. Hanson, "Old Testament Apocalyptic Reexamined,"
485-86.

[191]The later texts from Qumran or related to Qumran
thought, however, must be read in the light of the aim of the
members to "lead a life of continuous worship in which the sons
of Light on earth joined their voices to those of the celestial
choirs of angels" (G. Vermes, "Dead Sea Scrolls," *IDBSup*, 215).
The assimilation of priests to angels may have been understood
more "realistically."

[192]See above, pp. 146-47, for discussion of this text in
the light of *1 Enoch* 104:2, 6 and *Testament of Moses* 10:9.   In
Dan 12:12, the seer is told, "You will rest and will stand in
your allotted place (תַעֲמֹד לְגֹרָלְךָ) at the end of days."

[193]Y. Kaufmann, *The Religion of Israel* (New York: Schocken,
1972) 77.  Kaufmann speaks of the strict bounds set between
Yahweh who is one, and the host of *'elohim* who may not be worshipped (Exod 22:19).  Likewise, there is no worship in the OT,
he insists, of human beings, dead or alive, heroes or kings.
There is no concept of salvation through apotheosis in the manner of pagan mysteries, no idea of mystic absorption in God.
But the strange traditions concerning translations witness belief in a limited apotheosis, nonpagan because achieved not "by
a mystical regimen but by the grace of God" (p. 78).

[194]C. H. Talbert argues that Enoch and Elijah, because they
remained men and did not become "deities," do not really qualify
as "immortals" ("The Concept of Immortals in Mediterranean Antiquity," *JBL* 94 [1975] 429 n. 50).  But, however much Israel's
concept of the divine council differed from that of a pantheon,
we cannot rule out a priori an understanding of them as having
attained angelic or even divine status.  They are thought of as
existing in the world of the *'elohim*.  By the first century A.D.
Jewish writers had exalted other figures (Moses, Baruch, Ezra)
to the privilege of escaping death (see R. Baucham, "The Martyrdom of Enoch and Elijah: Jewish or Christian?" *JBL* 95 [1976]
451).

[195]The LXX with "theological caution" reads ὡς εἰς τὸν
οὐρανόν (J. A. Montgomery, *The Books of Kings* [ICC; New York:
Scribners, 1951] 356).  Josephus (*Ant.* 9.2.2) remarks that
"Elijah disappeared from among men and no one knows until today
anything of his death."  *Sukk.* 5a and other late traditions
deny that Elijah went up into heaven.  See Str-B 4.765-66 for
the rabbinic debate on this point.

[196]See above, p. 128, for the definition of this and related terms in this present work.

[197]Text 67, VI, 8-9 (C. H. Gordon, *Ugaritic Manual* [Rome,
1955] cited by Leah Bronner, *The Stories of Elijah and Elisha
as Polemics against Baal Worship* [Leiden: Brill, 1968] 127).
B. Childs ("On Reading the Elijah Narratives," *Int* 34 [1980]
131) warns against using Ugaritic parallels to argue that "what
appears in the OT as a historical narrative is really only a
construct of ancient mythological patterns transferred from one
deity to another."  The OT author regards Baal as a sheer delu-
sion and not a god at all.

[198]Whirlwind is associated with a "great cloud" in Ezek 1:4.

[199]Bronner, *Stories of Elijah and Elisha*, 54-77.

[200]Other critics have seen the chariot of fire and horses of fire as connected with the horses of the sun in which the sun god travelled through the heavens: "One may ask whether the translation takes place through the power of the sun-god, to the sun-god or even as the sun-god.  In the OT we are clearly no longer dealing with such conceptions, but with translation to the divine realm.  But the mythological background is unmistakable" (Fohrer, *History of Israelite Religion*, 222).

[201]P. D. Miller, Jr., "The Divine Council and the Prophetic Call to War," *VT* 18 (1968) 107; Cross, *Canaanite Myth*, 226; cf. 2 Kgs 6:15-19.

[202]See above, p. 156.

[203]J. L. Martyn, "We Have Found Elijah," 187.

[204]The task of restoration is seen in later tradition to involve reassembling the members of the people who have been taken away, determining which are genuine Israelites, reestablishing the purity of the corpus Israel.  He is also to clarify obscure points of Torah (cf. *'Ed.* 8:7).  Cf. Jeremias ("'Ηλ(ε)ίας," 931) and Martyn ("We Have Found Elijah," 188-89) for mention of all the functions attributed to Elijah in rabbinic literature, especially of his coming to the aid of the helpless and poor, and his bringing of peace.  See also above, p. 127.

[205]The Hebrew (MS B, Cairo) reads:
יה..... ך.../..אשר ראך ומת.  For reconstruction and interpretation of this verse, see A. E. Cowley and A. Neubauer, *The Original Hebrew of a Portion of Ecclesiasticus* (XXIX.15 to XLIX.11) (Oxford: Clarendon, 1897) 36; I. Levi, *The Hebrew Text of the Book of Ecclesiasticus* (1904; reprinted Leiden: Brill, 1963); W. O. E. Oesterley, *Ecclesiasticus* (Cambridge: Cambridge University, 1912) 328; T. Weber, "Sirach," *JBC*, 554.  On the basis of the Greek, the first line of the Hebrew is often emended and read: "Blessed (אשרי for אשר) was he who saw you and died" or "Blessed is he who sees you and dies."  The second line is too mutilated to be restored with certainty, but it has been conjectured that it read: "(But more) blessed are you, (Elijah), for you live (forever)" ([אשרי]ך [כי חיה תח[יה]).

[206]μακάριοι οἱ ἰδόντες σε
     καὶ οἱ ἐν ἀγαπήσει κεκοιμημένοι
     καὶ γὰρ ἡμεῖς ζωῇ ζησόμεθα
("Blessed are those who saw you and have fallen asleep in love. For we also surely will live").

[207]H. Duesberg and P. Auvray, *Le Livre d'Ecclésiastique* (Paris: Editions du Cerf, 1958) 214 n. a.  The blessed dead are compared to Elijah.  This seems to contradict Ben Sira's

frequently expressed disbelief in or lack of appreciation for
an afterlife (J. G. Snaith, *Ecclesiasticus* [London: Cambridge
University, 1974] 240); cf. 10:11; 11:28; 14:12-19; 17:1, 27-
30; 40:1. It may therefore have been added in view of the more
developed ideas of the afterlife that arose in the second century (Oesterley, *Ecclesiasticus*, 328). The Greek translator
models his hope of a future life on Elijah's fate.

[208]This tower, according to Milik (*Books of Enoch*, 43)
"units into a single place the first paradisiac abode of Enoch,
the heavenly palace, and the mountain-throne of God." The
Apocalypse of Weeks (*1 Enoch* 93:3-10 and 91:11-17) mentions
Elijah's assumption as the most important "event" between the
division of the Kingdom and 587 B.C.: in the sixth week "a man
shall ascend" (*1 Enoch* 93:8).

[209]So Jeremias, "'Ηλ(ε)ίας," 929. Milik (*Books of Enoch*,
45) identifies the ram, however, with Judas Maccabeus.

[210]*Sota* 9:15: "The resurrection of the dead will come
through Elijah of blessed memory."

[211]See Stiassny ("Le Prophète Elie," 212) for the late
Kabbalistic insistance that Elijah was not a man at all, but
an angel.

[212]Compare Ps 39:13 ("Look away from me, that I may know
gladness, before I depart and am no more"); Job 7:21 ("For now
I will lie in the earth; You will seek me and I shall not be").

[213]Gen 17:1: Abraham walked before (not with) God. Cf.
G. von Rad, *Genesis* (Philadelphia: Westminster, 1961) 69.

[214]Enoch's "walking with God" during his lifetime may have
been considered by authors of the pseudepigrapha in this sense:
heavenly journeys and initiation into the secrets of God,
dwelling with angels. In Sir 44:16 Enoch is called "a sign of
knowledge (אות דעת) for all generations." Throughout the
pseudepigrapha, Enoch is the transmitter of esoteric secrets
revealed before the flood.

[215]See U. Cassuto, *A Commentary on the Book of Genesis*
(2 vols.; Jerusalem: Magnes, 1961) 1.285.

[216]N. M. Sarna, "Enoch," *EncJud* 6, col. 793. Cf. Wis 4:
7-15, which will be discussed below. Other statements concerning the death of Enoch mention his wickedness or his repentance
from a former wicked life, and some deny his miraculous translation. Bowker considers these texts in part a reaction to
Christian use of the Enoch legend (*The Targums and Rabbinic
Literature* [Cambridge: Cambridge University, 1969] 143-47).
Cf. *Gen. Rab.* 25:1. According to *Tg. Onq.* (Gen 5:24), Enoch
"was not because the Lord caused him to die" (some MSS, however,
take the opposite point of view: "and he was not because the
Lord did not cause him to die" [Sperber U, y^b, d^1; cited by
Bowker, *Targums*, 147]).

[217]Cassuto, *Genesis*, 1.286.  He finds only faint echoes here of a translation tradition.

[218]Cf. Gen 5:24 LXX; Sir 44:16 LXX; Wis 4:10; Heb 11:5; 1 Clement 9:3.  These texts use the verb μετατίθημι, which means to transfer, take up, convey to another place, but also to change, to alter.  See also *Jub.* 4:23; *Tg. Ps.-J.* on Gen 5:24; Josephus, *Ant.* 1.85; Philo, *Ques. Gen.* 1.86; *1 Enoch* 70: 1-2; *Der. Er. Zut.* 1 (end).

[219]*Frg. Tg.*: "And Enoch served (or: worshipped) before the Lord in uprightness, and behold he was not, and we do not know what he was in his end, because he was taken away from before the Lord" (see Milik, *Books of Enoch*, 128).  *Tg. Neof.*: "And all the days of the life of Enoch were 365 years (a variant or marginal gloss reads: and he died and was gathered from the midst of the world).  And Enoch served in truth before the Lord and is not know (sic) where he is because he was taken away by a word (that came) from before the Lord" (ed. A. Diez Macho, 1968, p. 31).  There is no mention of Enoch in both Talmuds (Cassuto, *Genesis*, 1.284).

[220]Cassuto, *Genesis*, 1.26.  Cassuto does not consider Enoch an exception.

[221]Above, n. 212.  The phrase is associated with the absence of God.

[222]P. Grelot, "La Légende d'Henoch dans les Apocryphes et dans la Bible: origines et signification," *RSR* 46 (1958) 5-26, 181-210.

[223]Ibid., 208; cf. H. Odeberg, "'Ενώχ," 556-7.  The latter thinks that in Genesis "there may be hints of the myth of the original man," possibly of the idea of his representatives or bearers of his power in various ages of humanity.  Was Enoch seen as the second Adam, winning immortality while Adam lost it?

[224]Grelot, "La Légende," 205, 207, 210.

[225]Ibid., 208.

[226]See Y. Yadin (*The Ben Sira Scroll from Masada* [Jerusalem, The Israel Exploration Society and the Shrine of the Book, 1965] 30, 10) for the restoration of the verses concerning Enoch, and their order, in chapter 49.  The word פנים is difficult to translate.  There have been several suggestions: (a) it means "personally" or "in person" or "himself."  NEB translates "bodily."  (b) Some have emended to פתאם ("suddenly").  (c) Some have thought פנים could be understood in the sense of פנימה ("within"--that is, "into the heavens" or perhaps "into the presence of God").  See Oesterley, *Ecclesiasticus*, 335-36, and Odeberg, "'Ενώχ," 557.  Greenfield ("Prolegomena," xlvi n. 27) thinks it means "absorption into the heavenly presence, but not necessarily more than that."

[227]Odeberg, "'Eνώχ," 556.  Cf. Stone, "Book of Enoch,"
484-85.

[228]Cf. *Jub.* 4:23 (*Jubilees* is usually dated 150-125 B.C.;
the information concerning Enoch in 4:17-25; 7:38; 10:17; 10:
24-27 and 21:10 is based in part on ancient portions [200-160
B.C.] of the Enoch literature: *1 Enoch* 6-16; 23-26; 72-90);
*1 Enoch* 106:7-9 (cf. 18:5, 10); 70:3-4 (the Epistle of Enoch
[*1 Enoch* 91-108] contains the Book of Noah [*1 Enoch* 106-7]
which Milik regards as an ancient appendix probably to the
whole Enochic corpus [*Books of Enoch*, 57] but which he does not
date).  See Harrington, "Research," 156.

[229]Cf. *Jub.* 4:21; *1 Enoch* 106:7-8; 1QapGen 2:20-21 (Enoch
"is a beloved [חיד] and o[ne desired...and with the holy ones]
is his lot apportioned, and they make everything known to him").
J. Fitzmyer (*The Genesis Apocryphon of Qumran Cave 1* [Rome:
Biblical Institute, 1971]) dates this work in the first century
B.C.; he finds nothing in it to disprove Essene origin, and
argues that it depends on *1 Enoch* and *Jubilees* (pp. 16-17).
Others date it earlier, reversing the dependency.  Hengel, for
example, considers the *Genesis Apocryphon* pre-Maccabean (*Judaism
and Hellenism*, 2.117 n. 460).

[230]See above, p. 127.  In *2 Enoch* and *3 Enoch* there are
explicit statements of the angelicization or quasi-divinization
of Enoch.  Odeberg thinks that Enoch's exaltation in *2 Enoch* 11
(cf. chapter 18) is "his institution as the second archangel,
as a heavenly figure alongside the throne of God" ("'Eνώχ,"
558).  In *3 Enoch*, Enoch is identified with Metatron, given a
garment of glory and a royal crown, called "the little Yahweh"
(12:5; Exod 23:21 is the text behind this title), and transformed into fire (15:2).  Milik considers him here "an almost
divine being, an intermediary between God and creation" (*Books
of Enoch*, 127).

[231]Scholem, *Jewish Mysticism*, 67.

[232]He may also be identified with the herald of Isa 52:7,
the "anointed one of the Spirit" (line 18).  The preserved parts
of 11Q Melchizedek illustrate "a midrashic development which is
independent of the classic OT loci" (J. Fitzmyer, "Further Light
on Melchizedek from Qumran Cave 11," *JBL* 86 [1967] 31).  But
this text is regarded by some as grounded on exegetical conclusions drawn in part from the two OT passages in which Melchizedek is mentioned as an (unusual) human being.  It is not obvious
that the link with this character is broken.  See M. Hengel, *The
Son of God* (Philadelphia: Fortress, 1976) 81; Lindars, "Reenter,"
58; D. Flusser, "Melchizedek and the Son of Man," *Christian News
from Israel* 17 (1966) 25-26, 28; M. Delcor, "Melchizedek from
Genesis to the Qumran Texts and the Epistle to the Hebrews, *JSJ*
2 (1971) 127; Fitzmyer, "Further Light," 34.  In contrast, Milik
regards the Qumran Melchizedek as without human dimension; he is
more than a created angel or even the chief of the good spirits.
"Il est en réalité une hypostase de Dieu, autrement dit le Dieu
transcendent lorsqu'il agit dans le monde" (Milkî-sedeq et Milkî
resa' dans les anciens écrits juifs et chrétiens," *JJS* 23 [1972]

125; cf. 239).  The Qumran sectarians' understanding of themselves as partakers of the lot of the angels and as participants
in the heavenly council must be mentioned here as indicative of
the belief that the distinction between the human and the angelic or human and heavenly was not as clearcut as we might
think.

[233]T. F. Glasson, *The Second Advent* (London: Epworth, 1963)
2-7; idem, "The Son of Man Imagery: Enoch XIV and Daniel VII,"
*NTS* 23 (1976) 82-90; Charles, *The Book of Enoch*, 83-84; idem,
*Daniel*, 184; *APOT*, 2.170; Hengel, *Judaism and Hellenism*, 1.176,
2.117 nn. 458-60; Black, "The 'Parables' of Enoch," 7.  H. L.
Jansen (*Die Henochgestalt: eine vergleichende Religions-
geschichtliche Untersuchung*, 1939) found Enoch in heavenly form
behind the Son of Man in Daniel and later literature.  He
traced Enoch back to the Babylonian Ea/Oannes, god of ocean
and wisdom (cf. Colpe, "ὁ υἱὸς τοῦ ἀνθρώπου," 427 n. 207).

[234]Rowley, *Relevance*, 93-99, 57.

[235]Emerton, "The Origin of the Son of Man Imagery," 230.
They develop independently of one another, in dependence on
Ezekiel 1; Deut 32:2; Ps 68:17, etc.

[236]Russell (*Method and Message*, 342) argues that both
writers "may have been drawing on a common tradition which
would adequately explain the similarities between the two
texts."

[237]Enoch, who goes on a heavenly trip in subsequent chapters, is not said to touch down on earth in this and the following section, although in 29:1-3 (which seems to repeat chapters
12-16) a whirlwind (cf. 2 Kings 2; *1 Enoch* 52:2) carries him
off the earth.  Charles regards 39:1-3 as the account of a real
translation, and no dream as in 14:8-9 (*APOT* 2.210).  There is,
except for chapters 70-71, no description of a final ascent.
Enoch is spoken of as "at the ends of the earth" in the Noah
fragment (106:8).

[238]Milik, *The Books of Enoch*, 194-99.  Milik dates this MSS
paleographically to the early Herodian period or the last third
of the first century B.C. (p. 178).  He thinks the copy of 4QEn[c]
was made from a manuscript around 125 B.C. in which period an
Enochic corpus was already in existence (pp. 22, 183).

[239]Greek: οἱ ἅγιοι τῶν ἀγγέλων.

[240]The Greek adds: and waked me (ἤγειρεν με).  Cf. Zech 4:1
where an angel "wakes" the prophet like a man that is waked out
of his sleep.

[241]The Greek adds: ὁ ἄνθρωπος ὁ ἀληθινός, ἄνθρωπος τῆς
ἀληθείας, ὁ γραμματεύς.

[242]R. H. Charles translation (*APOT* 2.197-98); cf. *Apocalypsis Henochi* (ed. M. Black; Leiden: Brill, 1970) 28-29.

[243] There is no OT parallel for the stream(s) of fire, although Ps 50:3 comes to mind. In Daniel and *1 Enoch* we may have an interpretation of the lightning-fire and hashmal fire of Ezek 1:13-14, 27.

[244] There is no OT parallel for this phrase either, but it seems to be drawn from Zech 14:3-5; Ps 68:18 and/or Deut 33:2. Cf. *1 Enoch* 1:9; 40:1. The cherubim sides of the throne in *1 Enoch* are Ezekiel's *ḥayyoth* (cf. Ezek 10:15).

[245] Glasson, "The Son of Man Imagery," 82.

[246] Black, "The 'Parables' of Enoch," 7. Enoch also intercedes for the evil Watchers, whereas in the natural order of things they should intercede for humanity. As humanity is contrasted to animality in Daniel 7, in *1 Enoch* 14 (fallen) angelhood is contrasted with humanity. It seems to be implied that Enoch is superior to both good and evil angels.

[247] Milik, *Books of Enoch*, 34.

[248] Charles, *APOT* 2.195. This is in contrast to the one like a son of man in Daniel. It is the seer in Daniel who is made anxious, alarmed and pale by the vision (Dan 7:15, 28).

[249] Like the first three beasts in Daniel, the fallen Watchers live on, stripped of power. The evil spirits who proceed from the Giants, however, are not to be judged until the end (*1 Enoch* 15:8-16:1). While Daniel 7 gives clues to the identity of the human, historical dimension of the evil, in *1 Enoch* 14 evil procedes from the angelic sphere.

[250] The compiler and composer was a Judean, perhaps from Jerusalem, a trader who traveled widely. He lived under Egyptian (Ptolemaic) domination, during a time of active Hellenization in Palestine (Milik, "Problèmes de la Littérature Hénochique à la lumière des fragments araméens de Qumrân," *HTR* 64 [1971] 346). See G.W.E. Nickelsburg ("Apocalyptic and Myth in 1 Enoch 6-11," *JBL* 96 [1977] 389-90) for the argument that 4QEn[a] (dated by Milik to the first half of the second century B.C.) and 4QEn[b] (middle of the second century B.C.) almost certainly included the Enochic material in chaps. 12-16. As neither of these MSS appears to be an author's autograph, it is reasonable to date their composition to the third century (Stone, "Book of Enoch," 484). From the first half of the second century B.C. on, according to Milik, the Book of Watchers had essentially the same form as that of the Greek and Ethiopic versions (*Books of Enoch*, 25).

[251] Glasson, "The Son of Man Imagery," 84. Rowley (*Relevance*, 57, 97-98) weakly argues on the other hand that references to persecution may have been outside the purpose of the author. See Stone, "Book of Enoch," 487, 491-92.

[252] Glasson, "Son of Man Imagery," 86.

[253] See Black, "The 'Parables' of Enoch," 7.

[254]In *1 Enoch* 102:4-103:4; 104:1-2, Enoch is made the forceful spokesman for belief in life after death.

[255]Glasson ("The Son of Man Imagery," 83, and *Second Advent*, 4-5) calls Enoch "the original" of the Danielic one like a son of man; but this is claiming too much.

[256]Rowley, *Relevance*, 63 n. 2.

[257]The Enoch component will be re-emphasized in *1 Enoch* 71 and in Wis 4:10-15. Messianic interpretations re-emphasize the components of royal ideology and ritual that have gone into the composition of Daniel 7.

[258]In *1 Enoch* 14:8 the ascent is accomplished in the power of clouds, mist, lightning-flashes, thunders and winds, but it seems to be primarily the winds which do the lifting of Enoch. In Dan 7:13 the one like a son of man comes simply with or on the clouds of heaven.

[259]The schema of the four powers of world history (beasts) is drawn, however, from Daniel 2.

[260]Glasson and Emerton both make the mistake of considering that to hold either one of these two theories (that Daniel 7 was influenced by *1 Enoch* 14, or that Daniel 7 was influenced by Canaanite mythology probably via the royal traditions) is to render the other theory superfluous. Glasson ("The Son of Man Imagery," 83; cf. *Second Advent*, 5) argues that there is no need to invoke foreign mythologies to explain Daniel 7. Without a close examination of the several elements which cannot be considered related to *1 Enoch* 14, he simply insists Psalms 80 and 8 may provide the "general idea" of a contrast between man and beasts. Emerton ("The Origin of the Son of Man Imagery," 229) thinks that the view that Daniel 7 is an adaptation of *1 Enoch* 14 "fails to allow for the possibility that behind the present form of Dan vii lies a yet older tradition." He says that if Glasson's view could be substantiated, it would render his own theory (the Canaanite hypothesis) superfluous.

[261]We can speak in terms of a "general ideogram" of the heavenly ascent of a human figure. This is Borsch's term (*Son of Man*, 45 n. 3), by which he means something different than what is meant here. Borsch tends toward a post-Daniel date for *1 Enoch* 14, but remarks that even if Glasson's dating were correct, a general ideogram of an ascending man was too widespread to permit us to conclude the one like a son of man in Daniel 7 is Enoch. This, however, is not Glasson's contention.

[262]G. Scholem, *Kabbalah* (New York: Quadrangle, 1974) 11. See above p. 206 n. 143 on the use of the term "Merkabah." Stone ("Book of Enoch," 487) argues that *1 Enoch* 14 is not a mystical text, properly speaking, since the purpose of the ascent in it is the revelation of certain information rather than the perception of God's appearance on the Throne and cognition of the mysteries of the Throne world.

263It is twice stressed that Elisha must see Elijah as he
is being taken (2 Kgs 2:10, 12) if Elisha is to receive a
double portion of Elijah's spirit.  There seem to be others
present at some distance (fifty men of the sons of the prophets,
2 Kgs 2:7), but they do not see.

264The texts are not connected by use of the same word(s)
or identical expressions in each, but by synonyms and by similarity of motif.

265We have practically no information about haggadic exegesis before the time of Hillel (fl. 30 B.C.), except what we
can infer from early midrashic and apocryphal texts themselves
(J. W. Doeve, *Jewish Hermeneutics in the Synoptic Gospels and
Acts* [Assen: Van Gorcum, 1954] 63).  According to Doeve, to a
great extent haggadic exegesis did not have different methods
from halakic; but the *middoth* were employed for the former in a
freer manner.

266In part this must have been prompted by the analogy of
circumstance between Ezekiel 1 and Daniel 7: in both texts the
threatening of the temple and nation occasions the vision.

267See above, pp. 155, 157.

268See above, pp. 159-60.  This is not to say the author
was aware of the source of psalm imagery.

269Dan 7:1: "a dream and visions of (Daniel's) head as he
lay in his bed"; 7:2: "I saw in my vision by night...."

270M. Black, "Throne Theophany," 58.  Black takes as his
starting point W. Zimmerli's observation that there are two
classic forms of prophetic commission in the OT.  (1) The first
is the narrative type of call which consists of a dialogue between the prophet and Yahweh and the overcoming of the prophet's
reluctance by a divine command.  This type of commission is pre-
dominantly auditory.  Examples are the call of Moses and that of
Jeremiah.  (2) The second type is classically represented in
the call of Ezekiel.  Here the divine commission is preceded by
a "throne-vision" or "throne theophany."  Visionary experience
is combined with a verbal communication of the divine will for
the prophet.  Zimmerli places the throne-theophany prophetic
commission of Ezekiel in a line of developing tradition in the
OT traceable back through Isaiah 6 to 1 Kgs 22:10-23 (*Ezechiel*
[BKAT 13/1; Neukirchen-Vluyn: Neukirchener Verlag, 1969] 16-21).

271See above, pp. 163-64, for discussion of Black's theory
concerning the interpretation of Ezek 1:26-28 in Daniel 7.

272Black, "Throne Theophany," 61.  However, see below:
Daniel is not really a prophet, but an apocalyptic seer.

273In this case, the commission is to be rather than to do
something.

[274]Likewise, in *1 Enoch* 60 we find the throne theophany
(v. 2: "And the Head of Days sat on the throne of his glory,
and the angels and the righteous stood around Him").  Michael
explains to Enoch that this is a vision of the day of judgment
(vv. 5-6) but there is no explicit commission.  In *1 Enoch* 90
the throne theophany is in v. 20 ("And I saw till a throne was
erected in the pleasant land, and the Lord of the sheep sat
Himself thereon..."), but again there is no explicit commission.

[275]Cf. 8:6 ("Seal up the vision, for it pertains to many
days hence"); 12:9 ("Go your way, Daniel, for the words are
shut up and sealed until the time of the end"); 12:13 ("Go your
way till the end").

[276]Daniel differs from the prophets in that he cannot directly understand the mysterious vision given to him and is in
need of angelic interpretation.  He is not presented as a
prophet, but as a wise man, a practitioner of mantic wisdom
(Collins, *Apocalyptic Vision*, 87); nor is he classified as a
prophet in the Hebrew Bible.

[277]Ibid., 76.

[278]There is no reaction in 1 Kgs 22:19-23, but a spirit
volunteers.

[279]Hubbard, it will be recalled, makes no distinctions
between the two types of OT commissionings, arguing that Matt
28:16-20 conforms to the structure of a general "Hebrew Bible
Commissioning Gattung."  See above, pp. 122-23.

[280]Cf. 1 Kgs 2:16 and 18:12 for mention of the Spirit of
Yahweh as a translating force.

[281]Cf. the cloud and wind imagery in 1:4 and 10:3.

[282]See above, p. 207 n. 153.  The Spirit lifts or translates Ezekiel in 8:3 and 40:3.

[283]See above, pp. 173, 176.

[284]Lacocque, *Daniel*, 252.

[285]Hengel, *Judaism and Hellenism*, 1.233.

[286]Russell, *Method and Message*, 237; cf. Charles, *APOT*
2.531-32; p. 13 n. 27.

[287]Hengel, *Judaism and Hellenism*, 1.231.

[288]R. E. Clements, *God and Temple* (Philadelphia: Fortress,
1965) 132.

[289]Russell, *Method and Message*, 328.

[290]Cf. *1 Enoch* 69:11 (Similitudes); Dan 12:3.

[291] See the targums on Gen 5:24 where there is a naming of the power by which Enoch was taken. *Tgs. Pseudo-Jonathan* and *Neofiti I* say that he went up "by the (or: a) Word." The Samaritan version of Gen 5:24 reads, "The Angel took him."

[292] The interpretation offered here steers a middle course between the interpretations of Di Lella and Collins. In some respects it is close to the position presented by Lacocque (*Daniel*, 127-34, 145-47, 245-46) except that Lacocque, like Collins, thinks that the one like a son of man is identified with the angel Michael (p. 133); but see above, p. 154. Lacocque interprets Daniel 7 too much from the perspective of the later Qumran writings and does not give sufficient attention to the traditions the author is using in brilliant combination. Paul Ricoeur argues that the one like a son of man should not be determined in "too univocal a fashion" nor identified too hastily. Rather, "it is wise to leave *a bit of play* to this figure, to allow several concurrent identifications *play*..." (foreword to Lacocque, *Daniel*, xxii-xxiii). This, in my opinion, is part of the genius of this work, which Lacocque rightly calls a pioneering work (p. 146 n. 120).

[293] In Daniel 7 there is no explicit commission. The commission of Daniel as an apocalyptic seer, a "prophet" for the end time, occurs in 12:4 (cf. 8:6; 12:9; 12:13). See above, pp. 180-82.

[294] See above, pp. 89-93.

[295] See above, pp. 124, 183.

[296] See above, p. 2.

[297] Fuller, *Resurrection Narratives*, 83; cited above, p. 3.

# CHAPTER V

PASSAGES RELATED TO DANIEL 7 IN JEWISH LITERATURE
OF THE PERIOD BETWEEN THE COMPOSITION OF DANIEL
AND THE END OF THE NT PERIOD

One may not simply move from Daniel 7 to the NT uses of
Daniel 7 since, as has been emphasized in Chapter II, the NT
authors were heirs not only to the biblical text but to exegetical lines of development flowing from reflection on Daniel 7.[1]
Such reflection produced allusions to Daniel 7; indeed a whole
midrashic tradition may have developed around that text.  In
what follows I have confined myself chiefly to two passages
that are clearly related to Daniel 7 (and which I think resulted
from midrashic interpretation of Daniel 7).  There are several
other passages that personally I would judge to be also examples
of such midrashic interpretation, and at the end of this chapter
I shall briefly summarize what they might contribute to the picture.  However, since some would not find convincing the relationship that I see between such passages and Daniel 7, I shall
treat them as an addendum, so that the picture I draw may rest
on the two virtually certain adaptations of Daniel 7.  The debate over the question of the presence of an allusion to Dan 7:
14 LXX in Matt 28:18b illustrates the need for careful methodological controls and adequate proof of both linguistic and
conceptual affinity between texts,[2] so that discussion is of
true allusions, not of verbal and thought parallels.

## A. *1 Enoch* 71

*1 Enoch* 71 narrates the final translation of Enoch's
spirit[3] in stages, and his exaltation.  Ascending into the
heavens, he sees "the holy sons of God (the angels)[4] stepping
on flames of fire," and "two streams of fire."  He falls on his
face before the Lord of Spirits (v. 2).[5]  The angel Michael
seizes Enoch, lifts him up and introduces him "to all the secrets of righteousness" and of the ends of the heaven (vv. 3-4).
Finally, Enoch is translated into the heaven of heavens (v. 5).[6]
He sees the house built of crystals and fire, surrounded by
Seraphin, Cherubin and Ophanin, who guard the throne of glory,

and numberless other angels (vv. 5-8). The Head of Days[7] appears, coming out of the house with Michael, Gabriel, Raphael
and Phanuel and many angels (v. 10). Enoch (again) falls on his
face, but here experiences a transformation and utters praise
which is "well pleasing" before the Head of Days (vv. 11-12).

Then follows the passage which "has caused untold anguish
to the commentators":[8]

> V. 14. And he came to me and greeted me with his voice
> and said to me:[9]
> "You are the son of man who is born unto righteousness,[10]
> And righteousness abides over you,
> And the righteousness of the Head of Days forsakes you
> not."
> 15. And he said to me:
> "He proclaims unto you peace in the name of the world
> to come;
> For from hence has proceeded peace since the creation
> of the world,
> And so it shall be unto you for ever and ever.
> 16. And all shall walk in your ways since righteousness
> never forsakes you:
> With you will be their dwellingplaces and with you their
> heritage,
> And they will not be separated from you[11] for ever and
> ever and ever."

There have been several unsuccessful attempts to emend and
to rearrange this passage. Charles, considering it incomprehensible that the translated Enoch should be identified with
the preexistent Son of Man of the Similitudes, assumes that between verses 13 and 14 there was a passage now lost which described the Son of Man accompanying the Head of Days. It also
contained Enoch's question to one of the angels (as in 46:3).
concerning the Son of Man: who he was, and whence he was, and
why he went with the Head of Days. Verses 14 and 16, then, the
angel's answer, are emended by Charles from the second to the
third person: "*This is* the Son of Man who *is* born..." etc. The
whole speech which follows is about this figure.[12] However,
there is absolutely no manuscript evidence to support this
theory, and there is no reason to assume that Enoch would have
to ask twice (in chaps. 46 and 71) who this figure is. Black
thinks that 46:1b ("And with Him was another being whose counte-
nance had the appearance of a man and his face was full of
graciousness, like one of the holy angels") originally belonged
between 71:10 and 11. While this suggestion is the same as

Charles', Black's reasoning is quite different.  Black argues
that in chapter 71, Enoch does receive "a commission from the
Head of Days to be that 'Son of Man,' *yet there is nothing
corresponding in the vision.*"[13]  For the commission to make
sense, and for Black's understanding of the pattern of a throne-
vision (without the emendation, he thinks, defective) to be
restored, the insertion of the vision of the Son of Man in required.  Again, however, there is no manuscript evidence to
support this conjecture and, it will be argued, the phrase in
71:14 ("you are the son of man who...") is not a title and need
not refer to a previously described figure.  The scene is a
throne-theophany (like Ezekiel 1) even without the insertion,
as Enoch sees the Head of Days and the two streams of fire in
verse 2 probably refer to streams issuing forth from the throne.

Three theories exist explaining the relation of *1 Enoch*
70-71 to the rest of the Similitudes (chaps. 37-69).  It is
claimed that chapters 70-71 are (1) an integral part and the
climax of the Similitudes (Hooker, Sjöberg and others);[14] (2) a
later addition to the Similitudes (Flusser, Nickelsburg, Colpe,
Glasson and others);[15] (3) the oldest part of the Similitudes
(Black, Perrin).[16]  Here I opt for the theory that the Similitudes presuppose at least chapter 71, on the basis of the fact
that this chapter has close links with the Book of Watchers,[17]
and can be understood as an interpretation of Daniel 7 (and
Enoch traditions) which leads to the concepts of the
Similitudes.[18]

The verbal similarities between Daniel 7 and *1 Enoch* 71
are the following:

(1) *Dan 7:10:* "A stream of
fire issued and came forth
from before him" (cf. *1 Enoch*
14:19)

*1 Enoch 71:2:* "And I saw two
streams of fire..." (cf. v. 6:
"streams of living fire" issue
from the four sides of the
house)

(2) *Dan 7:9:* "...And one that
was ancient of days took his
seat; his raiment was white
as snow and the hair of his
head like pure wool" (cf.
*1 Enoch* 14:20 on the raiment
of the enthroned one).

*1 Enoch 71:10:* "And with [the
four angels] the Head of Days,
his head white and pure as wool,
his raiment indescribable."
*71:1:* "the garments [of the
holy sons of God] were white
and their raiment and their
faces shone like snow."

(3) *Dan 7:13:* "...with the
clouds of heaven there came
one like a son of man..."

*Dan 12:3:* "...and those who
turn many to righteousness
(shall shine) like the stars
for ever and ever." (Cf.
*1 Enoch* 15:1 where Enoch is
addressed as "righteous man
and scribe of righteousness")

(4) *Dan 7:10:* "A thousand
thousands served him, and ten
thousand times ten thousand
stood before him (cf. *1 Enoch*
14:22)

(5) *Dan 7:9:* "his throne was
fiery flames..." (cf.
*1 Enoch* 14:18)

*1 Enoch 71:14:* "You are the son
of man who is born unto righteousness..."[19]

*1 Enoch 71:8:* "And I saw angels, who could not be counted,
a thousand thousands, and ten
thousand times ten thousand..."
(cf. v. 13)

*1 Enoch 71:7:* "the throne of
his glory"

In addition, whereas in Dan 7:13-14 the one like a son of man
is presented to the Ancient of Days and given dominion over
all, in *1 Enoch* 71:14-17 there is a naming and sort of blessing
of Enoch and a promise of presence; he is told to be the righteous leader of all. Both texts can be considered to exhibit
aspects of an enthronement or installment form, but are more
properly classified as throne-theophany commissions.[20]

Several critics hold that the author of *1 Enoch* 71 is
working with Daniel 7 and with *1 Enoch* 14.[21] Besides the aspects of *1 Enoch* 14 mentioned in parentheses above in regard to
each of the five parallels between Daniel 7 and *1 Enoch* 71, the
influence of *1 Enoch* 14 is apparent primarily in *1 Enoch* 71 in
the description of the "house" or "structure built of crystals"
(or hail stones) in which sits the throne of God's glory,[22] and
in the explicit statement of Enoch's ascent to the divine presence. The prostration of Enoch is mentioned in both texts
(*1 Enoch* 14:14; 71:11), as is the angelic night guard of angels
(14:23 ["the most holy ones who were near to Him did not leave
by night nor depart from Him"]; 71:7 ["round about were Seraphin, Cherubin, and Ophanin: and these are they who sleep not
and guard the throne of His glory"]).[23] When *1 Enoch* 71 is
compared with *1 Enoch* 14, the "new element" in the former seems
to be the use and interpretation of Daniel 7.[24] From Daniel 7

comes the concept of exaltation and the phrases that describe
the two central figures, the son of man and the Head of Days.
Enoch's individuality has been reasserted.[25]  In *1 Enoch* 71,
then, we find not the identification or fusing of an earthly
figure with a pre-existent heavenly figure, but an interpretation of the (once earthly) figure *coming* (in a definitive manner) into the presence of the divine.[26]  Daniel 7, which used
Enoch traditions to speak of the limited apotheosis of the
faithful in Israel, is here used to speak of the limited
apotheosis of Enoch.[27]  What is given in *1 Enoch* 71 is an account of who that one like a son of man is (or was), how he was
elevated, and in what his dominion and power consist.[28]  Enoch
is commissioned as leader and abiding presence for all the
righteous (71:16).[29]  In place of an eternal kingdom (Dan 7:14),
there is an eternal state of peace "in the name of the world to
come" (*1 Enoch* 71:15).[30]

Is it possible that the dependency of which we are speaking, of *1 Enoch* 71 on Daniel 7, should be reversed, or at least
that *1 Enoch* 71 embodies traditions of Enoch's final translation and exaltation that were known to and used by the author
of Daniel 7?  Whereas *1 Enoch* 71 hints at transformation (see
v. 11 where Enoch's spirit is transfigured), his reception into
the heavenly court,[31] and his more-than-human destiny,[32] Daniel
7 may presuppose some such notions.  The figure of the one like
a son of man, it has been seen, has heavenly traits and is a
representative of the righteous in their fellowship with the
angelic world (Dan 12:3).  There are several indications, however, that *1 Enoch* 71 does not represent the *written* form of
the tradition known to the author of Daniel.  (1) The notion of
the Head of Days coming *out* of the crystal house to greet Enoch,
in contrast to the coming of the one like a son of man all the
way into the presence of the Ancient of Days, may be imagery
directed against interpretations that would read equality or
divinity or simply inappropriateness into Daniel 7.  (2) Emphasis on the translation and transfiguration of Enoch's *spirit*
seems to be a spiritualization of earlier ascent stories,[33] a
spiritualization not found in Daniel 7 (or 12:2-3).  (3) The
fact that *1 Enoch* 71 has a more developed conception of the

divine throne and its attendants[34] may also point in this
direction, though this is not necessarily so.

Concerning the possibility that both *1 Enoch* 71 and Daniel
7 represent a common ancestor, it has been noted above that
among the materials commonly regarded as oldest in *1 Enoch*,
there is no narration of his final ascent.[35] Twice, however,
the mountain-throne of God is mentioned. In the north-west
Enoch sees "a place which burns day and night, where there are
seven mountains of magnificent stones, three towards the east,
and three towards the south. And as for those towards the east,
(one) was of colored stone, and one of pearl and one of jacinth,
and those toward the south of red stone. But the middle one
reached to heaven like the throne of God, of alabaster, and the
summit of the throne was sapphire" (18:6-8).[36] Again in chapter
24 Enoch sees the seven mountains of magnificent stones. "And
the seventh mountain was in the midst of these, and it excelled
them in height, resembling the seat of a throne..." (24:3).
The angelic guide tells him, "This high mountain which you have
seen, whose summit is like the throne of God, is his throne,
where the Holy Great One, the Lord of Glory, the Eternal King,
will sit, when he shall come down to visit the earth with goodness" (25:3).[37] There is no account of Enoch's presentation
before God enthroned here, nor is there mountain imagery in the
description of the enthronement of the Ancient of Days in Daniel
7. There are indications, however, that there may have once
existed a scene in which the final ascent of Enoch to the
mountain-throne was narrated. In *Jub.* 4:23 Enoch is said to
burn the incense of the sanctuary, sweet spices "acceptable before the Lord on the Mountain." In *2 Enoch* 22:2, Enoch sees
the Lord's throne "very great and not made with hands." The
source of this image is the stone "cut out by no human hand" of
Dan 2:34.[38] "Something like the figure of a man" from the sea
in *4 Ezra* 13 flies to a region inaccessible to the seer, to
carve out for himself a great mountain (vv. 6-7). In the interpretation this is identified as Mount Zion, "the mountain
carved out without hands" (v. 36; cf. again Dan 2:34, 45). And
in the Similitudes, as in *4 Ezra*, there is evidence that the
אבן-בן wordplay mentioned above as related to Daniel 2 and 7[39]

is influential. Six mountains of different metals[40] melt before the presence of the Elect One (*1 Enoch* 52:1-6; cf. 1:6),
who seems to have been originally thought of as himself the
seventh mountain, the mountain that filled the whole earth.[41]

I offer the speculation that a (now lost) version of the
final translation of Enoch to the mountain-throne of God (a)
may have inspired the author of Daniel 7 to write his midrash
on Daniel 2, using mythological imagery which may be originally
Canaanite but which has probably reached the author indirectly;
and (b) lies behind *1 Enoch* 70-71.[42] Some of the elements of
the theophany which both texts share (the stream of fire, the
clothing of the enthroned one, mention of the throne, the thousands of angels and perhaps even the term "son of man" [drawn
from Ezek 2:1]) may have belonged to the common tradition.[43]
I have argued that the epithet "Ancient of Days" and description
of white hair is drawn from the Canaanite image of 'El, and
part of a complex of originally Canaanite elements used by the
author of Daniel 7.[44] The term "Head of Days" appears in
*1 Enoch* 71, but without the other Canaanite elements.[45] This
leads me to believe that *1 Enoch* 71 has also been influenced by
Daniel 7. The sequence of tradition-history of the visions--
as we have them--seems to be *1 Enoch* 14, Daniel 7 and *1 Enoch*
71.[46] The Danielic triad appears here as Head of Days, righteous son of man (Enoch) and the angels of the heavenly court.[47]
No interest is exhibited in the judgment or battle motifs of
Daniel 7. Attention is focused, rather, on the exaltation of
the righteous one who is henceforth master, guide and dwelling
of all the righteous. This attention will appear again in Matt
28:16-20.

A most important aspect of our study in this section is
the discovery of the (seven) mountain theme which may have been
related to a tradition of the exaltation of Enoch. The mountain
on which the risen Jesus appears in Matt 28:16 is the seventh
mountain of this Gospel.[48] If the mountain is regarded as the
throne of God, then the final Matthean pericope can be regarded
as a throne-theophany commission.

## B.  *4 Ezra* 10:60-12:51 and 13:1-58

Writing near the end of the first century A.D. and still
under the impact of the destruction of Jerusalem in 70 A.D.,[49]
the author of *4 Ezra* makes use of two traditional reinterpretations of Daniel 7 in order to answer the questions he raises
concerning the justice and mercy of God, the abandonment of
Israel to its enemies, and the fate of the righteous dead.   The
traditional reinterpretations, which do not reflect the disas-
ter of 70,[50] arise from a belief in the message of the author
of Daniel concerning Israel's right to rule.[51]   They indicate
how the Danielic vision, written during the Maccabean revolution to inspire hope in the eventual overthrow of the tyrant
Antiochus Epiphanes IV, was contemporized during the Roman
period to inspire hope in the annihilation of the Roman empire.

The reinterpretations are the fifth and sixth visions of
Ezra, the eagle-lion vision and the vision of the man from the
sea.   The Danielic passage has been fragmented and detached
from its matrix, the throne theophany and scene of final judgment.   In *4 Ezra*, the activity of the one who corresponds to
the one like a son of man initiates the era of the end but the
Most High alone brings it to a close, as the Most High alone
created (3:4; 6:6).   At the end, "the Most High will appear on
the judgment seat" and "the world that is not yet awake will be
aroused and what is corruptible will pass away" (7:33, 31).[52]
Several passages in this work indicate familiarity with the
practices and literary convention of visionaries who ascend into heaven,[53] but interest is centered on events which occur on
earth.[54]   The book in fact may embody a subtle and serious
polemic against the proponents of mystical practices and speculation.[55]   In this context the Danielic triad does not appear.[56]
We do find, however, important developments in the interpretation of the figure of the one like a son of man.

In the vision of the eagle and the lion (10:60-12:51),
both the fourth beast and the one like a son of man of Daniel 7
are radically reinterpreted.   The twelve-winged, three-headed
eagle with rival winglets or subwings rises from the sea and
spreads its wings over the whole earth, oppressively subjecting
everything under heaven.   It represents the Roman Empire with

its successive rulers and their challengers. The seer is told,
"The eagle you observed coming up out of the sea is the fourth
kingdom that appeared in a vision to Daniel, your brother. But
it was not interpreted to him in the same way that I now interpret (it) to you or as I have interpreted (it)" (12:11-12).[57]
A being like a ranging lion comes out of a forest and speaks
"in human language" (11:38) to the eagle, condemning it to destruction.[58] As the lion speaks, the eagle's remaining head
and wings vanish, and "the entire body of the eagle went up in
flames and the earth was aghast" (12:1-3).[59] The lion is identified as "the anointed one whom the Most High has reserved until the end of days, who will arise from the seed of David"
(12:32).[60] He is the liberator of "the remnant of my people
which is left in the land," to whom he grants "joy until the
end, the day of judgment about which I spoke to you at the beginning" (12:34). The vanishing of the beast means that "thus
the whole earth will be relieved and delivered from (its) power;
then it can hope for justice and the compassion of him who made
it" (11:46).[61]

     Several points are significant for our study here. (1) The
scene, a dream as in Daniel 7, is not set in the heavenly court,
but on earth.[62] (2) There is no mention of power having been
given to the lion; this is presumed. (3) Unlike the Danielic
one like a son of man, the lion is active, a warrior who destroys with the words of the Most High (11:38). He appears on
the scene at the peak of the sway of the fourth beast and
miraculously effects its destruction. Myers observes that "the
first task of the messiah is to free the land of foreign rule."[63]
(4) In the interpretation, his activity is described in legal
terms (12:32-33). The forensic formulation of the eschatological victory in Daniel 7 may have influenced the language used
here of the anointed one,[64] but the lion does not give the final
judgment.[65] (5) The lion does not receive an everlasting kingdom, but rules over a temporary (earthly) kingdom composed of
the remnant left in the land of Israel; nothing is said of the
subjection or service of the nations.[66] (6) Whereas the one
like a son of man in Dan 7:13-14 has both human and angelic or
theophanic traits (or is given superhuman privileges), the lion

in *4 Ezra* is at once pre-existent[67] or perhaps of heavenly
origin, *and* of Davidic descent.[68]

In this reinterpretation of Daniel 7, then, the one like a
son of man has become an individual messiah, distinct from the
remnant as its liberator, a warrior but with the weapon of
words. He is the beginning of God's intervention, and is to
function *until* the end. He is the rallying point of opposition
to Rome. Stone suggests that the eagle vision is an instance
of the traditional "Four Empires Vision complex" developed out
of Daniel 7 and characterized by at least the basic elements of
the symbolic vision form, the four empires schema and the
military-legal function of the messiah.[69] Two aspects of this
complex are paralleled in Matt 28:16-20: first, the notion of
one who speaks with God's authority,[70] and second, the notion
of an interim role for this figure (cf. 28:20b: "I am with you
always, *until* the close of the age"). Nothing of the forensic
or political aspects of the complex, however, occurs in the
final Matthean pericope, which in my opinion deals with the
in-breaking and composition of the Danielic kingdom in a
totally different way.

The sixth vision (14:1-58) is the climax of this apocalypse.[71] Again in a night dream, Ezra sees "a wind rising from
the sea that stirred up all its waves. As I kept looking that
wind brought up out of the depths of the sea something resembling a man,[72] and that man was flying with (*cum*) the clouds of
heaven" (13:2-3).[73] The man's ascent is described like a loud
and dangerous theophany: his glance shakes everything and his
voice melts those who hear it.[74] When an innumerable host of
human beings gathers to wage war against him, he carves out for
himself a huge mountain and flies upon it (13:6). Ezra is unable to see the region from which the mountain is carved.[75] The
man destroys his enemies with no weapon but with fire from his
mouth which cremates all. Afterward he comes down from the
mountain and summons to himself "another, peaceful host. Many
persons of (different) appearances joined themselves to him;
some were joyful, some sad, some in shackles, some leading
(others) of them as offerings" (13:12-13).[76]

In the interpretation, the man "represents the one whom the Most High has kept for many ages through whom to deliver his creation and he himself[77] will create (the new) order for those who survive" (13:26). He is called "my son" in verses 32, 37, 52 (cf. 7:28-29; 14:9).[78] While many critics have suggested that the Hebrew behind all these verses is עבדי and not בני, the Greek παῖς leading to the Latin *filius*,[79] we may have here an instance of the אבן-בן wordplay discussed above.[80] The titles "Son of 'El" and "Son of 'Elyon" appear in 4QpsDan A$^a$ 2:1, and the righteous one is called God's son in Wis 2:18 (cf. v. 13), both texts which are in my judgment related to Daniel 7 (see Addendum, below).

There are many elements of the vision that appear to have been drawn from Daniel 7: the wind stirring up the sea (13:2; cf. Dan 7:2); the four winds of heaven (13:5; cf. Dan 7:2); the stream of fire (13:10; cf. Dan 7:10); the night in which the vision occurs (13:1; cf. Dan 7:2, 13); the *quasi*-human aspect of the central figure (13:3; cf. Dan 7:13); the clouds on which he is borne (13:3; cf. Dan 7:13).[81]

In contrast to the silent and passive one like a son of man in Daniel 7, the man from the sea is above all a warrior, whose very glance and voice are cosmically destructive (13:3-4) and who spews forth fire to destroy the hostile multitude (vv. 5-11). Emerton is of the opinion that Canaanite mythological elements associated with Baal (rain-cloud and storm theophany, fire and lightning) are responsible for this dimension of the figure.[82] The man does not come to receive a kingdom in *4 Ezra* 13, but attracts or gathers the peaceful host to himself after battle. He plays a decisive part in the events preceding the end, as does the lion in the eagle vision. The events in chapter 13, though they begin in a "mysteriously cosmic remoteness," and continue on a "miraculously modified earth," "do not happen immediately under the eyes of the Ancient of Days. Heaven is not affected by them."[83] The figure of the deliverer is engaged in an independent activity of his own. "Sovereignty, power and honour do not have to be bestowed on him by the Ancient of Days, but are inherent in him from the beginning."[84]

The text is an answer to the unstated question, how will the promise of Daniel 7 come about? It is an answer that shows the mysterious figure actively taking possession of what he was previously given.[85] In the interpretation, this "how" is further elaborated. All the nations will turn from their plans of war against one another (13:31; cf. 4QpsDan A[a] 2:3 and Mark 13:8, pars.) to attack the man from the sea.[86] This figure will berate his enemies for their impiety, confront them with their evil designs and the tortures they are to undergo and "crush them effortlessly with the law," which is symbolized by the fire from his mouth (13:37-38). The peaceful host which the man summons to himself is interpreted as the ten captive tribes of Israel: they were led away across the river by the Assyrians, but escaped, says the author, even further beyond the Euphrates to "Azareth," where they were able to keep the statutes they had not kept in their own land. These will return and there will be a repeat of the stopping of the channels of the Jordan (cf. Josh 3:14-16) as they cross over (4 Ezra 13: 39-47). They join the survivors of the two tribes left in Israel (vv. 48-49). There is a universal dimension to this hope in the reconstruction of the nation, as the son is the one through whom the Most High delivers his creation (13:26).[87]

The motifs of (1) destruction from the mouth of a Davidic messianic figure, (2) the holy mountain, (3) the gathering of the dispersed people of Israel, and (4) return across waters which dry up are found joined in Isaiah 11. Here we read that the "shoot from the stump of Jesse" (v. 1) will "smite the earth with the rod of his mouth, and with the breath of his lips he shall slay the wicked" (v. 4). Peace will rule on "my holy mountain" (v. 9). The "root of Jesse" will himself be an ensign to the peoples (v. 10) and Yahweh will "raise an ensign for the nations, and will assemble the outcasts of Israel, and gather the dispersed of Judah from the four corners of the earth" (v. 12). The Reed Sea and the Euphrates will be crossed dryshod as they return (vv. 15-16). The first and third of these Isaian themes appear in the first century B.C. *Psalms of Solomon* 17,[88] and Perrin has called *4 Ezra* 13 "a kind of apocalyptic midrash" on *Ps. Sol.* 17.[89] In *4 Ezra* 13, Daniel 7 is

used to give a powerfully mysterious tone to the presentation
of the messianic warrior whose struggle will deliver "the peaceful host."[90]

There are subtle similarities between *4 Ezra* 13 and Matt
28:16-20, which lead me to posit that both texts may be drawing
on a common traditional complex.[91] Using Daniel 7, both present
an already-exalted figure on a mountain, both understand the
figure as one who speaks Torah,[92] both speak of the "son" (Matt
28:19b: "the Son"; *4 Ezra* 13:32, 37, 52: "my son"); and both
concern the gathering of a new people which must pass through
water.[93]

At the risk of oversimplification, the traditional vision
used in *4 Ezra* 13 can be considered a nationalistic, militaristic interpretation of Daniel, useful to some before and during
the war of 66-70. It was modified, perhaps after the war, by
someone who considered military rebellion impossible or unwise;
the fire by which Israel will destroy its enemies becomes the
Torah. In contrast to this adaptation of Daniel, stands Matt
28:16-20, in which no nationalistic or militaristic elements
are present. The figure of the risen Jesus disciples rather
than destroys by means of his Torah.[94]

### C. Elements from *1 Enoch* 71 and *4 Ezra* that may be Applicable to Matt 28:16-20

The intention in this chapter is to attempt to recover some
aspects of Jewish interpretation of Daniel 7 which may have
bearing on exegetical problems pertaining to Matt 28:16-20. It
is valuable at this point to take stock of the two works which
have an excellent claim to be midrashim on Daniel 7, by looking
at them through the lens of certain elements of the Matthean
pericope.

(1) *The exaltation of Jesus.* In Matt 28:18b we have seen
the probability that an allusion is made to Dan 7:14 LXX. The
risen Jesus speaks of a past transfer of all power to him. In
context it is implied that this transfer took place at his
death-resurrection, conceived as an assumption to heaven, from
which he appears. *1 Enoch* 71 speaks of the assumption of Enoch
to heaven, his final translation and exaltation. In *4 Ezra* 13,

the man from the sea flies up to a region inaccessible to the
seer (perhaps to heaven), to carve out for himself a mountain.
Both of these texts appear to understand Dan 7:13 as referring
to the movement of a human or humanlike figure to the heavenly
world.[95]  My suggestion is that the author of Matt 28:16-20, or
of the tradition behind this pericope, read Dan 7:13 in similar
fashion.  He referred it to the coming of Jesus into the divine
presence through the crucifixion, and intended this reading to
be evoked.

The promise of presence in Matt 28:20b (as in *1 Enoch* 71:
14-16) may implicitly counter a contention that the one who
like Enoch has been "taken" is separated from humanity, not to
be found.  Matt 28:20b (cf. 1:23; 10:32; 18:20) denies the
absence of Jesus from his community.

While *4 Ezra* indicates that the Danielic one like a son of
man was considered to be empowered as a fierce warrior or interim judge or prosecuting witness, *1 Enoch* 71 illustrates a
different interpretive tradition, one which emphasizes the
Wisdom component in the book of Daniel, probably drawing on the
connection which has been seen between Dan 7:13-14 and 12:2-3
(the exaltation of the *maṣdîqîm* or *maskîlîm*).  The exalted one,
that is, is regarded primarily as a *Maskîl*, one who knows and
communicates the way of righteousness (cf. *1 Enoch* 71:14, 16).
I understand the stress in Matt 28:19a on discipling, and in
verse 20a on the commands of Jesus, to be in line with this
tradition.[96]

The power of the risen Jesus is "all power in heaven and
on earth" (cf. Dan 4:14 LXX), that is, the full power of God.[97]
In *1 Enoch* 71:16, the role of Enoch resembles that of God ("all
will walk in your ways...with you will be their dwelling place
and with you their heritage...").  Claims such as these can
easily be understood as leading to speculation concerning "two
powers."[98]

(2) *Consequences of the exaltation, for Israel and for all
nations.*  In *4 Ezra* 13, a gathering is part of the scenario of
the eschatological age; the man from the sea summons to himself
a peaceable multitude, interpreted as the ten tribes who return
to join those who remained in Israel.  Annihilation of "all

nations" takes place in this vision (cf. the annihilation of
the eagle [Rome] in the lion vision). Emphasis here on the
universality of the Danielic kingdom has an imperialistic,
militaristic ring.[99] This is in a sense refined in *1 Enoch* 71:
all the righteous will follow the righteous Enoch, forming a
new community. In Matt 28:16-20, the eleven are sent to "make
disciples of all nations," by baptizing and teaching. Jesus'
exaltation is not seen as the exaltation of the nation Israel,[100]
but as the power behind the gathering of a group that is trans-
national. Each of these traditions explores the impact of the
exaltation on "all." The question of the place of the nation
Israel within "all nations" is not newly raised by Matt 28:
16-20,[101] but is one with which Daniel and his interpreters
struggled.

    (3) *The mountain*. In *4 Ezra* 13, the man from the sea ("my
son") carves out for himself a huge mountain, and stands on it
to wage war. This is identified in the interpretation as Mount
Zion, carved "by no human hand" (14:35-36). The place from
which the mountain is carved, I have suggested, is the heavenly
throne of God. There seem to have been two lines of interpretation of Daniel 2, one in which the stone-mountain is thought
of as the son (perhaps by means of wordplay),[102] and another in
which the mountain is thought of as God's throne. In *1 Enoch*
18:6-8; 24-25, seven mountains are spoken of, the seventh being
the throne of God. I have also explored the possibility that a
(now lost) version of the final translation of Enoch to the
mountain-throne of God lies behind *1 Enoch* 70-71.[103] It is
probable that in Matt 28:16 the mountain on which the risen
Jesus appears is related to the Danielic traditions in this
pericope. The fact that Matthew has referred to seven mountains
in his Gospel indicates that we may have a conscious use of the
mountain theme as it was developed especially in the Enoch literature. This mountain (in Galilee, but in a sense a heavenly
mountain, since Jesus is not said to descend to it or depart
from it) may be considered the kingdom of God which will never
be destroyed and whose sovereignty will not be left to another
(Dan 2:44). It may also symbolize the throne of God which has
been given to Jesus (cf. Dan 7:9, 14 with Matt 28:18b).[104]

(4) *The throne-theophany commission form*. I have argued
above, with Black, that Daniel 7 should be classified as a
throne-theophany commission. This form is found also in *1 Enoch*
71. If the mountain in Matt 28:16 is understood as the throne
of God, Matt 28:16-20 can be considered a development of this
form. The (throne) theophany is the vision of Jesus on the
mountain in 28:16. At some irrecoverable stage in the formation of this pericope, this first element may have been more
elaborate and explicit. On the other hand, it is possible that
in some circles, the symbol of the mountain was loaded and
evocative enough to need no elaboration. The words in 28:18b,
drawn from Dan 7:14 LXX (ἐδόθη μοι πᾶσα ἐξουσία) now interpret
the mountain symbol by alluding to the scene of the transfer of
power occurring where "thrones were set" (Dan 7:9). The second
element, the reaction, occurs in Matt 28:17. The third element
is the commission of the eleven to make disciples by baptizing
and teaching (28:19-20a). With the allusion to the last words
of the book of Daniel (12:13 LXX: εἰς συντέλειαν ἡμερῶν) in the
last words of the Gospel of Matthew (28:20b: πάσας τὰς ἡμέρας
ἕως τῆς συντελείας τοῦ αἰῶνος) a connection may also be acquired (by way of contrast) between the apocalyptic commission
of the seer Daniel[105] and the immediate sending forth of the
eleven.[106] The fourth element of the form, the word of reassurance, is the promise of presence, Matt 28:20b.

(5) *The triad*. A triad appears in *1 Enoch* 71: Head of
Days, angels, Enoch-righteous son of man. It occurs here in
the context of an exaltation and final translation. It is a
development of the Danielic triad, Ancient of Days, angels, one
like a son of man, occurring also in the context of an exaltation. This leads me to posit the theory that the Matthean triad
may be a shorthand expression for the event of Jesus' exaltation
and presence in the heavenly court. The triad does not appear
in *4 Ezra*, a work which exhibits no interest in angelology and
has a certain anti-mystical tendency, but the Man from the sea
is called in the interpretation "my son" (cf. "the Son" in Matt
28:18b). The Spirit does not appear in either of the two works
considered in this chapter, but in *1 Enoch* 71 there is emphasis
on the translation of Enoch's spirit, and one family of Ethiopic
MSS calls the translating power "a spirit."[107]

D.  Addendum: Survey of Some Other Passages
That May Be Related to Daniel 7

As I mentioned at the beginning of this chapter, there are other passages that I think make use of Daniel 7, but which some others would not find convincing.  Although I shall not be basing my conclusions about Matt 28:16-20 upon them, I present a brief survey so that the reader can know what they might have contributed to the picture of interpretive traditions flowing from Daniel 7.  Rabbinic material is omitted from the body of this survey because of its diversity and the impossibility of dating its traditions.  I hope at a later date to offer detailed support for the theory that allusions are present in the passages treated here, and to deal with the uses of Daniel 7 in rabbinic material.

1.  *1 Enoch* 90

This passage is the climax of the Animal Apocalypse (*1 Enoch* 85-90), in which the history of the world from Adam to the Messiah is recounted in symbolic imagery.  The faithful of the author's time are represented by sheep, and are being persecuted by four different kinds of birds (Daniel's four beasts?).  One of the sheep, probably representing Judas Maccabeus, develops a great horn (cf. the horns on the last beast of Daniel 7, especially the grotesque little horn).  The judgment scene begins with the setting up of a throne, the appearance of God (the Lord of the sheep) taking his seat, and the opening of the books.  Angels in attendance are mentioned, here called "the seven first white ones" (*1 Enoch* 90:21; cf. 87:2; 88:1).  The condemned are destroyed by fire, and all pay homage to the faithful sheep (90:30), fearing and making petition to the eschatological white bull (new Adam) born from this righteous community.[108]  A figure called "that man" who writes before God and who is one of the "seven first white ones" is mentioned (90:20, 22), and has variously been interpreted as Michael,[109] as the Danielic one like a son of man who is Michael,[110] or as the Danielic one like a son of man who is Enoch.[111]  However, this figure does not receive power.  I think the figure which most closely corresponds to the one like a son of man is the eschatological white bull.

This last Adam parallels the first Adam (85:3); he is born from the community and in line with the dominant symbolism of the Animal Apocalypse is understood as (super) human. Like the Danielic one like a son of man, he appears after the judgment; while he has no real function in the messianic kingdom, he receives homage from all (90:37; cf. Dan 7:14), and his transformation into a wild ox with great black horns symbolizes an extraordinary power.[112]

If this passage is related to the divinely granted exaltation of the one like a son of man and holy ones of the Most High in Daniel 7,[113] the following points concerning the use of Daniel 7 are most pertinent to an understanding of the *Nachleben* of that text. (1) In a pro-Maccabean political perspective (see *1 Enoch* 90:13-19), Daniel 7 is read as propaganda that inspires strong warriors with the hope of faithful Israel's annihilation of its enemies (cf. *4 Ezra* 10:60-12:51; 13:1-58) and the submission of all to Israel. (2) The Danielic one like a son of man is seen as a representative of the triumphant community, this figure's "messianic" and Adamic implications highlighted.[114] (3) The mention of "the seven white ones" as members of God's court may be related to and may facilitate a later understanding of the Spirit (with its seven powers; see Isa 11:2 LXX) given to the Son of Man.[115]

## 2.  4QpsDan A[a] (= 4Q246)

This unpublished fragment from Qumran[116] speaks of someone falling before a throne. A great affliction upon the earth is described, carnage among the countries, and the slavery or service of all to one named by the name of the Great King or God.[117] In Column II, the person who receives the service of all--or another person--is called "Son of God and Son of the Most High." Destruction reigns "until there arises the people of God." It (or he)[118] will give rest to all, will possess an eternal kingdom, judge the earth with righteousness, and be honored by all. The Great God will be its (or his) help, giving peoples into its (or his) power.

If this vision of the victory of the righteous is influenced by Daniel 7,[119] it may be evidence that (1) the Danielic

one like a son of man was given the titles "Son of God, Son of
the Most High";[120]  (2) this figure may have been interpreted or
at least open to interpretation as a Davidic messiah (cf. Luke
1:32-33, 35, where the same titles occur, apparently drawn from
2 Sam 7:8-16; Ps 2:7).[121]  He is not a warrior, but is righteous
judge of the earth and the object of the service and homage of
all.

Detailed discussion of this text must await publication of
the full text and editor's notes.  Its fragmentary nature may
preclude certain analysis.

3.  Testament of Job 33:2-5, 9

This Jewish work from the first century B.C. or A.D. depicts Elious wailing to Job, "Where is the splendor (δόξα) of
your throne?" (32:2-12).  Job promises to show him "my throne
and the splendor of its majesty which is among the holy ones."
He claims it is in the supra-terrestrial realm, "at the right
hand of the Father in the heavens" and is eternal.  "My kingdom
is forever and ever, and its splendor and majesty are in the
chariots of the Father" (33:2-5, 9).  The death of Job in this
work is narrated in terms of the translation of Elijah and of
Ezekiel's Merkabah vision, as the great chariot comes to take
his soul (52:2-5).[122]

If the idea and imagery of Job vindicated and enthroned in
heaven is related to the exaltation of the "one like a son of
man" of Daniel 7, that text has been made use of in the following ways.  (1) Daniel 7 contributes to the depiction of the
eternal, heavenly royalty of an individual just man.  The everlasting kingdom given to the people of the holy ones of the Most
High (Dan 7:27) and to the one like a son of man (7:14) is understood to belong to Job.  (2) Job's glory at the right hand of
the Father may be an interpretation of Ps 110:1 in terms of the
thrones set up in Dan 7:9.  The "chariots of the Father" (that
is, the thrones of the Father) appear to be thought of as the
support and foundation of the throne of Job, which exists even
while he is alive on earth, like the token of his vindication,
a place prepared for him.  (3) The coming of the Danielic one
like a son of man to the heavenly court to receive his kingdom,

read with Ezekiel 1 in mind and read as an ascent, underlies
the account here of the final translation of the righteous one
at death, his transcendence of death.  (4) The Danielic triad
becomes the triad of the just individual (Job), the holy ones
and the Father.[123]


4.  Wis 1:1-6:21

     In the so-called "book of eschatology" (Wis 1:1-6:11 and
6:17-21)[124] there is a description of the righteous who "will
shine and will run like sparks through the stubble" (Wis 3:7;
cf. Dan 12:3ϑ).  These "will judge nations and rule over
peoples" (3:8; cf. 5:15-16; 6:21; Dan 7:22, 14) and will understand truth (3:9; cf. Dan 12:10; 12:3; 11:33 LXX; 9:13ϑ).  In
this section there is a shift of focus from the righteous ones
to the righteous one *par excellence*, who seems to be their
representative and who is modeled in part on Enoch (cf. 4:10-
15).  This one is "numbered among the sons of God," with "his
lot among the holy ones" (5:5).  He is seen by his persecutors
"in the heavenly courtroom where he is exalted among the ranks
of angelic courtiers,"[125] a figure who has transcended death.
The sight of the exalted one in the heavenly court constitutes
a judgment in that it effects self-knowledge, self-condemnation
and repentance on the part of the ungodly (5:3-4).[126]
     If this depiction of the victory of the righteous is in-
fluenced by Daniel 7, the following aspects of Danielic reinterpretation are illustrated.  (1) The Enoch component of
Daniel 7 has been reasserted and developed (cf. *1 Enoch* 71) as
the new composition makes use of Daniel to portray the post-
mortem heavenly exaltation of the righteous individual (cf.
*Testament of Job*).  The "coming" of the one like a son of man
in Daniel 7 appears to have been understood in terms of Enoch's
being "taken up" (Wis 5:10-11) in death.  (2) The connection
between Dan 7:13-14 and 12:2-3 (that is, between the one like a
son of man and the *maskîlîm*) finds expression in Wisdom in the
oscillation between singular and plural righteous, and in the
portrayal of the exalted one as *Maskîl* or σοφός (4:17), who is
a champion of the Law (cf. 2:12)[127] and who understands the fate
of the just (2:16)--traits characteristic of the *maskîlîm* of

Daniel 11-12. His wisdom is considered to place him in a
father-son relation with the deity, whom he "knows" (2:13, 16;
cf. Dan 11:32).[128]   (3) The role of the righteous in judging
the nations, and that of the exalted one as a sort of witness
for the prosecution may be traced to an understanding of Dan
7:22 as referring to the power of judgment given to the holy
ones.[129]   The rule of the just over nations is understood in
Wisdom as a moral majesty and leadership influencing the political world (cf. Wis 1:1; 6:21).   (4) The apocalyptic, future-
oriented expectation of Daniel 7 has given way to interest in
eternal life, in the immortality of righteousness (Wis 1:15)
as an aspect of the relationship to God both before and after
death.   The righteous one represents all who are in touch with
their own immortality, living now the future life which is considered the real destiny of humanity.[130]   (5) The Danielic
triad appears here as God (by implication, the father of the
just one; 2:16-18), angels (sons of God, holy ones)[131] and
righteous one (child or son of God [2:13, 18], one who pleases
God [4:10, 14]).[132]   Again the triad occurs in the context of
an exaltation.[133]

NOTES TO CHAPTER V

[1] See above, p. 94.

[2] See above, Chapter III.

[3] In 71:1, 5, the Ethiopic uses the verb "hidden" as in 12:1; 10:1 (where it seems to mean withdrawal for the reception of revelation). Charles argues that this is the Ethiopic way of rendering μετέθηκεν (= הפל) in Gen 5:24 (*Book of Enoch*, 27).

[4] Ibid., 142.

[5] Perhaps this is intended to be an initial vision "from afar" as in *2 Enoch* 9 (Vaillant, p. 23). More likely it is evidence that two traditions have been unskillfully combined.

[6] The being intended by the final author or redactor as the translator of Enoch cannot be Michael, since Michael is mentioned below in vv. 8-9 going in and out of God's "house" with three other archangels, and in v. 13 as coming with the Head of Days. MSS B (v. 5) reads, "a spirit translated him." Charles considers the B form of the text late and secondary, although it occasionally presents the original text (*APOT*, 2.166).

[7] *Re'esa mawā'el* (= the sum of days) clearly echoes עַתִּיק יוֹמָיָא of Dan 7:13 (Colpe, "ὁ υἱὸς τοῦ ἀνθρώπου," 425 n. 194). Both terms must mean Aged One, Eternal One. In both texts the description of the white-haired head follows the title.

[8] Borsch, *Son of Man*, 151.

[9] It is not clear who comes and is speaking. Verses 14d and 15b make it seem unlikely that it is the Head of Days; the passage, however, concerns a sort of installment. The very ambiguity of the passage may be indicative of the author's reverential awe at the message he is writing; he may allow the impression that the Head of Days is speaking to coexist with the impression that it is another.

[10] Borsch compares this verse to "another royal naming oracle," Ps 2:7 ("you are my son"); *Son of Man*, 151 n. 5.

[11] The promise of presence—God with Enoch (v. 14) and Enoch with the righteous (v. 16)—may be intended to counter statements, such as those in the Targums (see above, p. 214 n. 219), of ignorance of Enoch's destiny and whereabouts, and/or to deny that the translated one is withdrawn from contact with humanity (cf. 70:1-2; 12:1).

[12] See Charles, *APOT*, 2.237, following Appel.

[13] Black, "Throne Theophany," 68-69. Contrast M. Casey, "The Use of the Term 'Son of Man' in the Similitudes of Enoch," *JSJ* 7 (1976) 11-29.

[14]Hooker (*The Son of Man*, 42-44) argues that chaps. 70-71
supply the solution and logical conclusion to the problem of
the Similitudes.  Cf. also T. W. Manson, "The Son of Man in
Daniel," 189; Rowley, *Relevance*, 114-15; Vermes, *Jesus the Jew*,
175; Casey, "Use of the Term," 19; C. L. Mearns, "Dating the
Similitudes of Enoch," *NTS* 25 (1979) 263-65.  E. Sjöberg (*Der
Menschensohn im Äthiopischen Henochbuch* [Lund: Gleerup, 1946]
160-67) tries to show that 70 and 71 form a united coherent
account, describing in three stages Enoch's translation and
exaltation; this analysis is opposed to treatments that regard
all or part of 70-71 as later additions.  Charles considers
chap. 70 the conclusion to the Similitudes, and thinks that
chap. 71 contains two misplaced visions which should precede
chap. 70.  He does not, however, deal with the questions of how
and why they were misplaced (*APOT*, 2.235; see below, nn. 15 and
17, for mention of Charles' earlier view).  Lindars ("Reenter,"
59) holds a similar opinion: he thinks chap. 71 should precede
chap. 69, which is the original conclusion of the work.  Milik
(*Books of Enoch*, 91) calls chaps. 70-71 "the epilogue...which
takes up the 'historical' framework of the work with the description of the removal of Enoch into the Paradise situated in
the North-West of the universe and his visit to the heavenly
Palace of God."  It is not clear whether he believes this section is by the author of the Similitudes or a later editor.

[15]Flusser, "The Son of Man," 230; Nickelsburg, *Resurrection*, 76; Colpe, "ὁ υἱὸς τοῦ ἀνθρώπου," 426-27 n. 203; Glasson,
*Second Advent*, 23, 40.  See Mowinckel (*He That Cometh*, 441 n. 2)
for references to other scholars who hold this position.  In
his 1893 edition of *The Book of Enoch* (pp. 183-84), Charles
concluded that chap. 71 is a later addition since it is "alien
alike in thought and phraseology to the Similitudes."  Charles
argued that chap. 71 was probably added by the same hand that
interpolated the Noachic fragments.  Several of his arguments
can be used to support position (3), that chap. 71 is the oldest part of the Similitudes (see below).

[16]Black ("The Eschatology of the Similitudes of Enoch,"
*JTS* 3 [1952] 8-9) suggested that chaps. 70-71 formed "an original constituent part of *1 Enoch*, out of which the Similitudes
have grown, by a rewriting of the Enoch legend in support of a
doctrine of a supernatural Messiah, foreign to the conception
of 1 Enoch."  In "Throne Theophany," twenty-five years later,
Black reaffirms his position concerning chap. 71.  He argues
that while it is unlikely that 70-71 was the work of anyone
other than the author of the secondary Greek version of the
Similitudes, it is possible that the Son of Man-Enoch tradition,
i.e., Enoch as Son of man (chap. 71) may have come from an
earlier source in the original Aramaic Enoch Pentateuch (p. 71).
Chapter 71 "could belong *either* to the original Enoch *or* to a
tradition earlier than the author of the book of Parables and
utilized by him" (p. 67).  Black dates chap. 71 to the first or
second century A.D. (p. 73).  Perrin (*Rediscovering*, 167) considers *1 Enoch* 70-71 pre-Christian, and the first use of the
imagery of Daniel 7 in subsequent apocalyptic.  The view of
Odeberg, if I understand him correctly, is similar.  He implies

that the Similitudes (in which a heavenly figure is equated
with the Messiah, and in which Enoch is only a visionary) are
an attempt on the part of "orthodox Judaism" to correct the
earlier Enoch tradition found in *1 Enoch* 70-71 (in which Enoch's
exaltation and "nomination" as the Son of Man is stressed); see
Odeberg, "'Ενώχ," 558.

[17]In chap. 71, as in the Book of Watchers, the immense distance (to be traveled) between God and humanity is emphasized,
whereas in the Similitudes one community of earth and heaven is
emphasized, God and the Son of Man dwelling with humanity (see
Charles, *Book of Enoch* [1893] 183). "Length of days" is promised to the righteous in 71:17, as though eternal life were
not already their lot (cf. 37:4; 40:9; 58:3; 62:14). Charles
argued that 71:17 probably showed the writer's acquaintance
with 3:9; 10:17; 25:6, in which long life (on earth) is promised (*Book of Enoch*, 184). The theophanic elements which
appear in chaps. 14 and 71 are treated below.

[18]Chapter 70 is not included in this discussion as it is
not a part of the midrashic history of Daniel 7. As already
noted, Charles considers this chapter the conclusion (as chap.
37 forms the introduction) of the Similitudes; its thought is
in keeping with the rest of this section (*Book of Enoch*, 141),
and it presents the fulfillment of Enoch's wish, expressed in
29:6-8. The fact that archaic material is preserved here can
be seen by comparison of 70:2-4 with *Jub.* 4:23 (cf. *1 Enoch*
106:8). See below, n. 42 on v. 3.

[19]In the context of the Similitudes, this verse has the
effect of identifying or joining the seer Enoch with the figure
he has previously seen (Elect One, Son of Man, Righteous One)
with the Lord of Spirits (Head of Days) in heaven. How this is
to be understood is the crux of interpretation of this passage.
Mowinckel (*He That Cometh*, 443-44) translates the phrase "son
of man" in 71:14 in lower-case letters, regarding it as a phrase
of common nouns. But in contrast, in 71:17 (as in 70:1), he
thinks the translator is using a technical expression. He argues that the intention of the author is to show that Enoch
("son of man who is born unto righteousness") is exalted to be
with (not to be) *the* Son of Man (p. 441; cf. p. 443). The
Ethiopic expression used in 71:14 (*walda be'esī*, with *we'etu*),
however, occurs also in 62:5 and twice in 69:29, where the
heavenly figure is clearly referred to (cf. Colpe, "ὁ υἱὸς τοῦ
ἀνθρώπου," 424; Colpe claims that the alternation of Ethiopic
expressions used for "Son of Man" in the Similitudes, plus the
use of demonstrative pronouns with the expression, show that
there is no Son of Man "title" in the Similitudes [p. 423]; cf.
also Vermes, *Jesus the Jew*, 175). There is nothing intrinsic
to chap. 71 which requires one to interpret v. 14 as a reference
to a previously described heavenly figure (cf. also 60:10 where
Noah is called "son of man").

[20]See above, pp. 180-83.

[21]There is no need to assume, as Perrin does, that *1 Enoch*
60 and 71 have been freshly modeled on Ezekiel 1 (*Rediscovering*,

167).  The imagery Perrin traces to Ezekiel 1 appears already
in *1 Enoch* 14 (with the exception of the phrase in *1 Enoch* 70:2,
"chariots of the spirit").  As I have shown, Ezekiel 1 had already been the inspiration of *1 Enoch* 14 and again of Daniel 7.
Here in *1 Enoch* 71 the influence of the Ezekiel merkabah scenes
continues to be felt, but this is because they are the presupposition and ground of interpretation, rather than a fresh influence and connection.  Black lays out the "basic structure
and recurring features" found in *1 Enoch* 14, 60, 70-71, whose
model in almost every case is Ezekiel ("Eschatology of the
Similitudes," 8-9).

[22] As in *1 Enoch* 14:9 (4QEn^C 1 vi 21-22), the crystal is
surrounded by tongues of fire (cf. *1 Enoch* 71:5).  In the latter text, however, only one house of God is mentioned (in contrast to the house within a house in *1 Enoch* 14:10, 15).  The
Head of Days comes forth *from* it, in contrast to *1 Enoch* 14
where Enoch approaches the open door of the second house *in*
which God sits.

[23] The wheels of the throne, which in 15:18 are "like the
disc of the sun," in 71:7 have become a class of angels, the
Ophanin.  Cf. 61:10.  This means the description of the throne
in *1 Enoch* 71 is more developed than in Daniel 7 (cf. Bowman,
"The Background of the Term 'Son of Man,'" 286) and in *1 Enoch*
14.

[24] Black, "Throne Theophany," 71.

[25] Glasson (*Second Advent*, 22-23) thinks the writer reasoned
in this way: Enoch and Elijah were the only two men who did not
die.  Elijah had already been designated the forerunner in
Malachi 4, and so Enoch remained to fulfill the role of Messiah.
This thinking confirmed the author's bold step in designating
Enoch as Son of Man and Messiah in *1 Enoch* 71.  Glasson, it
will be remembered (see above, p. 225), considers *1 Enoch* 71 a
later addition to the Similitudes; he thinks this explains the
inconsistencies (in some passages Enoch speaks of the Son of
Man as a different person from himself, but in chap. 71 he is
told that he is the Son of Man).  Glasson does not attempt to
explain why such an addition would be made, nor why the editor
did not bring the earlier chapters into harmony with his interpretation.  One problem with Glasson's interpretation is that
the forerunner in Malachi 4 is the forerunner of the "great and
terrible day of Yahweh" (cf. 3:1), not of the Messiah.

[26] The Danielic one like a son of man, in other words, is
present in this scene in *1 Enoch* 71, not as a heavenly vision
afforded the seer but as the seer himself, in the unemended
text.

[27] There is a certain parallelism between the interpretation
of *1 Enoch* 14 by Daniel 7, and the interpretation of *1 Enoch* 71
by the Similitudes: in both cases the translation of an individual human figure is regarded as the exaltation of a heavenly
figure who is in some sense corporate.

[28]His righteousness is that of the Head of Days (71:14).
Hahn connects the idea of Enoch's righteousness with the idea
of the image of God; he thinks that in *1 Enoch* 71, Enoch is not
identified with a preexistent Son of Man, but as the only righteous one among the early generations he is the representative
of humanity ('Adam) created in the image of God, and is taken
up as (son of) man. Hahn considers this a specifically Jewish
attempt to elucidate the concept of the archetypal man (which
was current and hovering in the background) in the light of the
biblical doctrine of creation (*Christologische Hoheitstitel*,
21 n. 4, cited by Fuller, *Foundations*, 41). Fuller objects
that this theory has the disadvantage of postulating the use of
the term "son of man" in two different senses in juxtaposed
contexts (i.e., in the Similitudes and in *1 Enoch* 71). He
concludes, therefore, that "the problem of 1 En 71 remains
unsolved." But it is precisely the distinction between the two
contexts that leads us to postulate that *1 Enoch* 71 is the
presupposition of the Similitudes.

[29]Hooker remarks that on this point the author is faithful
to the Danielic vision, in which the holy ones of the Most High
are obedient (*Son of Man in Mark*, 46); cf. Dan 12:3.

[30]Glasson considers Enoch "exalted to messianic dignity,"
a feature he argues is suggested by the language of Dan 7:14
(*Second Advent*, 23).

[31]The fact that Enoch's blessings and praise are "well
pleasing" to the Head of Days may indicate his angelic status
or his fellowship with the angels: he joins their choir of
praise.

[32]The language of 71:16 ("all will walk in your ways...
with you will be their dwelling places, and with you their
heritage") is similar to language used of Melchizedek in 11Q
Melchi 4-6. "(God) is going] to declare that they will become
part of the sons of heaven and (that they will participate) in
the heritage of Milkî-ṣedeq, f[or he is going to assign] them
a pa[rt in the portion of Milkî-ṣe]deq who is going to make
them enter into his [lot]..." (Milik translation, "Milkî-ṣedeq
et Milkî-reša'," 97-98).

[33]Hengel (*Judaism and Hellenism*, 1.204) considers *1 Enoch*
71 a spiritualized form of *1 Enoch* 14. It is no longer the
whole person but the spirit which shares in the journey. This
spiritualization Hengel finds characteristic of the Similitudes.
Here in *1 Enoch* 71, Enoch is not said to have died.

[34]See above, n. 23.

[35]*1 Enoch* 12:1-2 shows Enoch already in the eastern Paradise. Charles (*Book of Enoch*, 27-28) remarks that it is possible the editor intends the readers to understand that Enoch
has already been translated, yet the vision that follows does
not have this meaning. The author of *Jub.* 4:21 reads *1 Enoch*
12:2 as a reference to Enoch's "walking with God" during his

lifetime, before his translation (cf. Gen 5:22). According to
Milik, the four journeys of Enoch narrated in the Book of
Watchers are (1) his descent from paradise to the second chief
of the fallen Watchers; (2) his ascent to the palace of God
(14:8-16:4); (3) and (4) his "horizontal missions" to the West
(17-19, substantially rewritten in 21-25) and East (20, 26-36).
His final destination is the eastern Paradise (Charles, *Books
of Enoch*, 33-41).

[36]Charles notes the associations with Isa 14:13; Ezek 1:26
(the moving throne comes from the north) and 28:13-14 (*Book of
Enoch*, 41).

[37]Cf. *1 Enoch* 1:4-9, the introduction to the Book of
Watchers, in which the final epiphany of the Holy Great One on
Sinai is predicted. He will come "with ten thousand of his
holy ones" (v. 9) to judge.

[38]There is no influence of Daniel 7 on the narration of
the ascent and final translation of Enoch in *2 Enoch*.

[39]See above, pp. 144-45.

[40]Iron, copper, silver, gold, soft metal and lead.

[41]Charles notes that this passage is founded on Dan 2:31-
45, but he thinks the seventh mountain has been lost from the
text (*Book of Enoch*, 101-102).

[42]Cf. 70:3 where Enoch is said to be set "between the two
winds, between the north and the west." The mountain imagery
has been lost.

[43]Could this tradition have been the original ending of
the Book of Watchers? If it was a complement to *1 Enoch* 1:4-9
(see above, n. 37), it may have been a scene of final judgment
in which Enoch was translated in order to perform the function
of witness. As far as I know, no fragment of Enoch material
found at Qumran corresponds to this suggestion. But it is
plausible to suppose that a small section might be absent by
chance or not yet identified (cf. Milik [*Books of Enoch*, 5] on
the difficulty of identifying the majority of the fragments).

[44]See above, pp. 155, 177-78.

[45]A transfer of divine power does appear in *1 Enoch* 71:14,
16, but this is not royal power.

[46]Cf. Black, "The 'Parables' of Enoch," 8 n. 18.

[47]There is emphasis on the translation of Enoch's "spirit"
and in one family of Ethiopic MSS the translating power is
called "a spirit" (cf. above, p. 245 n. 6).

[48]See above, p. 59 n. 2.

[49] References to the fall of the city and temple occur in
10:20-23 and elsewhere, presented as though they refer to the
defeat of Judah by Babylon in 587 (cf. 3:1-2).  Identification
of the three heads of the eagle, the Roman Empire's insignia
(cf. 10:60-12:51), make it fairly certain that the book was
written during or soon after the reign of Domitian (81-96).
Some critics think it was touched up during the reign of Trajan
(100-135) and that it may also have Christian interpolations.
Box (*APOT*, 2) dates the final redaction around 120 A.D.   The
translation used here is that of J. M. Myers (*I and II Esdras*
[AB 42; Garden City, NY: Doubleday, 1974]).

[50] They may be based on material earlier than 70, but were
not necessarily drawn from written sources.  Most critics today
consider *4 Ezra* a unity, with minor insertions.  The author may
have used memories and traditions which produce certain inconsistencies and the impression of a mosaic, but this does not
mean the book is a compilation of major sources, as, for example, Box and Charles believed (see Myers, *I and II Esdras*,
119-21; Rowley, *Relevance*, 156-59).

[51] See Hooker, *Son of Man*, 50, 56.  The author of *4 Ezra*,
like Hooker, emphasizes the connection between Adam's lordship
(cf. 6:54-59) and the dominion promised in Daniel 7 (cf. 3:7).
E. Breech ("These Fragments I Have Shored Against My Ruins: the
Form and Function of 4 Ezra," *JBL* 92 [1973] 269-70, 274) argues
that the form of the work is constituted by Ezra's movement
from distress to consolation.  His distress (that of the be-
wildered post-70 community) is fully overcome only after he has
received the fifth and sixth dream visions ("the broken fragments of the community's traditions").

[52] Cf. 7:35-38; 14:35 with Dan 12:1-2, and *4 Ezra* 7:[97],
55[125] with Dan 12:3.

[53] The seeing of God is the central feature of the final
judgment (cf. 7:42, 87, 98).  The translation of Ezra himself
is narrated in summary fashion in the last two verses of the
book (14:49-50).

[54] Ezra's prayer or confession (8:20-36) opens with an invocation: "Lord, who lives forever, / Whose eyes are lifted
up, / (Whose) dwelling places are in the air, / Whose throne is
indescribable (Latin and Syriac read: immeasurable), / (Whose)
glory is incomprehensible, / Before whom angelic hosts stand
with trembling, / And at whose word they are converted to wind
and fire" (vv. 20-22; cf. Ps 104:4 LXX).  This passage is unusual for its mention of angels, since one of the most remarkable features of *4 Ezra* is the absence in it of interest in or
description or enumeration of different orders of angels and
angelic personalities, and absence of the sense of angelic influence in human affairs.

[55] Box (*APOT*, 2.542) argues that the purpose of the book as
a whole is "to commend the apocalyptic literature to certain
Rabbinical circles which were hostile and to secure for it a

permanent place within orthodox Judaism." To this end, the
"cruder elements of the older apocalyptic" were omitted, and
the compilation represents a fusion of apocalyptic and rabbinic
thought, with a strong heritage of wisdom tradition.  Compare
M. Stone, "Lists of Revealed Things in Apocalyptic Literature,"
420.  J. Neusner (*A Life of Yoḥanan ben Zakkai* [2d ed.; Leiden:
Brill, 1970] 132-33) discusses the differences in responses to
the destruction of 70 A.D. on the part of the authors of *4 Ezra*
and *2 Baruch*, on the one hand, and R. Yoḥanan ben Zakkai, on
the other hand.  The former rest on an eschatological expectation Neusner does not find in R. Yoḥanan's thought.

[56]Myers speaks of *4 Ezra* as a tract for an impatient revolutionary age, counseling "faith in a God who was alive to the
condition of his people, but who, at the same time, could not
be manipulated or hurried" (*I and II Esdras*, x).  In a sense,
this God does not appear in this work, but stands beyond and
above.  The readers are counseled to wait for God's intervention.

[57]As Myers remarks, this is an illustration of "the Jewish
concept of the vitality of scripture which contains certain
hidden meanings always susceptible to contemporary significance" (*I and II Esdras*, 297).

[58]"Your arrogance has reached the Most High, and your
haughtiness the Almighty" (11:44; cf. Dan 7:25).

[59]Cf. Dan 7:11, where, as the little horn is speaking
"great words," the body of the fourth beast is slain and burnt.

[60]The phrase about the anointed one being from the seed
of David is omitted in the Latin, but supplied here from the
Syriac; it is substantially present in all other oriental versions (Myers, *I and II Esdras*, 286).  The connection between
the lion and anointed one is probably an interpretation of Gen
49:9 (cf. 1 Macc 3:4 [Judas Maccabeus as a lion] and 1QSb 5:29
[the prince of the congregation as a lion]).  Nowhere else in
*4 Ezra* or in *1 Enoch* or in *2 Baruch* is the anointed one
referred to as a descendant of David.  In Rev 5:5 the Lamb is
given the titles "Lion of Judah" and "Root of David" in a
scene that reinterprets Dan 7:14.

[61]According to M. Stone, both 12:34 and 11:46 refer to the
final judgment after the end of the messianic kingdom, and not
to the eternity and universality of the theocratic messianic
kingdom ("The Concept of the Messiah in IV Ezra," *Religions in
Antiquity* [ed. J. Neusner; Leiden: Brill, 1968] 298).

[62]The forest from which the lion comes is not interpreted.
In *2 Baruch* 36-40 we find a "forest of wickedness" which is a
kingdom, perhaps Babylon (Charles, *APOT*, 2.501).

[63]Myers, *I and II Esdras*, 294.

[64]Perhaps we have the hint of a reading of Dan 7:22 which
understands that judgment (i.e., the power to judge) is given
*to*--not *for*--the holy ones of the Most High (see Montgomery

[*Daniel*, 310] on Wis 3:8; Matt 19:28; 1 Cor 6:2 and Rev 20:4 as
reminiscences of this interpretation of the Aramaic of Dan 7:22,
(וְדִינָא יְהִיב לְקַדִּישֵׁי עֶלְיוֹנִין).  But if so, this is the only indication in *4 Ezra* that the messiah is a corporate figure, although in 14:9 Ezra is told he will henceforth be with "my son
and those like you until the times are terminated" (cf. 14:50;
6:26) and in 7:28 it is said that "my son the messiah will be
revealed with those who are with him" (cf. 13:52).  Rowley
(*Relevance*, 116 n. 3) interprets 7:28 by 6:26, and Doeve (*Jewish Hermeneutics*, 126) by 14:9, arguing that nowhere in the
pseudepigrapha or rabbinic literature is the messiah ever pictured as coming with angels.  If these verses are all to be
understood in the light of one another, the messiah is in the
company of all the righteous or all the translated ones.

[65]See above, n. 61.  The eagle-lion vision is almost exclusively preoccupied with the destruction of Rome, although
its eschatology extends to the final judgment.  In Daniel 7,
in contrast, the judgment of the fourth beast is the final
judgment by the heavenly court (7:10, 26).

[66]It is difficult to harmonize the eschatological schema
here with that found in 7:26-30, where we also find the idea of
a temporary messianic kingdom.  In this passage, the anointed
one (*filius meus* in vv. 28, 29), like the Danielic one like a
son of man, plays no part in the events preceding the end, but
is revealed at the end of evils.  He brings joy to the survivors for 400 years and then dies.  After an interval of seven
days of primeval silence, the Most High appears for the final
judgment.

[67]Cf. 12:32; the two subwings and the head of the eagle
are also said to have been "reserved by the Most High for its
end" (presumably the end of the eagle; 12:30).  A clearer
expression of the preexistence of the messiah occurs in 13:52.

[68]Stone points out that "to the author of this document
the supposed incompatibility (between a transcendent and earthly messiah) did not seem important."  He compares the messiah
in 12:32 with the figure of Melchizedek in *2 Enoch* (born before
the flood and assumed to heaven in order to appear later at the
appointed time) and in 11Q Melchizedek ("The Concept of the
Messiah," 297, against Box, *APOT*, 2.614).  Preexistence also
does not preclude mortality (7:29).  This figure is no answer
to the problem of life after death, although his connection
with the translated ones is not forgotten.  There is a clean
break between the messianic age and the final judgment, with
which the resurrection is associated (7:32).

[69]His theory of the existence of this traditional complex
is based on the coincidence of a number of common elements in
the eagle vision and the vision of *2 Baruch* 38-43, which have
no literary connection.  Against Box (*APOT*, 2.608), who holds
that the vision is from an independent source already existing
in written form and excerpted by the redactor, Stone thinks
both the vision and its interpretation are the composition of
the author ("The Concept of the Messiah," 296-303).

[70]The figure of the one like a son of man in Dan 7:13-14 and its contemporizations in *1 Enoch* 71 and elsewhere in the Similitudes are silent.

[71]The seventh episode is not really a vision, but the legend of Ezra's restoration of the holy Scriptures and the esoteric books. It is "a necessary epilogue to the consolation of the prophet": his mediation of consolation to the community (Breech, "These Fragments," 274).

[72]This translation follows the Syriac and the other oriental versions. This part of the sentence is missing in the Latin MSS by homoioteleuton (Myers, *I and II Esdras*, 302; Box, *APOT*, 2.616). Cf. v. 32: "my son whom you saw as a man rising up." In vv. 3, 4, 12, 25, 51, the figure is simply called "that man" or "man"; the comparative sense is lost.

[73]This is obviously meant to be a continuation of the eagle-lion dream, as again a figure rises out of the sea. The function of the wind and clouds here in chap. 13 is different from their function in the preceding dream: there they did not bring the eagle out of the sea but buffeted its wings (11:2). But here, as in *1 Enoch* 14, they are the vehicle of the man, the impelling force of his ascent.

[74]See Ps 104:32 (Yahweh "looks on the earth and it trembles"); Ps 46:6 (Yahweh "utters his voice, the earth melts").

[75]As we have noted above (p. 228), this mountain is related to the stone cut out by no human hand, which broke the image and became "a great mountain and filled the whole earth" (Dan 2:34-35, 44-45). It is difficult, however, to trace the development of thought. Does the author intend the reader to understand that the man who cuts out the mountain is no merely human figure, since the stone is cut "by no human hand" (*4 Ezra* 13:36), and since the man here has access to the place (a huger mountain?, perhaps the throne of God as in *1 Enoch* 24:1-3; 18: 6-9?) which Ezra is unable to see? The man in *4 Ezra* stands on the mountain, identified in the interpretation as Mount Zion.

[76]This vision inspires in Ezra "excessive fear," but also the sense that those who live to see this event of the end time are better off than those who die before it happens (13:13, 15-20). The interpreter confirms this.

[77]Probably the man; cf. Myers, *I and II Esdras*, 310. This verse seems to be in contradiction with 5:56; 6:6; but cf. 13:29.

[78]In 13:32, the Ethiopic reads "that man"; Arabic[1] "my boy," "youth"; Arabic[2] "my servant." In 7:28, the Latin reads "my son Jesus"; Arabic[1] "my child, the messiah"; Syriac and other versions "the messiah." In 7:29 we have "my son Messiah." In 14:9, Arabic[1] "my youth"; Arabic[2] "my servant." See S. Gero ("My Son the Messiah," *ZNW* 66 [1975] 264-67) for the reading in Georgian MSS of 7:28 ("the elect, my anointed one") and 7:29 ("elect").

[79]Fuller, *Foundations*, 41; Stone, "Concept of the Messiah,"
303; Colpe, "ὁ υἱὸς τοῦ ἀνθρώπου," 428; Russell, *Method and
Message*, 333; cf. 336; Lohse, "υἱός," *TDNT* 8 (1974) 361; Tödt,
*Son of Man*, 25.

[80]Black believes that *4 Ezra* 13 contains the earliest
Jewish midrash on Dan 2:34-35. In it the mountain is interpreted as Daniel's stone, *filius mei* ("The Christological Use
of the OT in the NT," 13). That is, an explicit identification
of the mountain-stone and the man may have stood behind an
original בני in this text. In the text as it now stands, the
man flies to the mountain. But S. Gero ("My Son") believes on
the basis of the Georgian MSS that the original, ambiguous
Hebrew of 7:28 and perhaps later passages may have been ברי משיח,
with בר later interpreted as "son" (υἱός; cf. Prov 31:2; Ps 2:
11) as in the Latin and Syriac, and as "elect one" (ἐκλεκτός;
cf. Amos 5:11 LXX) as attested by the Georgian.

[81]The fact that the figure in *4 Ezra* rises out of the sea
like the beasts in Daniel 7, whereas in Daniel 7 the one like a
son of man "comes with the clouds of heaven" in contrast to them,
can be explained in either of two ways. (1) Either the author
of *4 Ezra* has access to material older than Daniel 7, which the
author of Daniel has changed in order to emphasize the difference between the one like a son of man and the beasts, or (2)
the author of *4 Ezra* has added this detail to link the vision
in chap. 13 with the eagle-lion vision in chaps. 11-12. Emerton ("The Origin of the Son of Man Imagery," 236) thinks the
former alternative is more likely. The sea is interpreted as
hiddenness, impenetrable mystery, in 13:52. A certain parallel
can be seen in the rising of the man from the sea and the
crossing of the river Jordan by the returnees, his people, in
13:47.

[82]Emerton, "The Origin of the Son of Man Imagery," 236-37;
cf. Myers, *I and II Esdras*, 308.

[83]Tödt, *Son of Man*, 27.

[84]Ibid. Perhaps the reader is meant to understand that
the bestowal of power takes place in the region where the man
flies to carve out the mountain. But the author of *4 Ezra* expresses the seer's inability to see that place, perhaps the
heavenly court (13:7). The coming of the man (down) to the
mountain on which he fights is in a sense his "second coming,"
following his coming up to heaven.

[85]See Bowman, "The Background of the Term 'Son of Man,'"
268.

[86]Have "all nations" become the fourth beast? The contemporization is not directed against the Roman government.

[87]Colpe ("ὁ υἱὸς τοῦ ἀνθρώπου," 428) remarks that this
eschatological Israel cannot be merely an historical continuation of the earlier one, but must represent the new aeon. Cf.

*2 Baruch* 72-74, where the Messiah summons all the nations.  As
in the eagle-lion vision, nothing is said in *4 Ezra* 13 of the
length of the new kingdom.

[88]The son of David (v. 23) will break in pieces the substance of the godless "with a rod of iron" and will destroy
them "with the word of his mouth" (vv. 26-27; cf. v. 35).  He
"will gather together a holy people, whom he will lead in righteousness" (v. 28; cf. v. 34, where nations come "bringing as
gifts her sons who had fainted").  The theme of the Spirit of
Yahweh resting on the son of David appears in Isa 11:2; *Ps. Sol.*
17:42, and in *1 Enoch* 62:2 ("and the spirit of righteousness
was poured out on [the Elect One] and the word of his mouth
slays all sinners"), but not in *4 Ezra* 13.  Although the Similitudes and *4 Ezra* have in common the use of Daniel 7 with
Isaiah 11, and some sort of notion of the preexistence of the
anointed one, Perrin argues that the Similitudes and *4 Ezra*
represent two independent cycles of tradition, independent uses
of Daniel 7 (*Rediscovering*, 165).  *4 Ezra* cannot be used to
supplement the Similitudes with reference to a Son of Man
"concept."  There is no titular use of the phrase "son of man"
in either work, no interest in his heavenly enthronement in
*4 Ezra*, and there are different developments of the idea of
the Danielic figure as judge.

[89]N. Perrin, "The Son of Man in Ancient Judaism and
Primitive Christianity," 19.  The author of *4 Ezra*, however,
has returned to Isaiah 11 for the fourth theme, the crossing
of waters.

[90]Glasson ("The Son of Man Imagery," 87) speaks of Daniel
7 suffering here a "sea change."  While the term "messiah" is
not used either in the vision or its interpretation in *4 Ezra*
13, the use of the messianic Davidic text Isaiah 11 implies
that the author has understood the one like a son of man as the
Davidic messiah (against Russell, *Method and Message*, 33).  See
also Stone, "Concept of the Messiah," 309-10.

[91]Discrepancies between the vision (*4 Ezra* 13:1-13) and
its interpretation (vv. 21-52), additional details found in the
interpretation, and the confusion of the interpretation itself
have led several critics to the conclusion that the vision is
independent material and contains mythological elements which
the author of *4 Ezra* may not have fully understood.  The interpretation is more in line with the thinking of the rest of the
book, in that it excludes or reinterprets all the cosmic aspects
of the vision and tones down the military formulation of the
*quasi*-human figure in favor of a forensic formulation similar to
that of the eagle vision.  Box and others have suggested that
the vision should be dated before 70 A.D. (*APOT*, 2.616; also
Tödt, *Son of Man*, 25; Emerton, "The Origin of Son of Man
Imagery," 226; cf. Hooker, *Son of Man*, 48 n. 2; Myers, *I and II
Esdras*, 316).  Stone thinks that in *4 Ezra* 13 the author is
writing his own interpretation of a "previously existing allegory" or reworking a previously existing interpretation which
is now submerged beyond recovery.  He does not venture to date
the tradition ("The Concept of the Messiah," 304-10).

[92]See above, p. 4, for the idea that Matt 28:20a ("teaching them to observe all that I have commanded you") refers implicitly to Jesus' radical reinterpretation of Torah. Already in Daniel, I have argued, the one like a son of man is representative of the *maskîlîm*, whose wisdom is based on the eschatological interpretation of scriptures and of visions (above, p. 194 n. 40).

[93]The returning tribes cross the stopped-up Jordan (*4 Ezra* 13:39-47), and all nations are to be made disciples through baptism (Matt 28:19b). Baptism is compared to a reversal of the Flood (Genesis 6-8) in 1 Pet 3:20-21, and to the crossing of the Reed Sea in 1 Cor 10:1. I am well aware that some will not find these parallels convincing.

[94]Aspects of a warrior interpretation of the Son of Man do appear, as will be seen, in the NT parousia texts and in Revelation.

[95]Late rabbinic traditions such as *b. Ḥag.* 14a, which speaks of the Messiah occupying one of the thrones of Dan 7:9, may presuppose the notion of assumption. Cf. *Midr. Ps.* 21:5 (Yalquṭ) on Dan 7:14 and Jer 30:21, dealing with the heavenly enthronement of the Messiah.

[96]In *4 Ezra* 13:37-38, the fire from the mouth of the man from the sea is interpreted as the law, used to overcome and destroy the man's enemies.

[97]Contrast *Pirqe R. El.* 11 where the power of the Messiah (spoken of in terms of Dan 2:35) extends only over the whole earth.

[98]This speculation is opposed in such texts as *Mek. R. Ishmael*, Shirata 4:23-24 (cf. Baḥodesh 5:24; *Pesiq. R.* 21:6), using Dan 7:9 and Exod 24:10.

[99]Josephus provides evidence that Daniel 2 and 7 were politically dangerous in his time. In *Ant.* 110.210, he is retelling the story of King Nebuchadnezzar's dream of the statue and stone, but he refuses to give the interpretation of the stone, indicating that it refers to "the hidden things that are to come." This evasiveness can only be due to the current messianic interpretation of the stone, taken as a symbol of the messiah or messianic kingdom which it was hoped would put an end to the Roman Empire. Likewise, Daniel 7 is completely omitted by Josephus in his summary of the book (see *Ant.* 10.263-69). In *J.W.* 6.5.4, #312-13, "an ambiguous oracle" is mentioned which "more than all else incited [the Jews] to war" against Rome in 66 A.D. Found in the sacred writings, it was an oracle "to the effect that at that time one from their own country would become ruler of the world. This they understood to mean someone of their own race, and many of their wise men went astray in their interpretation of it." Josephus adds that the oracle in reality referred to Vespasian. Some scholars think this oracle is Dan 7:13-14 (see, for example, Bruce, "The Book of Daniel," 221-22) but this is not certain (cf. Jeremias, *NT Theology*, 269 n. 4).

258                                    The Father, Son and Holy Spirit

[100] The "people of the holy ones of the Most High" in Daniel 7 are also not the nation of Israel. Lines are drawn between those considered faithful to the covenant and those considered apostate.

[101] See above, p. 59 n. 4.

[102] See *Tanḥuma* B Terumah #6 (46b) where the stone of Dan 2:34 is identified as the King Messiah who will destroy the whole world, smiting the earth with the breath of his mouth (Isa 11:4; cf. *4 Ezra* 13:10).

[103] In *2 Enoch* 9 the mountain-throne of God is clearly related to the "stone cut out by no human hand" of Daniel 2. The Elect One *is* the seventh mountain, before whom all other mountains melt, in *1 Enoch* 52. And in *Apoc. Ab.* 19, the seventh heaven is itself a mountain.

[104] If this is the case, rabbinic insistence that it is impossible for a human being to sit on God's throne (cf. *Exod. Rab.* 15:26; *Midr. Ps.* 72:2--both commenting on Dan 7:9) can be understood as a reaction to this sort of thinking.

[105] LXX: "And you, go, rest...." MT: "But go your way to the end...."

[106] I have also suggested that the phrase in Matt 28:16, οὗ ἐτάξατο αὐτοῖς ὁ Ἰησοῦς, should be translated "where Jesus commissioned them" (see above, p. 77 n. 201).

[107] See above, p. 245 n. 6. Cf. *1 Enoch* 70:2, where there is mention of "chariots of the spirit."

[108] This figure is transformed into an even more powerful wild ox (Milik, *Books of Enoch*, 44-45).

[109] By Hengel, Milik, Russell, R. H. Charles and others. "That man" is said to come down for the help of the ram (Judas Maccabeus) in v. 14; cf. 2 Macc 11:6-12.

[110] Glasson (*Second Advent*, 18) thinks this is the earliest interpretation of the one like a son of man, an interpretation which led to the attribution of the function of judge to the Son of Man in the Similitudes.

[111] Black, "Throne Theophany," 70.

[112] Glasson believes that the messianic figure of the white bull led to the attribution of the function of reigning to the Son of Man in the Similitudes, whose author has coalesced Michael and the white bull (*Second Advent*, 18).

[113] In my opinion, *1 Enoch* 90 is to be classified as "in the midrashic style," as it is not intimately based on Daniel 7, but merely inserts elements of that text into the climax of the Animal Allegory. In contrast, *1 Enoch* 71 and the two passages from *4 Ezra* have a better claim to be midrash in the broad sense of that term; see above, pp. 97-98.

[114]There is no great concern with the puzzle of martyrdom, or with faith in the transcendence of death. The "destroyed" (righteous dead) and the dispersed, however, do assemble with all the nations in the "new house" or new Jerusalem (90:27, 33).

[115]Charles argues that the order of seven archangels (cf. Tobit 12:15) is derived from the Zoroastrian Amshaspands (*Book of Enoch*, 212; cf. E. Schweizer, "πνεῦμα," *TDNT* 6 [1968] 450 n. 824). The seven spirits of God appear in the Book of Revelation. In Ezek 9:1-2, six "men" who are executioners and one who is a scribe are summoned to smite Jerusalem and mark the faithful before the departure of the *Kābôd*; the Persian tradition may have influenced the author of *1 Enoch* via Ezekiel.

[116]A transcription and translation of the text was given by its editor, Milik, at a public lecture in 1972 at Harvard. I am grateful to J. A. Fitzmyer for supplying me with a copy, and also to J. A. Sanders for making available to me a handwritten transcription with notes made in 1967 by Milik, and Sanders' own transcription and translation. Also, G. Blaszczak kindly loaned me an unpublished paper he had written at Harvard in 1974 on the text, along with a provisional reconstruction and translation by F. M. Cross. A portion of the text is discussed by Fitzmyer in "Qumran Aramaic and the New Testament," *NTS* 20 (1974) 393; idem, "The Aramaic Language and the Study of the New Testament," *JBL* 99 (1980) 14-15.

[117]The transcription by Milik and those of Fitzmyer and Cross are significantly different at this point (1:7-9) as are their interpretations.

[118]It is not clear how the third masculine singular should be translated in 2:5-9. Fitzmyer asks, Is the subject of this passage "'the people of God' (ii.4)? Is it an individual person? Or is it a person representing a collectivity (in the manner of the 'one like a son of man' in Dan vii.13 representing the 'holy ones of the Most High' in Dan vii.18)?" ("Qumran Aramaic," 392).

[119]According to Milik, this work is part of a Pseudo-Daniel cycle composed around 100 B.C. ("'Prière de Nabonide' et autres écrits d'un cycle de Daniel, fragments de Qumrân 4," *RB* 63 [1956] 407-15).

[120]In Milik's reconstruction there is a triad: Great God, angels (restored; against Fitzmyer), Son of God.

[121]See Brown, *Birth*, 310, 313. Fitzmyer ("Qumran Aramaic," 393) understands the Son of God in the Qumran text to be the son of an enthroned human king, possibly heir to the throne of David. But he cautions that there is no indication he is messianic ("Aramaic Language," 15).

[122]Compare *Apocalypse of Moses* 33:34, where the chariot which takes Adam's soul is the throne of God (cf. 37:3), called "the Father of all" (cf. 36:3: "the Father of light"). In *Life*

*of Adam and Eve* 25:1-3; 26:1-2 (drawing on Ezekiel 1 and
Daniel 7), Adam learns in a Merkabah experience of his own
death. M. Philonenko (*Le Testament de Job* [*Semitica* 18 (1968)]
302) remarks that the chariots have become "psychopompes": they
carry the soul of the just person to heaven.

[123]The title "Father" given to God in both *Testament of
Job* and *Apocalypse of Moses* may be pre-Christian or uninflu-
enced by Christian terminology. Is this an interpretation of
the great age of the Ancient of Days, modeled (perhaps unconsciously) on 'El, father of years, father of gods and men?
Cf. *Ascension of Isaiah* 8:18, where God is called "the primal
Father."

[124]This section prepares the way for the "book of Wisdom
proper," to use the terminology of W. Weber, E. Gärtner and
others who follow their lead. See J. M. Reese, *Hellenistic
Influence on the Book of Wisdom and Its Consequences*, xxx
(Rome: Biblical Institute, 1970) 35; D. Winston, *The Wisdom of
Solomon* (AB 43; Garden City: Doubleday, 1979) 10-11. Further
treatment of the use of Danielic traditions in this material
appears in my article, "Major Midrashic Traditions in Wisdom
1:1-6:25," forthcoming, *JSJ*.

[125]Nickelsburg, *Resurrection*, 48, 76, 60.

[126]These are those who "did not know the secret purposes
(μυστήρια) of God" (2:22). In Daniel 2, the word μυστήριον is
used eight times in both Greek translations concerning the
dream of the stone that smashes the statue.

[127]In *Midr. Ps.* 2:9, where Ps 2:7-8 is quoted after Dan
7:13-14, the promise of the nations for an inheritance is applied to the Lord Messiah, "because the Messiah occupies himself with Torah." *Num. Rab.* 11:1 interprets Dan 7:27 by 1 Sam
2:8 ("to make [Israel]...inherit a throne of glory") with a
similar emphasis: because Israel has observed the Torah, God
will restore its sovereignty and cause it to inherit a throne
of glory.

[128]Suggs (*Wisdom, Christology and Law*, 27) calls Wis 2:10
to 5 "no report of the fate of *a* wise man but a dogmatic statement concerning the destiny of Sophia's ideal representative."

[129]See above, pp. 252-53 n. 64. The scene in which the
exalted one is seen in the heavenly court, however, is not the
cosmic, final judgment.

[130]This development of thought should be pondered in the
light of Collins' comments concerning "incipient mysticism" in
Daniel (*Apocalyptic Vision*, 176).

[131]The term "holy ones" is used by the author to refer to
the human just, chosen ones in 3:9; 4:15, and in 18:13 the whole
people of Israel is called God's son. In *Midr. Ps.* 2:9 (Yalquṭ),
Ps 2:7 is interpreted as a declaration that the children of
Israel are God's sons; it is claimed that the Law (Exod 4:22),
the Prophets (Isa 52:13; 42:1) and the Writings (Ps 110:1; Dan
7:13-14) all declare this fact.

[132]There is emphasis throughout the Enoch traditions (see, for example, *1 Enoch* 71:12) on Enoch's having pleased God, an emphasis which may witness the application to him of Isa 42:1. Strong allusions to Psalm 2 are woven into Wis 1:1-6:21.

[133]The Danielic triad appears only once in rabbinic material which refers to Daniel 7: in *Midr. Ps.* 21:5 (Holy One, angels, King Messiah [Yalquṭ]; Holy One, angels, Israel [Buber ed.]), which speaks of angels drawing the third figure to the first. With very few exceptions, the rabbinic material almost studiously ignores the exaltation of the one like a son of man. In *b. Ḥag.* 13b-14a, the members of the Danielic triad are treated individually, for the most part in the light of Ezekiel 1.

CHAPTER VI

NEW TESTAMENT PASSAGES RELATED TO DANIEL 7
AND PERTINENT TO MATT 28:16-20

Just as one cannot leap from Daniel 7 to Matt 28:16-20 as
if there were no intervening Jewish reflection on the OT text,
so one cannot leap from the Jewish reflection discussed in
Chapter V to Matt 28:16-20 as if the author of Matthew were the
first Christian to reflect upon the Danielic passage. Rather,
Matthew stands within a broad line of Christian allusion to and
interpretation of Daniel 7.

In illustrating this below, I have limited my treatment of
NT passages in two ways. *First*, I have once again confined myself to allusions which are relatively clear and which most
scholars would classify as probable. For my own purposes, I
have made a list of some sixty-five other passages that, in
terms of relation to Daniel 7, would range from possible to
probable, and some of which I would be willing to defend as
constituting a connection between Daniel 7 and Matt 28:16-20.
But it would not be wise to give the impression that my conclusions are based on what many others would consider problematic.
*Second*, I have concentrated on interpretations of Daniel 7 that
throw some light upon Matt 28:16-20. The latter principle excludes many "Son of Man" passages, but let me devote a paren-
thetical paragraph or two to such passages.

Much of the vast literature on the "Son of Man problem" in
NT studies is of value here only indirectly. We are not presently concerned, for example, with the question of the authenticity of all or some of the NT Son of Man sayings, nor with
whether the phrase ὁ υἱὸς τοῦ ἀνθρώπου was used (in those sayings regarded by some as authentic) as a self-designation[1] or a
reference to a heavenly figure distinct from Jesus. The question of whether the Son of Man sayings were gradually "apocalyp-
ticized" or "reapocalypticized" in early Church exegesis is
also not dealt with. Not until these and other problems are
solved will we have a fully adequate understanding of the use
of Daniel 7 in the NT, and of the NT triad and its theological
bases, but these matters cannot be treated here.

I agree with the scholarly theory that there was no one
dominant pre-Christian Jewish apocalyptic expectation of the
Son of Man (with the phrase taken as a title) coming (to earth)
with the clouds as eschatological judge, victor and deliverer.
There was no clear "concept" of the Son of Man as transcendental Messiah, glorified as head of the final kingdom.[2]  Rather,
there were various uses of Danielic imagery, depicting a variety of understandings of the figure of the one like a son of man.
These range from the portrayal of the archetypical righteous
one who had been translated,[3] to the portrayal of an eschatological messiah, without function or with the function of warrior or judge, with corporate or individual traits.[4]  No titular use of the phrase בַּר אֱנָשׁ or its equivalents was found in
the survey reported upon in the previous chapter.  In first
century A.D. Judaism, then, there were various exegetical traditions based wholly or in part on Daniel 7,[5] and various concepts of the one like a son of man.[6]  What are seen in the NT
are processes of adaptation, unification and coordination of
themes drawn from the Danielic symbolism and its interpretations.

Returning from this digression on general "Son of Man"
passages and having now outlined the limitations of my treatment, let me begin treating the NT texts that I think reflect
the influence of Daniel 7 and help us to understand Matt 28:
16-20.

### A.  Exaltation Texts in Revelation
### (2:26-27; 7:9; 5:6-14 [1:4-8])

In my judgment, the book of Revelation as a whole can be
considered a creative Christian use of Daniel and of Danielic
traditions.[7]  Indeed, belief in the exaltation of Christ in
terms of Daniel 7 is in great part responsible for the theological tension and anguish facing the author's community.[8]  I suggest that  Dan 7:14 is the main text pondered, and it has influenced the entire composition.  It is read to mean that Christ,
the one like a son of man (1:13; 14:14) has by his death and exaltation received dominion over all and is Lord of the earth.
In the light of Dan 7:18, 22, 27, this is understood to mean
further that by virtue of their baptism and redemption Christians

share in Christ's kingship, as the representatives of God's
kingdom on earth.   These claims, however, are contradicted by
the Roman emperor's claim to divine honors and worldwide authority, and by the suffering and persecution of John's community, resulting from a refusal to adapt to the religious,
social, commercial and political life of Roman society, the
refusal of syncretism.[9]

The seer John argues that the contradiction is real, not
simply apparent: the claim of Rome is illegitimate and must be
rejected.[10]   The suffering and even martyrdom of Christians is
required, but death is being transcended.  According to
Fiorenza, the author of Revelation describes in three stages
how the dominion of God and Christ extends over the cosmos.
(1) It is established first in heaven: through his death and
enthronement in heaven Christ receives the kingship and reigns
there with God and with the martyrs (cf. 4:3-8; 5:9-10, 13;
12:9-13:18).  Satan is thrown down to earth (12:9).  The Christian community on earth acknowledges and represents God's rule
in the world, and so is the focal point of conflict with Satan,
the place of trial, witness, and martyrdom.[11]   (2) Next, the
kingdom extends to the whole earth with the eschatological
plagues and the parousia of CHrist (19:11-20:6).[12]   (3) Finally,
the underworld is destroyed (Satan, death and Hades: 20:7-15)
and in the last judgment a new and completely different heaven
and earth come down (21:1-22:5).[13]   Christians will then exercise their kingship with God and Christ in the cosmos which
again belongs to God.[14]   Within this structure, which I accept
as a working hypothesis, three passages use Dan 7:14 to express
belief in the exaltation of Christ and of Christians.

In Rev 2:26-27, the one like a son of man (1:13), Son of
God (2:18), promises that the one who conquers and keeps his
works until the end will be given power (ἐξουσίαν) over the nations, and will rule (or: destroy) them "with a rod of iron, as
when earthen pots are broken in pieces, even as I myself have
received (power) from my Father" (ὡς κἀγὼ εἴληφα παρὰ τοῦ
πατρὸς μου).  This is the fourth of the seven promises to the
seven churches,[15] all made to "the one who conquers," that is,
to the martyr.[16]   Each of the seven rewards involves a share in

Jesus' power; there is "unlimited inclusiveness and solidarity in both victory and heritage."[17] The promise in 2:26-27 to Thyatira combines a free rendering of Ps 2:8-9 with the allusion to Dan 7:14.[18]

The moment of Christ's past reception of power is his death-resurrection, his enthronement (see 3:21) in the heavenly realm among the angels (cf. 1:16, 20). The power is here understood as power to rule or perhaps to destroy the nations.[19] If to destroy, the interpretation of Daniel 7 would be in line with that of *4 Ezra* 13:5-11 (using Isa 11:4), in which the man from the sea cremates the hostile "innumerable multitude."[20] Elsewhere the author of Revelation, however, like Matthew, thinks of "all nations" being drawn to worship (cf. Rev 7:9; 14:6; 15:4).

Rev 7:2-8 depicts the "sealing" by angels of the servants of God,[21] twelve thousand from each of the "tribes of the sons of Israel." In the second phase of this vision, the seer sees "a great multitude which no one could number, from every nation, from all tribes and peoples and tongues" (ἐκ παντὸς ἔθνους καὶ φυλῶν καὶ λαῶν καὶ γλωσσῶν), a clear allusion to Dan 7:14.[22] This multitude stands before the throne and before the Lamb, and cries out, "Salvation belongs to our God who sits upon the throne[23] and to the Lamb" (Rev 7:10). In verse 17, the Lamb is said to be "in the midst of (ἀνὰ μέσον) the throne"; his exaltation is symbolized as the sharing of God's throne.[24] The throne angels respond with a sevenfold praise of God (vv. 11-12).

Revelation 4-5 constitutes the first heavenly throne-room vision in this work.[25] A revelation of "what must take place (ἃ δεῖ γενέσθαι) after this,"[26] it opens with the description of God enthroned in the midst of the twenty-four elders, "the seven torches (λαμπάδες) of fire, which are the seven spirits of God" (4:5),[27] and the "four living creatures" (Ezekiel's *ḥayyoth*, described with the features and functions of the seraphim of Isaiah 6; Rev 4:6-8). This is followed by a scene which is a dramatization of the eschatological meaning of Dan 7:14, the empowering and enthronement of the Lamb. "And between the throne and the four living creatures and among the elders,

I saw a Lamb standing,[28] as though slain, with seven horns and
with seven eyes, which are the seven spirits of God sent out
into the earth" (5:6). He alone in heaven, on earth, and under
the earth (v. 3) is found worthy to open the seven-sealed
scroll held by God, the scroll that contains the secret of the
events of the end time (cf. Dan 12:4, 9).[29] The Lamb, that is,
is alone worthy to be "the eschatological regent of the world."[30]
He receives the power to know and to set in motion God's final
plans.

Of special interest here is the statement that the Lamb
has seven horns and seven eyes (all power, omniscience), which
are the seven spirits.[31] He has received in his exaltation the
spirit of God in its fullness, probably explicated further in
5:12: "Worthy is the Lamb who was slain, to receive power and
wealth and wisdom and might and honor and glory and blessing."
Seemingly, the empowering[32] of the one like a son of man in
Dan 7:14 has been understood in terms of Isa 11:2, the prediction that the Spirit of Yahweh will rest on the shoot from the
stump of Jesse.[33] Acts 2:3 also places Jesus' reception of the
Spirit at the moment of his exaltation: "...being exalted at
the right hand of God, and having received from the Father the
promise of the Holy Spirit, he has poured out this which you
see and hear."[34]

The Lamb's power is celebrated in the "new song" of the
living creatures and elders, a song which interprets the vision.[35] They sing that the Lamb is worthy to take and open the
scroll because he was slain and by his blood ransomed for God
individuals "from every tribe and tongue and people and nation"
(cf. Dan 7:14), making them "a kingdom and priests to our God"
(cf. 1:6; 20:6).[36] "And they shall reign on earth" (5:9-10).[37]
The giving of an everlasting kingdom to the one like a son of
man in Dan 7:14 is here interpreted in terms of 7:18, 22, 27:
the kingship of Christ is the kingship of his followers, the
only difference being that not until the eschatological future
will their sovereignty be realized.[38]

To the voice of the elders and living creatures is joined
that of "many angels, numbering myriads of myriads and thousands
of thousands" (5:11; cf. Dan 7:10),[39] and finally that of "every

creature in heaven and on earth and under the earth and in the
sea and all therein" (5:13), glorifying God and the Lamb together.  It is made clear that it is God's power the Lamb receives, and that "all" serve him.  There are intimations of
equality between Christ and God, of an extraordinary coordination.[40]  There is a proliferation in this work of the third
member of the Danielic triad, the angels, in the mention of the
living creatures, elders and many angels.  But in 5:6-7 we find
a triad (God-Lamb-seven spirits).[41]  That the author sees special significance in this triad is evident from an examination
of the next text, Rev 1:4-5.

    These verses, modeled on the form of the letter prescript,[42]
name the sender (John) and the recipients (the seven churches in
Asia), and then give the salutation in triadic form: "Grace and
peace to you from him who is and who was and who is to come,[43]
and from the seven spirits who are before his throne, and from
Jesus Christ the faithful witness, the first born of the dead,
and the ruler of kings on earth."[44]  Grace and peace proceed
from the triad, that is, from the throne-complex as power-
source.[45]  Why has the author set this triad at the beginning
of his whole work, and what meaning does it hold for him?  One
may theorize that as the triad in Daniel 7 was a symbol by
means of which faithful Israel was to learn its identity and
destiny, and draw strength to act, so in Revelation the triad
is an expression of a similar political mysticism.  Thus, the
promise of Daniel would not be just repeated but reinterpreted
for the Christian of the 90s who, the author believes, is both
offered and denied participation in the exaltation of Christ.
The author would be challenging his audience to believe in the
accomplishment of the exaltation of Christ through death and
resurrection, and to see in this its own reality present and
future.[46]

    The use of Dan 7:14 in Revelation could then be very close
in meaning to its use in Matt 28:18b, in spite of the difference
in the communities' situations and the authors' perspectives.
Both authors may be influenced by and incorporate a traditional
understanding of the exaltation of Jesus in terms of the
Danielic text.  In the final chapter I will argue that as the

author of Revelation combats what he considers enthusiastic
misunderstanding of the corporate dimension of Jesus' exaltation, by maintaining the "eschatological reservation,"[47] so
Matthew (though for different reasons) combats this danger by
emphasizing in 28:16-20 the crucial importance of obedience to
Jesus' interpretation of Torah.

### B. The Giving of Power to the Son of Man in John 5:26-27

In several passages of John (3:35; 13:3; 17:2) we hear
that the Father has given "all things" or "power over all flesh"
to the Son.  I think that these statements (and Matt 11:25-27,
par. Luke 10:21-22) are related to the giving of power to the
one like a son of man in Dan 7:14, but let me show this by con-
centrating on John 5:26-27 where there is a specific reference
to the Son of Man who is given power to judge the living and
the dead.  The passage reads: "As the Father has life in himself, so he has given the Son of have life in himself, and has
given him authority to execute judgment because he is the Son
of Man" (καὶ ἐξουσίαν ἔδωκεν αὐτῷ κρίσιν ποιεῖν)[48] ὅτι υἱὸς
ἀνθρώπου[49] ἐστίν (cf. vv. 21-22).

The statement that the power of judgment is given to the
Son may be based either on (1) an understanding of the transfer
to the one like a son of man of the power of the Ancient of Days
and the heavenly court (Dan 7:10-12, 22)[50] or on (2) an understanding of Dan 7:22 which interpreted this verse to mean that
the holy ones are empowered to judge,[51] and then substituted the
figure of the one like a son of man for the group of holy ones
in the Danielic text.  In Daniel 7, it will be remembered, the
one like a son of man appears on the scene only after the heavenly court has sat in judgment and its judgment on the beasts
has been executed.  Moule speaks of the Son of Man here passing
from the role of defendant[52] to that of judge.[53]  We have already seen this process underway in the  two visions of *4 Ezra*
(cf. Wis 5:1-2; 4:16; 3:8).[54]

The allusion to Dan 7:14 in John 5:27 is joined to an allusion to Dan 12:2 in John 5:28-29.[55]  There is no verbal similarity between the two passages, but the sentence structure is
similar:

*Dan 12:2:* "And many of those
who sleep in the dust of the
earth
shall awake,
some to everlasting life,

and some to shame and
everlasting contempt."

*John 5:28-29:* "...all who are
in the tombs

will hear his voice and come forth,
those who have done good, to the
resurrection of life,
those who have done evil, to
the resurrection of judgment."

Lindars remarks, "Once the notion of the Son of Man's activity in performing the judgment has been reached, it is only
a short step to the idea that he is actively concerned in the
general resurrection which precedes it."[56]  The Gospel of John
takes the further step of considering the Son empowered to give
eternal life through his word in the present (the readers'
present as well as the present of the ministry of Jesus; see
5:21). This is the most explicit statement of the belief that
God holds nothing back in his transfer of ἐξουσία to the Son
of Man.

          C.  The Son of Man at the Right Hand of Power,
                  Coming on the Clouds of Heaven
              (Mark 14:62; Matt 26:64; Luke 22:69)

In the response of Jesus to the Sanhedrin we find these
words: Mark 14:62 "...and you will see the Son of Man sitting
at the right hand of Power, and coming with (μετά) the clouds
of heaven."  Matt 26:64: "...But I tell you, hereafter (ἀπ'
ἄρτι) you will see the Son of Man sitting at the right hand of
Power, and coming on (ἐπί) the clouds of heaven."  Luke 22:69:
"But from now on (ἀπὸ τοῦ νῦν) the Son of Man will be seated at
the right hand of the Power of God."

The allusion to Dan 7:13 in this saying may carry, at a
pre-gospel level, the primary meaning of exaltation or assumption, rather than that of parousia.  That is, the "coming" of
the Son of Man with or on the clouds may have been imagined as
a coming to heaven at the moment of his vindication, rather
than as a coming from heaven back to earth.  The use of Ps 110:1
supports the implication in Dan 7:13-14 that the one like a son
of man is coming to his enthronement.[57]  It is possible that the
death of the righteous one is thought of as an ascent to the
heavenly realm.[58]

Against the majority opinion--that the allusion to Dan 7:13
is intended at all levels of the tradition as a clear reference
to the parousia--a small number of critics has claimed that the
reply of Jesus to the high priest is, at an early stage, a
statement about his imminent vindication.  Standing before his
persecutors, Jesus is depicted as announcing the reversal of
the judgment against him, the intervention of God and the in-
auguration of Jesus' own reign.[59]  Both of the OT allusions
carry the same meaning: coming to God.

There are three objections to this theory as an explanation of the Markan and Matthean texts: (1) the first concerns
the sequence of the allusions, (2) the second concerns the prediction that the enemies will see the enthronement of the Son
of Man, and (3) the third concerns the fact that elsewhere in
the gospels there are statements about the coming of the Son of
Man which refer to his parousia.

(1) It is argued that if vindication were the meaning of
these texts, the reverse sequence ("coming" then "sitting")
would be more likely.  The placement of the allusion to Dan 7:13
in the texts supports the traditional understanding of these as
sayings concerning the parousia.[60]  Robinson, however, offers
the suggestion that session at the right hand and coming with
clouds are alternate, parallel expressions, one static and one
dynamic, for the same thing: ascension or exaltation.  The sequence is indifferent in the original saying, although subse-
quently Mark may have interpreted Dan 7:13 as a statement about
the parousia, in line with 13:26.[61]  Glasson holds that the
sequence may be due to the presentation first of the idea of
the personal exaltation of Jesus (using Ps 110:1), and then of
the corporate conception of the emergence of the new community
of "holy ones" (cf. Dan 7:27) in its representative (Dan 7:13).[62]

(2) The second objection to the theory that Mark 14:62 is a
statement of the exaltation of the Son of Man and not of the
parousia is based on the fact that it is declared here that the
enemies of Jesus will "see" the Son of Man sitting at the right
hand of Power and coming with the clouds.  It has been argued
that the verse must refer, as does Mark 13:28, to "visible por-
tents" of the end time which will be seen by all, and not to

objects of inward vision or realization, or to a mixture of
literal and symbolic seeing. Fuller, for example, thinks that
the verb ὄψεσθε can bear only the first meaning, literal seeing.
So Mark 14:62 means that "the Son of Man is revealed first (at
the parousia) sitting at the right hand of God, and then leaving
that position and coming on the clouds of heaven."[63] But it is
not certain that "seeing" must refer to the events of the
parousia. The verb ὁράω is used in several instances to refer
to recognition, perception, understanding,[64] and to resurrection
appearances.[65] There is, moreover, a tradition that translations may be witnessed,[66] even by enemies.[67] There is also an
emphasis in the Wisdom of Solomon on the enemies "seeing" both
the suffering and vindication of the righteous one. He "will
stand with great confidence in the presence of those who have
afflicted him, and those who make light of his labors. When
they see (ἰδόντες) him, they will be shaken with dreadful fear,
and they will be amazed at his unexpected salvation" (5:1-2).
If these traditions have influenced Mark 14:62, what is predicted is the shock of recognition and regret produced by the
sight of the exalted one--but without specification of when
this confrontation will occur.

(3) The third objection to an exaltation reading of the
tradition behind Mark 14:62 is that elsewhere in the gospels
there are statements about the coming of the Son of Man which
refer to his parousia. But even though this is the case, it is
possible that Dan 7:13 was interpreted in more than one way, in
the pre-Gospel tradition and perhaps even by individual
evangelists.[68]

Perrin's analysis of pre-Gospel traditions behind Mark
14:62 offers support to the efforts to understand the Dan 7:13
allusion as a reference to Jesus' ascent. According to Perrin,
just as the scribes of the Enoch saga in *1 Enoch* 70-71 interpreted the translation of Enoch in terms of Ezekiel 1 and Dan
7:13, so also, but "completely independently," the scribes of
earliest Christianity interpreted the resurrection of Jesus in
terms of two OT texts, Ps 110:1 and Dan 7:13. "Just as Enoch
became the Son of man on the basis of an interpretation of his
translation, so Jesus became Son of man on the basis of an

interpretation of his resurrection."[69]  Several aspects of
Perrin's theory need modification.  First of all, it is unlikely
that either Enoch or Jesus is considered to have "become" the
Son of man (with the term understood as a title and a coherent
concept), in the early stages of these traditions.[70]  Secondly,
it is also unlikely that these uses of Dan 7:13 are unrelated;
rather, they depend on a shared exegetical tradition.[71]

In my judgment, Perrin's most valuable contribution is his
placement of the allusion to Dan 7:13 in Mark 14:62 within the
context of the midrashic history of that OT text.  He considers
Mark 14:62 to reflect an earlier interpretation of Dan 7:13
than do the parousia sayings such as 13:26.[72]  The clearest
trace of the early exegetical tradition that used Dan 7:13 to
interpret the resurrection, he claims, can be found in Acts
7:55-56, and underlies the whole concept of the ascension, which
he considers an historicization of the pesher tradition.[73]  He
thinks that Acts 1:9 offers additional support for the thesis
that a tradition existed in primitive Christianity linking assumption and Son of Man.  Here Perrin finds an echo of Dan
7:13 in the mention of the cloud.[74]

At the level of Markan redaction, does 14:62 refer to the
exaltation or assumption of Jesus, or to the parousia?[75]  The
final chapters of Mark provide us with no sure answer to this
question.  The "young man" at the empty tomb tells the women,
"But go, tell his disciples and Peter that he is going before
you into Galilee; there you will see him, as he told you" (16:7).
The promise of seeing Jesus, and the reminder that this will
fulfill a prediction of Jesus himself (cf. 14:28), refer the
reader back to 14:62 and offer an interpretation of that verse.
But of what "seeing" is Mark thinking in 16:7?  His Gospel contains no accounts of appearances by the risen Jesus.[76]  A few
critics hold that Mark 16:7 focuses the attention of his readers
on the parousia, expected imminently in Galilee.  Mark 14:62 is
read by them as a reference to the parousia.  Mark regards the
risen Jesus as with God in the heavens; he will appear from
there as the Son of Man only at the parousia.[77]  It is more
likely, however, since Peter is singled out in 16:7, that the
reference there is to a resurrection appearance or appearances

known in the community.[78]  But since Mark 13:26-27 shows that
Mark does use Dan 7:13 to refer to the parousia, it is still
possible that this usage has colored Mark 14:62.[79]

At best I can suggest the possibility that Dan 7:13 was
used in the tradition behind Mark 14:62 to refer to the moment
of Jesus' vindication, his coming to God.  This would be in
line with the implication of the allusion to Ps 110:1.  Mark
may have known and preserved that tradition.  He knew as well
that Dan 7:13 had been used to refer to the parousia of Jesus;
again he preserved that tradition.  These meanings are possibly
held together in Mark 14:62, the latter interpretation not
cancelling out the former.[80]

Both the Lukan and Matthean parallels emphasize, by means
of an adverbial phrase (Luke: ἀπὸ τοῦ νῦν; Matthew: ἀπ᾽ ἄρτι )
meaning "from now on" or "henceforth,"[81] that the exaltation of
Jesus is thought of as beginning at this moment of the "trial."
The response to the high priest is intended as a statement of
the immediate exaltation of the Son of Man, in agreement with
the tradition which underlies Mark 14:62.  How is this agreement to be explained?  Some argue unconvincingly that Matthew
and Luke are reproducing a phrase originally found in Mark.[82]
Others consider the agreement to result from independent editorial activity on the part of Luke and Matthew, or from their
acquaintance with earlier tradition (perhaps oral).

The Lukan version is seen by most as the product of Lukan
redaction, in conformity with this Evangelist's distinctive
eschatology.[83]  More likely it is to be regarded as an earlier,
simpler version of Mark 14:62, from the oral tradition or from
Luke's special Passion Narrative source.[84]  According to this
theory, the saying fits in with Lukan theology with its de-
emphasis on the parousia and its focus on the interim reign of
Jesus,[85] but it is not a product of that theology.[86]

Matt 26:64[87] probably also draws the adverbial phrase from
a primitive form of the saying,[88] current in the oral tradition.[89]  What is the meaning of the saying from Matthew's view-
point?  It has been argued that it underlines the imminence of
the parousia,[90] or that it focuses attention on the glorification of the Son of Man, on which the coming with the clouds of

heaven (at the parousia) depends.[91] This latter view is to be
preferred, and it is possible that Matthew understands the saying as a statement about exaltation in death. Matthew's emphasis is on the process which begins now and initiates the reign
of the Son of Man. "*Within* Matthew's own redaction of the
Passion story there are indications that the glorification of
Jesus is linked on a literary and symbolic level with the *death*
of Jesus."[92]

Matthew gives us his comment on 26:64 in the triumphant
conclusion to his narration of Jesus' death. His distinctive
additions here indicate that for him the death has a cosmic
relevance, and in fact is *the* apocalyptic event, the turning
point of salvation history.[93] In death, Jesus' divine sonship
is manifested, and access to communion with God is obtained for
all humanity, including Gentiles (Matt 27:54).[94] What is most
important is the placement here of the "theological symbol" of
the raising of the holy ones (27:51-53). The expiration of
Jesus' spirit of life (27:50) triggers the resurrection which
is a victory over death itself. "And the earth shook, and the
rocks were split; the tombs also were opened, and many bodies
of the holy ones who had fallen asleep were raised, and coming
out of the tombs after his resurrection they went into the holy
city and appeared to many." These verses may be based on a
tradition which links Ezekiel 37 with Dan 12:2 to speak of the
relation of Jesus' exaltation to the resurrection. As in John
5:28-29, the correspondence with Dan 12:2 would be structural,
not verbal: Dan 12:2θ: πολλοὶ τῶν καθευδόντων ἐν γῆς χῶατι
ἐξεγερθήσονται; Matt 27:52b: πολλὰ σώματα τῶν κεκοιμημένων
ἠγέρθησαν.[95] The correspondences to Dan 12:2 in the Matthean
text are not strong enough for us to be certain that an allusion is present, rather than an appeal to a general belief in
the resurrection of the dead.[96] It has been noted that Dan 12:
1-3 is Daniel's climactic statement of the eschatological state
of salvation, corresponding to Dan 7:14, 22, 27,[97] and that in
John 5:28-29 an allusion to Dan 7:14 seems to be joined to one
with Dan 12:2 and Ezekiel 37.[98] If Matt 27:52b makes use of
Dan 12:2, the raising of the holy ones at the crucifixion scene
may form a sort of Danielic bridge between Matt 26:64 and 28:18b.

In any case, Matthew is stating that the death of Jesus inaugurates the final age,[99] and, in a certain sense, accomplishes his enthronement.[100] If Dan 12:2 can be brought to bear on Matt 26:64, this enthronement can be considered something of a corporate exaltation.

The Matthean "trial" scene should be read through the lens of the final pericope as well as through the lens of the scene of the death of Jesus. Matt 26:64 hints at the climax found in 28:16-20, and is tied to this conclusion.[101] Matt 28:18, 20 confirm the impression that in 26:64 Matthew is focusing our attention on the present and lasting state of the glorified Christ.[102] The death and resurrection of Christ have been seen as basically one pivotal event.[103]

I have argued that in Matt 28:18b there is a probable allusion to Dan 7:14, referring to the transfer of all power as an act already accomplished, presumably by the death-resurrection of Jesus. This allusion can be read as the complement and fulfillment of the allusion to Dan 7:13 in Matt 26:64, when the latter text is understood to refer to what is "from now on" happening in the passion: the coming of Jesus to God. That Matthew recognized the Danielic allusion in Mark 14:62 is clear from his redaction of that verse, bringing it into closer conformity with the LXX; he adds also, probably from the oral tradition, the adverbial phrase which makes the exaltation meaning clearer.[104] That Matthew recognized the allusion in 28:18b cannot be definitely shown. But Matthew has highlighted two aspects of his understanding of the "coming" of Jesus to God: (1) that this coming involves a corporate victory over death (27:51-53), and (2) that it results in the conferral of "all power in heaven and on earth" (28:18b). It can be said that at a redactional level whereas Mark 14:62 reminds readers of the resurrection accounts they knew (and, perhaps, of the parousia expectations they held), and Luke 22:69 emphasizes the intermediate reign of Jesus as well as the parousia, Matt 26:64 (with 27:51-53 and 28:18 in mind) announces the "event" of transcendence of death. This, however, does not exhaust Matthew's intent. As Mark does, but more often, Matthew uses Dan 7:13 to refer *also* to the parousia, which will be "the full manifestation

of the Son of Man coming on the clouds of heaven."[105]   It is
likely he intends the readers of his version of the Sanhedrin
scene to think of that final moment of judgment, when even the
enemies of the Son of Man will see his glory.[106]

The Danielic triad does not appear in Mark 14:62 or its
parallels.  If there is validity to the interpretation offered
here, the Son of Man is depicted at the pre-gospel level of
this saying[107] as exalted to the heavenly world, in the Matthean
and Markan versions coming on or with the clouds.  No angelic
retinue is mentioned, but this may not be far from the thinking
of the framers of this tradition.  In Dan 7:13 it is implied
that angels of the heavenly court present the one like a son of
man to the Ancient of Days.[108]  The thesis will be presented
below that the dynamic imagery of ascent and exaltation is basic
to an understanding of one aspect of the development of the NT
triad.

### D.  The Son of Man Bearing Witness in the Heavenly Court (Acts 7:55-56)

Allusions to Daniel 7 and 12 in Acts 7:55-56 and related
traditions present the Son of Man witnessing in the heavenly
court, and thus they illustrate the belief that the exalted one
"stands up for" those who confess him and who are caught up
somehow in the process of the Son of Man's vindication.  Acts
7:55-56 reads: "But (Stephen) full of the Holy Spirit gazed
into heaven and saw the glory of God and Jesus standing (ἐστῶτα)
at the right hand of God.  And he said, 'Behold, I see the
heavens opened, and the Son of Man standing at the right hand
of God.'"

In spite of the fact that verse 55 contains some distinctively Lukan terminology,[109] there is evidence that in both
verses 55 and 56 we are dealing with traditional material.[110]
The association of the Spirit with an allusion to Dan 7:13-14
and visionary or ecstatic experience may be traditional.[111]
The combination of "seeing the glory of God" (7:55) and "the
heavens opened" (v. 56) strongly evokes the vision of Ezekiel
by the River Chebar (Ezek 1:1, 28), and it is probable that
these two phrases belonged together in the pre-Lukan tradition.[112]

Here again, as often in the history of the interpretation of
Daniel 7, this text is joined with Ezekiel 1, this time in a
clear statement that the vision of the $K\bar{a}b\hat{o}d$ is the vision of
the exalted Son of Man.[113] In addition, the account of the
vision in 7:55-56 was most likely joined at a pre-Lukan stage
with the account of Stephen's transfiguration (6:15),[114] in
which Stephen's face is seen by those who sat in the council to
be "like the face of an angel."[115] Finally, apart from the citations of Dan 7:13 in Rev 1:13 and 14:14, Acts 7:56 is the
only place in the NT where the term "the Son of Man" or its
equivalent is used without direct reference to the words of
Jesus; the use here appears to be pre-Lukan.[116]

While it is true that the trial and death of Stephen is
modeled in part on the trial and death of Jesus,[117] it is not
the case that the Son of Man statement in Acts 7:56 is a creation of Luke's, "a conscious archaism" intended to "lend a
certain tone of primitiveness to his history" and reinforce the
parallel between Jesus and the martyr.[118] Acts 7:56 is related
in the tradition to Luke 22:69, in that both texts, using Ps
110:1 and Dan 7:13, speak of the Son of Man being at the right
hand of God, with no clear reference to the parousia or to the
final judgment. Acts 7:55-56 (cf. 1:6-11) may also be drawing
on Ezekiel 1. It is my contention that when the unique imagery
of Acts 7:55-56 (Jesus the Son of Man "standing" at the right
hand of God) is understood, this passage is seen to be related
as well to Luke 12:8-9; Mark 8:38 pars. and Rev 3:5, passages
in which the Son of Man appears as witness or advocate in the
heavenly court.

Acts 7:55-56 is the only text in which the Son of Man is
depicted standing,[119] and several explanations of this feature
of the text have been proposed. It has been regarded as indicative of the parousia or proleptic parousia motif,[120] or an
attribution to Jesus of predicates and powers of God.[121] It is
most likely, however, that the Son of Man's "standing" should
be read in line with the technical meaning of עמד in the OT and
intertestamental literature: as a term for participation, human
and angelic, in the heavenly council. The verb occurs in this
sense in a whole range of contexts: prophetic, military, judicial and priestly.[122]

As in Dan 12:1-3 (see Wisdom 5), a judicial connotation
is intended. It has been suggested that the Son of Man is
standing here because he has risen to take part in the final
judgment. His role is either that of judge[123] or, more probably, that of witness or advocate.[124] The function of the Son
of Man may be modeled on that of the exalted Enoch, scribe and
witness of the heavenly court (cf. *Jub*. 4:23; 10:17; Wis 2:16-
20; 5:1-5).[125] But nothing here in Acts indicates that this
scene is thought of as the final judgment. Moule sees the
scene as a double trial scene: as the witness Stephen confesses
Christ before the Sanhedrin, so Christ is standing to confess
him before the angels.[126] "Here Stephen is condemned and put
to death, but in the heavenly court where the books have been
opened,[127] this member of the Son of Man community is already
being vindicated by the head of that community--*the* Son of Man
*par excellence*."[128] The double trial motif appears also in
three other NT sayings which evoke the picture of the Son of
Man bearing witness in the heavenly court, and which we will
examine briefly.

These texts are the following. (1) Luke 12:8-9: "And I
tell you, everyone who acknowledges me (ὁμολογήσῃ ἐν ἐμοί) before men, the Son of Man will acknowledge before the angels of
God. But he who denies (ἀρνησάμενος) me before men will be
denied before the angels of God."[129] (2) Rev 3:5: "He who conquers will be clad thus in white garments[130] and I will not
blot his name out of the book of life;[131] I will confess (ὁμο-
λογήσω) his name before my Father and before his angels." (3)
Mark 8:38: "For whoever is ashamed (ἐπαισχυνθῇ) of me and of my
words in this adulterous and sinful generation, of him will the
Son of Man also be ashamed when he comes in the glory of his
Father with the holy angels."[132] Its Lukan parallel (9:26)
speaks of the Son of Man coming "in his glory and the glory of
the Father and of the holy angels."

It is widely held that (1) Luke 12:8-9 is a more original
version of (3) Mark 8:38.[133] But Borsch thinks that the verb
"to be ashamed" is more original than "to deny."[134] In any
case, the idea of shame may be drawn from Dan 12:2, where it is
said that some will wake to "shame and everlasting contempt."

Mark 8:38 par. explicates the shame of the condemned as the
just punishment of their having been ashamed of Jesus; whose
who rejected him will be rejected by the ashamed Son of Man.[135]

We cannot enter here into the discussion of whether or not
the original saying contained a reference to the Son of Man
(contrast Luke 12:8-9 with Matt 10:32-33),[136] nor into discussion of whether a distinction is being made in Luke 12:8-9 and
Mark 8:38, par. Luke 9:26 between Jesus and the Son of Man, a
distinct figure who would vindicate him at the judgment.[137]
Interest here is confined to the problem of how the vindication
hope and imagery of Daniel is used.  There is no allusion present in Matt 10:32-33, which is the stark statement that a decision for or against Jesus is mirrored in Jesus' confession or
denial before "my Father who is in heaven."  However, in the
three texts focused on here (Luke 12:8-9; Rev 3:5; and Mark 8:38
par.), the Son of Man, like an attorney for the defense and
prosecution, speaks in the heavenly court.  A formal, solemn and
binding declaration is thought of as pronounced before the angels.  Identification is being made in heaven of those who acknowledge Jesus (Luke 12:8; cf. Rev 3:5: "those who conquer")
and of those who deny him (Luke 12:9; cf. Mark 8:38, par. Luke
9:26: those who are ashamed of him and of his words).[138]  The
one like a son of man in Daniel 7, we have seen, has no juridi-
cal role; he appears to receive the kingdom only after judgment
has been pronounced and executed.  But the role of witness and
then of judge was attributed to him, I have argued, via a reading of Dan 7:22 which attributed the power of judging to the
holy ones, and/or via an understanding of him as sharing in the
power of God and of the heavenly court to judge (Dan 7:14).[139]
Has he been thought of in the sayings under consideration as
one who must testify for and identify those who belong to the
people of the holy ones (7:27)?[140]

The contexts in which the sayings occur link the idea of a
heavenly trial with that of earthly trials.  The Lukan context
especially, with mention of the disciples being killed (12:4-5)
and brought before "the synagogues and rulers and authorities"
(12:11), indicates that earthly trials are envisaged as the
proper moment to remember that the Son of Man takes part in the

heavenly court scene. Mark 8:38 appears in the context of a
discussion of saving and losing one's life. The following
verse (9:1) promises a vision of the kingdom before "some standing here" taste death. Stephen's trial and vision in Acts is a
dramatization of the double confession tradition.

Each of the texts considered in this section is triadic.
In Luke 12:8-9 we find Son of Man, angels, God. In Rev 3:5 the
triad is I (one like a son of man, 1:13),[141] my Father, his
angels. In Mark 8:38 (par. Luke 9:26), it is the Son of Man,
his Father, the holy angels; in Matt 16:27 the Son of Man, his
angels, his Father. The strange representation of God as the
Father of the Son of Man in the latter three texts (cf. Matt
25:34) may result from the use of terminology drawn from Daniel
7 and from Danielic traditions,[142] and perhaps also from early
Christian use of the term "Abba" for God.[143] The angels in Luke
12:8-9; Rev 3:5 are the angels of the heavenly court. In Mark
8:38 they are the retinue of the Son of Man, called "his angels"
in Matt 16:27 (cf. 13:41; 24:31; 25:31; 2 Thess 1:7), representing the transfer of power to the one like a son of man and even
his superiority to these beings.[144] In Acts 7:55-56 the Holy
Spirit, Son of Man (Jesus) and God are mentioned. The Holy
Spirit is related to the visionary experience, and may be
thought of as the power by means of which Stephen sees the vision of the Son of Man, or as the authority which legitimizes
the vision. The Son of Man is carefully identified with Jesus.

Each of these texts also presents the exalted Son of Man
as guarantee of the vindication of those who are faithful. The
context in Acts 7 of Stephen's martyrdom (cf. Rev 3:5) makes it
clear that vindication is by means of the transcendence of
death, not escape from death. The pre-Lukan tradition that
underlies Acts 7:55-56, of Jesus' exaltation as Son of Man,[145]
and the related traditions concerning the double confession
both have bearing on our understanding of the exaltation tradition behind Matt 28:18b.

> E.  A Commission Associated with the Theophany
>        of the Son of Man (Rev 1:12-16;
>     Rev 4-5; Acts 1; Mark 13:10 and par.)

One may posit almost the set throne-theophany commission
pattern for the scenes I wish to discuss here: (a) a theophany

(which sometimes involves a heavenly throne); (b) the reaction of the visionary; (c) the commission; and (d) the word of assurance.

In Rev 1:12-16 the vision of the one like a son of man is described with the features of a theophany drawn from the description of the Ancient of Days (Dan 7:9; Rev 1:14). Two elements of Ezekiel 1 are present here in Revelation. The voice of the one like a son of man (v. 15) is described in the terms Ezekiel uses for the sound of the *ḥayyoth*'s wings (Ezek 1:24) and for the coming of the *Kābôd* of Yahweh (43:2): "like the sound of many waters." The lampstands (λυχνίας) in the midst of which the one like a son of man stands (Rev 1:12) may be drawn from the mention of the appearance of lamps (λαμπάδων) in the midst of the *ḥayyoth* (Ezek 1:13 LXX). These features raise the possibility that the author of Revelation is thinking of "the likeness as it were of a human form" of Ezek 1:26-27. The seer John is commissioned to write what he sees, "what is and what is to take place hereafter" (Rev 1:19). The reaction appears in verse 17, and the reassurance in verses 17-18.

In another passage in Revelation (chaps. 4-5), there is a heavenly throne room, one who is seated on the throne, the Lamb and many attendants. It is true that the Lamb is not explicitly identified as the one like a son of man, but features of the scene indicate that Daniel 7 is being used.[146] Further, Ezekiel 1 is used abundantly in this passage, and the frequent association elsewhere of Ezekiel and Daniel (an association flowing from Daniel's own use of Ezekiel) encourages one to think Daniel may have been in mind. The commission of the seer does not occur here, although five chapters later (10:8-11) there is a commissioning modeled on the eating of the scroll in Ezek 2:8-3:4. The commissioning again evokes Daniel, for the seer is told, "You must again prophesy about many peoples and nations and tongues and kings" (cf. Dan 7:14).[147]

Still another text that may be mentioned, although with some hesitation, is Acts 1 where we are told the risen Jesus "was lifted up, and a cloud took him from their sight." I would argue that this cloud evokes the "great cloud" surrounding the chariot throne (Ezek 1:4) as well as the clouds on which the one

like a son of man comes (Dan 7:13). Yet, I recognize that
clouds are quite logically associated with heavenly journeys
and need not recall a specific text. In Acts 1:8 the apostles
are promised power when the Holy Spirit comes upon them, and
are commissioned to be witnesses in Jerusalem, Judaea, Samaria,
and to the ends of the earth. Of course, there is difficulty
in the fact that this commission preceeds the elevation of
Jesus; he appears at the beginning of the scene, however, as
the risen one.

In a way, Acts 1 is a bridge to another set of passages
which speak of the future coming of the Son of Man, but prefix
that coming with the idea that the gospel will be preached to
all nations, constituting a worldwide offer of membership in
the Son of Man's community. In the Markan version of the Little
Apocalypse, there is the warning that in the midst of interna-
tional sufferings and wars,[148] the disciples will be delivered
up to councils, beaten in synagogues, bear testimony before
governors and kings. "And the gospel must first be preached
to all nations" (Mark 13:10). Internal betrayals, and the hatred of the faithful by "all" are followed by the final abomi-
nation, "the desolating sacrilege," which is a sign for head-
long flight (vv. 14-16). At the peak of tribulation, associated with celestial phenomena which are drawn from OT theophanies on the Day of Yahweh, "they will see the Son of Man coming
in clouds with great power and glory. And then he will send
out the angels and gather his elect from the four winds, from
the ends of the earth to the ends of heaven" (vv. 26-27).[149]
The depiction is not of the Son of Man coming *to* God and bringing with him his elect; he comes, rather, in the place of God
and performs via the angels the functions of God. In Mark 13:
26-27 pars. the allusion to Dan 7:13 ("the Son of Man coming in
clouds") is expanded by an adverbial phrase ("with great power
and glory") inspired by Dan 7:14; this is an already-exalted
figure, thought of in Mark and Matthew as commanding angels.

Hartman argues that the main part of the Markan discourse
is based on a coherent midrash on portions of Daniel (2:31-45;
7:7-27; 8:9-26; 9:24-27; 11:21-12:4). The overlap and comple-
mentarity of these passages has been seen, and they have been

interpreted eschatologically, with the aid of other OT texts.[150]
Hartman outlines the stages by which the original nucleus of
the midrash was developed and linked more closely with Christian
experience,[151] at every stage the book of Daniel used as a basis to elucidate the present and future of the community and of
the world, to warn, comfort and prepare.[152] The basic theme of
the original midrash, retained in all its stages, is the struggle that precedes the end. Blasphemous resistance to God,[153]
persecution and deception will be overcome only when the Son of
Man is seen coming.

In Mark 13:10, inserted according to Hartman in one of the
closing stages of the development of the tradition,[154] is based
on an understanding of the disciples as maskîlîm (Dan 11:33;
12:3).[155] Matthew's reworking of this saying makes the allusion to Daniel firmer. He has transferred to his missionary
discourse in chapter 10 material from Mark 13:9, 11-12 concerning conflict with religious and civil authorities and within
families (cf. Matt 10:17-21). In its place here in this discourse Matthew inserts material concerning the martyrdom of
disciples and the hatred by all nations (24:9b), and concerning
apostasy, betrayal, the presence of false leaders and inner-
community deterioration (vv. 10-12). The allusions to Dan 11:
32-35; 12:1-4 are strong here,[156] and show that Matthew reads
Daniel as referring to false prophets (11:32 LXX: "those who
violate the covenant shall seduce with flattery"), to the
straying of many and to evil which increases until the end (see
12:4 LXX). He reads Daniel, that is, in terms of the situation
produced by leadership conflicts and ἀνομία (Matt 24:12) in his
own community, and reads his own situation in terms of Daniel.
Those who endure the tribulation and this tension will be saved.
"And this gospel of the kingdom"--the gospel, that is, of the
maskîlîm who as true prophets or teachers take the commandment
of love seriously[157]--"will be preached throughout the whole
world (ἐν ὅλῃ τῇ οἰκουμένῃ) as a testimony to all nations; and
then the end will come." This preaching is for Matthew the
promulgation of the standard by which all nations will be judged
by the Son of Man (25:31-46).

In Rev 14:6-7 an angel is seen "flying in midheaven, with
an eternal gospel to proclaim to those who dwell on earth, to

every nation and tribe and tongue and people" (cf. Dan 7:14).
What is proclaimed is that all should worship the God who
created heaven and earth, for the hour of judgment has come.[158]
This is a last summons to repentance and endurance. "One like
a son of man" (ὅμοιον υἱὸν ἀνθρώπου) appears in a sequel vision
(vv. 14-16) seated on the cloud and crowned with a golden crown.
He carries a sharp sickle, with which he reaps the earth.[159]
Jeremias maintains that the idea here of an apocalyptic event,
the angelic proclamation of God's final act, the "gospel" of
God's triumph, is earlier than the idea of a worldwide mission
of disciples. He argues that this is the original meaning of
the saying in Mark 13:10 (cf. also 14:9).[160] The early Christian community expected the ingathering of Gentiles in the hour
of final judgment, but without a Gentile mission; the angelic
summons is the signal to the nations for the eschatological
pilgrimage.[161] But Hahn, more correctly in my opinion, holds
that this is not the view behind Mark 13:10 par., but rather an
alternate view, that of particularist Jewish Christianity, with
a purely future hope in the extension of the kingdom to Gentiles
as an action reserved for God.[162] Matt 28:16-20, in line with
Mark 13:10 par., represents an understanding of mission based
on the belief in the nearness (even presence) of the eschatological reign of God, a belief Matthew traces back ultimately
to John the Baptist (Matt 3:2).[163] The preaching of the gospel
of the kingdom aims, for Matthew, at making disciples and
teaching (28:19-20).[164]

        Although there is no mention of a mission or preaching in
Matt 13:36-43, Matthew's interpretation of the parable of the
weeds, this passage can be regarded as a bridge text between
Matt 28:16-20 and 24:14. The exalted Son of Man[165] sows in the
kosmos "the good seed" which is "the sons of the kingdom." This
imagery has to do with preaching or teaching.[166] A link is
made between the activity of Jesus during his ministry and that
of the eleven after his resurrection, activity in which the
risen Jesus is considered present (28:20b).[167] "At the close
of the age" (13:39-40; cf. 28:20b; 24:3) comes the harvest, at
which the Son of Man sends "his angels" to gather out of his
kingdom "those who give him offense" (σκάνδαλα) and "those who

commit lawlessness" (ἀνομίαν),[168] and to execute their punishment in the "furnace of fire."[169]   Then follows the reward of the *maskîlîm* and their followers: "the righteous will shine like the sun in the kingdom of their Father" (13:43; cf. Dan 12:3).[170]   Again in this text we find the triad: Son of Man, his angels, Father (of the righteous, "sons of the kingdom").[171]

The texts considered in this section are evidence that the blend of wisdom and apocalyptic in Daniel gave rise to an interpretive tradition that grounds mission to all nations in the triumph of the one like a son of man.

### F.   Triads in the NT and Daniel 7

A number of NT passages associate the Father, Jesus (under some title) and angels.  These include:

Mark 13:32 (par. Matt 24:36): the angels, the Son, the Father
Matt 13:36-43: the Son of Man, his angels, Father (of the righteous)
Matt 25:31-43: the Son of Man, my Father, the angels
Mark 8:38: the Son of Man, his Father, the holy angels[172]
Luke 12:8-9: the Son of Man, angels, God
John 1:51: the Son of Man, angels, God
Acts 1:6-11: the Father, two "men" (angels), Jesus
1 Thess 3:13: our God and Father, our Lord Jesus, all his holy ones
1 Thess 4:13-18: the Lord, God, archangel
2 Thess 1:5-10: Lord Jesus, his mighty angels, God
Rev 1:4-7: his God and Father, the seven spirits (= seven angels?), Jesus Christ
Rev 5:6-7: the Lamb, the seven spirits, God
Rev 11:15-18: angel, our Lord, his Christ[173]

I would suggest that these passages reflect the triad of the Ancient of Days, one like a son of man, and the thousands/ tens of thousands of Daniel 7.  Moreover, they are a form of the triad we find in Matt 28:16-20 (Father, Son and Holy Spirit). Two steps are needed to make the latter assertion: first, to show how the titles for God and Jesus in these NT triads, especially "Son of Man," can be compared to the first two titles in Matt 28:19b, and second, how angels can be compared to Matthew's "the Holy Spirit."[174]

The Son-Stone wordplay (cf. Mark 12:10; Matt 16:13-18) may have been influential in abbreviating the phrase "one like a son of man" to "the Son."  In the NT, parabolic language and the

use of the address "Abba" for God influence the coordination of
the titles, "the Father" and "the Son." The idea of glory and
power given to the one like a son of man (Dan 7:14) so that he
becomes the bearer of the divine reality, contributes to the
fusion of Son of God/Son of Man terminology.[175]  Daniel 7 is
frequently used in conjunction with the vision of the *Kābôd* of
Yahweh in Ezekiel 1. Whether the one like a son of man was
identified with the humanlike figure on the moving throne, or
was considered as seated beside that form, this conjunction
fostered the notion of the attribution to the Danielic figure
of the divine glory.

I found no certain pre-Christian association of the Spirit
with the one like a son of man. But the links between Daniel 7
and Ezekiel 1 and Isaiah 11 lay the groundwork for that association, as does the mention of the Spirit in Dan 4:8-9.[176]
The inclusion of the Spirit in the triad may be a Christian
innovation, although the possibility exists that the link between the Danielic one like a son of man and the Holy Spirit
was first made by John the Baptist or his circle. We cannot
explore that possibility here.

Four further points are important in our exploration of
how and why the triad changed both in terminology and in theological significance.[177]  First, one may wonder whether at an
early stage the death-resurrection of Jesus was conceived along
the lines of the presentation of the one like a son of man by
angels to the Ancient of Days (Dan 7:13), that is, as an assumption to the heavenly court aided by angels. At most, we
have only traces in the NT of such a conception. The angelic
figures at the empty tomb and at the scene of the ascension in
Acts 1:6-11 do not assist Jesus but merely interpret the events.
But they *may* be relics of an earlier description of an assumption, related to the tradition preserved in the *Gospel of Peter*
9:35-10:40.[178]  The NT reduces the function of the angel(s) to
proclamation of the resurrection, perhaps out of reverence and
reluctance to depict the resurrection, but more likely because
of the belief that the exalted Christ is superior to the angels.
I would argue that the cloud imagery in Acts 1:9 may represent
a visualization of the assumption of Jesus partly in terms of

Ezekiel's throne-chariot, imagery used in association with the
death in *T. Job* 52 of Job. The association of similar imagery
with the translations of Elijah and Enoch (who according to
dominant tradition did not die, but escaped death) may have
made it eventually inadequate to fully express the Christian
belief in the resurrection as victory in and over death.

The inclusion of the Spirit in triads found in resurrection
contexts (e.g., Rom 8:11; 1:3-4) may be regarded as facilitated
by several related factors: (a) the tendency to call the figures
around the moving throne spirits rather than angels (cf. 4QS1
40, 24, 5-6: "most holy spirits," "spirits of the living God");
(b) the association of the Spirit with ascent in Ezekiel, and
with the translation of Elijah; (c) the spiritualization of the
idea of translation (e.g., *1 Enoch* 71:1)[179] and the effort to
express the belief that Jesus in death was transferred to a new
realm of existence;[180] (d) the consideration of the Spirit of
God as God's creative force which produces life (Gen 1:2; Ezek
37:9-10; cf. Rev 11:11). Dan 7:13-14 was used to contribute to
an understanding of the process by means of which Jesus was
vindicated. The substitution of Spirit for angel in the NT
triad is in part an articulation of that process.

Second, triadic imagery (drawn from Daniel?) is related in
several NT contexts to visionary or pneumatic experience.[181] In
apocalyptic texts angels transport the seer to another, heavenly
dimension. They are regarded as facilitating intellectual and
spiritual access to heavenly secrets and eschatological mysteries; they enable the seer to understand what is seen in vision,
and thereby understand the sacred prophecies of the past and
the turmoil of the present. In an interiorization of this experience, the Spirit was spoken of as an invasive or specially
given energy from God, the source of insight or wisdom, the
power by means of which new reality is grasped. The presentation of Jesus as *Maskil* and as eschatological prophet would
have led to the belief that he was endowed in this way with the
Spirit, and hence to the idea that his followers were also.
Fuller speaks of the NT triad developing under the pressure of
the "triadic implications" of the early community's experience
of the gospel: "in faith the believer is brought by the Spirit

to the eschatological presence of God in Jesus."[182]   In addition to the literary conventions of Wisdom and Apocalyptic, it
is probable that we should take into account the influence of
mystical practices and imagination on the development of NT
triadic passages.  I have shown that Ezekiel 1, the source
text of Merkabah mysticism, was drawn upon in the creation of
Daniel 7, and then linked often with that text in its interpretive history.  This study suggests that elements of early
Christian tradition should be further explored as facets of the
early phase of Merkabah mysticism.[183]

Thirdly, the exaltation of the Son of Man, the transfer to
him of power and dominion (Dan 7:14), seems to have been interpreted in the NT with the use of Isa 11:2, to mean that his
exaltation is his reception of the fullness of the Spirit.  This
idea was apparently retrojected from Easter to the ministry,
baptism and conception of Jesus.[184]

A fourth aspect in the development of the NT triad is adjustment of heavenly court imagery.  In several texts the Son
of Man stands as a witness for or against those who confess or
deny him, before the Father and the angels.  In other texts the
role of the Son of Man is that of eschatological judge, with
the angels appearing as his retinue and as executioners of the
punishment he decrees.  His superiority to the angels is indi-
cated by the fact that he commands them as his host.  In Revelation there is a tendency to represent the angels of the heavenly
court by the "seven spirits" around the throne.  I would speculate that the development of the idea of Spirit as advocate or
Paraclete of the elect (see Matt 10:20) took place when the
role of witness was left vacant by Jesus' elevation beyond the
angelic.

In the course of development that I have posited here, the
triad originating in various interpretations and uses of Daniel
7 does not assume the character of a static symbol.  It appears
in texts that deal with the dramatic acts, past and present and
future, in which faith is considered to be grounded: the vindication of Jesus of Nazareth, the conquering of death, the dis-
pensation of ultimate justice, the gathering of the dispersed
community, the uniting of all humanity under one rule and in

mutual service. There is an eschatological and cosmic dimension to the triadic traditions, emphasized again and again by
NT authors. In a sense, the triad is "open" in that there are
indications in some texts considered that the figure of the Son
(of Man) is understood as corporate, or (in Moule's term) as an
"inclusive personality."[185] Other texts emphasize that this
figure is a force that draws authentic humanity to itself and
into the transcendent realm.[186]

## G.  Summary

We have considered five NT texts or grouping of texts related to Daniel 7. By way of summary, here are the significant
points seen in those texts which will be useful for the study
of Matt 28:16-20 in the next chapter.

(1) The exaltation texts in Revelation are evidence that
Dan 7:14 was used to express the belief that Christ by his
death and exaltation received dominion over all and is Lord of
the earth, the eschatological regent of the world and one who
shares God's throne. He has received the power to know and to
set in motion God's final plans, and to him belong the "seven
spirits" of God. It has been argued that the exaltation of
Christ is understood to involve the exaltation of Christians:
they share in his power now by virtue of their baptism, and in
the future by virtue of the extension of his reign throughout
the universe. A triad (but with different titles than those
found in Matt 28:19b) is set at the beginning of this work.
There is evidence that Dan 7:13-14 has been combined with Isa
11:2.[187]

(2) John 5:26-27 has been seen as an example of the use of
Dan 7:13-14 to explicate the power received by Jesus as the
power of God himself (in this case, God's power to judge the
living and the dead). In this text it is emphasized that Jesus
exercises that power in the present, in his ministry.[188]

(3) In the pre-gospel tradition behind Mark 14:62, and to
some extent in the redactional meanings of this saying, Dan 7:13
is alluded to and combined with Ps 110:1, probably to predict
the coming of Jesus to God in his passion and resurrection, his
translation into the heavenly realm.

(4) Acts 7:55-56 and related texts depict the exalted Son of Man witnessing and participating in the heavenly court. These texts are triadic, showing different stages of development of the Christian triad. The vindication of the Son of Man is considered to involve the vindication of his followers.

(5) Several texts have been examined which associate a commission with the theophany of the Son of Man. In one (Rev 1:12-16), we find the full pattern (theophany, reaction, commission, word of reassurance) found in Daniel 7 (-12), in *1 Enoch* 71 and Matt 28:16-20. In other NT passages there are elements of this pattern and/or what appears to be an adjustment of its sequence.

(6) A number of NT passages have been listed which associate the Father, Jesus (under some title) and angels. In my opinion, they reflect the triad in Daniel 7, and are a form of that triad found in Matt 28:19b. Based on the study of Danielic traditions, I have made proposals concerning the factors which led to the development of the triad, its titles, contexts and meanings.

This examination of selected passages which would be accepted by most critics as allusions to Daniel 7 strengthens the case for the presence of an allusion to Dan 7:14 LXX in Matt 28:18, and supports the theory that the allusion functions there to depict the exalted Jesus. He is given "all power in heaven and on earth"--God's power--in his death and resurrection. This power is exercised in the work of the eleven, who are themselves empowered to "make disciples" and with whom Jesus is always present. The grounding of the commission of the eleven in the theophany of the exalted one is probably evidence of the use of a traditional pattern. It is likely that the Matthean pericope presupposes and evokes the notion that Jesus has been assumed into the heavenly realm; the prediction of his coming to God in terms of Dan 7:13 would then be regarded as fulfilled. The triad in Matt 28:19b can be reasonably considered to be related to the proposed Danielic allusion in 28:18, and should therefore be explicated in light of this relationship.

These inquiries into aspects of the interpretation and adaptation of Daniel 7 will aid in the attempt to separate tradition from redaction in Matt 28:16-20, and to provide a focused treatment of the statements made at both levels.

[1]As a self-designation, the phrase might imply Jesus' identification with the heavenly figure of Daniel 7, with a traditional reinterpretation of that figure, or (in idiomatic use) represent the avoidance of the first person singular. There is disagreement, however, about this last point. Black and Vermes argue that the phrase was used as a circumlocution in certain contexts for the first or second personal pronoun, but Fitzmyer, Colpe and Jeremias think that this cannot be proven. Cf. Vermes, *Jesus the Jew*, 162-63; Stephen S. Smalley, "The Johannine Son of Man Sayings," *JTS* 15 (1968/69) 286-87; Bowker, "The Son of Man," 20-32; Fitzmyer, "Aramaic Language," 20-21; M. D. Hooker, "Is the Son of Man Problem Really Insoluble?" *Text and Interpretation* (ed. E. Best and R. McL. Wilson; New York: Cambridge University, 1979) 157-59, 165-68.

[2]See above, p. 119.

[3]Emphasis in *1 Enoch* 71 (cf. Wisdom 1-6) is on the Enochic aspects of this figure.

[4]In addition, the usages of Daniel 7 with Ezekiel 1 suggest, though they do not prove, that the one like a son of man may have been interpreted (as well as partially conceived) in the light of "the likeness as it were of a human form" on the moving throne of Ezekiel's vision. I have, however, found no text in the pre-Christian material examined which identifies the two figures.

[5]The exegetical traditions are seen as elements of living religious consciousness and practice, not as elements of a purely literary interest.

[6]Lindars argues that "although the Son of Man is not the designation of a particular figure in Judaism, apocalyptic thought embraces the concept of an agent of God in the coming judgment, who may be a character of the past reserved in heaven for this function at the end time" ("Reenter," 54; cf. 56-57). In some cases this figure is presented as of higher rank than the angels. Identification of the figure with Jesus is fundamental to Son of Man christology, found in widely separated strands in the NT; in the sayings tradition of the gospels only, the designation "Son of Man" was applied to Jesus in this role. Lindars stresses that "we are not dealing with a single, defined concept which could be taken over ready-made into Christian thinking" ("Reenter," 60; see pp. 61-62 for his discussion of the "scheme" of this christology). I see this scheme and concept as *an* aspect of the NT use of Daniel 7, but neither as unified nor as influential as Lindars suggests. Without exception, those scholars who argue that there was *a* dominant pre-Christian concept of the Son of Man accept the Similitudes (or at least extensive, recoverable traditions behind the Similitudes) as pre-Christian. J. P. Meier, without a thorough examination of the problem of dating the Similitudes, for

example, presupposes a Son of Man concept ("glorious eschatological champion or judge") and title (*Vision of Matthew*, 77;
cf. 59, 169). But even if the Similitudes were proven to be
pre-Christian, this would still not mean there was *a* dominant,
unified pre-Christian concept of the Son of Man.

[7]The scholarly consensus is that Revelation is the theological work of one author, and that the book is a carefully
composed unity with a startling coherence (E. Fiorenza, "Revelation, Book of," *IDBSup*, 744). J. M. Ford's revival of the
theory that the two Jewish apocalypses have here been redacted
by a Jewish Christian disciple of John the Baptist (*The Revelation of John* [AB 38; New York: Doubleday, 1975]) has been
severely criticized for ignoring the unity of the work's language and symbol system (see, for example, the review by E.
Fiorenza, *CBQ* 39 [1977] 347).

[8]Many of the image-clusters and symbol associations woven
into the fabric of Revelation and repeated with incredible
variation are drawn directly from Daniel 7: throne, beasts,
heavenly court, worship of all, prolongation of the life of the
beasts, punishment by fire, reign of the people, judgment, the
books, etc. This contributes to the unified impact of Revelation, in spite of the fact that the author also makes extensive
use of pagan and Jewish mythologies and early Christian
traditions.

[9]E. Fiorenza, *The Apocalypse* (Chicago: Franciscan Herald,
1976) 47; A. Y. Collins, "The Political Perspective of the
Revelation to John," *JBL* 96 (1977) 253.

[10]This is so because the kingdom of God, says the author,
is cosmic, political and universal, and is not to be confined
to the realm of individual piety, of the purely spiritual. This
stance, according to Fiorenza, is in contrast to a rival Christian theology which advocated adaptation, submission, and focus
on the detached, superior Christian's spiritual share and rule
in the heavenly world (*The Apocalypse*, 48-52). For the author
of Revelation, the apocalyptic question, "Who is lord of the
world?" is central, and the main theological symbol is the
throne (Fiorenza, "Revelation," 745).

[11]E. Fiorenza, "The Eschatology and Composition of the
Apocalypse," *CBQ* 30 (1968) 552, 559. She argues that between
the exaltation of Christ and his parousia, the Kingdom of God
is an already present reality on earth in the Christian community. "The end does not affect a manifestation of God's Kingdom, but an extension of the priestly-kingly community of salvation to the whole world" (559 n. 115).

[12]Christ and the victorious Christians assume the kingship
on earth for a thousand years, the two beasts are imprisoned
and Satan is thrown into the abyss.

[13]Note that as in the two visions considered in *4 Ezra*,
the last judgment is detached from the scene of the exaltation
of the one like a son of man. In that apocalypse, final

judgment is in the realm of God which is presently inaccessible.
In Revelation, however, the heavens are in a sense open to the
Christian.

[14]See Fiorenza, "Revelation," 746; idem, "Eschatology,"
569.

[15]It is the only double promise: in v. 28 it is said that
the conqueror will also be given the morning star.  Turner argues that the parallelism has been misunderstood: the translation should read, "As I myself received from my Father, so will
I give him the morning star."  He thinks this may be a reminiscence of Job 38:12, and may mean that what was denied to Job
(all the power of God and knowledge of the deep things of God)
will be granted to the overcoming Christian.  Christ received
power and knowledge from God and he passes them on ("Revelation,"
*PCB*, 1048).  It is unlikely, however, that the author of Revelation understands the morning star as a symbol for knowledge; in
22:16 he has Christ describe himself as the morning star.

[16]Cf. 12:11: "and they have conquered (the accuser) by the
blood of the Lamb and by the word of their testimony, for they
loved not their lives even unto death."  Christ himself is depicted as a conquerer in 3:21; 5:5; 17:14.

[17]P. Minear, *I Saw a New Earth* (Washington: Corpus, 1968)
60.  He notes that the one basic promise is conveyed in multiple
images, and each of the promises is taken up again in later
chapters.  Those who conquer share Christ's throne (3:21) and
are called God's sons (21:7).

[18]There is extensive use of Psalm 2 in Wis 1:1-6:21.  Here
in Rev 2:26-27 the one who conquers (as in Psalm 2, the anointed
one), not God, destroys, in contrast to Wis 4:19.

[19]The verb ποιμανεῖ in Rev 2:27 may mean "to destroy"; see
R. H. Charles, *The Revelation of St. John* (ICC; 2 vols.; Edinburgh: T. & T. Clark, 1920) 1.75-76.  Actual destruction of the
heathen may be implied (cf. 19:15), and also the activity of
the martyrs as members of the heavenly army (cf. 17:14; 19:13-
14).  In 19:15, Isa 11:4 and Ps 2:9 are combined to depict
Christ the warrior-judge (cf. *Pss. Sol.* 17:23-42).

[20]"All the nations" in 13:34, distinguished from the
peaceable multitude which is the reconstructed Israel.

[21]The action is modeled on the marking of the faithful
which occurs before the destruction of Jerusalem and the departure of the *Kābôd* in Ezek 9:4-6.

[22]This may be a free citation, from memory, or, according
to Charles, may presuppose either the existence of a translation of Dan 7:14 differing from both the LXX (πάντα τὰ ἔθνη τῆς
γῆς κατὰ γένη καὶ πᾶσα δόξα αὐτῷ λατρεύουσα) and Theodotion
(πάντες οἱ λαοί, φυλαί, γλῶσσαι αὐτῷ δουλεύσουσιν), though
closer to the latter, or the independent use of an Aramaic text
of Daniel older than that preserved in the canon (*Revelation*,

1.148).  The four terms "nation and tribes and peoples and
tongues" occur but in different order also in 5:9; 11:9; 13:7
and 14:6; in no two instances is the order the same.  In 10:11
and 17:15 they recur, but with βασιλεῦσιν for φυλαῖς in the
former, and ὄχλοι for φυλαί in the latter.  See also *4 Ezra* 3:7:
*gentes et tribus, poluli et cognationes.*

[23]God is identified over ten times in this work simply as
the one who sits on the throne.

[24]Cf. 3:21: "The one who conquers, I will grant to sit
with me on my throne, as I myself conquered and sat down with
my Father on his throne."  The throne itself is called "the
throne of God and of the Lamb" in 22:1, 3.

[25]As the second of three commissions (cf. 1:12-20; 10:1,
11, 14), it can be classified as a throne-theophany commission.
(The commission does not occur until Rev 10:8-11.)  The parallels with and allusions to Isaiah 6, Ezekiel 1, *1 and 2 Enoch*,
later texts such as *T. Levi, b. Ḥagigah, Ascension of Isaiah*
and other similar works are numerous, as Charles details in his
commentary.  The author has mastered the sources and products
of early Merkabah mysticism available to him, and draws on them
lavishly.  Mearns ("Dating," 364-65) thinks *1 Enoch* 40 is a
cruder prototype of Revelation 4, but I do not agree.

[26]See Rev 1:1, 19.  The allusion is to Dan 2:28, 29 (LXX
and Θ), 45 (Θ), where δεῖ "signifies conformity with an apocalyptic eschatological regularity"; only here in Jewish apocalyptic literature is δεῖ used strictly with this meaning (Tödt,
*Son of Man*, 188).  The "apocalyptic δεῖ" appears also in the
Synoptic passion predictions.

[27]The seven spirits in Revelation are derived, via Ezek
1:13 and Zech 4:2, 10, from the concept of seven archangels
(see *1 Enoch* 20; 90:21).  They are considered here as concrete
beings, perhaps identical with the seven angels of Rev 8:2;
15:1.  But in a sense they may represent the fullness of the
Spirit of God or God's own action (E. Fiorenza, "Redemption as
Liberation: Apocalypse 1:5f and 5:9f," *CBQ* 36 [1974] 222 n. 8).
In this regard, it is possible to see an allusion intended here
to Isa 11:2, which becomes clearer at Rev 5:6.

[28]The standing may symbolize his resurrection, or indicate
that he appears as a witness in the heavenly court (cf. Wis 5:1).

[29]See Charles (*Revelation*, 1.137-39) on various opinions
concerning the contents of the scroll.  He relates it to the
heavenly tablets which contain the future destinies of the world
and the blessings in store for the righteous (cf. *1 Enoch* 81:1;
93:1-3; 106:19; 107:1; 103:2).

[30]Fiorenza, "Redemption as Liberation," 227.

[31]In 3:1, Christ "has the seven spirits of God and the
seven stars."  The latter symbolize the angels of the seven
churches (v. 20).

[32]Horns represent evil power in Daniel 7, but here in Rev 5:6 (as in *1 Enoch* 90:9, 37, 38) the power of God.

[33]See above, n. 27. Isaiah 11 is linked with Daniel 7 in *4 Ezra* 13, but without mention of the reception of the Spirit. In *1 Enoch* 61:11-12 seven spirits animate the praise of the angels. The Elect One is presented in *1 Enoch* 49:2-3, standing before the Lord of Spirits; an allusion to Isa 11:2 occurs here for the purpose of showing that judgment of the former is just and penetrating. Again in the judgment scene of *1 Enoch* 62, Daniel 7 is found in conjunction with Isa 11:2, 4. There is no direct literary relationship between these texts from the Similitudes and Rev 5:6, 12 (or John 3:34-35), but the combination of texts shows the authors are drawing on common midrashic tradition. There is no need to assume the priority of the Similitudes.

[34]Cf. 1 Tim 3:16; Rom 1:4. Haenchen (*Acts*, 183) remarks that it is a later view that the exalted Lord only acquired the Spirit in order to share it abroad.

[35]This *axios* acclamation parallels the one addressed to God in 4:11.

[36]Exod 19:6ϑ comes into play in the idea that the redeemed are installed not only to kingship but as priests (Haenchen, *Acts*, 226).

[37]See Metzger (*Textual Commentary*, 738) and Fiorenza ("Redemption as Liberation," 222 n. 6) on the MSS variants of the verb tense. The future βασιλεύσουσιν is preferred; cf. 22:5; 2:26-27.

[38]In Rev 1:5-6, a similar unit is found, probably belonging to the early Christian baptismal tradition; in this text redemption and salvation are emphasized as an already accomplished reality. See Fiorenza, "Redemption as Liberation," 223-27. She notes that the formula and hymn are open to "enthusiastic misunderstanding" and illusion. The exaltation of Christ, that is, is celebrated in baptism, and this rite is understood as an incorporation into the kingdom given to the one like a son of man. The emphasis on *future* reigning in 5:10 is the author's check on this tradition. He uses the Danielic tradition to encourage resistance, confirming that Christians have become kings by virtue of Christ's exaltation in which they participate baptismally; but he adds that this reign is now only potential.

[39]Rev 5:11: μυριάδες μυριάδων καὶ χιλιάδες χιλιάδων. Dan 7:10ϑ: χίλιαι χιλιάδες...μύριαι μυριάδες.

[40]The symbol of the shared throne, similar worship and hymns offered to both, and their joint rule (cf. 11:15, 17; 12:10) are these intimations. Charles (*Revelation*, 1.cxii) argues that the relation is one of subordination rather than of equality. It is never stated that God and Christ are one, nor is Christ called God. "And yet He is to all intents and purposes God...a true revelation of God in the sphere of human history."

[41]The seven spirits are in part drawn from (and still not completely distinct from) the seven angels.

[42]Verses 5-6 then parallel the thanksgiving; see Fiorenza, "Redemption as Liberation," 224 and n. 22.

[43]This description of God stems from the tradition connected with Exod 3:14, but is also linked by its third part (ὁ ἐρχόμενος) to the coming of Christ (Charles, *Revelation*, 1.10). God is here the one who spans all time; he is not only "the Ancient of Days."

[44]Each of the titles given to Christ here may interpret his role in terms of Daniel 7 traditions. As "faithful witness" (cf. 3:5, 14), he testifies in the heavenly court, as the Son of Man does in Luke 12:8-9; Mark 8:38. The phrase "first born of the dead" reflects a traditional Christology as found in Rom 8:29; 1 Cor 15:20; Col 1:18, and is a hint of the second Adam motif. He is "ruler of the kings on earth," considered either as set over all those kings who are on the side of the beast or Satan, or as leader of his followers who have become kings (cf. Dan 7:18, 22, 27). See the discussions by Fiorenza ("Redemption as Liberation," 223 n. 18) and Minear (*I Saw a New Earth*, 14) on the genitive "of kings." Both prefer the second alternative.

[45]In almost all the NT epistles, grace and peace (or grace, mercy and peace) are said to be sent forth not from the triad, but from God our (or: the) Father and Jesus Christ (Rom 1:7; 1 Cor 1:3; 2 Cor 1:2; Gal 1:3; 1 Thess 1:1; Eph 1:2; Phil 1:2; 2 Thess 1:2; 1 Tim 1:2; 2 Tim 1:2; Titus 1:4; Phlm 1:3; 2 Pet 1:2; 2 John 1:3). Only in two passages is a triad set at the beginning of a letter: in Rom 1:3-4 and 1 Pet 1:2.

[46]The Christian is "son," ruler, witness, transcender of suffering and death. As Fiorenza stresses, the author struggles against a blurred distinction between present and future. Visions of the heavenly liturgies draw that future into the present, but fleetingly, with hard realism.

[47]Fiorenza, "Redemption as Liberation," 221.

[48]The phrase κρίσιν ποιεῖν occurs elsewhere in the NT only at Jude 14-15 which is a quotation of *1 Enoch* 1:9. Here Jude is referring to the parousia of the Lord Jesus, although in *1 Enoch* the reference is to the coming of the great Holy One for judgment.

[49]This is the only instance in the gospels where the phrase is anarthrous, as it is in Dan 7:13 (cf. Rev 1:13; 14:14). In John 5:27, however, it appears without the comparative preposition. The absence of the definite article may be an indication of closeness to the OT text, or may be due to the word order of the sentence (C.F.D. Moule, *The Origin of Christology* [Cambridge: Cambridge University, 1977] 16-17 n. 15). Borsch (*Son of Man*, 294) denies the presence of an allusion here to Daniel.

But the constellation of elements that have affinity to the
Danielic text, and the fact that these appear to be related to
similar constellations elsewhere in the NT on the basis of a
traditional interpretation of Daniel 7 indicate there is an
allusion here.  Leivestad ("Exit," 252) also denies the presence of an allusion; he argues the phrase υἱὸς ἀνθρώπου simply
means "human"; Jesus can judge human beings because he is human
(cf. *T. Abraham* 13; Bultmann, however, thinks that this text
has been influenced by John 5:27 [*Gospel of John*, 261 n. 5]).

[50] Since a primary function of the king is to judge, the
gift of the kingdom to the one like a son of man (7:14) is the
gift of the power to judge.

[51] See above, pp. 252-53 n. 64.

[52] The Son of Man appears as a witness in the heavenly
court in Acts 7:55-56; Mark 8:38; Luke 12:8-9; (Rev 3:5).

[53] C.F.D. Moule, "From Defendant to Judge--and Deliverer:
An Enquiry into the Use and Limitations of the Theme of Vindication in the New Testament," *Studiorum Novi Testamenti Societas
Bulletin* 3 (1952) 48; cf. Smalley, "Johannine Son of Man Sayings," 293.  Brown distinguishes two types of judgment texts in
the Fourth Gospel: those in which it is denied that Jesus judges
(in the sense of condemns; e.g. 3:17; 12:47), and those in which
it is insisted that Jesus does judge (in the sense that his
presence provokes self-judgment which has eternal consequences;
e.g., 3:19; 12:48; 9:39; 5:22); R. Brown, *Gospel According to
John*, 1.345.

[54] John 5:27, as many critics have seen, has affinities with
*1 Enoch* 69:27, in which it is said that the "sum of judgment"
(cf. John 5:22: πᾶσαν τὴν κρίσιν) is committed to the Son of Man
who sits on the throne of his glory and executes vengeance.  His
throne, as in Revelation, is the throne of God (cf. *1 Enoch* 47:
3; 51:3; 45:3; 55:4; 62:3, 5).  This passage from the Similitudes, however, is not a literary influence on John 5:27.

[55] Cf. Colpe, "ὁ υἱὸς τοῦ ἀνθρώπου," 465 n. 441; B. Lindars,
"The Son of Man in the Johannine Christology," *Christ and the
Spirit in the New Testament* (ed. B. Lindars and S. Smalley;
Cambridge: Cambridge University, 1973) 52; A.J.B. Higgins, *Jesus
and the Son of Man* (Philadelphia: Fortress, 1964) 165; Brown,
*Gospel According to John*, 1.220.

[56] Lindars, "The Son of Man in the Johannine Christology,"
58.  The parallelism of the two Danielic texts has been seen by
the framers of this tradition.  Both John 5:27-28 and Matt 27:
51-53 may use a tradition which links Ezekiel 37 with Dan 12:2,
the Matthean text associating this resurrection with the death
of Jesus and the Johannine text associating the command that
the prophet "prophesy to the רוּחַ" and call it to breathe on the
dry bones (Ezek 37:9) with the voice of the Son of Man calling
forth the dead.  The going forth of the word of that Son of Man,
probably a reference to his role as advocate (Mearns, "Dating,"
366) is mentioned in *1 Enoch* 69:29.

[57]Psalm 80 may also have had a part in the formation of
these NT texts.  Dodd thinks that Ps 80:17, which identifies
"God's right hand man" with the divinely strengthened Son of
Man may have provided scriptural justification for the fusion
of Ps 110:1 and Dan 7:13 (*According to the Scriptures* [London:
Nisbet, 1952] 101-2).  O. F. J. Seitz also argues that Psalm 80
was the unseen "catalyst" which brought together the Son of Man
and the right hand of God.  But Seitz's position is further
that Ps 80:17 rather than Dan 7:13 was the primary reference to
the Son of Man; the allusion to the clouds of Daniel 7 was only
an afterthought ("The Future Coming of the Son of Man: Three
Midrashic Formulations in the Gospel of Mark," *SE* VI [= TU 112
(1973)] 481-85, summarized by Moule, *Origin*, 24-25).  This is
unlikely, as *T. Job* may join Ps 110:1 with allusions to Daniel
7.

[58]See above, pp. 241-42, on the death of Job in *T. Job* 52,
and p. 242 on the post-mortem exaltation of the just one in
Wisdom 4-5.  *1 Enoch* 71 narrates the translation of Enoch's
spirit, but he is not said to have died.

[59]Cf. Glasson, *Second Advent*, 55-59; Robinson, *Jesus and
His Coming*, 44-47; Hartman, "Scriptural Exegesis," 146, 144.
We will not enter here into discussion of the question of the
authenticity of the saying.

[60]H. K. McArthur, "Mark XIV.62," *NTS* 4 (1958) 156-58; cf.
Tödt, *Son of Man*, 39.  Hay argues that the sequence makes it
clear that when Jesus comes on clouds at the parousia he will
have the authority and might of the one sitting at God's right
hand (*Glory at the Right Hand*, 66).  According to Lindars,
"coming with clouds," which follows the heavenly session, denotes Jesus' transport for his apocalyptic function as Judge;
Lindars thinks this phrase may be an expansion of the NT text
(*NT Apologetic*, 49).

[61]Robinson, *Jesus and His Coming*, 49.  Hooker also thinks
the order is unimportant, since the citations are metaphorical
and parallel, "though not necessarily identical in meaning"
(*Son of Man*, 170-71).  Borsch argues that what we have here are
"two ideograms referring to the same conception, the beginning
of the reign of the figure in heaven.  The Son of Man is soon
to appear exalted" (*Son of Man*, 391).  Schweizer agrees with
Robinson concerning the original meaning of the verse, but says
that Mark may have inverted the sequence (*Lordship and Discipleship* [Naperville, IL: A. Allenson, 1960] 39 n. 4; idem, "The
Son of Man," *JBL* 79 [1973/74] 120).

[62]T. F. Glasson, "The Reply to Caiaphas (Mark XIV.62),"
*NTS* 7 (1960) 91.

[63]Fuller, *Foundations*, 146; cf. Hay, *Glory at the Right
Hand*, 65-66.  Fuller's analysis is in agreement with Hahn's
opinion that Mark 14:62 represents the oldest form of the primitive concept of Jesus as the future Messiah.  The thought
captured here is that of a return of Jesus from heaven, visible

to all the world (F. Hahn, *The Titles of Jesus in Christology* [trans. F. Knight and G. Ogg; New York: World, 1969] 163, 285). Both Ps 110:1 and Dan 7:13 have been understood eschatological- ly: the enthronement and the coming are to take place before all at the parousia. Reading Mark 14:62 in this way, and in line with his reconstruction of Christological development, leads Hahn to insist that this is the only place in the NT where Ps 110:1 has been understood as a reference to the parou- sia; elsewhere it represents an exaltation christology (*Titles*, 130, 134 n. 10). But Hahn's schematization seems to have forced this interpretation, and as Donahue points out, the schematization is itself inadequate (*Are You the Christ?*, 145-47).

[64]Cf., for example, Acts 8:23; Heb 2:8.

[65]John 20:18, 25, 29; cf. 1 Cor 9:1.

[66]Elisha saw (ἑώρα) the whirlwind taking Elijah (2 Kgs 2:12). In the *T. Job* and *Assumption of Moses*, there are wit- nesses (Job's daughters and Eve) who see the ascents of the souls of Job and Adam.

[67]See Rev 11:12. In the *Gospel of Peter* 34-42, Roman soldiers, the centurion and Jewish elders witness the exit from the tomb.

[68]See above, p. 134 n. 21, and pp. 124-26, 128. Several critics accept the theory that a shift of application occurred in the interpretation of this text.

[69]N. Perrin, "The Son of Man in Ancient Judaism," 26; idem, *Rediscovering*, 168, 173.

[70]See above, pp. 247 n. 19, 291 n. 1, 264.

[71]In broad terms, this tradition uses Daniel 7 to speak of the exaltation or final assumption of the righteous one (Enoch himself in *1 Enoch* 71; cf. *T. Job* 52; Wis 1:1-6:21).

[72]Perrin claims, in fact, that 14:62 is from the Christian exegetical tradition that began all Son of Man speculation. He argues that the section of the verse that reads "the Son of Man sitting at the right hand of Power" contains no parousia refer- ence but only reference to an ascension. "You will see" and the further allusion to Dan 7:13, "coming with the clouds of heaven," are also pre-Markan but from another Christian pesher tradition that originated in an interpretation of the cruci- fixion and was expanded by the addition of a further (parousia) use of Dan 7:13. It is only at this stage, according to Perrin, that a parousia expectation entered the picture ("Mark XIV.62: The End Product of a Christian Pesher Tradition?" *NTS* 11/12 [1964/66] 151, 154; idem, *Rediscovering*, 173-85). On the basis of other NT uses of Zech 12:10, Perrin claims that the verb ὄψεσθε in Mark 14:62 is drawn from that prophetic text. How- ever, the tradition dealing with either witnessed translations

or the confrontation between persecutors and the exalted one
may be responsible for that verb here in Mark 14:62, and may
have later suggested the connection with Zech 12:10.  F. H.
Borsch ("Mark XIV.62 and 1 Enoch LXII.5," *NTS* 13/14 [1966/68]
565-67) points out that three items (they see, Son of Man, sitting) are linked in the same order in both these texts.  He
suggests that this is not a case of parallel Jewish and Christian developments using the same texts, but an indication of
the influence on both of older common conceptions.  It is possible to read both parts of the Dan 7:13 allusion in Mark 14:62
as references to an exaltation or ascent.

[73]Perrin, "Mark XIV.62," 151; cf. Lindars, *NT Apologetic*,
257.

[74]Perrin, *Rediscovering*, 179.

[75]Perrin (see above, n. 72) argues that the second part of
the saying refers to the parousia even at the pre-Markan stage.
He finds in 14:62 little or no trace of Markan redaction or
composition ("Creative Use of the Son of Man Traditions by
Mark," *USQR* 23 [1967/68] 360).  J. Donahue, on the other hand,
argues for Markan redaction here of previous exegetical traditions which used Daniel 7 to speak of both the resurrection and
the parousia.  He thinks that Mark turned these various exegetical traditions into a developed Son of Man Christology, composing the climactic statement of his Gospel (*Are You the
Christ?*, 180-83; idem, "Temple, Trial and Royal Christology,"
*The Passion in Mark* [ed. W. Kelber; Philadelphia: Fortress,
1976] 71).

[76]We are assuming that 16:8 is the original ending of the
Gospel.

[77]See Perrin, "Towards an Interpretation of the Gospel of
Mark," *Int* 30 (1976) 38; idem, "The High Priest's Question and
Jesus' Answer (Mark 14:61-62)," *Passion in Mark*, 81.  References
to the similar opinions of Lohmeyer, R. H. Lightfoot, Michaelis
and Marxsen are given by Fuller (*Resurrection Narratives*, 206
nn. 31-34).  See T. J. Weeden (*Mark--Traditions in Conflict*
[Philadelphia: Fortress, 1971] 11-13) for the view that resurrection appearances are suppressed in Mark because they belonged to
the *theios aner* christology which he opposed.  Mark's emphasis
on the parousia is seen as an attempt to counteract the traditions of the resurrection appearances.  This theory is challenged by D. L. Tiede (*The Charismatic Figure as Miracle Worker*
[Missoula, MT: Scholars] 257-60) and Moule (*Origin*, 44-45).

[78]Fuller, *Resurrection Narratives*, 63-64.  It is difficult
to see why Peter should be singled out if the reference is to
the parousia.  Mark may be alluding to the two appearances
listed in 1 Cor 15:5, to Cephas and to the twelve.  See also
J. Alsup, *The Post-Resurrection Appearance Stories of the Gospel
Tradition: A History of Tradition Analysis, with Text-Synopsis*
(Calwer Theologische Monographien, Series A; Bibelwissenschaft,
5; Stuttgart: Calwer, 1975) 93; R. Brown et al., *Peter in the
NT*, 71-72.

[79]Donahue wisely speaks of the ambiguity of Mark 14:62 in its context as perhaps due to a deliberate tension in Mark between resurrection and parousia (*Are You the Christ?*, 143, 170, 180).

[80]Schweizer, on the contrary, thinks that although Mark 14:62 in the original version may have meant Jesus' exaltation to God's throne, in Mark the Dan 7:13 allusion refers to the parousia ("The Son of Man Again," 259). See also Hay (*Glory at the Right Hand*, 64-68) who argues Mark did not understand or intend his readers to understand the Dan 7:13 allusion in its original sense, but only as a description of the parousia. This goes beyond the evidence.

[81]The phrases are synonyms and favorite expressions of each Evangelist. The thesis that the Matthean phrase is a misreading of ἀπαρτί ("exactly," "certainly") from an earlier source (BDF, 8) has not met with acceptance (cf. Robinson, *Jesus and His Coming*, 47; Senior, *Passion Narrative*, 178). Others have attempted to attribute a different nuance to the Matthean phrase. Hay (*Glory at the Right Hand*, 68) argues it means not "from now on" but "at a later time"--i.e., the parousia; so also W. Allen (*St. Matthew*, 284), Trilling (*Das Wahre Israel*, 68) Tödt (*Son of Man*, 84), Schweizer (*Good News*, 499). But the phrase is used elsewhere in Matthew to speak of the end of one significant period in Jesus' life and the beginning of another (23:39; 26:29).

[82]Glasson, *Second Advent*, 56; Robinson, *Jesus and His Coming*, 48-49. The manuscript evidence is too slight to support this theory; moreover, both of these critics insist that Matthew could only have intended 26:64 to refer to the parousia.

[83]The insertion of ἀπὸ τοῦ νῦν is seen to conform to the omission of the phrase "coming with the clouds of heaven." This is considered in line with Luke's tendency to tone down the eschatology of his sources and allow the parousia to recede into the distant future. His focus is rather on the present exaltation of the Son of Man during the period of the church. For him the enthronement of Christ took place from the resurrection onward (cf. 24:26), but the coming on clouds is reserved for the future. See Tödt, *Son of Man*, 102, 305, 349, 382-83; H. Conzelmann, *The Theology of St. Luke* (trans. G. Buswell; New York: Harper and Row, 1961) 113-20, 84-85; cf. Lindars, *NT Apologetic*, 48. Actually, however, Luke uses the cloud imagery of Dan 7:13 (and perhaps of Ezekiel 1) not just for the parousia but for the ascension (Acts 1:9, 11).

[84]This simpler version speaks only of exaltation in line with the original imagery of Dan 7:13. According to this schema, the parousia emphasis has not yet been added in the tradition. Jeremias (*NT Theology*, 266 n. 2) thinks Acts 7:56 confirms Luke 22:69 as an early formulation. It is probable, he says, that the earliest conception was that the revelation

of the Son of Man would come about in the form of an assumption
to God (cf. *1 Enoch* 71); this assumption is reflected in Luke
22:69. Colpe ("ὁ υἱὸς τοῦ ἀνθρώπου," 435) also argues for the
antiquity of the saying. He regards it as from Luke's special
Passion Narrative source (also [with caution] V. Taylor, *The
Passion Narrative of St. Luke* [SNTSMS 19; Cambridge: Cambridge
University, 1972] 82-83).

[85]See, however, the cautions of C. H. Talbert ("Shifting
Sands: The Recent Study of the Gospel of Luke," *Int* 30 [1976]
386, esp. n. 36).

[86]The primitive conception of resurrection-assumption-
exaltation as one act is split in Luke-Acts into the two events
of resurrection and ascension.

[87]Matthew has brought the two OT citations closer to their
LXX form: he has put the participle καθήμενον before ἐκ δεξιῶν
τῆς δυνάμεως so that the Ps 110:1 quotation is more faithfully
reproduced (κάθου ἐκ δεξιῶν μου), and has changed Mark's μετὰ
τῶν νεφελῶν to ἐπί (cf. the similar correction of Mark 13:26 at
Matt 24:30).

[88]A. Feuillet ("Le triomphe du fils de l'homme d'après la
déclaration du Christ aux Sanhédrites (Mc. xiv, 62; Mt. xxvi,
64; Lc. xxii, 69)," *La Venue du Messie* [RechBib 6; Brugge, 1962]
156-57, cited by Senior, *Passion Narrative*, 178 n. 5). Feuillet
thinks the saying originally had reference to the establishment
of the reign of Christ over the universe; only later were the
words taken to refer to the parousia. Senior himself remarks
that it is possible to understand the phrase as Matthew's addition within his redactional perspective, "without need to deny
the secondary character of 26:64." He does not raise the question of an early tradition behind Mark 14:62.

[89]It is the opinion of most critics that Matthew in his
passion narrative is using no written source other than Mark
(Senior, *Passion Narrative*, 310; N. Dahl, "Die Passionsgeschichte
bei Matthäus," *NTS* 2 [1955/56] 17-32; A. Descamps, "Rédaction et
christologie dans le récit matthéen de la Passion," *L'Evangile
selon Matthieu* [ed. Didier; Gembloux: Duculot, 1972] 360).

[90]See Kingsbury, *Matthew*, 74, 114; Strecker, *Der Weg*, 115,
236; Trilling, *Das Wahre Israel*, 68; Tödt, *Son of Man*, 82, 84,
288; P. Lamarche, "Le 'Blasphème de Jésus devant le Sanhédrin,'"
*RSR* 50 [1962] 78. These scholars regard the adverbial phrase
as redactional.

[91]According to this view, the saying concerns two separate
moments or events in the Son of Man's future: his glorification
and his coming in judgment. The weight falls in Matthew on the
first moment. Cf. Senior, *Passion Narrative*, 182 n. 1; McArthur,
"Mark XIV.62," 157.

[92]Senior, *Passion Narrative*, 182. Senior argues that ἀπ'
ἄρτι in 26:64 emphasizes the strong contrast between past and
future, without trying to narrowly specify the span of time

referred to, i.e., without heavily emphasizing immediate glorification. He finds it possible that a heightened christological perspective motivates a "foreshortening" of Jesus' prophecy of glorification.

[93]See Meier, *Vision of Matthew*, 33, 204.

[94]A. Vanhoye, "Structure et théologie des récits de la Passion dans les évangiles synoptiques," *NRT* 89 (1967) 159.

[95]On John 5:28-29, see above, p. 270. In Matt 27:51, the earthquake, the opening of graves and other elements, recall Ezek 37:7 LXX. See Senior, *Passion Narrative*, 320-22; idem, "The Death of Jesus and the Resurrection of the Holy Ones (Mt. 27:51-53)," *CBQ* 38 (1976) 312-29; Meier, *Vision of Matthew*, 34.

[96]Senior thinks that Matthew himself has constructed 27:51b-53, drawing simply on the motif of the eschatological resurrection of the dead, current in intertestamental Judaism, on Ezekiel 37 and on a rich fund of apocalyptic imagery. The possibility that Matthew was aware of Dan 12:2 in his composition of 27:52b "is tantalizing but cannot be established with certitude" (*Passion Narrative*, 320).

[97]Above, pp. 192 n. 18, 146.

[98]A related tradition may be found in 1 Thess 4:13-18, in which I would argue are found traces of the linking of Ezekiel 37 and Dan 7:13; 12:2, but in a different context. Here the resurrection of the holy ones is connected not with the death and resurrection of Jesus but with his parousia, in the depiction of what L. Hartman (*Prophecy Interpreted* [Lund: Gleerup, 1966] 186) and Robinson (*Jesus and His Coming*, 20) call a "corporate parousia." "For since we believe that Jesus died and rose again, even so, through Jesus God will bring with him those who have fallen asleep" (1 Thess 4:14). Jesus is pictured descending from heaven, perhaps with the archangel whose call--along with Jesus' (?) cry of command and the trumpet blast--seems to wake the dead. The gathering of the faithful is in two stages: first the dead rise, then the living will be "caught up together with them in clouds to meet the Lord in the air" (v. 17). The cloud imagery of Dan 7:13 appears to have been applied to the faithful; a multitude is brought forward with Jesus to God. Again, the allusion to Dan 12:2 cannot be proven.

[99]H. W. Bartsch ("Die Passions und Ostergeschichten bei Matthäus. Ein Beitrag zur Redaktionsgeschichte des Evangeliums," *Basileia* [Stuttgart, 1959] 27-41) sees the wonders that accompany Jesus' death in Matthew's Gospel not as eschatological "signs" but as part of the eschatological events themselves. He considers these wonders as traces of an original account which linked the death of Jesus with the beginning of the parousia. But see J. Meier, *Law and History in Matthew's Gospel: A Redactional Study of Mt. 5:17-48* (Rome: Biblical Institute, 1976) 32 n. 15. In Matthew's perspective, death leads to messianic

enthronement, but only the missionary activity of the disciples
(28:16-20) will unite this enthronement with the final parousia.

[100]Schweizer remarks that "in a manner faintly reminiscent
of John, the torment of Jesus is seen not only as necessary for
but in fact a part of his enthronement at the right hand of God"
(*Good News*, 499-500).  Glasson reads Matt 26:64 as roughly corresponding to John 13:31 (*Second Advent*, 22 n. 2).  Matt 19:28;
25:31 should not be understood as dating the act of the Son of
Man's enthronement at the parousia.  These scenes are the beginning of the final judgment (cf. Dan 7:9).

[101]H. Conzelmann, "History and Theology in the Passion Narratives of the Synoptic Gospels," *Int* 24 (1970) 194.  Conzelmann argues that "the passion is a stage on a way that runs like
a straight line to the enthronement (Matt 28:16-20)" (p. 193).
The enthronement, however, does not take place in the final
pericope; it is simply revealed to the disciples.

[102]Descamps, "Redaction et christologie," 410.

[103]Meier's stress on the unity of insight in Matt 27:51-54;
28:2-3; 28:16-20 (*Law and History*, 30-40) is, in my opinion,
closer to Matthew's perception than Conzelmann's linear schematization (above, n. 101).

[104]Fuller (*Resurrection Narratives*, 209 n. 22) calls Matt
26:64 "the case *par excellence* for the shift of a christology
based in part on Dan 7:13f from the parousia to the exaltation."
If Matthew understood Mark 14:62 to refer to the parousia, he
has indeed made a shift--but not from a primitive parousia
christology to a later exaltation christology; the shift would
be back to an emphasis on the meaning of the earlier tradition
behind Mark 14:62.  But there is no evidence that Matthew so
understood Mark 14:62, which cannot be read as an unambiguous
reference to the parousia.

[105]Meier, "Salvation History in Matthew," 211 n. 17.  See
above, p. 128.

[106]The prediction that the Sanhedrin will "see" is obviously not fulfilled in the final Matthean pericope.  In his
redaction of Mark 13:26, Matthew makes it clear that "all the
tribes of the earth" will mourn at the parousia (24:30).

[107]And, to a certain extent, at the redactional levels.

[108]Clouds and wind are spoken of in Enoch's translation in
*1 Enoch* 14:8; in *1 Enoch* 70:2 he is raised aloft on "chariots
of the spirit."  Angels bearing a seer to the heavenly world
are a common feature of intertestamental scenes; they may appear
as vestiges of this idea in the NT empty tomb narratives and in
the ascension in Acts 1.

[109]The phrase "full of the Holy Spirit," occurs in Luke
4:1; Acts 6:3, 5; 11:24.  The verb ἀτενίζειν (to gaze) is used
twelve times in Luke and Acts.  The singular οὐρανός is Lukan,
occurring twenty-four times in Acts.  Note the plural in Acts
7:56, used elsewhere only in Luke 10:20; 12:33; Acts 2:34.

[110]Colpe, to the contrary, assumes that Luke found v. 56 in the tradition and introduced it in his own words in v. 55 ("ὁ υἱὸς τοῦ ἀνθρώπου," 642). So also Hay (*Glory at the Right Hand*, 74 n. 96) who argues that v. 55 "explains the vision in terms of a momentary fulness of the Spirit in Stephen and tells the reader that the Son of Man (7:56) is Jesus"; the redundancy of v. 56 indicates that a source is being used there.

[111]See Rev 1:10; 4:2; Luke 10:21-22; John 3:34; 3:1-11.

[112]The plural οὐρανοί in v. 56 is traditional, and Colpe believes that θεωρῶ and διηνοιγμένους are pre-Lukan as well ("ὁ υἱὸς τοῦ ἀνθρώπου," 462 n. 417). Tödt also concludes that the motif of the opening of the heavens is traditional (*Son of Man*, 304). Hay (*Glory at the Right Hand*, 74 n. 96) thinks that the phrase about God's glory may have been added simply to prevent the tautology of 7:56 from being too tedious; he says the phrase has no other obvious function.

[113]Jesus here seems to be seen within the *Kābôd*, at the right hand of God.

[114]Hay (*Glory at the Right Hand*, 73) agrees with Dibelius (*Studies in the Acts of the Apostles* [London: SCM, 1956] 168) that the author of Acts interpolated his account of Stephen's speech into a narrative in which the statement about Stephen's transfiguration in 6:15 was followed directly by the report of the vision. Cf. Haenchen, *Acts*, 295.

[115]This description is probably drawn from descriptions of the shining of the righteous ones in apocalyptic writings. Cf. Dan 12:3; *4 Ezra* 7:97; *2 Apoc. Bar.* 51:10-12. It is stated explicitly in *2 Apoc. Bar.* 51:8, 11 that transfiguration is the effect of vision of the other world. In *1 Enoch* 46:1, the face of the Son of Man is described as having "the appearance of a man, and his face was full of graciousness, like one of the holy angels." See also the Matthean and Lukan transfiguration accounts.

[116]See C. K. Barrett ("Stephen and the Son of Man," *Apophoreta* [Berlin: A. Töpelmann, 1964] 34-35) for a summary of the attempts of O. Cullmann, W. Manson, and M. Simon to analyze the particular strain of early Christology that produced the statement in Acts 7:55-56.

[117]There are, for example, parallel charges concerning the temple (Acts 6:13; Mark 14:58; missing in Luke), and blasphemy at the mention of the Son of Man (Acts 6:11; Mark 14:64; Matt 26:65; missing in Luke), and prayers for the forgiveness of executioners (Acts 7:60; Luke 23:34). Stephen also commits his spirit to Jesus (Acts 7:59) as Jesus commits his spirit to his Father (Luke 23:46).

[118]Borsch (*Son of Man*, 235) inclines to this explanation of the saying. Barrett also, but for a different reason, considers the saying in essence distinctively Lukan (see below, n. 120).

[119]Hay (*Glory at the Right Hand*, 36) points out that it is
not the only Christian passage alluding to Jesus' position at
the right hand of God which does not indicate that Jesus is
seated. Several passages leave open the question of whether or
not he is seated (Rom 8:34; Acts 2:33; 5:31; 1 Pet 3:22;
*Apocryphon of James* 14:30-31). In Rev 5:6 the Lamb is standing.

[120]H. P. Owen ("Stephen's Vision in Acts VII.55-56," *NTS* 1
[1955] 224-26) and Fuller (*Foundations*, 137 n. 72) think that
the Son of Man is standing because he is about to return;
Stephen sees a proleptic vision of the parousia and of his own
vindication. But we would expect some clearer reference to the
coming. Barrett has offered a modified version of the theory
that this is a proleptic parousia scene. He argues that the
Son of Man is standing to welcome Stephen and come to him in
distress, as in the moment of death the martyr ascends to heav-
en (cf. 7:59). Barrett attributes to Luke here the insight
that the individual Christian death was *an* eschaton, though not
*the* eschaton, a private and personal *parousia* of the Son of Man
("Stephen," 35-36). Barrett relates this interpretation to
Luke 24:43. Barrett also sees a similarity to traditions which
depict Elijah as the guide of souls to the heavenly world (p.
38). On a redactional level, Barrett's theory may be accurate.

[121]Colpe believes, with reservations, that the participle
ἐστῶτα is an adaptation of the idea that God rises up to come
forth in wrath on behalf of his children, or to confront his
enemies, or to accomplish salvation. The Son of Man, in the
tradition behind Acts 7:56, "takes God's place by ushering in
the end in judgment and salvation." A Samaritan predicate for
God ("the standing one") may have here been transferred to the
Son of Man, but the meaning of the divine "standing" is not
clear from the examples we have; Colpe, "ὁ υἱὸς τοῦ ἀνθρώπου,"
462-63. Other suggestions are discussed by Barrett ("Stephen,"
32-34), Jeremias (*NT Theology*, 273 n. 6), Hay (*Glory at the
Right Hand*, 75 n. 100).

[122]See above, pp. 194 n. 38 and 210 n. 183. The verb may
imply an understanding of Jesus exalted to the status of angel
(cf. Tödt, *Son of Man*, 303-4; Borsch, *Son of Man*, 233 n. 2).
See Dan 12:1; Wis 5:1, 5. It is clear, however, that an angel
or angel-like christology is already being superseded in Acts
7:55-56 (Higgins, *Jesus and the Son of Man*, 145; Barrett,
"Stephen," 33).

[123]Cf. Acts 10:42, the claim that the witnesses to the
resurrection were commanded to preach to the people "and to
testify that he is the one ordained (ὡρισμένος) by God to be
the judge of the living and the dead." Haenchen (*Acts*, 353)
comments that this is the function of the Son of Man in the
earliest passages in the Synoptics; it is probably more accurate
to say, however, that the Son of Man functions as witness in the
earliest Synoptic traditions (Robinson, *Jesus and His Coming*,
38). The verb ὁρίζω, it has been claimed, is traceable back to
the term חֹק in Ps 2:7; the idea is of an effectual royal decree
involving the giving of the kingdom to David's promised heir

(L. C. Allen, "The Old Testament Background of (ΠΡΟ)ΟΡΙΖΕΙΝ in
the New Testament," *NTS* 17 [1970/71] 104-108).  The decree is
the same as a divine appointment (K. L. Schmidt, "ὁρίζω," *TDNT*
5 [1967] 453).  In this text in Acts, and in the one mentioned
in the following note, the resurrection is understood as the
moment of appointment, along the lines of Daniel 7.

[124]Cf. Acts 17:31, a call to repentance because God "has
fixed a day by which he will judge the world in righteousness
by a man whom he has appointed (ἐν ἀνδρὶ ᾧ ὥρισεν), and of this
he has given assurance to all by raising him from the dead."
Here again we have a weak Danielic allusion (cf. Lindars,
"Reenter," 61-63; Barrett, "Stephen," 34; against Haenchen,
*Acts*, 526 n. 3; Borsch, *Son of Man*, 234 n. 3).  On the Son of
Man standing in a judicial role in Acts 7:55-56, see Cullmann
(*Christology*, 157-58, 183), Theo Preiss (*Life in Christ* [London:
SCM, 1954] 50), Hay (*Glory at the Right Hand*, 132-33), Higgins
(*Jesus and the Son of Man*, 145).

[125]See Schweizer, "The Son of Man Again," 261, 258-59.  He
sees the Son of Man in Acts 7:55-56 as the decisive witness who
brings about the judgment of God.  He is at once counsel for
the defense and for the prosecution in one person.

[126]Moule, "From Defendant to Judge," 46-47.

[127]Cf. Dan 7:10; 12:1.

[128]Moule, "From Defendant to Judge," 47; cf. Higgins,
*Jesus and the Son of Man*, 145-46.

[129]The parallel in Matt 10:32-33 reads: "So everyone who
acknowledges me before men, I also will acknowledge before my
Father who is in heaven; but whoever denies me, I also will
deny before my Father who is in heaven."

[130]See Charles (*Revelation*, 1.84): the white garments are
the spiritual bodies, bodies of light, in which the faithful
are to be clothed in the resurrection life.  They probably also
represent the garments received at baptism.

[131]Dan 12:1 concerns the deliverance of everyone whose
name is found written in the book.

[132]Lindars remarks that this is "the only Markan saying
showing the Son of Man performing the eschatological judgment"
("The Son of Man in the Johannine Christology," 57 n. 33).
Actually, however, the reference here may be to his function as
witness, not judge.  Hooker ("Insoluble," 162) argues that the
role of judge is never predicated of the Son of Man in Mark.
The "coming" may have originally referred to the Son of Man's
coming to God (cf. Jeremias, *NT Theology*, 274; Higgins, *Jesus
and the Son of Man*, 59) or the clause about coming may have
been added in the course of transmission (Robinson, *Jesus and
His Coming*, 54-55, 93-94, 129), referring now to the coming to
earth.

[133]See, for example, Tödt, *Son of Man*, 54, 89; Higgins, *Jesus and the Son of Man*, 58-59; Perrin, *Rediscovering*, 186; Donahue, *Are You the Christ?*, 162-63.

[134]Borsch, *Christian and Gnostic Son of Man*, 18; see also Hooker, *Son of Man*, 118. Jeremias (*NT Theology*, 7 n. 2) suggests that the Semitic verbs behind "to deny" and "to be ashamed" are כפר and חפר. The bifurcation of the tradition took place during the course of oral tradition in an Aramaic speaking milieu. Heb 2:11 understands shame as a denial of relationship: "he is not ashamed to call them brothers."

[135]Shame is frequently spoken of in the Similitudes in connection with the confrontation between the mighty and the Son of Man. There, however, the mighty are filled with shame and darkness and their faces downcast; nothing is said of the Son of Man being ashamed of them. Cf. *1 Enoch* 46:4-8; 48:4-10; 62:5-16; 63:7-11. In Wisdom 5 the oppressors of the righteous one are filled with fear, amazement, anguish, repentance. The chief offense of the sinners in the Similitudes is that they have "denied (the name of) the Lord of Spirits" (*1 Enoch* 38:2; 41:2; 45:2; 46:6-7; 63:7) or "denied the Lord of Spirits and His Anointed" (48:10) or "the name of the dwelling of the holy ones and the Lord of Spirits" (45:1). In 46:5, the kings are blamed because they do not extol and praise him (presumably, the Son of Man). Cf. 60:6 where judgment is pronounced against those "who worship not the righteous law, and for those who deny the righteous judgment, and for those who take his (the Lord of Spirits') name in vain." A subtheme is that of the wickedness of the mighty in their oppression of the righteous ones (46:5; 53:2-7; 62:11; cf. 47).

[136]Cf. Perrin, "The Son of Man in Ancient Judaism," 27; Colpe, "ὁ υἱὸς τοῦ ἀνθρώπου," 442; Jeremias, *NT Theology*, 262-63. In Matt 25:31-46, Matthew will present his understanding of the relation between earthly commitment *to* the Son of Man and heavenly commitment *by* the Son of Man.

[137]Cf. Bultmann, *Theology of the NT*, 1.29-30; Fuller, *Foundations*, 122-23; Jeremias, *NT Theology*, 276; P. Vielhauer, "Jesus und der Menschensohn," *JTC* 60 (1963) 141-42; Bowker, "Son of Man," 22-23, 25, 27, 44-45; M. Casey, "The Son of Man Problem," *ZNW* 67 (1976) 150-51; Hooker, "Insoluble," 165-67 for a survey of the wide range of opinions on this point.

[138]Luke 12:8-9 par. and Mark 8:38 par. Luke 9:26 exhibit the form discussed by Käsemann as a "sentence of holy law": the same verb describes in the protasis and apodosis both human guilt and divine judgment, in order to characterize the precise correspondence of the two in content and their logical connection. An eschatological *jus talionis* is being promulgated. The proclamation of judgment is more than a threat: "in it a process of being judged is already under way" ("Sentences of Holy Law in the New Testament," *New Testament Questions of Today* [trans. W. J. Montague; Philadelphia: Fortress, 1969] 67-68). The confession is to be the standard of judgment on the last day.

¹³⁹See above, pp. 252-53 n. 64, 269.

¹⁴⁰T. W. Manson claims that the Son of Man is here represented as a corporate figure (*The Teaching of Jesus* [Cambridge:
Cambridge University, 1931] 263-70, 332-33), but there is no
evidence here that this is the case.  There is an alternate
reading, "mine" (i.e., my followers) for "my words" in Mark
8:38 and in some MSS in Luke 9:26, and Hooker thinks this offers some support to the idea that the Son of Man is conceived
as a corporate entity (*Son of Man*, 120).  But the shorter reading is probably due to accidental omission, facilitated by the
similarity of the endings of the words ἐμοὺς λόγους (Metzger,
*Textual Commentary*, 99-100).

¹⁴¹Rev 1:5: "Jesus Christ the faithful witness"; 2:18:
"the Son of God."

¹⁴²Cf. the use of the term "Father" for God in *T. Job* 33:9;
Wis 2:16, and the use of "son" in Wis 2:18; 4QpsDan Aᵃ and
*4 Ezra* 13:32, 37, 52.  W.R.G. Loader ("The Apocalyptic Model of
Sonship: Its Origin and Development in New Testament Tradition,"
*JBL* 97 [1978] 525-54) notes that Father-Son terminology features
especially in contexts and sayings (among which he lists Mark
13:32; 8:38 pars.; Luke 12:8-9; Matt 25:31-46; 13:36-43; John
5:22-27) which refer to Jesus' apocalyptic function, mostly as
Son of Man.  But he does not discuss a pre-NT background for
this phenomenon.

¹⁴³See Jeremias, *NT Theology*, 61-68; Loader, "Apocalyptic
Model," 528, 538.

¹⁴⁴See Tödt, *Son of Man*, 45.  In Mark 13:27 (cf. Matt 13:
41), the Son of Man sends out the angels to gather the elect,
indicating that he has the power to command them.  It is also
possible that we have the transfer here to the Son of Man of
the idea of God coming with his angels (cf. *1 Enoch* 1:9 and
Jude 14-15).  Luke's inclination, as Tödt points out, is to
make the angels subject to God alone (*Son of Man*, 104); but
Luke speaks of glory which belongs to all three members of the
triad (9:26).  See Robinson (*Jesus and His Coming*, 109-10) for
his reconstruction of the development of the tradition behind
these texts; he thinks there is "a progressive detachment of
both the glory and of the angels of the Son from those of the
Father."  Angels are associated with the Son of Man in the
Similitudes, but are not the retinue which accompanies him (see
Glasson, *Second Advent*, 31); Charles emends *1 Enoch* 62:11.

¹⁴⁵See Perrin, "Son of Man," *IDBSup*, 836; idem, *Rediscovering*, 179; Schweizer, "The Son of Man Again," 261; Lindars, "Reenter," 62 n. 1.

¹⁴⁶I have argued that the empowering of the Lamb in 5:6-14
is a dramatization of the eschatological meaning of Dan 7:14.
The "new song" makes this clear when it declares he has ransomed
individuals "from every tribe and tongue and people and nation"
(v. 9; cf. Dan 7:14).  His horns recall the horns of the fourth
beast of Daniel 7.  See above, pp. 266-68.

312     The Father, Son and Holy Spirit

[147]The element of reassurance is missing from this text,
and there is no reaction of the seer to his vision except for
his weeping in 5:4.

[148]Compare 4QpsDan A$^a$ 2:3; *4 Ezra* 13:31; Mark 13:8 pars.

[149]The parallel in Matt 24:30-31 contains additional apocalyptic details.  Luke 21:27 merely states that "then they will
see the Son of Man coming in a cloud with power and great glory."
There is no mention of the gathering.  See Conzelmann (*Theology
of Luke*, 130-31) and Tödt (*Son of Man*, 100) on Lukan redaction
here.  Luke thinks of the angels as subject only to God, and
the parousia as unobservable, indescribable (cf. 17:20).

[150]Hartman, *Prophecy Interpreted*, 146-47, 189.  A comparison of Mark 13 with 1 Thess 4:13-5:11 and 2 Thess 2:1-17 indicates to Hartman that a form of this discourse, including elements of the Matthean and Lukan versions, and parenetic material,
was known to Paul.

[151]Ibid., 207-9, 226-45.  He thinks the midrash originated
in the teaching of Jesus (pp. 245-48) but this point and contrasting theories cannot be discussed here.

[152]Hartman has overlooked the allusion in Mark 13:32, par.
to Dan 12:6-7.  It is generally considered that Mark 13:28-32
is a logia composition, joined secondarily to the discourse;
Hartman thinks it is outside the compass of the reconstructed
midrash (*Prophecy Interpreted*, 223).  Verse 32, however, is a
reply to the question asked in Mark 13:1 ("When will this be,
and what will be the sign when these things are all to be accomplished?") which resembles Dan 12:6-7 (the seer asks, "How
long shall it be till the end of these wonders?" and receives
the answer that "when the shattering of the holy people comes
to an end, all these things will be accomplished").  Dan 12:7,
11, 12 are attempts to be precise about the length of the time
of oppression, but no such calculations are attempted in the NT
discourse.  Whereas in Daniel, an angel knows the time of the
end and tells Daniel, Mark 13:32 (par. Matt 24:36, with minor
variations) insists that "of that day or that hour no one knows,
not even the angels in heaven, nor the Son, but only the Father."
Daniel is being alluded to, and disagreed with.  The triad angels, the Son, the Father, appears here in ascending hierarchy.

[153]The "desolating sacrilege" (Mark 13:14, par. Matt 24:15),
based on the Zeus altar set up by Antiochus Epiphanes IV in the
Jerusalem temple (cf. Dan 11:31; 12:11; 9:27), refers to some
form of blasphemy which seems to be intentionally not described.
As Hartman notes, in the NT texts as they now stand, the devas-
tation of Jerusalem and Judea in 70 A.D. is associated with the
blasphemy (*Prophecy Interpreted*, 152).  It is probable that the
discourse was updated in both 40 (when Caligula demanded that
his statue be set up in the Jerusalem temple) and in 70 A.D.,
when its significance was seen from new perspectives.  On the
relation of the discourse to the events of 70, compare the
opinions of A. Feuillet ("Le Sens du Mot Parousie dans l'Evangile

de Matthieu," *The Background of the New Testament and Its Eschatology* [ed. W. D. Davies and D. Daube; London: SPCK, 1956] 261-80), Robinson (*Jesus and His Coming*, 124-25 n. 3), and D. R. Hare (*The Theme of the Jewish Persecution of Christians in the Gospel according to St. Matthew* [Cambridge: Cambridge University, 1960] 178-79).

[154]No parallel appears in the Lukan version, but there is mention of "our gospel" in 2 Thess 2:14.

[155]Hartman, *Prophecy Interpreted*, 171. The "apocalyptic δεῖ" from Dan 2:28 appears in Mark 13:10. The "many" whom the *maskîlîm* make wise and righteous are understood as "all nations." The preaching in Mark 13:10 must happen "first" before the parousia. Hahn (*Mission*, 74) sees this text as a stage of development parallel to Matt 28:18-20 and Mark 16:15-18. In the latter two passages the task of the Gentile mission is defined "fundamentally by Christology" (that is, by "the exaltation concept"); in the former "a far-reaching modification of the apocalyptic tradition was undertaken, and the old idea of God's latter-day message to the Gentiles [see below] was taken up in a new form by reference to the fact of missionary preaching among all the nations." Given the connection in both passages, however, with the work of the *maskîlîm* in Daniel, it is likely these are related, not parallel, developments.

[156]Hartman, *Prophecy Interpreted*, 169-72. Cf. 11:41 LXX.

[157]Schweizer, *Good News*, 451. Matt 4:23 and 9:35 refer to Jesus "preaching the gospel of the kingdom."

[158]This angel is one of three who announce the coming judgment (vv. 6-11).

[159]On the difficulties of this text, see Charles, *Revelation*, 2.18-25; Turner, "Revelation," *PCB*, 1053; D'Aragon, "Apocalypse," *JBC*, 485. The reaping imagery here is derived from Joel 4:13.

[160]Jeremias, *Jesus' Promise*, 22-23. Mark and Matthew, however, understand the saying in terms of human proclamation. Charles (*Revelation*, 2.12) relates the phrase in Rev 14:6 (εὐαγγέλιον αἰώνιον) to that in 10:7 (τὸ μυστήριον τοῦ θεοῦ), insisting that it must not be translated as if it were τὸ εὐαγγέλιον. "It is a proclamation of the impending end of the world and of the final judgment, which, while it is a message of good tidings to the faithful, constitutes for all nations a last summons to repentance." He regards this gospel as "based on a purely theistic foundation" and compares this text to Mark 1:15 (p. 13).

[161]Jeremias, *Jesus' Promise*, 56, 69.

[162]Hahn, *Mission*, 58, 67-68.

[163]Hahn, *Mission*, 122. Jeremias (*Jesus' Promise*, 51) points to the boldness of the Baptist's threat in Matt 3:9 par. (Q); he thinks that Jesus, like the Baptist, warned that the place of his Jewish hearers might be taken by Gentiles, and even

further, promised Gentiles a share in the kingdom, expecting their ingathering in the hour of final judgment (p. 55). But Hahn sees in Jesus' work an eschatology in the process of being realized: in Jesus' acceptance of individual Gentiles the eschatological event began to be realized. Hellenistic Jewish Christianity took seriously the universalistic aspects of Jesus' ministry (*Mission*, 33, 68).

[164]Hahn, *Mission*, 121. Hahn notes that Matthew consistently distinguishes between κηρύσσειν and διδάσκειν, the first relating to the message of God's reign and the second to the exposition of the law. Preaching the gospel is announcing and promising salvation.

[165]He is represented as the one to whom the field, which is the world (13:37), belongs, as his kingdom (v. 41). "The resurrection has made him cosmocrator, something he was not before" (Meier, *Vision of Matthew*, 92). Contrast Tödt, *Son of Man*, 72-73, 79. Those besides Meier who understand 13:36-43 and 28:16-20 to concern the activity and presence of the exalted Son of Man in the period between Easter and the Parousia include Kingsbury (*Parables*, 99), Vögtle ("Mt. 28, 18-20," 290-91), Lohmeyer (*Matthäus*, 223-24), Barth ("Matthew's Understanding," 134).

[166]In the parable (13:24-30) the seed most likely refers to the Word, as in the parable of the sower, but here in the interpretation the seed is persons in whom the Word has taken hold. See Jeremias' discussion (*Parables*, 79) of the fusion here of two concepts: of the Word as God's seed (e.g., *4 Ezra* 9:31) and of people as God's planting (*4 Ezra* 8:41; cf. *1 Enoch* 10:16; 62:8). What is spoken of in 13:38 is a communication of a share in "sonship" (cf. Meier, *Vision of Matthew*, 92).

[167]As Meier puts it, in 28:16-20 the eleven are given the mandate to sow good seed throughout the world. He considers the explanation of the parable of the weeds "an excellent explanation of 28:16-20" (*Vision of Matthew*, 93).

[168]Kingsbury, *Parables*, 102, 104-5.

[169]"Angels of punishment" appear in the Similitudes (*1 Enoch* 53:3; 56:1; cf. 62:11; 63:1; 66:1, etc.). In *1 Enoch* 53:6, Michael, Gabriel, Raphael and Phanuel cast sinners into the burning furnace.

[170]If Matthew is thinking at all of the LXX version of Dan 12:3, the reference to preaching or teaching is strengthened. Here, instead of the term "the righteous," we find οἱ κατισχύοντες τοὺς λόγους μου (which Montgomery [*Daniel*, 473] thinks is a misreading of מצדיקי הרבים as מחזיקי דברי; the "misreading," however, may be an interpretation). Theodotion has ἀπὸ τῶν δικαίων τῶν πολλῶν.

[171]No consistent distinction is made by Matthew between
the kingdom of the Son of Man and the kingdom of God; each have
both present and future significance (Hahn, *Mission*, 123 n. 3;
Kingsbury, *Parables*, 98; Strecker, *Der Weg*, 166 n. 7; Trilling,
*Das Wahre Israel*, 151-54).  Contrast Colpe, "ὁ υἱὸς τοῦ ἀνθρώπου," 461 n. 414; Dodd, "Matthew and Paul," 54-57; Walker, "The
Kingdom of the Son of Man," 575-77; Bultmann, *History*, 187 n. 3.
Several motifs are shared by Matt 13:36-43 and *1 Enoch* 62:7-16
(mention of the Son of Man, the "sowing" of his congregation,
deliverance of the wicked to angels for punishment, the glorification of the righteous).  There are, however, no verbal
parallels and many significant differences between the texts.
I find no literary relationship here.

[172]Par. Matt 16:27: the Son of Man, his angels, his Father;
Luke 9:26: the Son of Man, the Father, the holy angels.

[173]The last two references should perhaps be excluded from
our list of triads, since these texts depict a huge cast of
characters in the heavenly world.

[174]The other NT passages which I think are related to Dan
7:13-14, and which mention the Spirit in a triad are: Luke 10:
21-22 (the Holy Spirit, the Father, the Son); John 3:34-35 (the
Spirit, the Father, the Son); 3:13-14; cf. vv. 5-6 (the Spirit,
the Son of Man, God); Acts 7:55-56 (the Holy Spirit, God, the
Son of Man).  None of these triads nor the ones in the list
above appears to be influenced directly by a specific triad in
the Similitudes (see above, pp. 95, 85 n. 280).

[175]See Doeve, *Jewish Hermeneutics*, 151 (on Matt 16:27;
25:31-46), 159-60.  Loader writes, "the self description of
Jesus as Son, derived from his own use of *abba*, was linked ini-
tially especially with what he or at least the very early tradition saw as his function at the eschaton as Son of Man.  But
we also find a tendency for the designation Son itself to take
up connotations once primarily associated with Jesus' future
role as Son of Man.  And further, Jesus as the Son is increasingly understood to perform this role not just at the parousia
but also in the exercise of authority in the present" ("Apocalyptic Model," 538).  He argues also that cross fertilization
and synthesis took place between the apocalyptic model of sonship as it developed and sonship of the royal messianic tradition.  Wisdom and prophetic traditions also feed into the NT
meaning of "Son of God."  This article offers many valuable
insights which support the thesis presented here.  For Kingsbury's views on Matthew's understanding of the relation between
the titles Son and Son of Man, see above, pp. 38-39.

[176]In *4 Ezra* 13, Isaiah 11 is linked with Daniel 7, but
Isa 11:2 is not used.  The Spirit is thought of as given to the
Messiah (using Isa 11:2) in such texts as *Psalms of Solomon* 17.
Daniel 7 and Isa 11:2 are found joined in *1 Enoch* 62, but, as
we have seen (above, p. 297 n. 33), it cannot be determined that
this passage from the Similitudes has influenced any NT text.
The "spirit of righteousness" is spoken of in *1 Enoch* 62:2.

[177]See above (pp. 52-54) for the attempts of Lohmeyer and
Fuller to illustrate and to explain the changes in the NT triad
from (1) Son of Man, Father, angels, to (2) Father, Son, angels,
to (3) Father, Son, Spirit.

[178]Matt 28:2-4 is the nearest the canonical gospels come
to narrating the resurrection. "An angel of the Lord" rolls
back the stone; the earthquake recalls OT theophanies. See
Fuller, *Resurrection Narratives*, 51, 56-57, 74-75. Acts 12:
1-17, the story of Peter's release from prison by an angel before Passover, has been shown to be parallel in many respects
to the gospels' resurrection stories (M. Smith, "The Report
about Peter in 1 Clement V. 4," *NTS* 7 [1960/61] 86-88). Again,
we may have a hint of a tradition which attributed a helping
role to an angel with regard to the resurrection of Jesus.

[179]"Chariots of the spirit" are mentioned in *1 Enoch* 70:2.

[180]Cf. the flesh/spirit antithesis in 1 Pet 3:18; 1 Tim
3:16. On the presentation of Jesus as a "new Enoch" in 1 Pet
3:18-22, see W. J. Dalton ("Interpretation and Tradition: an
Example from 1 Peter," *Gregorianum* 49 [1968] 34; J.N.D. Kelly
(*A Commentary on the Epistles of Peter and of Jude* [London:
Adam and Charles Black, 1969] 156); Bo Reicke (*The Epistles of
Peter, James and Jude* [AB 37; Garden City: Doubleday, 1964] 109.
J. T. Sanders argues that the original behind 1 Pet 3:18-19, 22
may have been an earlier form of this hymn than that quoted in
1 Tim 3:16 (*NT Christological Hymns*, 18).

[181]Acts 7:55-56; Rev 1:10; 4:2; Luke 10:21-22; John 3:34;
3:1-11.

[182]Fuller, *Resurrection Narratives*, 87, cited above, p. 53.

[183]See above (pp. 52-53) for Lohmeyer's insistance that
John the Baptist's teaching was of great importance in the
development of the NT triad.

[184]See R. E. Brown, *Birth*, 124-25. He speaks of the relation of the Holy Spirit to Jesus' divine sonship articulated
first in reference to the resurrection, then to his baptism and
then to his birth.

[185]Moule, *Origin*, 87, 95-96. By this Moule means that
Christ is thought of as more than individual, more than a representative; in short, like the omnipresent God. In Danielic
terms, the holy ones of the Most High, or *maskîlîm* and their
followers, are embodied in the one like a son of man, who suffers their fate and sums up their existence and experience in
himself. T. W. Manson calls the NT Son of Man the remnant, the
true Israel; it is a name for Jesus and for those who follow
him, suffer with him, are glorified with him (*Teaching of Jesus*,
265-70 [on Matt 25:31-46 especially]; idem, "The Son of Man in
Daniel, Enoch and the Gospels," 190-91). On the inadequacy of
H. W. Robinson's idea of "corporate personality," see J. W.
Rogerson, "The Hebrew Conception of Corporate Personality: A
Reexamination," *JTS* 21 (1970) 1-16.

[186]Moule agrees with C. H. Dodd that the NT conception of the Son of Man "challenges the mind to discover a doctrine of personality, which will make conceivable this combination of the universal and the particular in a single person" (*Interpretation of the Fourth Gospel*, 249; cited by Moule, *Origin*, 51).

[187]Rev 5:6, 12; see also John 3:34-35; *1 Enoch* 62:2; 49:2-3.

[188]Contrast the expression of final or future eschatology in John 5:26-30.

CHAPTER VII

MATT 28:16-20 AND ITS TRIADIC PHRASE

In this chapter I will return to the question of tradition
and redaction in Matt 28:16-20[1] on the basis of the preceeding
examination of Danielic interpretive traditions.  First I will
attempt to distill a pre-Matthean "narrative midrash" from the
pericope, and will offer suggestions concerning its provenance
and function.  Interest is in the meaning of the triadic phrase
within this tradition.  Second, I will discuss Matthean redaction of the midrash, in particular as this shows how Matthew
understood the triadic phrase and set it in the context of his
grasp of the demands and powers of authentic discipleship.  The
chapter concludes with a statement of the results of this study
and with a set of open questions for further study.

A.  The Pre-Matthean Midrash

1.  The Separation of Tradition and Redaction

Let me begin with a recapitulation of the most important
theories, discussed above in Chapter I, concerning the tradition behind Matt 28:16-20.  By an analysis of the common elements found in Matt 28:16-20, Luke 24:36-53, John 20:19-23 and
the Markan Appendix 16:14-20, and by removing from each passage
elements he considers redactional, Hubbard concludes that a
common tradition, a proto-commission, lay behind these passages.
He reconstructs it as follows:

> Jesus appeared to the eleven.
> When they saw him they were glad,
> though some disbelieved.
> Then he said:
>     Preach (the gospel)
>     to all nations.
>     (Baptize) in my name
>     for the forgiveness of sins.
>     (And behold) I will send
>     the Holy Spirit upon you.[2]

Hubbard argues that the universalistic emphasis ("to all nations") was added by someone involved in the Gentile mission,
and that this proto-commission was a written(?) statement of

credentials for preaching.  It is based on the actual narration
by one of the eleven of a Christophany and commissioning.  Among
the elements that Hubbard thinks Matthew added in his redaction
are (a) the mention of the mountain, verse 16; (b) the emphasis
on the authority of the risen one, verse 18b, drawn directly
from Dan 7:14 and indirectly via Matt 11:27; (c) the triadic
phrase, verse 19b, from his community's liturgical practice;
(d) the promise of presence, verse 20b.  Hubbard sees no intrinsic connection among these four, only the third of which is
traditional.[3]

Based on an analysis of the elements in Matt 28:16-20 which
appear elsewhere in the gospel tradition but are never isolated
logia, and on a study of Matthean terminology and linguistic
patterns, Strecker's contention is that a traditional liturgical "word of revelation" stands behind Matt 28:18-20:

> All power in heaven and on earth has been given to me.
> Baptize in the name of the Father and of the Son and
> of the Holy Spirit.
> I am with you all days.[4]

Meier finds in Acts 1:6-12 a tripartite schema similar to that
in Matt 28:16-20, dealing with (a) the exaltation of Jesus,
(b) the command to start a mission, and (c) the promise of assistance.  Furthermore, both pericopes concern an appearance
of the risen Jesus on a mountain.  This structural similarity
and the study of Mattheanisms in Matt 28:16-20 lead Meier to
argue that Strecker's reconstruction should be expanded.  The
tradition behind Matt 28:16-20 involved:

> (a) an appearance of the risen Christ in Galilee on a
>     mountain to which he had ordered his disciples to go;
> (b) a statement concerning exaltation or enthronement;
> (c) a command to baptize or, alternately, some sort of
>     command to start a mission;
> (d) perhaps a promise of continuing divine support in
>     this mission.[5]

The possibility is raised, then, that some of the elements assigned by Hubbard and others to Matthean redaction, or considered
by critics like Fuller as independent units of tradition, were an
integral tradition at the pre-Matthean stage.

My analysis from a linguistic and conceptual standpoint
indicates that the distinctively Matthean terms and phrases in
28:16-20 are the underlined (those that do not seem to be due
solely to Matthean redaction are marked with dashes):

> 16. Now the e̱le̱ve̱n disciples went to̱ G̱a̱li̱le̱e̱, to the
> mountain where Jesus commissioned them.  17. And when
> they saw him they worshipped him; but some doubted.
> 18. And Jesus came and said to them, "All authority
> in heaven and on earth has been given to me.  19. Go
> therefore and ma̱ke̱ di̱sci̱ple̱s of all nations, ba̱pti̱zi̱ng̱
> them in the name of the Father and of the Son and of
> the Holy Spirit, 20. teaching them to observe all
> that I have commanded you; and lo, I am with you all
> days, to̱ the cḻo̱se̱ of the age."[6]

The removal of Mattheanisms of which I am reasonably certain
leaves us with this statement:

> (The eleven) went (to Galilee) to the mountain where
> Jesus commissioned them.  Jesus (said): "All authority
> in heaven and on earth has been given to me.  Make
> disciples of all nations; baptize[7] them in the name
> of the Father and of the Son and of the Holy Spirit.
> I am with you (to) the close of days.

It has been shown in Chapter III that the clause "all authority...has been given to me" in Matt 28:18b and the phrase
"all nations" in verse 19a are probably drawn from Dan 7:14 LXX,
referring to all authority given to the one like a son of man
and to the service of him by all nations.  Moreover, the claim
in Matt 28:18b that the authority of Jesus is "all" authority
"in heaven and on earth" probably rests on Dan 4:14 LXX, where
it is said that "the Lord of heaven has authority over all in
heaven and upon earth."  Finally, the phrase "all days, to the
close of the age" in Matt 28:20b may allude to Dan 12:13 LXX,
where the seer Daniel is told that he will rest and stand in
his glory "at the close of days."[8]

Study of the midrashic history of Daniel 7 convinces me
that several other aspects of the Matthean pericope may be drawn
from Danielic interpretive tradition.  (1) *The mountain* (v. 16)

to which the eleven come, where they see Jesus and are commissioned, could be ultimately related to the mountain of Daniel 2,
the final kingdom which develops from the stone "cut out by no
human hand." That stone in Daniel strikes the image of world
empires and destroys it, and becomes a great mountain that
"filled the whole earth" (Dan 2:35), interpreted as the kingdom
which will never be destroyed (2:44). Daniel 7 is itself a
"midrash" on Daniel 2, in which the one like a son of man and
the kingdom given to him interpret the stone.[9] A seventh mountain appears in Enochic literature as the throne of God (*1 Enoch*
18:6-8; 24-25; cf. *2 Enoch* 9 where the mountain-throne is clearly related to the stone of Daniel 2.

        (2) *The triad* of the Father, the Son and the Holy Spirit
very likely is a development of the Danielic triad, Ancient of
Days, one like a son of man and angels. The particular titles
in Matt 28:19b are found together elsewhere in the NT only in
Luke 10:21-22 (cf. John 3:34-35), which may also be an allusion
to Dan 7:14 LXX.[10] A close coordination of three figures into
what can be considered like Matt 28:19b a triadic *phrase* is
found in only two other places in the NT Danielic material which
has been analyzed. Rev 1:4-5 blesses the seven churches in
epistolary style with grace and peace "from him who is and who
was and who is to come, and from the seven spirits before his
throne, and from Jesus Christ the faithful witness, the first-
born of the dead and the ruler of kings on earth." Luke 9:26
speaks of the Son of Man coming "in his glory and the glory of
the Father and of the holy angels."

        (3) The idea which I have claimed is presupposed in Matt
28:16-20, of the risen *Jesus* as one *assumed into heaven*, would
then be based on an interpretation of Dan 7:13 as a heavenly
ascent or translation to the divine council. It has been seen
that Daniel 7 is used in this fashion (influenced by Ezekiel 1)
in *1 Enoch* 71, and the pre-gospel tradition behind Mark 14:62
pars. may use Dan 7:13 to speak of Jesus' coming to God. The
exaltation texts in Revelation, and Acts 7:55-56, I have argued,
adapt the role of the Danielic one like a son of man to depict
Jesus empowered in the havenly realm. The promise of presence
in Matt 28:20b, which bears some similarity to *1 Enoch* 71:14-16,
can be understood within the context of a translation tradition:

against the claims that the translated one has simply disappeared or is removed from contact with humanity, it is
asserted that he is present in a new and total way.[11]

(4) Finally, the presentation in Matt 28:20a of the risen
Jesus *commissioning the eleven to teach* all nations to keep the
commands he had given during his earthly ministry--commissioning
them, that is, to publish his interpretation of Torah--is
similar to two aspects of Danielic interpretation which have
been considered in the preceding chapters. First, Jesus is depicted in the final Matthean pericope as himself a teacher, the
source of the teaching of the eleven. In *4 Ezra* 13, the man
from the sea appears as a warrior sending forth fire from his
mouth. The fire is identified as Torah (13:38), and it destroys
his enemies (drawing on Isa 11:4; cf. Rev 1:13-16).[12] In Matt
28:16-20 there is no indication that the teaching of Jesus is
destructive. Four other NT passages which I would relate to
Dan 7:14 LXX link reception of πάντα or ἐξουσία with knowledge
or inspired speech. The ability to utter the words of God and
to command an obedience that leads to life are the powers given
when the Father gives "all things" into the hand of the Son in
John 3:34-35. John 13:3 states that Jesus knew that the Father
had given all things into his hands and that he had come from
God and was going to God. John 17:1-5 interprets the eternal
life which Jesus is believed to be empowered to give as knowing
God and Jesus Christ. Matt 11:25-27, par. Luke 10:21-22, speaks
of the Son as the one to whom all things have been delivered
and as the only one who knows and can reveal the Father.[13] Each
of these four passages, in a distinctive way, stresses the notion of Jesus' "wisdom" and may link it with the power given him
in terms of Dan 7:14. As Matt 28:20a focuses on the obligation
to observe the commands given during the ministry of Jesus, John
3:36 contrasts belief in and disobedience to the Son.[14]

Secondly, the commission based on the appearance of the
risen Jesus in Matt 28:16-20 is similar to the commissions associated with the theophany of the Son of Man in Rev 1:12-16;
4-5;[15] Mark 13:10, par. and with appearance and ascension (in a
cloud) of the risen Jesus in Acts 1.[16] In the first passage,
the seer John, who thinks of himself as a (Christian) prophet

and witness (Rev 1:1-3), is commissioned to write what he sees,
"what is and what is to take place hereafter" (1:19); the commission associated with the second theophany is a commission to
prophesy "about many peoples and nations and tongues and kings"
(10:11). The disciples' preaching of "the gospel" to all nations precedes the final parousia of the exalted Son of Man in
Mark 13:10 par.[17] The commission of the apostles in Acts 1 is
to be the witnesses of the risen Jesus throughout the world
(1:8). In contrast to *4 Ezra* 13, where there is no commission
by the man from the sea,[18] each of these passages connects a
mission to a theophany, the latter as ground or climax of the
former. The commission of the eleven to "make disciples" in
Matt 28:19-20, grounded in the announcement that "all authority
in heaven and on earth" has been given to Jesus (v. 18), appears
to be an example of this Danielic interpretive tradition.

If we return to consider the statement that resulted when
Mattheanisms were removed from Matt 28:16-20 (above, p. 321),
we find that the following appear in the distillation: the
words and phrases alluding to Dan 7:14; 4:14 and 12:13 LXX, the
mention of the mountain, the triadic phrase, and the promise of
presence. The symbolism of the mountain, the statement about
"all authority in heaven" and the promise of permanent presence
all indicate that Jesus is thought of as appearing from a heavenly dimension. The two major elements from Matt 28:16-20 which
do not appear in the distillation are: (a) the disciples' reaction, a mixture of worship and doubt (v. 17) and (b) the phrase
"teaching them to observe all that I have commanded you" (v.
20a). The first is an expression of the Matthean understanding
of the tension inherent in discipleship.[19] The second, related
to other aspects of Danielic interpretation (number 4 above),
in line with the constant emphasis in Matthew on the binding
and freeing nature of the Law as interpreted by Jesus.[20] These
two elements are Matthean redaction, which will be considered
below.

The tradition which results from removal of the Mattheanisms I consider a "narrative midrash" basically on Daniel 7.
Strecker, as has been seen, speaks of Matthew receiving a tripartite "liturgical tradition." His reconstruction consists

only of logia. Meier considers the narrative framework of
verses 16-17 mostly redactional, but argues that hints of previous tradition may be seen at the end of verse 16.[21] The mention of the eleven going to a designated mountain where they
encountered Jesus makes the reconstruction proposed here a narrative. It is a (throne-)theophany commission, with the three
elements of the theophany,[22] the commission,[23] and the word of
assurance. It is missing the element of reaction. This is a
presentation of the exalted Jesus commissioning the eleven, in
terms indicating that the book of Daniel and elements of its
later interpretation have been the vehicle for understanding
and expressing a distinctive belief in the ultimate exaltation
of Jesus, its universal consequences, and the obligations open
to the disciples.

That Matthew is not the author of the midrash, but rather
inherited it, cannot be proven simply by pointing to the fact
that the midrash has no Mattheanisms. By its very allusive
nature we would not expect it to. The fact, however, that there
are found elsewhere (1) an exaltation use of Dan 7:14 (Rev 2:
26-27; Revelation 5);[24] and (2) a combination of motifs similar
to those of Matt 28:16-20, and in the context of an allusion to
Daniel 7 (*4 Ezra* 13; cf. Acts 1:1-12)[25] shows that Matthew is
using traditional material. Moreover, there is probably no
direct literary connection between any of the above texts and
the pre-Matthean midrash.

Allusions to Dan 7:14; 4:14 LXX may appear in Matt 11:25-27
par. Luke 10:21-22,[26] and this observation could suggest that
Matthew has composed his final pericope largely out of that Q
tradition.[27] The Lukan version also contains the triad of
Father, Son, and Holy Spirit; the Spirit is mentioned perhaps
because of a further allusion to Dan 4:5 LXX and/or to Isa 42:1,
or because of the influence of Ezekiel's association of the
Spirit with visionary experience.[28] It is possible that Matthew
knew a version of the saying that included mention of the Holy
Spirit.[29]

In spite of the common allusions and parallels, the differences between the two traditions (the midrash behind Matt 28:
16-20 and the Q saying) are striking. The midrash presents the

exalted Jesus after Easter on a mountain.  Having been given
God's total power in heaven and on earth, he commands that all
nations be drawn into discipleship by baptism.  The Q saying,
on the other hand, presents Jesus in a pneumatic experience
during his ministry thanking God, the Lord of heaven and earth,
for the revelation of eschatological secrets.  He announces
that "all things" have been given to him by the Father, involving intimacy between Father and Son, and the power of the latter
to reveal the former.  It has been suggested that originally
this saying referred to Jesus' baptism by John,[30] and that at
some stage it was a baptismal hymn, expressing some sort of belief in the baptized one's identification with or incorporation
into the exalted Christ and a share in his knowledge.[31]  As
such, it can be regarded as a step on the way to a strong spiritualization of baptism through its identification with gnosis.[32]
No such emphasis is apparent in the midrash extracted from Matt
28:16-20, which stresses the rationale and performance of a rite.

In my opinion, then, the midrash does not depend on the Q
saying, nor do both depend on a common tradition.  The midrash,
commanding baptism because of the exaltation of Jesus, may have
produced in some circles the hymn's enthusiastic description of
baptism (Jesus' and the believer's).  I see no direct dependence
of Matt 28:16-20 on the Q saying, but think that Matthew redacted both in line with his special concerns (see below).

Behind Matt 28:16-20, then, I find a traditional midrash.
The essence of its wording is recoverable.  There is no compel-
ling reason to regard it as having grown in stages by the addition of Danielic allusions.[33]  The only phrase that makes me
hesitate with regard to this point is the final phrase, "the
close of days," an allusion to Dan 12:13 LXX.  But most likely
Matthew found this in the midrash and changed it to accommodate
the formula he uses with other Son of Man passages, "the close
of the age."[34]  The mention of "all nations" is integral, drawn
from Dan 7:14 LXX,[35] which means that there is a universalism
present at this stage, but not necessarily that debates concerning the necessity of circumcision and the observance of other
Torah legislations must be presupposed to have already occurred.
The Danielic theme of the subjection of the nations has been
replaced by that of the discipling of the nations.

## 2. The Triad

The triadic phrase in the context of the midrash is short-hand for the eschatological theophany, or for the event of exaltation. For those acquainted with the throne symbolism of the mountain, and who catch the allusions and recognize the form of the midrash, the phrase evokes the imagery of the heavenly court. The figure of the exalted one, here named the Son, has been presented at the heavenly throne of the one called the Father. If he is imagined as himself enthroned, the exalted one may be thought of in terms not only of Dan 7:14, but also in terms of "the likeness as it were of a human form" of Ezek 1:26-28, a manifestation of the *Kābôd* of God. Both the power of the heavenly world and the power that brings one to the heavenly world may be captured in the phrase "the Holy Spirit." If angelic members of the court are symbolized or represented here, the Holy Spirit can be considered as a personal being, and this would mean that the phrase in the midrash meets one of the two conditions for being considered trinitarian.[36] It is impossible, however, to be sure of this, as the author may have used the term "the Holy Spirit" simply to interpret the impersonal ἐξουσία of Dan 7:14.[37] Concerning the second condition, the intention to express the unity in holiness of the three figures, in my judgment the author of the midrash joins the three figures in the triadic phrase to indicate that they are to be mentioned during the baptismal rite, the act of drawing the baptized into the realm of the holy. The second condition is met. In the boldness and terseness of the midrash's triadic phrase lie the seeds of perplexity and controversy, as the author celebrates but does not explicate the mysteries of the celestial world. The triadic phrase stands here as a statement of belief that death has been transcended in the case of Jesus of Nazareth who, like Enoch, has been assumed. As part of the baptismal command, the triadic phrase is also a statement of hope in the ultimate vindication of authentic Israel, of all drawn into participation in this event of exaltation. In baptism in the name of the Father, the Son and the Holy Spirit, the exaltation of Jesus becomes a communal experience, one that could be regarded as the keeping of the promise to Daniel's *maskîlîm* and their followers.

3. Origin of the Midrash

The fact that a mission to all nations is commanded by the risen Jesus in the midrash seems to some to be proof that the midrash was composed toward the end of the first century, as an articulation of Christian experience of that period. Such a clear mission given immediately by the risen Jesus would apparently make the history recorded in Acts unintelligible, since there the Jerusalem apostles do not seem to know that they are to go to the Gentiles.[38] Although in Acts 1:8 the eleven are told by Jesus before his ascension that they will be his witnesses "in Jerusalem and in all Judea and Samaria and to the end of the earth,"[39] they do not consistently behave in the subsequent narrative as though they had in fact received such a clear mandate. According to Luke, no real Gentile is admitted into the Christian community until Peter admits Cornelius, and he does that only after being shown in an extraordinary divine intervention that he may associate with or visit someone "of another nation" (ἀλλοφύλῳ) and that no one is unclean (10:28). Moreover, Peter defends himself against the objections of "the circumcision party" not by appeal to a divine commission but by appeal to his vision and by appeal to the Gentiles' reception of the Holy Spirit (11:5-17). The apostles in Acts do not go to the geographical "end of the earth"; instead, it is Paul who essentially carries out this mission. In short, for Luke, Acts 1:8 defines for the Church the terms of its commission, and as the apostles are only the Church's representatives, they may quietly stay in Jerusalem and allow Paul to undertake the main mission.[40]

Even if it be argued that one of Luke's interests is in the mission's movement from circumcized "Gentiles" (the Samaritans) to Gentile whose circumcision might be meaningless (the eunuch) to uncircumcized Gentile (Cornelius), and that it is the question of whether or not circumcision is necessary that needs to be settled by further revelation, still the representatives of the Jerusalem apostles do not behave as though they are under a mandate from Jesus to undertake a Gentile mission. Acts is evidence that others besides the eleven began this work. What authorization did they claim? Hahn thinks that the command

to missionize among nations is "old" and that Matt 28:16-20
represents the Hellenistic Jewish Christian view of mission.[41]
The pre-Matthean midrash does not mention circumcision, a silence that can be interpreted as indicating (1) that the tradition was composed after the issue was settled,[42] or (2) that it
was composed to ground the authority of those who believed circumcision was not necessary, or (3) that circumcision was taken
for granted.[43] If the second of these possibilities is the
case, as I am inclined to believe, a further question must be
raised: would those who held this view have linked it to a tradition associated with the eleven?[44] Since this is not likely,
that association may be secondary; the midrash may originate in
the wider circle of Jesus' disciples.

     Further questions concerning the origin of the midrash and
its *Sitz im Leben* are left as open questions demanding further
study, and will be mentioned below in section C.

### B.  Matthean Redaction of the Midrash

     Matthew has made minor changes of style and vocabulary in
the midrash,[45] and two important insertions. In his redaction,
he places a sobering stress on the nature of discipleship as he
understands it. This focus offers clues to Matthew's interpretation of the triadic phrase in 28:19b.

     The eleven are called disciples in verse 16. The last time
these have appeared in a scene in this Gospel is at Gethsemane,
when "all the disciples forsook (Jesus) and fled" (26:56). The
incompleteness of the group gathered at the mountain in Galilee
is highlighted by the fact that Matthew has narrated at length
the betrayal and death of Judas (26:14-16, 25, 50; 27:3-10),
and earlier recorded a promise that "in the new world" when the
Son of Man will sit on his glorious throne, those who have followed him will also sit on twelve thrones, judging the twelve
tribes of Israel (19:28; cf. Luke 22:28-29).

     If Matthew is responsible for the reference to Galilee in
verse 16, drawn from Mark 16:7 (cf. 14:28), this would have
bearing on his use of the mountain symbol. The interpretation
of the mountain as the divine throne for Matthew may be jarring
to some, since the gospels do not incorporate unchanged aspects

of "heavenly ascents" like those in the pseudepigrapha and
later literature. Christian incarnational religious experience
and theology, in the insistence that God in Jesus communicates
with humanity in the concrete world, is considered to have
burst the bonds of Jewish apocalyptic.[46] It is possible that
the mountain in the midrash was thought of as a celestial mountain, in line with the meaning of the symbol in other literature we have examined. But even if the reference to Galilee is
traditional, and not Matthew's addition, the six other mountains in his Gospel seem to indicate that he understands the
seventh as both celestial and earthly. The theme of the divine
throne may be transmuted in Matthew.[47] In some sense we may
speak here of a manifestation of the throne of God on earth,
though the tension between heaven and earth is not dissolved.

In verse 17, Matthew makes his first *major* addition, the
statement about the reaction of the eleven to the sight of the
risen Jesus: worship is mixed with doubt (cf. 25:8, where fear
is mixed with great joy). The form of the midrash, a throne
theophany commission, may have suggested the inclusion of the
reaction to the numinous, but its meaning here is specifically
Matthean. Unlike the pericope about the walking on the water
(14:22-33), the final scene does not end with the overcoming of
doubt and a confession of faith. For Matthew discipleship involves terror and unresolved tension, which it is never his
habit to minimize. It involves also, however, the capacity to
worship Jesus.[48] A certain realism about the actual past per-
formances of the disciples, and perhaps as well an intimation
of difficulties ahead, prevent Matthew from presenting the moment of encounter with the risen Jesus as one of ecstasy and
joy (contrast Luke 24:32, 52-53). This reserve is a message
Matthew directs to certain groups or individuals in his church.[49]
The use of the verb μαθητεύω in verse 19a indicates that the
task given is understood as the work of expanding the kingdom
of God into the whole earth (cf. Dan 2:35, 44). The two other
uses of this verb in Matthew show that he associates it with
mention of the kingdom. In 13:52 he speaks of a scribe who has
been trained for or instructed about (μαθητευθείς)[50] the kingdom of heaven. In his description of Joseph of Arimathea as

having become a disciple (ἐμαθητεύθη) of Jesus (27:57), Matthew
is summarizing Mark's remark that Joseph "was also looking for
the kingdom of God" (Mark 15:34).

For Matthew two activities (not one, as in the midrash)
are integral to making disciples.  The mention of baptism is
followed by the second *major* Matthean addition, mention that
the disciples must teach all nations to observe all that Jesus
has commanded them (28:20a), the commands, that is, that have
been given during the earthly lifetime of Jesus to the eleven.[51]
One becomes a disciple by being baptized "in the name of the
Father and of the Son and of the Holy Spirit" *and* by observing
the Torah as Jesus has interpreted it.[52]  Baptism without
obedience would be inadequate, and perhaps in Matthew's mind
would be the equivalent of cheap words divorced from the actual
doing of the will of God (cf. 7:21; 25:44).  Even the reception
of the deepest revelation (see 11:25-27) does not make a person
a disciple without acceptance of the yoke of Jesus (11:28-30).
Matthew's addition of verses 28-30 to 11:25-27 makes the same
point as his addition of 28:20a to the midrash behind the final
pericope.  Jesus speaks in the Q saying (11:25-27) of a revelation to "babies" of the eschatological nature of certain
events;[53] he himself is presented as the one to whom all things
have been delivered, the only person who knows and is known by
the Father, and as the revealer of the Father.[54]  The saying
expresses belief that the disciple can participate in the Son's
knowledge and intimacy.  Matthew's addition of the invitation
to "all who are heavy laden" to take on the yoke of Jesus' discipline and learn from him (11:28-30) depicts Jesus in the role
of Wisdom and Torah incarnate.[55]  Submission to the teaching of
Jesus completes the revelatory experience.

Baptism is related to righteousness (3:15; 21:32, on the
baptism of John the Baptist), perhaps as identity is related to
life style.  Only in Matthew is the behavior demanded of disciples called righteousness (cf. 5:6, 10, 20; 6:33).  Matthew
conceives of a disciple as both a prophet and a righteous one
(cf. 10:41-42), a charismatic and one who keeps the Torah.[56]
This is the disciple who is in a sense equated with the master
(10:40, 24-25).[57]  Matthew shows that the disciple shares the

power of the risen one and faithfully transmits the teaching
of the earthly Jesus.[58]

The Evangelist may be affirming what he considers the
positive traits of opposing groups in his church, and integra-
ting these traits into his presentation of an ideal.  In this
Gospel we find both a positive evaluation of prophecy and
charismatic deeds and *revelatory insights*,[59] and emphasis on
the importance of *doing all the law*.[60]  The excesses of both
anomistic and legalistic behavior are condemned, the first in
the Christian "false prophets" and charismatic miracle workers
who do not do the will of God (24:11-12; 7:15-23), and the
second in those Pharisees who are hypocrites (23:1-36).  Matthew
warns against "Christians of an easy morality,"[61] and takes his
stand against a "post-Easter exegesis by a Church for which
Jesus' own deeds and teaching would no longer be of unambiguous
authority."[62]  Matthew warns also against those Pharisees who
"are a walking contradiction of visible justice (doing God's
will) and hidden lawlessness (rebellion against God's will)."[63]
These are those who lay heavy burdens on the shoulders of others
(23:4), who exalt themselves as pious but persecute and murder
the truly righteous, who "shut the kingdom of heaven against
people," neither entering themselves nor allowing others to
enter (23:13).

The addition in 28:20a of the stress on teaching the
earthly Jesus' commands illustrates Matthew's method of combat-
ing "uncontrolled prophetism."  The method used here is not to
emphasize the suffering and martyrdom that face the faithful,[64]
nor the "not-yet" of the eschatological life.[65]  It is, rather,
to emphasize obedience.  The balance between enthusiasm and
Torah-keeping is all-important in Matthew.  He is expressing
this balance by joining verse 20a to verses 18-19.[66]

If this is so, some further conclusions can be drawn about
the meaning of baptism "in the name of the Father and of the
Son and of the Holy Spirit" as it was understood in Matthew's
community.  The phrase seems to have summarized, as one might
have expected, the *enthusiastic experience*.  Baptism is an insertion into the exaltation of Jesus; it is the exaltation of
the disciple, the disciple's sharing in the power given to Jesus

(v. 18b). The association at the baptism of Jesus of the gift
of the Spirit with the (Father's) declaration of Sonship, and
this same association at the resurrection of Jesus (cf. Rom 1:
3-4; Acts 2:33; Heb 5:5) is most likely the ground of a connection made between Christian baptism, the gift of the Spirit to
the Christian and the Christian's adoption (cf. Gal 3:26-4:7;
Rom 8:14-16). The enthusiasts may have spoken of baptism "in
the name of the Father and of the Son and of the Holy Spirit"
as the moment of reception of their power in union with the
risen Jesus, the source of their abilities to prophesy, perform
miraculous healings, exorcise. Perhaps like some in Corinth
and in communities to which the author of Revelation writes,
they thought of themselves as "already reigning" (cf. 1 Cor 4:8;
Rev 1:6) and transferred proleptically to the divine realm.
This attitude is open to spiritualizing and individualizing
tendencies, and to an evaluation of the life of the baptized as
one in radical and total discontinuity with the life of Torah-
demands.

Matthew does not deny the connection between Jesus' exaltation and baptism. In fact, by inserting οὖν in verse 19a he
makes it clear that the command to baptize is a consequence of
that exaltation. But he understands the exalted one to be the
one of the ministry, not removed from the concerns of that ministry, nor totally transformed by new power. The final exaltation of Jesus is not for Matthew the moment of Jesus' reception
of the Spirit. Jesus was conceived "of the Holy Spirit" (1:18,
20),[67] which came upon him at his baptism (3:16). The Spirit
empowered his ministry (12:18-21, 28). Jesus is called God's
Son from his infancy (2:15), and for Matthew his baptism was
simply a proclamation of that fact (3:17). What the exaltation
means for Matthew is primarily the *full extension* of Jesus'
power (28:18). Already in Jesus' ministry the Spirit had
spoken through the twelve sent on their first mission (10:20).
The new power imparted to the eleven in virtue of the exaltation is the power to teach. Jesus' exaltation is the exaltation of the disciples and of those they disciple only insofar
as they engage in doing and teaching to do the will of God.
This must be so for Matthew because the heaven to which Jesus

has been exalted is the "place" where God's will is done (6:10).
The disciples' teaching is to make all nations responsible before the final judgment, at which all will be judged on the
basis of their treatment of the least (25:40, 45).  In a sense,
Matthew like Luke asks his audience why they stand "looking
into heaven" (Acts 1:11); Matthew redirects their gaze to the
human community.[68]

Matthew sees baptism "in the name of the Father and of the
Son and of the Holy Spirit" as a statement of a *theologia
gloriae* which must be explicated not by a *theologia crucis* but
by a *theologia caritatis*.  Incorporation into the new exalted
life of Jesus[69] is paradoxically incorporation into his old
life before death; this is the way Matthew understands the
transcendence of death.  Of the baptized are demanded serious
intellectual effort[70] and serious love even of enemies (5:44;
7:12; 22:34-40).  Earlier in the Gospel, it is not the act of
being baptized, but the act of loving by which people become
"sons" of the Father in heaven (5:45).[71]  "Sons of the kingdom"
are sown by the Son of Man in the world before the close of the
age (13:37-40).  This does not contradict Matthew's stress on
the uniqueness of Jesus' sonship,[72] but it does give it a corporate dimension.[73]  In the final pericope this dimension must
be remembered.  A person is introduced by baptism into the corporate life of the community.[74]

While I do not find Matthew's understanding of the triadic
phrase in 28:19b to be "trinitarian" in the sense in which I
have defined this term, I can safely say that Matthew's conception of God and of the Holy Spirit is centered in the revelation of and by Jesus of Nazareth.  The conception of Jesus in
this Gospel, on the other hand, is centered in the belief that
his source and destiny are one: in God and through the Holy
Spirit.  Matthew does not move directly to confront this as a
new insight into the divine.  Instead, his mind has leapt in-
tuitively to ponder the "old" command which will eventually be
regarded by others as endangered, or superceded, or re-expressed:
the *Shema'*.  From different angles, as Gerhardsson has shown,
the Gospel of Matthew affirms that the oneness of God is pro-
fessed and proclaimed perfectly in its unfolding narrative.[75]

We are privileged to witness a theological mind at work crea-
tively, generating insights which other generations will treat
as problems.  In the "unfinished" quality of this work lies its
fascination.

One pressing problem concerns the relation of Matthew's
community to the synagogue.  The image of the Danielic one like
a son of man empowered and enthroned, if it is an image clearly
recognized by Matthew in the midrash, may have been offered as
the climax of his Gospel in the light of the implications Matthew saw in it, as an image of reconciliation.  In Daniel we
have seen that the figure is a divine representative, both
heavenly and human, of the people of the holy ones of the Most
High (Dan 7:27), the *maskîlîm* and their followers.  His coming
to the Ancient of Days and his reception of the kingdom is a
statement of the ultimate triumph of authentic and faithful
Israel over all enemies--internal and external, and including
death.  He sums up the eternal value of the people of Israel,
the heavenly dimension of its existence and its position with
regard to all nations.  In the context of the book of Daniel,
and in the context of one important aspect of the midrashic
history of Daniel, that position is not simply to be the people
who will be served by all, but to be a people who will be a
revelation of righteousness for "many."  In *1 Enoch* 71:16 the
translated, transfigured one provides a way of righteousness
for all to walk.  Matthew innovates in his addition of verse
20a to the midrash, on the basis of this tradition which interprets the one like a son of man in terms of Israel's righteousness and wisdom.  What Black calls the "apotheosis of Israel"
occurs for Matthew in the full exaltation of the righteous
Jesus.  In his person the Evangelist sees Israel itself having
come and coming to its God, and drawing all nations to the God
of Israel.


## C.  Conclusions and Open Questions

The most important conclusion of this study is that the
triadic phrase in Matt 28:19b, naming the Father, the Son and
the Holy Spirit, is a development of the triad found in Daniel
7: Ancient of Days, one like a son of man and angels.  It is not

to be traced to the triad found in the Similitudes, although
evidence has been found of the use of common Danielic traditions.[76] The NT development is more than the adjustment and
alteration of titles; it is the process of "organic growth"
from the original Danielic vision, which is transmuted and kept
alive by adaptation. The Matthean triad and Matthew's understanding of it are integral parts of an interpretation of Daniel
which emphasizes the wisdom and apocalyptic elements of that
work, highlighting the theme of transcendence of death on the
part of authentic Israel and highlighting the importance for all
nations of Israel's exaltation. In Christian belief in the exaltation of the historical person Jesus of Nazareth, the mythological and semi-mythological elements of the book of Daniel
and of its interpretive tradition come to a new a distinctive
focus. The vision of the eschatological theophany is not left
"in the world of myth." Joined to the commission to make disciples, it is presented as inspiration and impetus for the
renewal of history by means of the formation of a new community
of the Son of Man.

I conclude also that behind Matt 28:16-20 a traditional
midrash, containing the triadic phrase, can be isolated. This
midrash may have functioned as a liturgical tradition associated
with the rite of baptism, possibly seen by some as the fulfillment and extension of the rite of John the Baptist. Matthew
has redacted this midrash in line with his emphasis on the essential importance of obedience to Jesus as ultimate *Maskil*,
whose life and teaching offer a hermeneutical key to the interpretation of Torah for the present age. The Matthean pericope
is a statement of the Evangelist's ideal of balance between
enthusiasm and righteousness.

I conclude further that there is not sufficient evidence
to indicate that the triadic phrase, either at the midrashic or
at the Matthean redactional stage, is trinitarian. But two aspects of the thought world out of which it originates could
impel toward trinitarian thinking: (a) the assimilation of
angels and Holy Spirit, of the "personal" beings of the heavenly
court and the impersonal power of the divine; (b) the image of
the human yet heavenly figure now permanently in the divine

council.  In the NT, hierarchical triadic texts which subordinate the angels to the Son of Man show the progressive conception of that figure as more than angelic.  The "limited apotheosis" of human figures in OT and intertestamental texts here
breaks through its limits.  In the Matthean triadic phrase, the
Father, the Son and the Holy Spirit are linked closely in a way
that has not yet required explanation.  In several pre-Matthean
Danielic traditions and in the Gospel of Matthew itself there
are indications that the Son (of Man) retains a corporate
dimension.

Finally, this study, conceived as a phase of a comprehensive effort critically to examine the biblical bases of the
Trinitarian dogma, leads to the conclusion that there is a wide
field for exploration of this topic, which can open up perspectives concerning the importance of these bases as statements
of fundamental early Christian belief and self-understanding.
Whatever the idea of the Trinity became, in its triadic origins
it was neither boring nor a contemplation of the inaccessible
and irrelevant.

The following are areas in which further research and coordination are necessary in order to bring us to firmer conclusions regarding the triadic phrase in its Matthean and biblical
context.

(1) More thorough use of the method of comparative midrash
will enable us to see more clearly the distinctive streams of
interpretation and adaptation of Daniel, and their interplay.
Deeper knowledge of that variety will give us a better sense of
the choices made by interpreters.  For example, the relationship between the Son of Man traditions in the Similitudes and
in the NT must be more carefully probed in order to place the
understanding of Danielic traditions in a broader spectrum and
acquire more clues to the sociological matrixes of these traditions.[77]  Passages such as those treated in the Addendum to
Chapter V and many NT texts not treated here can be brought to
bear on this study only when adequate and convincing methodological controls are developed to make sure that simple parallels
of language and concept are not mistaken for true allusions,
adaptations and interpretations of the OT text.

(2) The question of the precise understanding of baptism
in the circle in which the pre-Matthean midrash was written
should be explored.  In my opinion, this may have some relationship to the expectations and baptismal practices of John
the Baptist.  Further, I think there are clues that an interpretation of Daniel 7 in the context of early Merkabah thought
and experience is involved in materials concerning the Baptist.
These suggestions should be tested analytically.

(3) No effort has been made here to examine the problem of
the relation between NT triads which appear in the context of
allusions to Daniel and those which appear without such allusions.  The full picture of NT trinitarianism, incipient or
developed, requires this effort.

(4) Examination is needed of the relationship between the
midrash behind Matt 28:16-20 and the post-resurrection commissionings of the other gospels and of Acts 1:1-11.  This study
might provide information about the *Sitz im Leben* of the
midrash.

(5) The use of Merkabah traditions by different groups in
first century Judaism, and different perceptions of the messianic implications of Daniel 7 should be further explored,
especially in the light of responses to the war of 66-70 and
belief in the survival of Israel in that political crisis.  In
my opinion, the lines of development of triadic imagery (in the
context of Danielic interpretations) which I have attempted to
trace in this present work suggest that there was Christian use
of Merkabah imagery and mystical tradition which has not yet
been adequately appreciated.

It is my hope that in the course of this discussion "raw
material" has been generated for the systematic theologian in-
terested in the roots of Trinitarian thought.  In the interests
of dialogue, I raise the following questions which are beyond
the scope of my competence to deal with, but part of the concern that motivated this work.  What light does this investigation of Matt 28:19b shed on the post-NT creation of Trinitarian
theologies, those later judged both heretical and orthodox?
Käsemann has argued that "beginnings are decisive for the time
to follow, and that, however obscurely and strangely, they

contain the laws of the future."[78]   Can this principle be illustrated by a study of the dogma of the Trinity which traces
it from elements of Jewish apocalyptic, transmuted into a
Christian exaltation theology?   Do developments in terms of
Greco-Roman philosophy work out some of the biblical insights
recovered?   Or are the latter noninfluential, ignored or misunderstood, so that the history of the dogma is primarily a
process of forgetting, or of breaking free of the origins?

Paul Van Buren states that "the church's characteristic
doctrine--that of the Trinity" should be seen to express the
peculiarly Gentile (in contrast to Jewish) apprehension of the
One God of Israel.   He regards this doctrine as simple and inevitable, expressing "nothing less than the only possible Gentile apprehension of the God of the Jews.   It comes out of
their own Gentile experience.   Drawn by the divine spirit, by
way of the Jew Jesus, only in this way can Gentiles apprehend
the God of Israel" as the God of Israel.[79]   But I have argued
that the Matthean triadic phrase is not, contrary to some past
scholarly opinion, primarily a statement by and/or for Gentiles,
but a statement of Jewish and early Jewish Christian eschatological hope and mystical experience.   Is it correct to sense
that critical attention to pre-trinitarian thinking and imagery
may open up possibilities of understanding a new phase of Jewish Christian theology, in the context of the resurgence and
transformation of old mythologies and under the pressure of the
events of the life and death of Jesus of Nazareth and belief in
his resurrection?   Attention especially to the Danielic component in pre-trinitarianism suggests a rethinking of the differences between Jewish and Gentile apprehensions of God.[80]

How are we to understand the relation of myth and symbol
to analogical and literal talk about God?   Is it possible in
this specific case to retrace the way poetic language eventuates
in conceptual language, the way symbol gives rise to thought?
Have we--or should we have--any means of looking with what
Ricoeur calls "secondary naiveté" at the symbolic base discovered?

Finally, has this probe of an aspect of the background of
Trinitarian dogma offered material to support the suggestion of

some scholars that rethinking of this dogma is of value today
as an alternative to or correction of static concepts of God?
If something of the dynamic, event-centered imagery traced
from Daniel 7 to Matthew 28 is retained and carried forward
into Trinitarian thinking, does it eventuate in an understanding of God as involved in the process of vindication and reconciliation through and beyond death?  Braaten has remarked that
"the apocalypticists grasped the idea that the whole universe
of reality is being drawn through struggle, conflict and pain
into the final unity of God."[81]  In the traditions examined is
found the hint of an idea of God as the one to whom, with whom
and by whom humanity is or could be travelling.  In different
phases of the interpretive tradition associated with Daniel 7
there is evidence of the continuation of what Collins calls the
"political mysticism" of the original, which Matthew captures
in a new key in his vision of the enthusiastic and righteous
world community.  If this tradition retains its vitality as it
contributes to the formation of dogma, then it is difficult to
see that dogma as irrelevant "mystery."

[1] See above, pp. 29-42.

[2] Hubbard, *Matthean Redaction*, 122-23. See above, p. 33.

[3] Fuller speaks also of a pre-Matthean tradition of a post-resurrection missionary charge. He thinks it read simply, "Preach the gospel," and contained a command to baptize. There was, however, no pre-Matthean "narrative" of the charge. Fuller believes that Matthew combined this tradition with two other traditional sayings: one about authority (28:18b) and the other about the presence of Jesus (20b). See above, pp. 31-32.

[4] Strecker, *Der Weg*, 210. See above, pp. 34-35.

[5] Meier, "Two Disputed Questions," 412, 416; see above, p. 36. He does not attempt to recover the wording of this tradition.

[6] See above, pp. 43-44. An infinitive (such as "to make disciples") may be understood after "commissioned them" in v. 16).

[7] I have argued that the verb μαθητεύω is a Mattheanism, and the coordination of the circumstantial participles βαπτί-ζοντες (v. 19a) and διδάσκοντες (v. 20a) with this finite verb is a Matthean stylistic pattern. But the combination of "making disciples" and baptizing is found in John 4:1; this may indicate that the association of these ideas in Matt 28:19 is traditional (see above, pp. 43-44.

[8] See above, p. 114.

[9] We have seen that the stone-son wordplay appears in the history of Danielic interpretation.

[10] Four other NT passages which I think may use Dan 7:14 LXX speak of the Father and the Son. Cf. John 5:19-29; 13:3; 17:1-5 and Rev 2:26-27 (the Son [of God] is mentioned in v. 18). Aspects of Father-Son terminology appear frequently in wider Danielic contexts (Mark 13:32; 8:38 pars.; Matt 25:31-46, etc.). See above, p. 311 n. 142, citing Loader.

[11] A parallel but with different stress is found in the promise of Jesus' future presence in Acts 1:11 (see above, p. 36).

[12] In an Addendum to Chapter V, I have mentioned also that the exalted righteous one of Wis 1:1-6:21 is portrayed as a *Maskîl* or σοφός (4:17) and champion of the Law (2:12). In my opinion, this figure is an adaptation of the figures of the one like a son of man of Daniel 7 and the *maskîlîm* of Dan 12:3. See above, pp. 242-43.

[13]The Lamb worthy to open the scroll of eschatological secrets and to activate God's final plans for the end time appears in Revelation 5, which I have considered in part a dramatization of the eschatological meaning of Dan 7:14.

[14]See also Matt 11:28-30, where Jesus' "yoke" and "burden" are offered. This material was not, in the opinion of Suggs, originally joined to 11:25-27 (*Wisdom, Christology and Law*, 79-81).

[15]The Lamb, as noted, is not explicitly identified as the one like a son of man, but features of this scene indicate that Daniel 7 is being evoked. See above, p. 311 n. 146 and pp. 266-67.

[16]See Section E of the previous chapter.

[17]Compare the proclamation of "an eternal gospel" by an angel to all who dwell on earth in Rev 14:6-7 (see above, 284-85).

[18]And in contrast to Matt 13:36-43, where there is no theophany but the mention of the "sowing" (preaching or teaching?) of the exalted Son of Man in the kosmos. At the end the Son of Man "sends" his angels to gather evildoers and punish them.

[19]See above, p. 78 n. 204. Hubbard understands this as Matthean redaction of an element in the proto-commission, of the statement that those who saw the risen Jesus were glad, though some disbelieved. But Meier is not certain that any reaction of the disciples was mentioned in the pre-Matthean tradition ("Two Disputed Questions," 416 n. 37). The theme of disbelief does appear in the Markan Appendix 16:14 and Luke 24:31-41, and perhaps an original expression of doubt was transferred by the Evangelist from John 20:19-23 to the separate episode in 20:24-29 (see Hubbard, *Matthean Redaction*, 105, citing Brown, *Gospel According to John*, 2.1028). It is important to note that the doubt in Mark 16:14 and John 20:24-29 is doubt concerning the testimony that Jesus has been seen alive. In Luke 24:37-41 the physical nature or identity of the one being seen is doubted (cf. Luke 24:25: doubt concerning the testimony of the prophets). There is no reaction similar to these in Acts 1:1-11. The doubt in Matt 28:17 is not explained, but expresses an immediate reaction to the sight of Jesus.

[20]See Hamerton-Kelly, "Matthew," 581.

[21]Meier, "Two Disputed Questions," 411.

[22]I am assuming that the mountain symbolized God's throne in the midrash as in the final Matthean pericope. The midrash may have spoken of the seventh mountain. Or, more likely, Matthew understood the symbolism and made it (subtly) clearer by giving his readers six other mountain scenes. But, as will be seen, Matthew may not have understood the symbol in precisely the same way as the author of the midrash.

[23]Strecker and Meier think that Matthew is responsible for redacting the liturgical tradition "to make it a vehicle of (a) the one great post-resurrection appearance of Jesus to the eleven in Galilee; and (b) the great missionary commission" which is a universal mission to all nations ("Two Disputed Questions," 411). But the phrase "all nations" is part of the original midrash, drawn from Dan 7:14 LXX. And mention of making disciples by baptizing may also be pre-Matthean (cf. n. 7 above). The tradition already contains the element of a world-wide commission.

[24]Matt 13:36-43, as we have seen, presents the exalted Son of Man at work in the kosmos before the parousia. There is no allusion to Dan 7:14 in this text, however. Acts 7:55-56; Rev 1:12-16 and 14:14 use Dan 7:13 to depict the exalted Jesus in a heavenly appearance.

[25]On Acts 1:1-12, see discussion of Meier's position (above, p. 36) and discussion of this scene as a theophany commission (above, pp. 282-83). In *4 Ezra* 13, it will be recalled, we find an exalted Danielic figure, called Son, on a mountain, effecting the gathering of a new people of Israel, some of whom must pass through water to return (above, p. 235).

[26]In addition, L. Cerfaux claims (I think rightly) that the Q pericope uses Dan 2:19-23 and perhaps Isa 42:1 ("Les Sources scripturaires de Mt., XI, 25-30," *ETL* 31 [1955] 333, 335 n. 21). "These things" (Matt 11:25) may be an allusion to Dan 11:32 LXX: the *maskîlîm* are preparing the people "who know these things." Both sayings seem to be references to knowledge of God and apocalyptic secrets (on the Q saying, see W. D. Davies, "'Knowledge' in the Dead Sea Scrolls and Matthew 11: 25-30," *HTR* 46 [1953] 137; Meier, *Vision*, 79-80).

[27]Because of parallels between the passages, Lange claims that Matt 28:16-20 is a "new edition" of the central articulation of the Easter experience of the people behind Q, of their existence, self-understanding and missionary activity (*Erscheinen*; see the review by E. L. Bode, *CBQ* 37 [1975] 125-26). Bacon thinks that Matthew adapted 11:27-30 to the form of a post-resurrection commission (*Jesus, the Son of God* [New Haven: Yale University, 1911] 3). Kingsbury calls 11:27 the pre-Easter counterpart to the post-Easter passage 28:18b (*Matthew*, 59). See also E. P. Blair, "Jesus and Salvation in the Gospel of Matthew," *McCormick Quarterly* 20/21 (1966/68) 301-8.

[28]John 3:34-35, which contains the triad of the Father, the Son and the Spirit, may combine an allusion to Dan 7:14 LXX with an allusion to Isa 11:2.

[29]The phrase ἠγαλλιάσατο ἐν τῷ πνεύματι τῷ ἁγίῳ in Luke 10:21 is without Scriptural parallel. Although most critics believe that it is Lukan, I think we would expect, rather, the common Lukan phrase, "full of the Holy Spirit." Mention of the Spirit appears several times before passages I consider allusions to Dan 7:13-14: in John 3:34; 3:1-11; Rev 1:10; 4:2; Acts

7:55.  Matthew may have dropped the phrase (1) because of his placement of the pericope, and (2) because, being wary of ecstatic Christianity without moral substance, he may have been reluctant to run the risk of presenting Jesus as an ecstatic (see E. Käsemann, "The Beginnings of Christian Theology," *JTC* 6 [1969] 19-20, 28; R. Scroggs, "The Exaltation of the Spirit by Some Early Christians," *JBL* 84 [1965] 359-60).

[30]Jeremias, *NT Theology*, 61.  The discussion in Mark 11:27-33 (pars. Matt 21:23-27; Luke 20:1-8) linking Jesus' ἐξουσία with the baptism of John may indicate that Dan 7:14 was drawn on to describe that baptism, but I make no judgment here on the authenticity of Matt 11:25-27 par.

[31]Suggs, *Wisdom, Christology and Law*, 78, 82; M. Rist, "Is Matt 11:25-30 a Primitive Baptismal Hymn?" *JBL* 15 (1935) 69-77.  Like John 3:34-35; 13:3; 17:2; 5:26-27 (cf. Mark 2:10), Matt 11:27 appears to transfer back into the ministry of Jesus the original reference to his empowering at Easter, reapplying Dan 7:14.

[32]See *Apocalypse of Adam* 85:22-26 for mention of "the hidden knowledge of Adam which he gave to Seth--which is the holy baptism of those who know the eternal knowledge" (*Gnosis*, 2.23).  R. McL. Wilson describes this apocalypse as a non-Christian gnostic document.  Christian material is not present in it, "or at least is not mentioned openly and without disguise."  It originated in Jewish baptist circles in the first or second century and was later revised in a gnostic sense (*Gnosis*, 2.15).  G. MacRae speaks of the indication in this work that "the practice of baptism has given way to a spiritualized concept of baptism as the reception of gnosis" ("Adam, Apocalypse of," *IDBSup*, 10).

[33]Contrast Hartman's theory concerning Mark 13, pars. (above, pp. 283-84).

[34]See above, p. 44; against Gundry (above, p. 114) who argues that Matthew prefixed the phrase, "all days," to gain the allusion.  If the suggestion made here is correct, it may be an indication that Matthew did recognize an allusion to Dan 7:14 in the midrash.

[35]Contrast Hubbard's position (above, p. 319), and that of Strecker and Meier (above, p. 343 n. 23).

[36]See above, pp. 7, 23.

[37]As far as I can tell from an analysis of the use of the term Holy Spirit in the Gospel of Matthew, to Matthew it denotes an impersonal force or power (see above, pp. 23-24, 26).

[38]See Brown, "Difficulties," 151; cf. above, p. 73 n. 143.

[39]A world mission is decreed there, presupposing that salvation is not restricted to Israel (Haenchen, *Acts*, 144).  Using Isa 49:6, Acts 13:46-48 interprets "ends of the earth" to mean Gentiles.

[40]Ibid., 144.

[41]Hahn, *Mission*, 51. He does not think the exaltation
Christology found in this pericope, however, belongs to the
earliest tradition.

[42]This *may* have been the dominant understanding of the
midrash by Matthew's time. Meier holds that the fact that the
command in 28:19 does not include the requirements of circumcision or adherence to food laws, plus the fact that the pericope shows an apparent lack of concern about the delay of the
parousia, are indications that the Gospel of Matthew is relatively late, perhaps between 80-90 A.D. (*Law and History*, 7).

[43]That is, that the midrash was originally at home in a
Law-observant mission to all nations. This possibility awaits
proof that there was such a mission that was not simply a reaction against the mission that abrogated the Law in some sense.

[44]It has been argued above that the midrash may mention the
eleven, though it is impossible to be certain of this (see pp.
43, 321).

[45]See above, pp. 43-44, on Mattheanisms in Matt 28:16-20.

[46]I owe these reflections to J. P. Meier (in a letter to
me). Cf. W. G. Rollins ("The New Testament and Apocalyptic,"
*NTS* 17 [1970/71] 472): in proclaiming Jesus of Nazareth as
Messiah, the early church "broke ground for the reclamation of
history and of 'world' as the locus of God's self disclosure."
One may wonder, however, to what extent incarnational theology
may be post-Matthean, and how precisely Jewish and Christian
mysticism differ in respect to the meaning of such symbols.

[47]The possibility that still in Matthew the seventh mountain is not a specific geographical location but a locus of
revelation is recognized by many recent scholars who, unlike
their predecessors, do not attempt to identify a specific mountain (Tabor or Hermon), speaking rather of mythical imagery
here; see above, pp. 33, 89, 238. H. Koester speaks of Christian
language in the NT "caught between myth and history" ("The Role
of Myth in the New Testament," *ANQ* 8 [1968] 184). But see now
the exploration of G.W.E. Nickelsburg ("Enoch, Levi and Peter:
Recipients of Revelation in Upper Galilee," *JBL* 100 [1981] 575-
600); he takes seriously the geographical data in texts (to
which Matt 28:16-20 should be added) which point to the area
around Tell Dan and Mount Hermon as sacred territory associated
with visionary activity.

[48]Of the thirteen times the verb προσκυνέω is used in
Matthew, eleven times Jesus is its object (see above, p. 78 n.
204, for the list of the five times it is redactional alteration of Mark). It is used nine times in Revelation with God
enthroned as the object (4:10; 5:14; 7:11; 11:16; 14:7; 15:4;
19:4, 10; 22:9). No other NT writer uses it as Matthew does,
of persons approaching Jesus during his ministry as well as
after his resurrection. The verb often means prostration, and
is a response to royalty and divinity.

[49]Kingsbury argues that the disciples represent the Christians of Matthew's church.  They are not idealized, but insights are attributed to them during the ministry that the other gospels insist are post-resurrection insights (*Matthew*, 33).  On the other hand, Matthew links the term "disciples" to the twelve chosen by Jesus, to make it clear that the only true discipleship is that of the earthly Jesus (U. Luz, "Discipleship," *IDBSup*, 233).

[50]Kingsbury, *Matthew*, 157.

[51]Ellis argues that this means that custody of the messianic Torah of Jesus has been given to them, and that the eleven now replace the Pharisees as the leaders of the true Israel (*Matthew*, 138).  But focus here is more likely on the earthly Jesus as teacher, not on some centralized teaching authority claiming descent from the eleven and opposing the Jamnian rabbis.  This is not simply the substitution of one power group for another, but a rethinking of the proper uses of power.

[52]The Torah is still valid for Matthew, interpreted by the standard of Jesus' teachings and conduct.  Matthew's Jesus warns against lawlessness (7:21-23; 24:10-12) primarily because it leads to the cooling off of most people's love.  And love is considered the epitome of all religious obligation laid down in the Torah and the Prophets (7:12).  The obligation to love even enemies is the summation of Jesus' interpretation (5:44).  The Torah of Moses is in this sense the Torah of Jesus the Messiah.  Cf. Hamerton-Kelly, "Matthew," 581.

[53]Suggs (*Wisdom, Christology and Law*, 95) argues that "these things" in 11:25 refers to the mighty works (11:20-21) as eschatological signs (see also Davies, *Setting*, 207; Kingsbury, *Matthew*, 62 n. 57).

[54]See Suggs, *Wisdom, Christology and Law*, 77.  Meier (*Vision*, 79-80) understands "these things" as the totality of apocalyptic secrets, "reducible to one basic mystery: the mutual knowledge and relationship between the Father and the Son."

[55]Suggs, *Wisdom, Christology and Law*, 95-96, 100-6; Hamerton-Kelly, "Matthew," 582; H. D. Betz, "The Logion of the Easy Yoke and of Rest (Matt 11:28-30)," *JBL* 86 (1967) 22; H. Conzelmann, "Wisdom in the NT," *IDBSup*, 958.

[56]As Kingsbury points out, the itinerant missionaries sent out to proclaim the gospel of the Kingdom to Jews and Gentiles are also called the "wise" and "scribes" (23:34); "The Figure of Peter in Matthew's Gospel as a Theological Problem," *JBL* 98 (1979) 78 n. 37.

[57]Authentic disciples perform the same miracles as Jesus (10:1, 7 with 9:35; 4:23; 11:5), their activity considered a continuation of his.  Their preaching of repentance (10:7) repeats the preaching of the Baptist (3:2) and of Jesus (4:17).  And, finally, they are commissioned to teach as and what he taught.

[58]U. Luz, "Die Jünger im Matthäusevangelium," *ZNW* 62
(1971) 141-71, cited by Harrington, "Matthean Studies," 381.

[59]See Strecker, *Der Weg*, 137 n. 4. E. Käsemann, on the
other hand, thinks that Matthew wants nothing to do with the
enthusiastic movement in his church, but is rather himself an
"ethical rigorist" and representative of a "budding Christian
rabbinism." He finds enthusiasm and imminent apocalyptic expectation not characteristic of Matthew himself ("Beginnings,"
19, 20, 30).

[60]Ellis, *Matthew*, 141.

[61]E. Schweizer, "Observance of the Law and Charismatic
Activity in Matthew," *NTS* 16 (1970) 216 n. 2.

[62]Ibid., 217. In modern terms, says Schweizer, Matthew is
skeptical about "a kerygma theology, in which the Gospel would
be totally identified with the preaching after Easter without
being safeguarded by a strict faithfulness to Jesus' own
teaching"; see pp. 218-19.

[63]Meier, *Vision*, 164.

[64]As has been noted, Matthew does not use the term baptism
as a metaphor for Jesus' death, a metaphor which does appear in
Mark 10:38-39; Luke 12:50; Rom 6:3-8; cf. Col 2:12. Matthew,
of course, does elsewhere underline his belief that the life of
the disciple involves the traumas of dissent, persecution and
betrayal (10:17-21) and death (24:9).

[65]He does, with the phrase συντέλεια τοῦ αἰῶνος in v. 20b,
evoke the memory of his descriptions of the final "coming" of
the Son of Man, when the elect will be gathered (24:3, 30-31),
the wicked damned (13:38-42) and the righteous exalted (13:43).
In terms of the Gospel as a whole, the stress on the parousia
is a strong counterweight to an exaltation theology.

[66]Critics have wondered why the formulation "make disciples
...baptizing...teaching" (1) contains no mention of the preaching of the kerygma and of acceptance of Jesus by faith, and (2)
places baptizing before rather than after teaching. In Acts 8:
26-39 we find the sequence: instruction, profession of belief,
and then baptism. Matthew is seen to be departing in 28:19-20
from the normative missionary procedure because "he takes for
granted the preaching of the kerygma and the subsequent act of
faith in Jesus which is the *sine qua non* of discipleship. His
concern in the formulation, therefore, is not with the prelimi-
naries of discipleship which he takes for granted, but with the
perfection or essence of discipleship" (Ellis, *Matthew*, 135).
Ellis thinks the Gospel is written for those who are already
Christians and for catechumens who are on the way to becoming
Christians. Matthew is not concerned with the totality of the
missionary enterprise. But the formulation of Matt 28:19a-20a
is dictated in part by the formulation of the pre-Matthean
midrash, perhaps already in a liturgical tradition.

[67]See Brown (*Birth*, 161) for the idea that for both Matthew and Luke the birth of Jesus constituted his coronation as Davidic king.  We are moving in the Infancy Narratives toward the concept of Jesus' pre-existence, which will eventually drastically influence interpretation of the Matthean triadic phrase.

[68]It is debated whether Matthew intended "the least" in the parable of the last judgment (25:31-46) to be understood as (a) disciples of Jesus, Christian missionaries, or (b) all those human beings in need.  The first view is based mainly on the fact that in other NT texts solidarity between Jesus and his disciples is expressed (cf. Matt 10:40; Luke 10:16; Matt 10:42; Mark 9:41), and the fact that Matthew elsewhere calls the disciples "little ones" (cf. 10:42; 18:6, 10, 14).  See L. Cope, "Matthew XXV:31-46 -- The Sheep and Goats Reinterpreted," *NovT* 11 (1969) 32-44; J. Lambrecht, "The Parousia Discourse; Composition and Content in Mt XXIV-XXV," *L'Evangile selon saint Matthieu*, 333-40; Kingsbury, *Matthew*, 156; Jeremias, *Parables*, 207-9.  The second view, which I accept here, is more in line with Matthew's presentation of Jesus' demands and examples, and his awareness that the disciples themselves are subject to the judgment.  See Tödt, *Son of Man*, 75; Ellis, *Matthew*, 93; Schweizer, *Good News*, 477-79; Meier, "Nations or Gentiles," 99 n. 18, and other references given there.

[69]Trilling, it will be recalled, speaks of baptism here as "into life in God" (*Gospel According to St. Matthew*, 269).

[70]This Gospel stresses that disciples must understand Jesus and have knowledge of his ἐξουσία.  Understanding is based on revelation, not human achievement, but it is also recognition (see G. Barth, "Matthew's Understanding of the Law," 110).  The discipled scribe's intellectual effort is spoken of in 13:52. The hermeneutical key to the Torah is thought of as having been given to be used.

[71]Matthew's version of this saying is about a "sonship" in the present, in contrast to Luke's version (6:35; cf. Matt 5:9). Rev 21:7 also places the conqueror's "sonship" in the future world; Rev 2:26-28 applies Ps 2:8-9 to him at "the end."  See Schweizer (*Good News*, 95) on the Matthean insistence that "this miracle can take place on earth if a person grows into total obedience" and becomes like God in action.

[72]Cf. Kingsbury, "Peter," 77.

[73]In Matt 25:31-46 the identity between the Son of Man and the least is conceived realistically (cf. Schweizer, *Good News*, 476).  It is not a question of acts of love shown to the king and judge "personally" or as an individual, but to the least (his "brothers") and through them to himself (Jeremias, *Parables*, 207).  This pericope indicates that for Matthew the Danielic one like a son of man was an inclusive person.

[74]See Strecker, "The Concept of History," 229.

[75]See above, pp. 25-26.  Matthew's focus on the *Shema'* is not an answer to the problem of the interrelationship among the members of the triad.  The interrelationship is not yet seen as a problem.

[76]See above, pp. 296 n. 25, 297 n. 33, 299 n. 54, 301-2 nn. 71-72, 315 n. 171, 315 n. 176.  Further, the judgment scenes in Matt 25:31-46 (a triadic text) and *1 Enoch* 45, 62-63 may draw on common tradition involving the transfer to the one like a son of man of the power of judgment.  The theme of recognition of the righteous one from Isaiah 52-53 has also influenced this tradition, vis Wisdom 2, 4-5.  Contrast Hindley, "Towards a Date," 545 n. 1; Nickelsburg, review of Milik, *Books of Enoch*, *CBQ* 40 (1978) 417-18; Mearns, "Dating," 365; J. Theisohn, *Der auserwählte Richter* (Göttingen: Vandenhoeck & Ruprecht, 1975) 152-82, refuted by Knibb, "Date," 357.  Knibb is skeptical about supposed NT dependence on the Similitudes, which he dates to the late first century A.D.

[77]On the basis of the limited investigation here, it seems possible that the Similitudes and certain related NT texts are the products of groups which shared a similar background but eventually grew apart.  That group in which the Similitudes was produced may have either maintained or reasserted its "conservative" Jewish identity more strongly, or developed a strange type of Christianity in which the messianic figure was closely assimilated to that of Enoch and understood primarily as eschatological judge.  See Schweizer ("Son of Man Again," 260) for different but related speculations.

[78]Käsemann, "Beginnings of Christian Theology," 17.

[79]P. Van Buren, "Affirmation of the Jewish People: a Condition of Theological Coherence," *JAAR* 45 (1977) 1075, 1094-97.

[80]A dialogue by P. Lapide and J. Moltmann furthers this rethinking (*Jewish Monotheism and Christian Trinitarian Doctrine* [Philadelphia: Fortress, 1981]).

[81]Carl E. Braaten, "The Significance of Apocalypticism for Systematic Theology," *Int* 25 (1971) 497.

SELECTED BIBLIOGRAPHY

I. Texts and Translations

A. Bible and Apocrypha

Aland, K.; Black, M.; Martini, C. M.; Metzger, B. M.; Wikgren, A., eds. *The Greek New Testament*. 2nd ed. New York: American Bible Society, 1968.

Kittel, R., ed. *Biblia Hebraica*. 7th ed. Stuttgart: Württembergische Bibelanstalt, 1966.

May, H. G., and Metzger, B. M., eds. *The Oxford Annotated Bible with the Apocrypha* (Revised Standard Version). New York: Oxford University, 1965.

Rahlfs, A., ed. *Septuaginta*. 2 vols. Stuttgart: Württembergische Bibelanstalt, 1971.


B. Pseudepigrapha, Targums and Rabbinic
Literature, Josephus

Black, Matthew, ed. *Apocalypsis Henochi Graece*. Leiden: Brill, 1970.

Bonner, Campbell, ed. *The Last Chapters of the Enoch in Greek*. Darmstadt: Wissenschaftliche Buchgesellschaft, 1968 (reprint of 1937 ed.).

Charles, R. H., ed. *The Apocrypha and Pseudepigrapha of the Old Testament, in English*. Vol. 2: *Pseudepigrapha*. Oxford: Clarendon, 1969 (reprint of 1913 ed.).

_____. *The Book of Enoch*. Oxford: Clarendon, 1893, 1912.

Diez-Macho, Alejandro, ed. *Neofiti I. Genesis*. Eng. trans. by M. McNamara and M. Maher. Madrid: Consejo Superior de Investigaciones Cientificas, 1968.

Epstein, I., ed. *The Babylonian Talmud. Ḥagigah*. Trans. I. Abrahams. London: Soncino, 1938.

Freedman, H., and Simon, Maurice, eds. *Midrash Rabbah*. 10 vols. London: Soncino, 1961 (reprint of 1939 ed.).

Josephus. 9 vols. LCL. Ed. by H. St. J. Thackeray, R. Marcus, A. Wikgren, and L. H. Feldman. Cambridge: Harvard University, 1926-65.

Kraft, R. A.; Attridge, H.; Spittler, R.; and Timbie, J., eds. *The Testament of Job*. Missoula, MT: Scholars, 1974.

*Midrash on the Psalms*. Vols. 1 and 2. Trans. William G.
    Braude. New Haven: Yale University, 1959.

Sperber, Alexander, ed. *The Bible in Aramaic*, Vol. 3: *The
    Latter Prophets According to Targum Jonathan*. Leiden:
    Brill, 1962.

Vaillant, A. *Le Livre des Secrets d'Hénoch*. Paris: Institut
    d'études slaves, 1952.


                          C. Qumran Scrolls

Barthelemy, D. and Milik, J. T., eds. *Qumran Cave 1*. DJD 1.
    Oxford: Clarendon, 1955.

Dupont-Sommer, A. *The Essene Writings from Qumran*. Trans.
    from the 2nd French edition of 1960 by G. Vermes.
    Cleveland: World, 1969.

Fitzmyer, Joseph A., ed. *The Genesis Apocryphon of Qumran
    Cave 1*. Rome: Biblical Institute, 1971.

Milik, Jozef T., ed., with the collaboration of Matthew Black.
    *The Books of Enoch: Aramaic Fragments of the Qumran Cave 4*.
    Oxford: Clarendon, 1976.

Vermes, G. *The Dead Sea Scrolls in English*. Baltimore:
    Penguin, 1973.


                      II. Other Literature

Albright, W. F. and Mann, C. S. *The Gospel According to
    Matthew*. AB 26. Garden City, NY: Doubleday, 1971.

Allen, Leslie C. "The Old Testament Background of (ΠΡΟ)OPIZEIN
    in the New Testament." *NTS* 17 (1970/71) 104-108.

Allen, Willoughby C. *The Gospel According to St. Matthew*.
    ICC. New York: Scribners, 1925.

Alsup, John E. *The Post-Resurrection Appearance Stories of the
    Gospel Tradition: A History of Tradition Analysis, with
    Text-Synopsis*. Calwer Theologische Monographien, Series A:
    Bibelwissenschaft 5. Stuttgart: Calwer, 1975.

Barr, James. "Daniel." *PCB*. Ed. by M. Black and H. H. Rowley.
    London: Nelson, 1962.

Barrett, C. K. "Stephen and the Son of Man." Pp. 32-38 in
    *Apophoreta*, Festschrift E. Haenchen. Berlin: A. Töpel-
    mann, 1964.

Barth, Gerhard. "Matthew's Understanding of the Law." *Tradi-
    tion and Interpretation in Matthew*. Ed. by G. Bornkamm,
    trans. by Percy Scott. Philadelphia: Westminster, 1963.

Barth, M. "Baptism." *IDBSup*, 85-89. Nashville: Abingdon, 1976.

Beasley-Murray, G. R. *Baptism in the New Testament*. London:
    Macmillan, 1962.

Bentzen, Aage. *King and Messiah*. London: Lutterworth, 1955.

Betz, H. D. "The Logion of the Easy Yoke and of Rest."
    *JBL* 86 (1967) 10-24.

Black, Matthew. "Die Apotheose Israels: eine neue Interpreta-
    tion des danielischen 'Menschensohns.'" Pp. 92-99 in
    *Jesus und der Menschensohn*. Ed. by Rudolph Pesch and
    Rudolph Schnackenburg. Freiburg: Herder, 1975.

_____. "The Christological Use of the Old Testament in the
    New Testament." *NTS* 18 (1971/72) 1-14.

_____. "The Eschatology of the Similitudes of Enoch."
    *JTS* 3 (1952) 1-10.

_____. "The 'Parables' of Enoch (1 En 37-71) and the 'Son
    of Man.'" *ExpTim* 78 (1976/77) 5-8.

_____. "The Throne-Theophany Prophetic Commission and the
    'Son of Man': A Study in Tradition-History." Pp. 57-73
    in *Jews, Greeks and Christians*, Vol. XXI of *Studies in
    Judaism in Late Antiquity*. Ed. by R. Hamerton-Kelly and
    Robin Scroggs. Leiden: Brill, 1976.

Blair, Edward P. "Jesus and Salvation in the Gospel of
    Matthew." *McCormick Quarterly* 20/21 (1966/68) 301-308.

_____. *Jesus in the Gospel of Matthew*. New York: Abingdon,
    1960.

Bloch, Renée. "Midrash." *DBSup*, Vol. 5, cols. 1263-81.
    Paris: Letouzey, 1957.

Borgen, Peder. *Bread From Heaven*. Leiden: Brill, 1965.

_____. "Response" to B. Lindars, "The Place of the Old
    Testament in the Formation of New Testament Theology."
    *NTS* 23 (1977) 67-75.

Bornkamm, Günther. "The Risen Lord and the Earthly Jesus:
    Matthew 28:16-20." *The Future of Our Religious Past*.
    Ed. by M. Robinson, trans. by Charles E. Carlston and
    Robert P. Sharlemann. London: SCM, 1971.

Borsch, Frederick H. *The Christian and Gnostic Son of Man*.
    London: SCM, 1970.

_____. "Mark XIV.62 and 1 Enoch LXII.5." *NTS* 13/14
    (1966/68) 565-67.

_____. *The Son of Man in Myth and History*. Philadelphia:
    Westminster, 1967.

Bowker, John W.  "The Son of Man."  *JTS* 28 (1977) 19-48.

_____.  *The Targums and Rabbinic Literature*.  Cambridge:
    Cambridge University, 1969.

Bowman, John.  "The Background of the Term 'Son of Man.'"
    *ExpTim* 58/59 (1947/48) 283-88.

Breech, E.  "These Fragments I Have Shored Against My Ruins:
    The Form and Function of 4 Ezra."  *JBL* 92 (1973) 262-74.

Bronner, Leah.  *The Stories of Elijah and Elisha as Polemics
    Against Baal Worship*.  Leiden: Brill, 1968.

Brown, Raymond E.  *The Birth of the Messiah*.  Garden City, NY:
    Doubleday, 1977.

_____.  "Difficulties in Using the New Testament in American
    Catholic Discussions."  *Louvain Studies* 6 (1976) 144-58.

_____.  *The Gospel According to John*.  AB 29, 29A.  Garden
    City, NY: Doubleday, 1966, 1970.

Bruce, F. F.  "The Book of Daniel and the Qumran Community."
    *Neotestamentica et Semitica*.  Ed. by E. Earle Ellis and
    Max Wilcox.  Edinburgh: Clark, 1969.

Bultmann, Rudolf.  *The Gospel of John*.  Trans. by G. R. Beasley-
    Murray, R.W.N. Hoare and J. K. Riches.  Philadelphia:
    Westminster, 1971.

_____.  *History of the Synoptic Tradition*.  Trans. by John
    Marsh.  New York: Harper and Row, 1968.

_____.  *Theology of the New Testament*.  2 vols.  Trans. by
    K. Grobel.  New York: Scribners, 1951, 1955.

Casey, Maurice.  "The Corporate Interpretation of 'One Like a
    Son of Man' (Dan VII 13) at the Time of Jesus."  *NovT* 18
    (1976) 167-80.

_____.  "The Son of Man Problem."  *ZNW* 67 (1976) 147-54.

_____.  "The Use of the Term 'Son of Man' in the Similitudes
    of Enoch."  *JSJ* 7 (1976) 11-29.

Cassuto, U.  *A Commentary on the Book of Genesis*.  Vol. 1.
    Trans. by Israel Abrahams.  Jerusalem: Magnes, 1961.

Cerfaux, L.  "Les Sources scripturaires de Mt., XI, 25-30."
    *ETL* 31 (1955) 331-42.

Charles, R. H.  *A Critical and Exegetical Commentary on the
    Book of Daniel*.  Oxford: Clarendon, 1929.

_____.  *The Revelation of St. John*.  2 vols.  Edinburgh:
    Clark, 1963 (reprint of 1920 ed.).

Charlesworth, James H.  *The Pseudepigrapha and Modern Research*.
Missoula, MT: Scholars, 1976.

_____.  "The SNTS Pseudepigrapha Seminars at Tübingen and
Paris on the Books of Enoch."  *NTS* 25 (1979) 315-23.

Childs, Brevard S.  "The Canonical Shape of the Book of
Daniel."  Unpublished paper delivered at the SBL Annual
Meeting, October, 1975.

Collins, John J.  "Apocalyptic Eschatology as the Transcendence
of Death."  *CBQ* 36 (1974) 21-43.

_____.  *The Apocalyptic Vision of the Book of Daniel*.
Missoula, MT: Scholars, 1977.

_____.  "The Court Tales in Daniel and the Development of
Apocalyptic."  *JBL* 94 (1975) 218-34.

_____.  "The Mythology of Holy War in Daniel and the Qumran
War Scroll."  *VT* 25 (1975) 596-612.

_____.  "The Son of Man and the Saints of the Most High in
the Book of Daniel."  *JBL* 93 (1974) 50-66.

_____.  "The Symbolism of Transcendence in Jewish Apoca-
lyptic."  *BR* 19 (1974) 5-22.

Colpe, Carsten.  "ὁ υἱὸς τοῦ ἀνθρώπου."  *TDNT* 8 (1972) 400-77.

Conybeare, F. C.  "Three Early Doctrinal Modifications of the
Text of the Gospels."  *HibJ* 1 (1902) 96-113.

_____.  "The Eusebian Forms of the Text. Mt. 28:19."  *ZNW* 2
(1901) 275-88.

Conzelmann, Hans.  "History and Theology in the Passion
Narratives of the Synoptic Gospels."  *Int* 24 (1970)
178-97.

_____.  *The Theology of St. Luke*.  Trans. by G. Buswell.
New York: Harper and Row, 1961.

Cooke, G. A.  *The Book of Ezekiel*.  ICC.  Edinburgh: Clark,
1951 (reprint of 1936 ed.).

Cooke, Gerald.  "The Sons of (the) God(s)."  *ZAW* 76 (1964) 22-47.

Cope, O. Lamar.  *Matthew: a Scribe Trained for the Kingdom of
Heaven*.  CBQMS 5.  Washington: Catholic Biblical Association of America, 1976.

Coppens, J.  "Le Fils d'Homme Daniélique et les Relectures de
Dan. VII, 13, dans les Apocryphes et les Ecrits du Nouveau
Testament."  *ETL* 37 (1961) 5-51.

_____.  "Miscellanées bibliques 85: La vision du Très-Haut
en Dan., VII et Hén. ethiopien, XIV."  *ETL* 53 (1977) 187-89.

Cross, Frank Moore. *Canaanite Myth and Hebrew Epic*.
     Cambridge: Harvard University, 1973.

_____. "The Council of Yahweh in Second Isaiah." *JNES* 12
     (1953) 274-78.

Cullmann, Oscar. *Baptism in the New Testament*. Trans. by
     J.K.S. Reid. London: SCM, 1950.

_____. *The Earliest Christian Confessions*. Trans. by
     J.K.S. Reid. London: Lutterworth, 1949.

Dahl, Nils Alstrup. "The Neglected Factor in New Testament
     Theology." *Reflection* 73 (1975) 5-8.

Daniélou, Jean. *The Theology of Jewish Christianity*. Trans.
     and ed. by John A. Baker. Chicago: Henry Regnery, 1964.

Davies, W. D. *The Setting of the Sermon on the Mount*.
     Cambridge: Cambridge University, 1964.

Delcor, M. *Le Livre de Daniel*. Paris: J. Gabalda, 1971.

Denis, Albert-Marie. *Introduction aux Pseudépigraphes Grecs
     d'Ancien Testament*. Leiden: Brill, 1970.

Descamps, A. "Rédaction et christologie dans le récit matthéen
     de la Passion." Pp. 359-415 in *L'Evangile selon Matthieu*.
     Ed. by M. Didier. Gembloux: J. Duculot, 1972.

Dequeker, L. "Les Saints du Très-Haut en Daniel VII." *ETL* 36
     (1960) 353-92.

DiLella, Alexander. "The One in Human Likeness and the Holy
     Ones of the Most High in Daniel 7." *CBQ* 39 (1977) 1-19.

_____ and Hartman, L. F. *The Book of Daniel*. AB 23.
     Garden City, NY: Doubleday, 1978.

Dodd, C. H. "Matthew and Paul." *New Testament Studies*.
     New York: Scribners, 1952.

Doeve, J. W. *Jewish Hermeneutics in the Synoptic Gospels and
     Acts*. Assen: Van Gorcum, 1954.

Donahue, John R. *Are You the Christ? The Trial Narrative in
     the Gospel of Mark*. Missoula, MT: Society of Biblical
     Literature, 1973.

*Early Christian Fathers*. LCC 1. Trans. and ed. by Cyril C.
     Richardson. Philadelphia: Westminster, 1953.

Eichrodt, Walther. *Ezekiel*. Trans. by Cosslett Quin.
     London: SCM, 1970.

Eissfeldt, Otto. *The Old Testament: An Introduction*. Trans.
     by Peter R. Ackroyd. New York: Harper and Row, 1965.

Ellis, E. Earle.  "Midrash, Targum and New Testament Quota-
     tions."  *Neotestamentica et Semitica*.  Ed. by E. E. Ellis.
     and Max Wilcox.  Edinburgh: Clark, 1969.

Ellis, Peter.  *Matthew: His Mind and His Message*.  College-
     ville, MN: Liturgical Press, 1974.

Emerton, J. A.  "The Origin of the Son of Man Imagery."
     *JTS* 9 (1958) 225-42.

Ferch, A. J.  "Daniel 7 and Ugarit: A Reconsideration."
     *JBL* 99 (1980) 75-86.

Feuillet, A.  "Le Fils de l'Homme de Daniel et la Tradition
     Biblique."  *RB* 60 (1953) 170-202, 321-46.

Filson, Floyd V.  *A Commentary on the Gospel According to
     St. Matthew*.  London: P. Adam and Charles Black, 1960.

Fiorenza, Elizabeth Schüssler.  *The Apocalypse*.  Chicago:
     Franciscan Herald, 1976.

_____.  "The Eschatology and Composition of the Apocalypse."
     *CBQ* 30 (1968) 537-69.

_____.  "Redemption as Liberation: Apocalypse 1:5f and
     5:9f."  *CBQ* 36 (1974) 220-32.

_____.  "Revelation, Book of."  *IDBSup*, 744-46.

Fitzmyer, Joseph A.  "The Aramaic Language and the Study of
     the New Testament."  *JBL* 99 (1980) 5-21.

_____.  "The Contribution of Qumran Aramaic to the Study
     of the New Testament."  *NTS* 20 (1973/74) 382-407.

_____.  "Implications of the New Enoch Literature from
     Qumran."  *TS* 38 (1977) 332-45.

Flemington, W. F.  "Baptism."  *IDB*, 2:348-353.

Flusser, David.  "The Conclusion of Matthew in a New Jewish
     Christian Source."  *ASTI* 5 (1966/67) 110-30.

_____.  "The Son of Man: Jesus in the Context of History."
     *The Crucible of Christianity*.  Ed. by Arnold Toynbee.
     New York: World, 1969.

Fortman, Edmund J.  *The Triune God: A Historical Study of the
     Doctrine of the Trinity*.  Philadelphia: Westminster, 1972.

Fuller, Reginald H.  *The Formation of the Resurrection Narra-
     tives*.  New York: Macmillan, 1971.

_____.  *The Foundations of New Testament Christology*.
     New York: Scribners, 1965.

_____.  "On Demythologizing the Trinity."  *ATR* 43 (1961)
     121-31.

Gerhardsson, Birger.  "The Hermeneutic Program in Matthew
    22:37-40."  Pp. 129-50 in *Jews, Greeks and Christians*.
    Ed. by Robert Hamerton-Kelly and Robin Scroggs.  Leiden:
    Brill, 1976.

_____.  "Du Judéo-Christianisme à Jésus par le Shema."
    *RSR* 60 (1972) 23-36.

_____.  "Monotheism och högkristologi i Matthews-evangeliet."
    *SEÅ* 37/38 (1972/73), summarized in *NTA* 18 (1973/74) 297.

Gerd, S.  "My Son the Messiah: A Note on 4 Esr 7:28-29."
    *ZNW* 66 (1975) 264-67.

Ginsberg, H. Louis.  *Studies in Daniel*.  New York: Jewish
    Theological Seminary of America, 1948.

Glasson, T. Francis.  *The Second Advent*.  3rd ed.  London:
    Epworth, 1963.

_____.  "The Son of Man Imagery: Enoch XIV and Daniel VII."
    *NTS* 23 (1976) 82-90.

Goulder, M. D.  *Midrash and Lection in Matthew*.  London: SPCK,
    1974.

Grant, Robert M.  *The Early Christian Doctrine of God*.
    Charlottesville: University of Virginia, 1966.

Greenfield, J. C. and Stone, M.  "The Books of Enoch and the
    Traditions of Enoch."  *Numen* 26 (1979) 89-103.

_____.  "The Enochic Pentateuch and the Date of the
    Similitudes."  *HTR* 70 (1977) 51-65.

Grelot, Pierre.  "La Légende d'Hénoch dans les apocryphes et
    dans la Bible: Origine et Signification."  *RSR* 46 (1958)
    5-26, 181-210.

Gundry, Robert Horton.  *The Use of the Old Testament in St.
    Matthew's Gospel*.  Leiden: Brill, 1967.

Haenchen, Ernst.  *The Acts of the Apostles*.  Trans. by Bernard
    Noble and Gerald Shinn, rev. by R. McL. Wilson.  Phila-
    delphia: Westminster, 1971.

Hahn, Ferdinand.  *Mission in the New Testament*.  Trans. by
    F. Clarke.  Naperville, IL: Allenson, 1965.

_____.  *The Titles of Jesus in Christology*.  Trans. by
    Harold Knight and George Ogg.  New York: World, 1969.

Hamerton-Kelly, R. G.  *Pre-existence, Wisdom and the Son of Man:
    A Study of the Idea of Pre-existence in the New Testament*.
    SNTSMS 21.  Cambridge: Cambridge University, 1973.

_____.  "Matthew, Gospel of."  *IDBSup*, 580-83.

Hanson, Paul D. *The Dawn of Apocalyptic*. Philadelphia:
    Fortress, 1975.

_____. "Jewish Apocalyptic Against Its Near Eastern
    Environment." *RB* 78 (1971) 31-58.

_____. "Old Testament Apocalyptic Re-examined."
    *Int* 25 (1971) 454-79.

Hare, Douglas R. A. and Harrington, Daniel J. "Make Disciples
    of All the Gentiles (Mt. 28:19)." *CBQ* 37 (1975) 359-69.

Harrington, Daniel J. "Matthean Studies Since Joachim Rohde."
    *HeyJ* 16 (1975) 375-88.

_____. "Research on the Jewish Pseudepigrapha During the
    1970s." *CBQ* 42 (1980) 147-59.

Hartman, Lars. "Into the Name of Jesus." *NTS* 20 (1973/74)
    432-40.

_____. *Prophecy Interpreted*. Lund: Gleerup, 1966.

_____. "Scriptural Exegesis in the Gospel of Matthew and
    the Problem of Communication." *L'Evangile selon Matthieu*.
    Ed. by M. Didier. Gembloux: J. Duculot, 1972.

Hartman, Louis F. and DiLella, Alexander. *The Book of Daniel*.
    AB 23. Garden City, NY: Doubleday, 1978.

Hay, David M. *Glory at the Right Hand: Ps. 110 in Early
    Christianity*. New York: Abingdon, 1973.

Heaton, E. W. *The Book of Daniel*. London: SCM, 1956.

Hengel, Martin. *Judaism and Hellenism*. 2 vols. Trans. by
    John Bowden. Philadelphia: Fortress, 1974.

_____. *The Son of God*. Trans. by John Bowden. Phila-
    delphia: Fortress, 1976.

Higgins, A.J.B. *Jesus and the Son of Man*. Philadelphia:
    Fortress, 1964.

Hindley, J. C. "Towards a Date for the Similitudes of Enoch."
    *NTS* 14 (1968) 551-65.

Hooker, Morna D. *The Son of Man in Mark*. Montreal: McGill
    University, 1967.

_____. "Is the Son of Man Problem Really Insoluble?"
    Pp. 231-43 in *Text and Interpretation*. Ed. by E. Best and
    R. McL. Wilson. Cambridge: Cambridge University, 1979.

Hubbard, Benjamin Jerome. *The Matthean Redaction of a Primitive
    Apostolic Commissioning: An Exegesis of Matthew 28:16-20*.
    SBLDS 19. Missoula, MT: Scholars, 1974.

Jeffery, Arthur. "Daniel." *IB*, Vol. 6. New York: Abingdon, 1951.

Jeremias, Joachim. "'Ηλ(ε)ίας." *TDNT* 2 (1964) 928-41.

_____. *Jesus' Promise to the Nations*. Trans. by S. H. Hooke. London: SCM, 1958.

_____. *New Testament Theology*. Trans. by John Bowden. New York: Scribners, 1971.

_____. *The Parables of Jesus*. Trans. by S. H. Hooke. New York: Scribners, 1963.

Johnson, Marshall D. "Reflections on a Wisdom Approach to Matthew's Christology." *CBQ* 36 (1974) 44-64.

Johnson, Sherman E. "Matthew." *IB*, Vol. 7.

Käsemann, Ernst. "The Beginnings of Christian Theology." *JTC* 6 (1969) 17-46.

_____. "Sentences of Holy Law in the New Testament." *New Testament Questions of Today*. Trans. by W. J. Montague. Philadelphia: Fortress, 1969.

Kaufmann, Yehezkel. *The Religion of Israel*. Trans. and abridged by M. Greenberg. New York: Schocken, 1972.

Kelly, J.N.D. *Early Christian Creeds*. London: Longman, 1972.

Kilpatrick, G. D. *The Origins of the Gospel According to St. Matthew*. Oxford: Clarendon, 1950.

Kingsbury, Edwin C. "The Prophets and the Council of Yahweh." *JBL* 83 (1964) 279-86.

Kingsbury, Jack Dean. "The Composition and Christology of Matt. 28:16-20." *JBL* 93 (1974) 573-84.

_____. "The Figure of Peter in Matthew's Gospel as a Theological Problem." *JBL* 98 (1979) 67-83.

_____. *Matthew: Structure, Christology, Kingdom*. Philadelphia: Fortress, 1975.

_____. *The Parables of Jesus in Matthew 13*. Richmond: John Knox, 1969.

Knibb, M. A. "The Date of the Parables of Enoch: A Critical Review." *NTS* 25 (1979) 345-59.

Kosmala, Hans. "In My Name." *ASTI* 5 (1967) 87-109.

_____. "The Conclusion of Matthew." *ASTI* 4 (1965) 132-47.

Kretschmar, Georg. *Studien zur frühchristlichen Trinitäts-theologie*. Tübingen: J.C.B. Mohr, 1956.

Labuschagne, C. J. *The Incomparability of Yahweh in the Old Testament*. Leiden: Brill, 1966.

Lacocque, André. *The Book of Daniel*. Trans. by D. Pellauer. Atlanta: John Knox, 1979.

Lagrange, M.-J. *Evangile selon Saint Matthieu*. 7th ed. Paris: Gabalda, 1948.

Lange, J. *Das Erscheinen des Auferstandenen im Evangelium nach Matthäus*. Forschung zur Bibel 11. Würzburg: Echter, 1973.

Larcher, Chrysostome. *Etudes sur le livre de la Sagesse*. Paris: J. Gabalda, 1969.

Lebreton, Jules. *History of the Dogma of the Trinity*. Vol. 1. Trans. by Algar Thorold. London: Burns, Oates and Washbourne, 1939.

LeDéaut, R. "Apropos a Definition of Midrash." *Int* 25 (1971) 259-82.

Leivestad, Ragnar. "Exit the Apocalyptic Son of Man." *NTS* 18 (1971/72) 243-67.

Levey, Samson H. "The Targum to Ezekiel." *HUCA* 46 (1975) 139-58.

Lindars, Barnabas. "The Apocalyptic Myth and the Death of Christ." *BJRL* 57 (1974/75) 366-87.

_____. *New Testament Apologetic*. Philadelphia: Westminster, 1961.

_____. "The Place of the Old Testament in the Formation of New Testament Theology: Prolegomena." *NTS* 23 (1977) 61-66.

_____. "Re-enter the Apocalyptic Son of Man." *NTS* 22 (1975) 52-72.

_____. "The Son of Man in the Johannine Christology." Pp. 43-60 in *Christ and the Spirit in the New Testament*. Ed. by B. Lindars and S. Smalley. Cambridge: Cambridge University, 1973.

Loader, W.R.G. "The Apocalyptic Mode of Sonship." *JBL* 97 (1978) 525-54.

Lohmeyer, Ernst. *Das Evangelium des Matthäus*. Ed. by Werner Schmauch. Göttingen: Vandenhoeck und Ruprecht, 1962.

_____. "Mir ist gegeben alle Gewalt." *In Memoriam Ernst Lohmeyer*. Ed. by Werner Schmauch. Stuttgart: Evangelisches Verlagswerk, 1951.

362                          The Father, Son and Holy Spirit

Luz, U. "Discipleship." *IDBSup*, 232-34.

McArthur, H. K. "Mark XIV.62." *NTS* 4 (1958) 156-58.

McBride, S. D. "The Yoke of the Kingdom." *Int* 27 (1973) 273-306.

McNeile, Alan Hugh. *The Gospel According to St. Matthew*. London: Macmillan, 1915.

Malina, Bruce J. "The Literary Structure and Form of Mt. XXVIII:16-20." *NTS* 17 (1970/71) 87-103.

Manson, T. W. "The Son of Man in Daniel, Enoch and the Gospels." *BJRL* 32 (1950) 171-93.

Martyn, J. Louis. *History and Theology in the Fourth Gospel*. New York: Harper and Row, 1968.

_____. "We Have Found Elijah." Pp. 182-219 in *Jews, Greeks and Christians*. Ed. by R. Hamerton-Kelly and Robin Scroggs. Leiden: Brill, 1976.

Massaux, Edouard. *Influence de l'Evangile de saint Matthieu sur la littérature chrétienne avant saint Irénée*. Louvain: Publications Universitaires de Louvain, 1950.

Mearns, C. L. "Dating the Similitudes of Enoch." *NTS* 25 (1979) 360-69.

Meeks, Wayne A. "'Am I a Jew?' Johannine Christianity and Judaism." Pp. 163-86 in *Christianity, Judaism and Other Greco-Roman Cults*, Part I. Ed. by J. Neusner. Leiden: Brill, 1975.

_____. "The Man from Heaven in Johannine Sectarianism." *JBL* 91 (1972) 44-72.

Meier, John P. *Law and History in Matthew's Gospel: A Redactional Study of Mt. 5:17-48*. Rome: Biblical Institute, 1976.

_____. "Nations or Gentiles in Matthew 28:19?" *CBQ* 39 (1977) 94-102.

_____. "Salvation-History in Matthew: In Search of a Starting Point." *CBQ* 37 (1975) 203-15.

_____. "Two Disputed Questions in Matt. 28:16-20." *JBL* 96 (1977) 407-24.

_____. *The Vision of Matthew: Christ, Church and Morality in the First Gospel*. New York: Paulist, 1979.

Michel, Otto. "Der Abschluss des Matthäusevangeliums." *EvT* 10 (1950/51) 16-26.

Milik, J. T.  "Milkî-ṣedeq et Milkî-rešaʿ dans les anciens
     écrits juifs et chrétiens."  *JJS* 23 (1972) 95-144.

_____.  "Problèmes de la Littérature Hénochique à la
     lumière des fragments araméens de Qumrân."  *HTR* 64 (1971)
     333-78.

Miller, Merrill P.  "Midrash."  *IDBSup*, 593-97.

_____.  "Targum, Midrash and the Use of the Old Testament
     in the New Testament."  *JSJ* 2 (1971) 29-82.

Miller, Patrick D.  "The Divine Council and the Prophetic
     Call to War."  *VT* 18 (1968) 100-107.

Minear, Paul.  *I Saw a New Earth*.  Washington: Corpus, 1968.

Montgomery, James A.  *The Book of Daniel*.  ICC.  Edinburgh:
     Clark, 1950.

Moor, Johannes C. de.  "Ugarit."  *IDBSup*, 928-31.

Moore, George Foot.  "Christian Writers on Judaism."  *HTR* 14
     (1921) 197-254.

Moule, C.F.D.  "From Defendant to Judge--and Deliverer: An
     Enquiry into the Use and Limitations of the Theme of
     Vindication in the New Testament."  *Studiorum Novi
     Testamenti Societas Bulletin* 3 (1952) 40-53.

_____.  "The New Testament and the Doctrine of the Trinity:
     A Short Report on an Old Theme."  *ExpTim* 88 (1976) 16-20.

_____.  *The Origin of Christology*.  Cambridge: Cambridge
     University, 1977.

Mowinckel, S.  *He That Cometh*.  Trans. by G. W. Anderson.
     New York: Abingdon, 1954.

Muilenberg, James.  "The Son of Man in Daniel and the
     Ethiopic Apocalypse of Enoch."  *JBL* 79 (1960) 197-209.

Myers, Jacob M.  *I and II Esdras*.  AB 42.  Garden City, NY:
     Doubleday, 1974.

Nickelsburg, George W.E.  "Enoch, Book of."  *IDBSup*, 265-68.

_____.  *Resurrection, Immortality and Eternal Life in
     Intertestamental Judaism*.  HTS 26.  Cambridge: Harvard
     University, 1972.

Neiman, D.  "Council, Heavenly."  *IDBSup*, 187-88.

Noth, Martin.  "The Holy Ones of the Most High."  Pp. 215-28 in
     *The Laws in the Pentateuch and Other Essays*.  Trans. by
     D. R. Ap-Thomas.  Philadelphia: Fortress, 1966.

Odeberg, Hugo. "ʾΕνώχ." *TDNT* 2 (1964) 556-60.

Oepke, A. "βαπτω, βαπτίζω." *TDNT* 1 (1964) 527-44.

Perrin, Norman. "Creative Use of the Son of Man Traditions by
      Mark." *USQR* 23 (1967/68) 357-65.

_____. "The High Priest's Question and Jesus' Answer (Mark
      14:61-62)." *The Passion in Mark: Studies on Mark 14-16*.
      Ed. by Werner H. Kelber. Philadelphia: Fortress, 1976.

_____. "The Interpretation of the Gospel of Mark."
      *Int* 30 (1976) 115-24.

_____. "Mark XIV.62: The End Product of a Christian Pesher
      Tradition?" *NTS* 11/12 (1964/66) 150-55.

_____. *Rediscovering the Teaching of Jesus*. New York:
      Harper and Row, 1967.

_____. "The Son of Man in Ancient Judaism and Primitive
      Christianity: A Suggestion." *BR* 11 (1966) 17-28.

*Peter in the New Testament*. Ed. by Raymond E. Brown, Karl P.
      Donfried, John Reumann. Minneapolis: Augsburg, and New
      York: Paulist, 1973.

Porteous, Norman W. *Daniel*. Philadelphia: Westminster, 1965.

Quispel, Gilles. "Qumran, John and Jewish Christianity."
      Pp. 137-55 in *John and Qumran*. Ed. by James H. Charles-
      worth. London: Geoffrey Chapman, 1972.

Rad, Gerhard von. *Genesis*. Trans. by J. H. Marks.
      Philadelphia: Westminster, 1961.

_____. *Old Testament Theology*. Vol. 2. Trans. by D.M.G.
      Stalker. New York: Harper and Row, 1965.

Rahner, Karl. "Person," "Trinity." *Theological Dictionary*.
      Ed. by C. Ernst, trans. by R. Strachan. New York:
      Herder and Herder, 1965.

_____. *The Trinity*. Trans. by J. Donceel. New York:
      Herder and Herder, 1970.

_____. "Trinity, Divine," 296-303. "Trinity in Theology,"
      303-308. *Sacramentum Mundi*. Vol. 6. Ed. by K. Rahner.
      New York: Herder and Herder, 1970.

Reese, James M. *Hellenistic Influence on the Book of Wisdom
      and Its Consequences*. Rome: Biblical Institute, 1970.

Rhodes, Arnold B. "The Kingdom of Men and the Kingdom of
      God." *Int* 15 (1961) 411-30.

Rist, Martin. "Is Matt. 11:25-30 a Primitive Baptismal Hymn?"
      *JR* 15 (1935) 63-77.

Robinson, John A.T. *Jesus and His Coming*. London: SCM, 1957.

Rohde, Joachim. *Rediscovering the Teaching of the Evangelists*. Trans. by D. M. Barton. London: SCM, 1968.

Rowley, H. H. *The Relevance of Apocalyptic*. 3rd ed. London: Lutterworth, 1963.

Russell, D. S. *The Method and Message of Jewish Apocalyptic*. Philadelphia: Westminster, 1964.

Sanders, James A. "From Isaiah 61 to Luke 4." Pp. 75-106 in *Christianity, Judaism and Other Greco-Roman Cults*, Part 1. Ed. by J. Neusner. Leiden: Brill, 1975.

Sanders, Jack T. *The New Testament Christological Hymns*. New York: Cambridge University, 1971.

Schmidt, K. L. "ὁρίζω." *TDNT* 5 (1967) 452-56.

Scholem, Gershom G. *Jewish Gnosticism, Merkabah Mysticism and Talmudic Tradition*. New York: Jewish Theological Seminary of America, 1965.

_____. *Major Trends in Jewish Mysticism*. New York: Schocken, 1973 (reprint of 1954 ed.).

Schweizer, Eduard. *The Good News According to Matthew*. Trans. by David E. Green. Atlanta: John Knox, 1975.

_____. *Lordship and Discipleship*. Naperville, IL: Allenson, 1960.

_____. "Observance of the Law and Charismatic Activity in Matthew." *NTS* 16 (1970/71) 213-30.

_____. "The Son of Man." *JBL* 79 (1960) 119-29.

_____. "The Son of Man Again." *NTS* 9/10 (1963/64) 256-61.

_____. "πνεῦμα πνευματικός." *TDNT* 6 (1968) 396-451.

_____. "υἱός in the New Testament." *TDNT* 8 (1972) 363-92.

Scott, R.B.Y. "Behold, He Cometh with the Clouds." *NTS* 5/6 (1958/60) 127-32.

Scroggs, Robin. "The Exaltation of the Spirit by Some Early Christians." *JBL* 84 (1965) 359-73.

Senior, Donald. "The Death of Jesus and the Resurrection of the Holy Ones (Mt. 27:51-53)." *CBQ* 38 (1976) 312-29.

_____. *The Passion Narrative According to Matthew*. Louvain: Leuven University, 1975.

Sjöberg, E. *Der verborgene Menschensohn in den Evangelien*. Lund: Gleerup, 1955.

Smalley, Stephen S.   "The Johannine Son of Man Sayings."
      *NTS* 15 (1968/69) 278-301.

Speiser, E. A.   *Genesis*.   AB 1.   Garden City, NY: Doubleday,
      1964.

Stauffer, Ethelbert.   *New Testament Theology*.   Trans. by John
      Marsh.   London: SCM, 1955.

Stendahl, Krister.   "Matthew."   *PCB*, 769-98.

_____.   *The School of St. Matthew and Its Use of the Old
      Testament*.   Lund: Gleerup, 1969.

Stone, Michael.   "The Book of Enoch and Judaism of the Third
      Century B.C.E."   *CBQ* 40 (1978) 479-92.

_____.   "The Concept of the Messiah in IV Ezra."   Pp. 295-
      312 in *Religions in Antiquity*.   Ed. by Jacob Neusner.
      Leiden: Brill, 1968.

Strecker, Georg.   "The Concept of History in Matthew."
      *JAAR* 35 (1967) 219-30.

_____.   *Der Weg der Gerechtigkeit*.   Göttingen: Vandenhoeck
      und Ruprecht, 1962.

Suggs, M. Jack.   *Wisdom, Christology, and Law in Matthew's
      Gospel*.   Cambridge: Harvard University, 1970.

Talbert, Charles H.   "The Concept of Immortals in Mediterranean
      Antiquity."   *JBL* 94 (1975) 419-36.

Tödt, Heinz Eduard.   *The Son of Man in the Synoptic Tradition*.
      Trans. by D. M. Barton.   London: SCM, 1965.

Trilling, Wolfgang.   *The Gospel According to St. Matthew*.
      2 vols.   Trans. by K. Smyth.   London: Burns and Oates,
      1969.

_____.   *Das Wahre Israel*.   München: Kösel-Verlag, 1964.

VanderKam, James C.   "Enoch Traditions in Jubilees and Other
      Second-Century Sources."   Pp. 229-51 in *SBL 1978 Seminar
      Papers*, Vol. 1.   Ed. by P. J. Achtemeier.   Missoula, MT:
      Scholars, 1978.

Vermes, Geza.   *Jesus the Jew*.   New York: Macmillan, 1974.

Vögtle, A.   "Das christologische und ekklesiologische Anliegen
      von Mt. 28, 18-20."   *SE* 2 (1964) 266-94.

Wainwright, Arthur W.   *The Trinity in the New Testament*.
      London: SPCK, 1962.

Walker, William O., Jr.   "The Kingdom of the Son of Man and
      the Kingdom of the Father in Matthew."   *CBQ* 30 (1968)
      573-79.

Whybray, R. N.  *The Heavenly Counsellor in Isaiah XL, 13-14.*
    Cambridge: Cambridge University, 1971.

Winston, D.  *The Wisdom of Solomon.*  AB 43.  Garden City, NY:
    Doubleday, 1979.

Wright, Addison G.  *The Literary Genre Midrash.*  Staten Island,
    NY: Alba, 1967.

Zevit, Ziony.  "The Structure and Individual Elements of
    Daniel 7."  *ZAW* 80/81 (1968/69) 385-96.

Zimmerli, Walther.  *Ezechiel.*  BKAT 13/1.  Neukirchen-Vluyn:
    Neukirchener Verlag, 1969.

Zumstein, Jean.  "Matthieu 28, 16-20."  *RTP* 22 (1972) 14-33.